Voice and Video Conferencing Fundamentals

Scott Firestone, Thiya Ramalingam, and Steve Fry

Cisco Press

800 East 96th Street
Indianapolis, IN 46240 USA

Voice and Video Conferencing Fundamentals

Scott Firestone, Thiya Ramalingam, and Steve Fry

Copyright© 2007 Cisco Systems, Inc.

Published by:
Cisco Press
800 East 96th Street
Indianapolis, IN 46240 USA

Printed in the United States of America 1 2 3 4 5 6 7 8 9 0

First Printing: March 2007

ISBN-10: 1-58705-268-7

ISBN-13: 978-1-58705-268-2

Library of Congress Cataloging-in-Publication Data

Firestone, Scott.

  Voice and video conferencing fundamentals / Scott Firestone, Thiya Ramalingam, and Steve Fry. -- 1st ed.

    p. cm.

  ISBN 978-1-58705-268-2 (pbk.)

  1. Videoconferencing. 2. Internet telephony. I. Ramalingam, Thiya. II. Fry, Steve. III. Title. IV. Title: Voice and videoconferencing fundamentals.

  HF5734.7.F57 2007

  006.7--dc20

  2007003879

Warning and Disclaimer

This book is designed to provide information about voice and video conferencing. Every effort has been made to make this book as complete and as accurate as possible, but no warranty or fitness is implied.

The information is provided on an "as is" basis. The authors, Cisco Press, and Cisco Systems, Inc., shall have neither liability nor responsibility to any person or entity with respect to any loss or damages arising from the information contained in this book or from the use of the discs or programs that may accompany it.

The opinions expressed in this book belong to the author and are not necessarily those of Cisco Systems, Inc.

Corporate and Government Sales

Cisco Press offers excellent discounts on this book when ordered in quantity for bulk purchases or special sales.

For more information please contact: U.S. Corporate and Government Sales 1-800-382-3419 corpsales@pearsontechgroup.com

For sales outside the U.S. please contact: International Sales international@pearsoned.com

Feedback Information

At Cisco Press, our goal is to create in-depth technical books of the highest quality and value. Each book is crafted with care and precision, undergoing rigorous development that involves the unique expertise of members from the professional technical community.

Readers' feedback is a natural continuation of this process. If you have any comments regarding how we could improve the quality of this book, or otherwise alter it to better suit your needs, you can contact us through email at feedback@ciscopress.com. Please make sure to include the book title and ISBN in your message.

We greatly appreciate your assistance.

Trademark Acknowledgments

All terms mentioned in this book that are known to be trademarks or service marks have been appropriately capitalized. Cisco Press or Cisco Systems, Inc., cannot attest to the accuracy of this information. Use of a term in this book should not be regarded as affecting the validity of any trademark or service mark.

Publisher: Paul Boger

Associate Publisher: Dave Dusthimer

Executive Editor: Kristin Weinberger

Managing Editor: Patrick Kanouse

Development Editor: Dayna Isley

Senior Project Editor: San Dee Phillips

Team Coordinator: Vanessa Evans

Book and Cover Designer: Louisa Adair

Composition: Mark Shirar

Indexer: Tim Wright

Cisco Representative: Anthony Wolfenden

Cisco Press Program Manager: Jeff Brady

Technical Editors: Jesse J. Herrera, Nermeen Ismail

Copy Editor: Keith Cline

Proofreader: Gayle Johnson

Americas Headquarters
Cisco Systems, Inc.
170 West Tasman Drive
San Jose, CA 95134-1706
USA
www.cisco.com
Tel: 408 526-4000
800 553-NETS (6387)
Fax: 408 527-0883

Asia Pacific Headquarters
Cisco Systems, Inc.
168 Robinson Road
#28-01 Capital Tower
Singapore 068912
www.cisco.com
Tel: +65 6317 7777
Fax: +65 6317 7799

Europe Headquarters
Cisco Systems International BV
Haarlerbergpark
Haarlerbergweg 13-19
1101 CH Amsterdam
The Netherlands
www-europe.cisco.com
Tel: +31 0 800 020 0791
Fax: +31 0 20 357 1100

Cisco has more than 200 offices worldwide. Addresses, phone numbers, and fax numbers are listed on the Cisco Website at **www.cisco.com/go/offices.**

About the Authors

Scott Firestone holds a master's degree in computer science from MIT and has designed video conferencing and voice products since 1992, resulting in five patents. During his 10 years as a technical leader at Cisco, Scott developed architectures and solutions related to video conferencing, voice and video streaming, and voice-over-IP security.

Thiya Ramalingam is an engineering manager for the Unified Communications organization at Cisco. Thiya holds a master's degree in computer engineering and an MBA from San Jose State University. He holds several patents issued and pending, related to voice and video over IP. Thiya is currently leading the development of multimedia conferencing products at Cisco.

Steve Fry is a technical leader in the Unified Communications organization at Cisco. For the past several years, Steve has been involved in the design and development of telephony and conferencing products. Prior to his conferencing projects, he was a principal engineer on the CallManager MGCP gateway products. He is currently leading product development in video conferencing.

About the Technical Reviewers

Jesse J. Herrera is a senior systems analyst for a Fortune 100 company in Houston, Texas. Mr. Herrera holds a bachelor of science degree in computer science from the University of Arizona and a master of science in telecommunication management from Southern Methodist University. His responsibilities have included design and implementation of enterprise network architectures, including capacity planning, performance monitoring, and network management services. His recent activities include engineering and support roles in electronics business and retail system services.

Nermeen Ismail is a technical leader in the TelePresence Systems Business Unit in Cisco. She has more than 15 years of experience in academia and industry, focusing on multimedia communications over packet networks. Nermeen has an engineering degree from Cairo University and a master of science degree from University College London.

Acknowledgments

Nermeen Ismail provided a cover-to-cover review of the book, lending considerable expertise in video and voice over IP.

Jesse Herrera also provided a full review, verifying all parts of the text in minute detail.

The authors are particularly grateful to Stuart Taylor for providing a number of suggestions and comments on the introduction and architecture chapters; to Tripti Agarwal for taking time to review the H.323 section and provide her insight on CallManager signaling implementation details; to Judy Gulla for doing a thorough review of the SIP chapter and providing valuable comments; to William May for reviewing the media control chapter; and to Dan Wing, who was instrumental in reviewing the security chapter.

We thank all the folks at Cisco Press. We especially thank Kristin Weinberger and Dayna Isley, who helped take the basic material and create a real Cisco Press book. Thank you.

Thiya Ramalingam: I want to thank Johnny Chan, Shantanu Sarkar, and Walter Friedrich for believing in me and encouraging me in every way with my career at Cisco. I also want to say thank you to the architects and engineers who worked with me on the distributed video conferencing project that was the inspiration for me to start this book.

Steve Fry: I want to thank Thiya Ramalingam for inviting me to collaborate with him on this book and to Scott Firestone and the reviewers for their assistance in developing my contribution.

This Book Is Safari Enabled

The Safari® Enabled icon on the cover of your favorite technology book means the book is available through Safari Bookshelf. When you buy this book, you get free access to the online edition for 45 days.

Safari Bookshelf is an electronic reference library that lets you easily search thousands of technical books, find code samples, download chapters, and access technical information whenever and wherever you need it.

To gain 45-day Safari Enabled access to this book:

- Go to http://www.ciscopress.com/safarienabled
- Complete the brief registration form
- Enter the coupon code PTDS-3U4C-1TB7-52CT-L4PT

If you have difficulty registering on Safari Bookshelf or accessing the online edition, please e-mail customer-service@safaribooksonline.com.

Contents at a Glance

Contents

Chapter 4   Media Control and Transport   105

Icons Used in This Book

Protocol Translator   CallManager   Conference Server   Phone   Relational Database   Video

File Server   Proxy Server   Webcam   Router   Catalyst Switch   MCU

SCCP Video Phone   IOS Firewall   Label Switch Router   H.323 Gatekeeper   VPN Concentrator   H.323 Video Terminal

Firewall Switch Module   External NAT/Firewall

Command Syntax Conventions

The conventions used to present command syntax in this book are the same conventions used in the IOS Command Reference. The Command Reference describes these conventions as follows:

- **Boldface** indicates commands and keywords that are entered literally as shown. In actual configuration examples and output (not general command syntax), boldface indicates commands that are manually input by the user (such as a **show** command).

- *Italic* indicates arguments for which you supply actual values.

- Vertical bars (|) separate alternative, mutually exclusive elements.

- Square brackets ([ ]) indicate an optional element.

- Braces ({ }) indicate a required choice.

- Braces within brackets ([{ }]) indicate a required choice within an optional element.

Foreword

I still remember the first video conferencing network I helped implement almost 20 years ago. It was an H.320-based system that used multiple ISDN channels to connect endpoints at the relatively high (for the time) speed of 768 kbps. However, building the video conferencing network was actually easier than using it. Users had to navigate through a complex array of parameters such as service provider IDs (SPID) and telephone IDs (TID) using a 30-button remote control just to set up the session. A common joke at the time was that video conference meetings would always start 20 minutes after the scheduled start time; this gave the users enough time to get the proper connections up and running.

And that was just for video. The audio conference was provisioned independently, usually by dialing into an expensive operator-assisted service that used a completely different network than the video conference.

Today, collaboration has moved far beyond old-fashioned circuit-based audio and video conferencing. The nature of communications in many industries has been changed forever by the widespread adoption of mobile technologies, the emergence of global markets and supply chains, and an increasingly distributed workforce. At the same time, broadband and IP have enabled collaboration as a virtualized service that can connect users any time, anywhere. This new paradigm for collaboration is no longer based on SPIDs, TIDs, and dial tone, but rather on a portfolio of unified, presence-enabled services that bring together the worlds of voice and video, the PC and the telephone, and wired and wireless networks.

New standards, more-efficient ways of encoding audio and video signals, and breakthroughs in chronic roadblocks such as firewall traversal are enabling companies to communicate and collaborate more effectively than ever before across both geographic and organizational boundaries. The impact of these changes can help streamline virtually every business process in an organization, decreasing the time it takes to develop new services or products, driving efficiencies in how products are manufactured, reducing the sales cycle, enabling competitive differentiation, and improving customer loyalty. In the new "networked virtual organization," the barriers between businesses, partners, and customers are beginning to dissolve.

As technology has advanced, the design of conferencing and collaboration systems has become more complex. *Voice and Video Conferencing Fundamentals* provides a comprehensive view of audio and video conferencing concepts, and a clear and concise description of the information needed to understand and administer modern conferencing systems; it is a reference book for how we collaborate in the twenty-first century. Thiya, Scott, and Steve have used their practical, hands-on knowledge and expertise to provide insights not only into the fundamentals of building today's IP-based collaboration systems, but also into avoiding the most common pitfalls of deploying next-generation conferencing and collaboration systems.

Donald R. Proctor
Senior Vice President
Voice Technology Group
Cisco Systems, Inc.

Introduction

In past years, video conferencing has been something of a novelty, and there has been a certain tolerance for quality problems. As audio and video conferencing move more into the mainstream, however, customers and end users will demand greater performance, reliability, security, and scalability from their systems.

Voice and Video Conferencing Fundamentals provides readers with in-depth insight into the conferencing technologies and associated protocols. The information provided will enable information technology managers and technicians to understand basic concepts of video conferencing. The characteristics of video streams, encoding and decoding schemes, and conference control features are important aspects of deployment. The valuable information found in this book will prove extremely helpful during deployment and when performing vendor evaluations and making buying decisions.

Voice and Video Conferencing Fundamentals presents the architectural and technology basics of implementing audio and video conferencing over IP networks. Written by technical leaders who have years of experience in voice and video conferencing systems at Cisco, this book delivers the most authoritative coverage of the conferencing technologies. Professionals who are working or starting to work on these areas will find clear discussions of the concepts and principles of audio and video conferencing systems. More-comprehensive coverage is given for the advanced video architectures, such as emerging video codecs, audio and video synchronization, and distributed implementations. Related protocols, such as Session Initiation Protocol (SIP) and H.323, with specifics on how to use them for conference signaling, are also explained in detail.

Goals and Methods

The book has three major goals:

- To provide an understanding of different video conferencing deployment models, including centralized and distributed architectures, by using real-world examples.
- To explain how video conferencing infrastructure uses signaling standards to establish synchronized, secure conference connections. The book uses call flow diagrams to show each signaling message needed to create a conference.
- To provide a comparison of the most widely used video codecs, in a concise reference format.

Who Should Read This Book?

This book is intended for use by network and system administrators, development and technical support engineers, Cisco customers, solution partners, and graduate students who are involved in the design, development, deployment, and support of audio and video conferencing products.

How This Book Is Organized

Chapter 1 provides an overview of the conferencing models and introduces the basic concepts. Chapters 2 through 8 are the core chapters and can be read in any order. If you intend to read them all, the order in the book is an excellent sequence to use.

The chapters cover the following topics:

- **Chapter 1, "Overview of Conferencing Services"**—This chapter reviews the elementary concepts of conferencing, describing the various types of conferences and the features found in each. It also provides an overview of endpoint types and their characteristics.

- **Chapter 2, "Conferencing System Design and Architecture"**—This chapter reviews conferencing system design and the underlying components used in their construction.

- **Chapter 3, "Fundamentals of Video Compression"**—This chapter discusses the basics of video compression algorithms used by four major codecs: H.261, H.263, H.264, and MPEG-4 part 2. This chapter also includes a discussion of scalable video codecs.

- **Chapter 4, "Media Control and Transport"**—This chapter discusses the basics of Real-Time Transport Protocol (RTP) and Real-Time Transport Control Protocol (RTCP) and their usage in conferencing systems. This chapter also includes a discussion of RTP packetization formats for video codecs and different types of conferencing devices.

- **Chapter 5, "Signaling Protocols: Conferencing Using SIP"**—This chapter discusses the fundamentals of Session Initiation Protocol (SIP) and its relevance to audio and video conferencing. The session description formats for the video codecs are covered in detail with examples.

- **Chapter 6, "Signaling Protocols: Conferencing Using H.323"**—This chapter provides a brief overview of the H.323 protocol, with an emphasis on conferencing systems. It also describes the mechanisms for creating and managing media connections.

- **Chapter 7, "Lip Synchronization in Video Conferencing"**—This chapter analyzes the end-to-end data pipeline of a video conferencing system and discusses the process of achieving lip synchronization in an RTP-based video conferencing product.

- **Chapter 8, "Security Design in Conferencing"**—This chapter goes into depth on many aspects of video conferencing security, including encryption, authentication, attack prevention, firewall traversal, and network-level hardening.

- **Appendix A, "Video Codec Standards"**—This appendix explains the detailed operation of four major codecs: H.261, H.263, H.264, and MPEG-4 part 2.

This chapter covers the following topics:

- Conference types

- Voice and video conferencing components

- Voice conferencing modes

- Types of endpoints

- Video controls: far-end camera control

- Text overlay

CHAPTER 1

Overview of Conferencing Services

As voice over IP (VoIP) technology becomes mainstream, the conferencing and collaboration markets are following its lead. Enterprise networks are deploying new conferencing technology using IP networks, and Internet service providers (ISP) are hosting new services.

Gains in the speed of digital signal processors (DSP) allow newer endpoints to use more advanced compression algorithms to provide better voice and video quality over a range of bit rates. In addition, communication transport costs have dropped drastically over the past few years, making voice and video conferencing across geographic regions extremely cost-effective. These technologies, together with integrated web collaboration, result in conferencing systems that bring significant productivity gains to businesses. For example, integrated web collaboration allows presenters to share their presentation or their PC desktop with other participants in the meeting using a browser. Participants may invoke chat sessions publicly or privately during the meeting, thus providing a common experience for all the participants and eliminating the need to e-mail documents to other meeting members in advance.

This chapter covers the various types of voice/video conferences, along with the associated conference characteristics and features.

Conference Types

The three main conferencing models are ad hoc, reservationless, and scheduled conferencing modes.

Ad hoc conferencing is the most basic model and has the fewest features. It is also the easiest for the end user to create, because ad hoc conferences are simply created with the Conference button on the user's phone.

Reservationless conferencing is the next most basic model and usually is created using the telephone keypad, after the user has called into the conference bridge. Both ad hoc and reservationless are immediate meetings, created quickly for this instant in time.

Scheduled conferences are more complex and have the largest set of conferencing features. They are placed on the system calendar for some point of time in the future and require more input from the meeting organizer than reservationless meetings.

Ad Hoc Conferences

As previously stated, ad hoc conferences are the simplest form of meeting. Phone users create them in two ways:

- When the meeting host presses the Conference button on the phone. The conference functionality enables a user to escalate an existing two-party call into one with multiple participants.

- By using the Meet Me option on the phone.

Ad hoc meetings do not reserve resources in advance and do not require participants to interact with a voice user interface before joining the meeting.

Ad Hoc Conference Initiation: Conference Button

The Conference button on the phone creates an ad hoc conference by expanding a two-party call into a multiparty conference.

Consider the following call scenario:

1. Bob places a call to Alice, and Alice answers.

2. Bob decides to include Fred in the call. Bob presses the Conference button to put Alice on hold.

3. Bob places a call to Fred, and Fred answers. Bob announces that he will include Fred in the preexisting conversation with Alice.

4. Bob presses the Conference button again to connect Fred into the previously established call with Alice, creating an ad hoc conference among the three participants.

Any one of the participants can repeat this sequence of steps to invite more people, until a maximum number of participants (set by the system administrator) have been added to the conference.

Ad hoc conferences created using the Conference button are "dial-out" meetings only; external participants may not dial into the meeting, because the conference has no specific telephone access number or meeting identification.

In addition, participants join ad hoc meetings directly; they do not hear prompts, and the system does not play prompts to other participants as callers join or leave.

The conference initiator also has the option to remove the last participant added, via another button on the phone. Reasons for removing the last participant include times when only brief consultation is desired with the last caller, and the person is not needed for the remainder of the meeting. Another possibility is that the last person called was not there, and the call entered the voice-mail system. For Cisco Unified CallManager systems, the RmLstC button provides this feature. Depending on the type of phone and display system, the phone might present a list of participants. For these phones, other users can be selected for removal, in addition to the last person added.

Ad Hoc Conference Initiation: Meet Me Button

A Meet Me conference is one in which a number of destination telephone numbers are set aside for conferencing purposes. Each number corresponds to a unique conference that users can join on an ad hoc basis. Administrators set up these numbers by configuring the local phone system to forward these calls to a conference server. After the phone system redirects the calls, the conference server manages them independently. When these numbers are known, any caller can join them.

Security consists of the conference system playing specific tones to the conference when callers join or depart. The meeting participants can then ask new participants to identify themselves.

Consider the following call scenario:

1. Bob presses the Meet Me button on the telephone to create a conference.

2. Bob enters a desired Meet Me telephone number. If the number is not currently in use, a conference server creates the conference immediately, and Bob connects to the conference.

3. After Bob sets up the conference, Alice and Fred simply dial the Meet Me telephone number to join the conference on the conference bridge. Anyone knowing the number may call in. When you use a Cisco Unified CallManager phone system, the default maximum number of participants is four. This is a configurable value.

Meet Me conferences may optionally play entry or exit tones as participants join and leave the conference.

Reservationless meetings are more feature-rich implementations than Meet Me conferences. The following section describes reservationless meetings.

Reservationless Conferences

Reservationless meetings are an alternative to scheduled meetings and are used when the meeting organizer quickly wants to place a meeting on the calendar without specifying the number of expected callers or the duration. For this conference type, the meeting organizer specifies a meeting name and creates a meeting identifier (or may request that the system generate one).

Unlike scheduled meetings, reservationless conferences are created immediately upon request. Resources are managed on a first-come, first-served basis.

The person hosting the meeting generally dials into the conferencing system and creates a meeting instance via the Interactive Voice Response (IVR) system.

Another type of reservationless meetings is an open-ended or continuous meeting. This meeting type is always active and can be joined at any time.

Scheduled Conferences

Scheduled conferencing allows the meeting organizer to specify resource-related items such as the number of participants, via a user interface provided by the conferencing system. Scheduled and reservationless meetings can be published on a roster or web page, allowing participants to locate and join the conference.

Some schedulers provide a telephone user interface (TUI) for participants who need to schedule conferences via their telephone keypad.

Another key feature of many conference systems is integration with calendaring systems such as Microsoft Outlook. This integration provides the meeting organizer with a central point for creating a meeting, inviting participants, and reserving the required conferencing resources.

A scheduled conferencing system has the real, practical advantage of allowing the system to be sized smaller than the peak demand. For example, if you cannot reserve at 10 a.m., perhaps you will hold your meeting at a less-busy time during the day instead. This is far superior to getting a busy signal, which is what happens if a reservationless system is undersized.

Setting Up Scheduled Conferences

When creating a scheduled meeting, the meeting organizer might specify the resources required to support the number of participants and whether a meeting should support video callers. The organizer also specifies the start and end times of the meeting.

Because conferencing system resources such as dial-in capacity and audio processing power are finite, the scheduling system must manage these facilities. The conferencing system's scheduler must ensure that a meeting will actually have the resources available at the specified time to accommodate the expected number of callers. This accounting is generally referred to as a *reservation*.

Resource reservation guarantees the required resources will be there when the meeting begins. Schedulable resources in a conferencing system include some number of access ports. For each caller, one port is consumed. For non-IP-based systems, such ports may be channels on a digital telephone trunk line. In the case of IP-based systems, there is generally a system limit on the number of allowed media connections.

Depending on the configuration, this guarantee can be somewhat of an illusion because of the practice of overbooking. When the system administrator configures a conferencing system for overbooking, it is possible to reserve more access ports than actually exist. The main benefit of overbooking is to allow real resource utilization to be maximized, because many times ports that are reserved for a meeting go unused. Participants might not call in, or the person scheduling the meeting overestimates the attendance. These ports are then available for other meetings. The downside to using overbooking is that it is possible that some reservations might not be honored at meeting time.

Scheduled and reservationless meetings have identifiers in the form of a meeting name and meeting identification number, also called the meeting ID. The meeting ID is a string of digits that allows callers to identify and join the desired meeting. When joining by telephone, the participant specifies the desired meeting by entering the digit string from the telephone keypad. The meeting organizer may specify the digit string or request that the conferencing system generate it automatically.

Common methods for creating scheduled meetings include the following:

- **Web browser interface**—Most conference scheduling interfaces provide a central, web-based conferencing portal. A portal is a web server providing browser access to the conferencing system's user and administrative interfaces. The portal allows users to log in and schedule conferences, view future conferences, and join and control active conferences. The conference portals also list the dial-in access information for conferences.

- **Via the telephone**—This method allows a user to dial into the conferencing system, log in, and schedule meetings by means of the telephone keypad. The user follows voice prompts, entering the required information.

- **Microsoft Outlook integration**—Some conferencing systems are integrated with e-mail and calendaring systems, such as Microsoft Outlook. With this option, a plug-in is installed into the Outlook calendaring application, which communicates with the conference server. After installation, Outlook presents a new page/tab in the calendar where the meeting details can be entered directly. This integration eliminates the need for the user to bring up a separate browser program.

After the meeting organizer enters the meeting details, the conferencing system reserves resources for the time period specified. This resources reservation ensures that they are available for callers when the conference starts. After the system successfully completes this task, it returns a summary of the information necessary for users to join the conference. This information usually includes the telephone number of the conferencing system, a confirmation of the conference date and time, and some sort of meeting identification number or other identifier. This information can then be sent as a meeting invitation or listed in a meeting roster.

Joining a Scheduled or Reservationless Conference

At meeting time, each participant in a scheduled or reservationless conference typically dials the access number provided, which usually connects to an IVR system. The IVR prompts the participant to enter the meeting ID number and might ask the participant to "speak your name at the tone" for a recorded name announcement. When the IVR connects the participant to the conference, the IVR plays the recorded name for all participants to hear. Alternatively, each participant might enter a predefined "profile" number, which the conference server uses to track the participant in the conference. The profile may have a previously recorded name, which is used to announce the new participant.

Depending on how the conferencing system is configured, new participants may be prompted to record their name before joining the meeting. The conference server may then play the recorded name announcement at the time participants join and leave the conference.

After the participant enters the meeting ID and records his name, the conference server might move a new caller to a temporary waiting room until the meeting organizer joins the conference. Or, the meeting organizer can specify that participants proceed directly to the conference.

In another variant of the reservationless meeting, the meeting is tied to a specific dial-in phone number. In this mode, the participants just call the number and are placed directly into the conference, without having to interact with the IVR system.

It is fairly common for conferences to be announced through distribution of a URL link, which brings the users into a multimedia meeting without having them dial in and use the TUI. The user just clicks the provided link through the web browser, and the system identifies the user and dials the user's phone directly. Over time, this will likely become the predominant attendance method for both voice and video meetings.

Scheduled and Reservationless Conference Features

Features available during the conference are called *in-conference controls*. These features enable meeting coordinators to control certain aspects of the meeting. Other features include allowing a participant to initiate a collaboration session. This section provides details about the most common conferencing features.

Whiteboard Collaboration

The whiteboard collaboration feature allows users to share an application window on their computer or their entire desktop with others in the conference. The person sharing might be demonstrating an application or walking through a spreadsheet or other document with the rest of the group. Optionally, other participants can take control and interact with the shared computer, controlling the keyboard and mouse.

Muting and Ejecting Participants

The muting and ejecting participants feature allows a conference administrator to mute the incoming voice stream from a participant or remove a participant from the conference. A participant might need to be muted when calling from an environment with much background noise or when the participant has placed the call on hold and music on hold is configured on the participant's phone.

When a meeting agenda changes, it might be necessary to restrict the attendee list and remove certain participants from the meeting.

Using Talk-Over Mode

Another feature is *talk-over mode*. This feature lowers the volume at which other participants are heard so that the administrator can be heard clearly when speaking.

Dialing Out to Participants

Sometimes a meeting chairperson or initiator might want to perform a dial-out operation, either as a courtesy or to control toll charges. Meeting participants can also initiate a dial out to their own phone number, using a web interface.

Sidebar Conferences

Sidebars allow participants in a main conference to move to a smaller breakout session. A breakout session is generally used by a small group to work on some aspect of the main topic, after which they may rejoin the main conference. Some sidebar conferences offer a whisper mode, in which participants in a sidebar conference can hear the main conference, but with a reduced volume. This whisper mode enables them to track the activities in the main conference while still discussing the sidebar agenda items.

Voice and Video Conferencing Components

A typical centralized video conferencing system requires a device that acts as the core entity to receive and redistribute streams. This device is known as a multipoint control unit (MCU).

The MCU terminates all voice and video media streams in a conference and consists of two types of logical components:

- A single multipoint controller, generally referred to as an *MC* or *focus*

- One or more multipoint processors, generally referred to as an *MP* or *mixer*

The MP and MC might reside in separate servers or co-reside in a single server.

> **NOTE** Note that the terms *MP* and *MC* are used by the International Telecommunications Union (ITU) and are generally associated with H.323 signaling. The terms *focus* and *mixer* are used by the Internet Engineering Task Force (IETF) in reference to systems using Session Initiation Protocol (SIP) signaling.

The MC controls the conference while it is active and operates on the control (signaling) plane. The control plane is simply the part of the system that manages conference creation, endpoint signaling, and in-conference controls. It negotiates the session parameters with each endpoint and controls all voice and video conferencing resources. The MC does not process the media streams directly.

Whereas the MC exists on the control plane, the MPs operate on the media plane and receive media streams from each endpoint. A basic MCU typically has a single audio MP for audio mixing and a single video MP for composing the video streams. The MPs generate output streams and send them back to the conference participants.

A video MP might be capable of implementing one of several video composition schemes. The MCU is responsible for configuring the MP for the type of video layout (1×1, 2×2, and so on) sent to each participant. The video display output from the MP may vary from participant to participant.

Figure 1-1 shows an example of a video conferencing deployment consisting of a variety of video endpoints and devices. This deployment includes VoIP gateways providing connectivity to the public switched telephone network, endpoints that use SIP and H.323 signaling protocols, and an H.323 gatekeeper (see Chapter 6, "Signaling Protocols: Conferencing Using H.323," for a discussion of gatekeepers). The diagram also shows other types of video devices, such as endpoints that use H.320 signaling and others that use the Cisco Skinny Call Control Protocol (SCCP).

Figure 1-1   *Video MCU Network Connectivity, with a Variety of Endpoints, Connected via LAN and PSTN Networks*

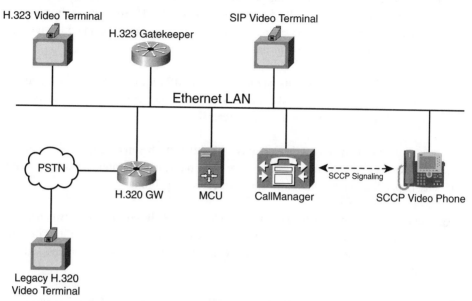

Cisco SCCP devices work together with Cisco Unified CallManager and may appear to the network as either SIP or H.323 devices. The H.320 device is an older type of video endpoint that uses ISDN lines for transporting audio, video, and signaling. For it to participate in the meeting, it connects via an H.320 gateway, which converts the H.320 to the H.323 protocol. Each of these devices may participate in the same video conference if the MCU control plane supports the same list of protocols.

The two main video composition schemes are *voice-activated switching* and *continuous presence*. Other schemes may include a combination of voice-activated and continuous presence modes, in which some windows are fixed and others contain the active speaker.

Video Conferencing Modes

This section describes the various operating modes and features of common video conferencing systems.

Voice-Activated Conferences

In voice-activated switched (VAS) mode, the MCU switches who is seen by others in the conference based on the incoming voice energy level from the various participants. When a new person speaks, the MCU forwards the video stream of the loudest speaker to each endpoint, with one exception: The loudest speaker usually receives a stream of the previous loudest speaker. The reason is that because most endpoints provide a "self view" for each participant, the loudest speaker does not need another self-view stream from the MCU. Some users, however, prefer to know when their image is being transmitted, and MCUs often provide an option in which the active speaker is the only image transmitted.

Because the MCU contains both the audio and video MP for the conference, the audio mixer reports changes in the loudest speaker to the MC, which then commands the video MP to switch to a new set of current and previous video streams.

Because endpoints may have video streams with different stream characteristics from other endpoints (codecs, bit rate, frame rate, picture size), the video MP might need to convert the video streams, depending on the endpoints' specific receive capabilities.

For example, if endpoints are using different video codecs, the conversion between one codec and another is called *transcoding*. If the endpoints have different receive capabilities in terms of bit rate, the MCU must adjust the rate at which video is transmitted, using a process called *transrating*.

Transcoding or transrating requires the video MP to fully decode and then re-encode the video. These processes require DSPs on the MCU. For a voice-activated conference, the processing load is less than what is required for the continuous presence mode. You can find more information in the next section.

Another variant of voice-activated mode is called *image passthrough* or *stream switching mode*. In this mode, all endpoints send and receive video streams with the same parameters (codec, bit rate, frame rate, and image size). Because all video streams have the same characteristics, the video MP requires no transrating or transcoding functions.

For this scenario, the MP just forwards the loudest speaker's video stream to all endpoints except the loudest speaker, after replacing the Real-time Transport Protocol (RTP) headers in the source stream with appropriate RTP headers for each destination endpoint.

Conferences in this mode must have homogenous input and output video streams, each with the same parameters. The video MP does not process the video payload and therefore does not require a DSP.

Continuous Presence Conferences

Continuous presence (CP) conferences have the benefit of displaying two or more participants simultaneously, not just the image of the loudest speaker. In this mode, the video MP tiles together streams from multiple participants into a single composite video image, as illustrated in Figure 1-2. CP conferences are also referred to as *composition mode conferences* or *"Hollywood Squares" conferences*. The video MP can either scale down the input streams before compositing or maintain the sizes of input streams, generating a larger-size video composite for the output. In CP mode, most MCUs send the same composite video image to all participants.

Figure 1-2 *Continuous Presence Display Example*

The manner in which the output stream is divided into subpictures is called the *layout*, and the mapping of input streams to subpicture locations is called the *floor control*.

For example, in a 2×2 layout, the screen is divided into four quadrants, and the MCU assigns a participant to each quadrant of the screen, as shown in Figure 1-3.

Figure 1-3 *2×2 Subpicture Layout*

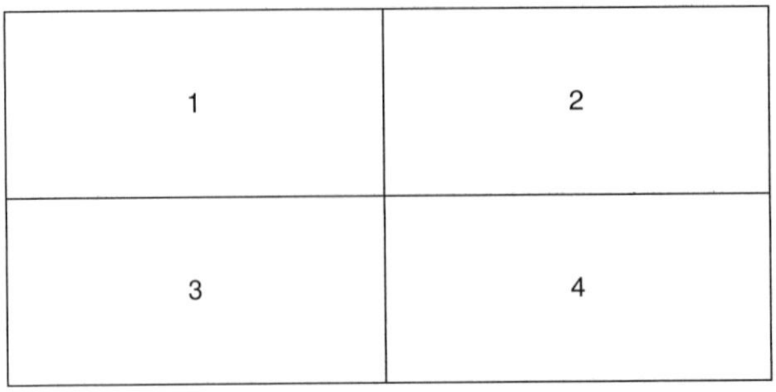

Many layouts are possible. For instance, the layout may have one subpicture that is substantially larger than the other windows. More-advanced MCUs may allow each end user to select a different layout, selectable via the telephone keypad, a conference portal web page, or special buttons on an IP phone. Cisco 79xx IP phones have a vid-mode button that enables users to toggle between two preconfigured layouts.

Some conference bridges can support a large number of simultaneously displayed participants. However, unlike VAS conferences, CP conferences require a significant amount of processing power, because the video MP must decode all video streams included in the composite video image. The number of simultaneously supported layouts is usually quite limited because of the processing power required to generate the various composite images.

Layouts with multiple pictures may have fixed image locations, or they can change dynamically as participants join and depart. Dynamic subpictures may display different participants over time. One dynamic layout option displays a variable number of subpictures; when a new participant joins the conference, the MC creates a new layout with an additional subpicture for that participant. As participants depart, the MC changes the layout to show fewer (but larger) subpictures.

Within a layout, the *floor control* policy determines how the media processor maps participants to subpictures. In addition, the floor control decides whether subpictures are locked or dynamic. A locked subpicture continues to display the same participant until that person leaves the conference or the conference organizer changes the subpicture source stream.

Floor control also allows certain privileged users to gain access to a shared resource, such as a remote device or media stream, and change the behavior for themselves or others. For example, a moderator might need to reposition a remote camera.

Some MCUs may also support a hybrid presentation, using a combination of both voice-activated and composition mode. For instance, voice-activated switching can be used for the largest subpicture, to show the person who is currently speaking. Other nonspeaking participants appear in smaller subpictures, as illustrated in Figure 1-4. The maximum number of pictures shown in a layout is a configurable option, set by the system administrator.

Figure 1-4 *Other Layout Examples for a Composition Session*

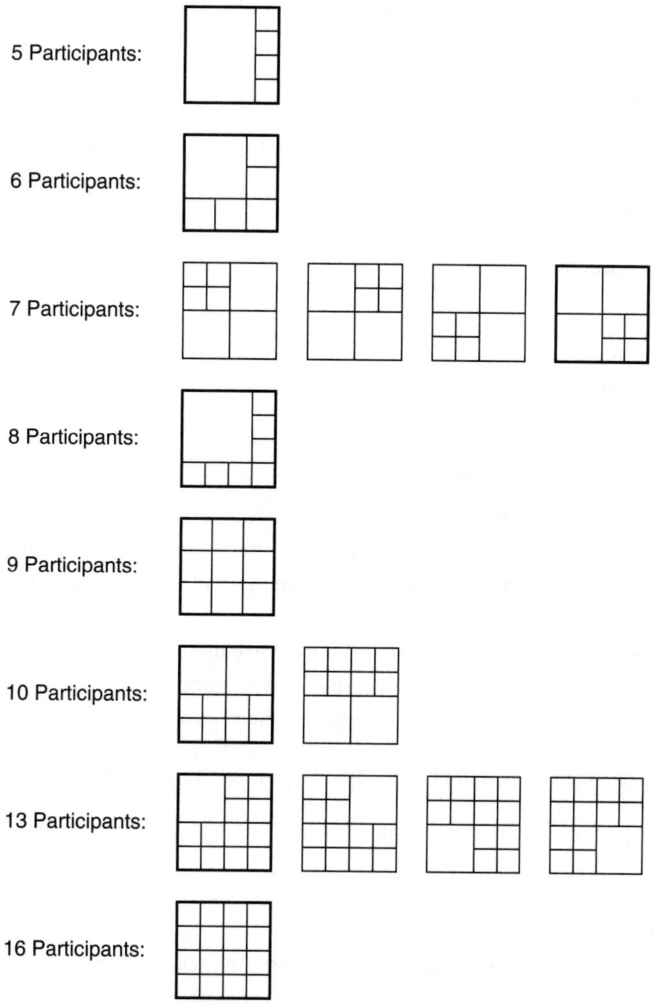

5 Participants:

6 Participants:

7 Participants:

8 Participants:

9 Participants:

10 Participants:

13 Participants:

16 Participants:

Lecture Mode and Round-Robin Conferences

One presentation variant is called *lecture mode*. This mode uses a layout with a large subpicture showing the lecturer. Video streams of students occupy smaller subpictures. The lecturer subpicture is locked, and the student subpictures operate in continuous presence mode with voice-activated priority, so that a student asking a question becomes active in one of the smaller subpictures.

The lecturer may receive a video stream with a different layout than the layout presented to students. The lecturer's video stream could display a single picture in which a different student is shown based on a time interval.

Another floor control variation is called *round-robin mode*. In this mode, the main image cycles through all the participants over a period of time.

Types of Endpoints

Conferencing endpoints fall into three categories, based on the feature set:

- Low-end desktop systems

- High-end room systems

- Ultra-high-end telepresence systems

The following sections describe all three categories.

Desktop Conferencing Systems

Low-end video conferencing products include desktop endpoints. When compared to high-end systems, the main difference is the maximum bit rate supported by the encoder in the sending direction. Other components in desktop endpoints include the following:

- An inexpensive camera that generates more noise than a high-end model, which paradoxically results in a higher encoded video bit rate for the same quality. In addition, the fixed cameras do not allow remote control via far-end camera control (FECC).

- For PC-based systems, client-side encoding or decoding on the PC rather than on DSPs.

- Video display on a computer monitor, which is often too small to use in a conference room.

Room Conferencing Systems

High-end room conferencing systems are common in medium- to large-size companies. These systems have high-quality optics and dedicated real-time codecs, which produce excellent video quality at bit rates that range up to 1922 kbps. They support one or more S-video/composite displays and often support computer monitors at resolutions up to 1024×768.

Telepresence Systems

At the extreme high end of room conferencing is the telepresence system. These systems use studio-quality high-definition cameras, large display systems, and special room lighting to provide a life-size view of the remote conference room and participants. Discrete multichannel, high-quality speaker systems and spatial audio codecs provide a vastly improved experience over traditional room conferencing systems.

Some systems such as the Hewlett-Packard HALO video collaboration system require a special HP-managed fiber-optic network to provide features that require very high bandwidth.

Telepresence systems generally include an additional high-resolution camera for sharing the image of a physical object, illustration, or design.

Video Controls: Far-End Camera Control

Far-end camera control (FECC) enables a user to control the camera position of a remote endpoint and is a feature often found in high-end room systems. It typically requires a camera with a motorized pivot that can rotate with two degrees of freedom (up/down and left/right). Options for control include zoom, pan (left/right rotation), and tilt (up/down rotation).

Video conferencing systems use one of two FECC protocols:

- **H.323**—H.323 annex Q describes the standard FECC protocol for IP networks.

- **H.224**—The second, older scheme (pre-annex Q) uses an ISDN-like H.224-based High-Level Data Link Control (HDLC) frame.

In both cases, endpoints open a low-bandwidth data channel to carry the FECC transmissions encapsulated in IP packets. The packets are transmitted from the endpoint initiating the camera movement to the MCU. The MCU then relays the packets to the far-side endpoint with the camera to be moved. Depending on the protocol used by the endpoints for FECC, the MCU might have to convert the FECC messages from annex Q to H.224 or vice versa. To save bandwidth, the FECC channel might close after a period of inactivity.

At connection time, endpoints exchange FECC protocol capabilities and negotiate which protocols to use, if any. If the remote device indicates it does not support FECC, the user interface on the local device often shows the FECC option "grayed out" (not selectable).

In H.323, two endpoints negotiate FECC protocol formats using the Terminal Capabilities Set (TCS) messages. Older endpoints support only the H.224 scheme, and others use the annex Q mechanism. Some H.323 endpoints support both annex Q and H.224 protocols.

The Internet Engineering Task Force (IETF) has not yet defined any standards for how to transport FECC messages between endpoints. Therefore, endpoints using IETF call signaling standards such as SIP generally use proprietary methods to transport FECC. This has resulted in interoperability issues among different manufacturers.

Because proprietary methods of FECC may also appear in H.323 endpoints, FECC interoperability among different endpoint manufacturers is problematic at best.

Text Overlay

Video image processing within the conferencing server may allow a text overlay within a presentation window (subpicture). This text overlay can display identifying information such as the caller's name or phone number. The text generally appears as a small semitransparent overlay on top of the video image. The conference organizer can often configure the degree of opacity, font, font size, and color.

Summary

This chapter provided an overview of voice and video conferencing systems. The chapter discussed the various modes in which conferencing systems operate and briefly described the components that comprise a system. In addition, you learned about the features available in each conference type and how the user interacts with and invokes them.

The chapter closed with a description of the three tiers of video conferencing endpoints currently available in the marketplace and a description of their features.

The next chapter provides an in-depth look at conferencing architectures and the components that comprise a conferencing system.

This chapter covers the following topics:

- Components of a conferencing system

- Conferencing architectures

- Advanced conferencing scenarios

CHAPTER 2

Conferencing System Design and Architecture

This chapter examines various conferencing system architectures, their design, and the interactions of the modules that comprise the system. Details are provided about the user interface, conference control, and control and media planes from which conferencing systems are constructed.

The later sections of this chapter discuss architectural models. In addition, specific conferencing system features and operational modes are reviewed in detail. Topics include the role of a conference moderator, floor control, lecture and panel mode.

Components of a Conferencing System

A conferencing system is composed of several components, including a user interface, a conference policy manager, media control, a player/recorder, and other subsystems. This section explores these individual elements, providing details about the functionality found in each service and how together they make up a conferencing system.

Figure 2-1 shows the major layers of a conferencing system:

- **User interface**—The user interface typically consists of several separate interfaces:

    — A scheduler to arrange conferences in advance.

    — A web portal for system access and control via a browser.

    — A voice user interface (VUI) to allow users to manage the conference after participants join.

    — A Meet Me button to create a conference. In the most basic user interface, conference creation can be accomplished by having the user press the Meet Me button on a phone and enter a conference number.

    — An Interactive Voice Response (IVR) system to deliver voice prompts to users who dial into the conference. The user may interact with this system via the telephony user interface (TUI) or via voice recognition.

- **Conference control**—Conference control performs resource allocation, conference management, and call routing. The user interface and scheduler interact with conference control to create meetings, insert and remove users from meetings, and connect them to the IVR based on user input.

- **Control plane**—The control plane contains the signaling stacks, such as H.323 or Session Initiation Protocol (SIP). It controls incoming and outgoing connections and negotiates session parameters based on the server's media capabilities.

- **Media plane**—The media plane consists of the video and audio mixers, which have inputs and outputs for media streams. In addition, the player/recorder subsystem resides in the media plane. Under the control of the VUI, the player can read audio files and play them to the user. The VUI may also direct the recorder to record a stream. Recorded streams may be from an endpoint, such as when recording a user's name for playing into the conference, or it may record the entire conference call for later retrieval.

  Transcoding services are used for converting streams from one compression algorithm to another. Transcoders use digital signal processors (DSP) and reside in the media plane.

> **NOTE**   The control plane and the media plane are the principal elements of conferencing but exist at a lower level and are not visible to the end user.

- **Administrative interface**—The administrative interface provides access for the system administrator to control and configure the system. It can interact with the conference control, control plane, and media plane layers. Configuration options can include the following:

  — Setting resource allocation defaults, such as the minimum number of ports each scheduled meeting will reserve

  — Configuring the number of overbook and floater ports

  — Specifying the maximum meeting length

  — Enabling and configuring the signaling protocols and defining which one should be used when the system initiates an outbound call

  — Configuring a system name

  — Configuring audio codecs and preferences

  — Setting video capabilities and bandwidth limitations

  — Adding and configuring system users and capabilities

  — Adding or updating recorded prompts

  — Setting the system to an enabled or disabled state

Figure 2-1 *Hierarchy of Conferencing System Layers*

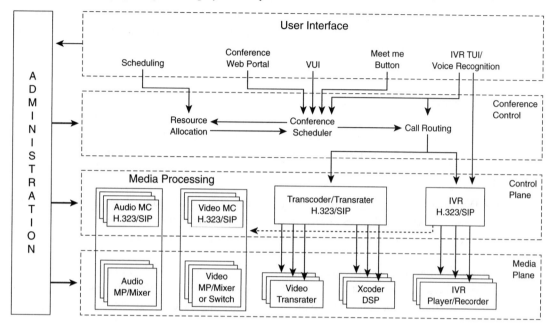

The following sections describe each layer in more detail.

User Interface

The user interface enables the user to interact with and control the conferencing system. The user can schedule new meetings, attend meetings, and have access to a set of in-conference controls. The two main interfaces are a web browser interface and the telephone.

Web Portal

The web portal provides a web browser interface to the conferencing system. It allows a user to log in, schedule meetings, attend meetings, view the active speaker list, and perform moderator functions. Such functions include muting and unmuting participants and controlling the audio volume of certain callers. When joining a meeting, users may request that the system initiate an outbound call directly to the user's phone, eliminating the need for users to call in and re-authenticate themselves. They can also eliminate the need to enter the meeting identification number, because the system already knows which meeting the user wants to attend from the browser session.

Voice and Telephony User Interface

The IVR is the user interface externally visible to the caller. The interface generally consists of a series of menus, allowing the caller to interact with the system based on a set of context-sensitive scripts running on the IVR. Callers can input requests by using the telephone keypad, or sometimes by means of voice recognition.

The initial script may play a welcome prompt and present some high-level menu choices. Then, depending on the user's selection, new scripts are executed that control that specific context. At some point, the user enters the meeting ID and is connected. Meetings can also be access protected, requiring the user to enter a password or authentication code too before being allowed to join.

The IVR interacts with the user by means of a set of prerecorded audio prompts, which may be either bundled with the devices or recorded by the system administrator. These prompts may be recorded in the various languages supported by the conferencing system.

While a meeting is in progress, participants and moderators can invoke in-conference controls. These features include operations such as allowing a caller to mute the outgoing stream to the conference, initiating a roll-call announcement, or moving the caller to a breakout conference.

These in-conference features constitute a Voice User Interface (VUI). Participants can often access these features via a website hosted by the conference server.

Conference moderators may use the VUI to control other aspects of the conference. One especially useful feature of a VUI is the ability to identify callers who are contributing excessive background noise to the conference by showing them in the active speaker list. The moderator can then mute or eject these disruptive participants. Users can mute and unmute their own input streams by pressing a key sequence on the phone. This feature enables them to participate in meetings when they are in environments with excessive background noise without disrupting the meeting.

Another often used VUI feature enables the moderator to play announcements to meeting participants in breakout sessions, requesting they rejoin the main meeting.

Meet Me Button

For simple conference systems, the telephone of the end user may have conference control buttons, such as the Meet Me or Conference button, used for creating ad hoc conferences. You can read about their use in Chapter 1, "Overview of Conferencing Services."

Conference Control

The conference control layer has three main functions:

- Resource allocation

- Conference management and scheduling

- Call routing

The conference scheduler works with the resource allocation module to reserve ports during the time window when meetings are scheduled to be active. The resource allocation module is aware of how the administrator has configured the system with respect to conferencing, floater, and overbook ports and uses this information when responding to resource allocation requests.

At meeting time, after the user has entered a meeting ID, the scheduler checks the resource availability for the conference and then directs the call routing module to add the caller to the meeting.

The conference scheduler is responsible for managing resources used for current and future conferences. Conference servers typically have a capacity measured in ports, and each connected conference participant consumes a port. The conference scheduler and resource allocation module keep track of the total number of ports available and the number of ports used. When a user schedules a conference, the scheduler may optionally reserve ports in advance. The conference scheduler must keep track of meeting start and end times along with port reservations for those periods. The scheduler also provides utilization statistics, and may have log files for billing purposes.

The scheduler may separate the entire pool of ports into partitions and use different partitions in different ways: one partition might be used for reserved conferences, another might be used for overbooked ports, and another might be used for ad hoc conferences.

The scheduler uses the overbook pool whenever the number of ports to be reserved exceeds the actual number of available ports on the system. In this case, if the overbook pool contains available ports, the scheduler can assign these ports to a scheduled conference, allowing the scheduling request to complete successfully. Overbooking allows more-complete utilization of the system, because some number of reserved ports may go unused. Floater ports are a pool of ports that are accessed when the number of actual participants in a meeting exceeds the reservation. Floater ports may not be reserved and are used to handle overflow conditions.

Before a participant is allowed to enter a meeting, the conference scheduler performs a number of checks. First, it verifies that the requested meeting is valid and scheduled for the current time. If the meeting is valid and the participant is the first to join, the scheduler creates the meeting instance. If a suitable port is available, the scheduler allocates a port for the conference, debits the port pool, and adds the incoming party to the meeting. As each participant departs, the scheduler returns the port used by that participant to the available port pool.

One significant challenge for the resource management aspects of the scheduler is how to deal with the various types of media streams and their characteristics at run time. The resource allocation originally made for an audio port might be inadequate if the caller calls in with a high-complexity codec. These calls take more compute power from the DSP, and the DSP cannot process as many of these stream types. Unfortunately, it is not often possible to know in advance how many of these types of callers may want to participate in a conference.

Video stream characteristics have a similar impact, because video streams have a variable bit rate. In these cases, a particular conference might need to be configured with a bit rate maximum. Even though some callers might call in at a lower rate, the only way to have a deterministic outcome is for the scheduler to assume that all callers will use the maximum rate allowed. Another factor is the number of transrating and transcoding resources to be reserved. Depending on the network topology, the types of video endpoints in use, and where the calling endpoints reside in the network, varying numbers of transcoding and transrating resources might be needed at meeting time.

Control Plane

The control plane of the conference server is responsible for establishing a signaling channel with each endpoint, negotiating the type of media, and connecting the endpoints with the mixers on the media plane. The control plane opens H.323 or SIP ports, listens on those ports, and waits for incoming connections. When an endpoint connects to the control plane, the control plane provides the endpoint with the audio and video session capabilities of the conference server as part of media negotiations. As discussed in Chapter 5, "Signaling Protocols: Conferencing Using SIP," and Chapter 6, "Signaling Protocols: Conferencing Using H.323," the capability negotiation may occur in the form of the H.323 terminal capabilities exchange or a SIP offer/answer.

After the control plane and the endpoint complete the media negotiations, the two sides open logical channels for media streaming. If the connection fails at any time during the call, the control plane must notify the underlying layers. This allows the lower layers to free allocated resources associated with the session.

Different standards refer to two different terminologies when discussing the conferencing server, depending on the signaling protocols in use. In H.323 mode, the International Telecommunications Union (ITU) term *multipoint control unit* (MCU) may be used when referring to the conference server. In SIP mode, the Internet Engineering Task Force (IETF) term *focus* is frequently referenced.

After the user has entered the meeting ID, the IVR notifies the conference scheduler. The conference scheduler then performs the final step of connecting the user to the meeting, and media streaming begins.

The IVR also controls the player/recorder, providing functions such as recording a user's name and playing it as an announcement to the main conference upon joining and departing.

Media Plane

The media plane contains the infrastructure that processes media streams and includes the audio and video mixers. The media plane manages Real-time Transport Protocol (RTP) and Real-time Transport Control Protocol (RTCP) port allocation and may control a DSP for setting audio and video stream characteristics. Stream characteristics include elements such as the codec, the RTP payload type, the picture size, the frame rate, and so on.

The media plane is also responsible for RTCP message exchanges and for detecting stream failures. Media stream failures may take the form of incoming RTP stream loss or Internet Control Message Protocol (ICMP) port unreachable events. ICMP events are errors returned by the remote device when network error conditions arise. As an example, an ICMP port unreachable error occurs when the receiving device detects packets are arriving for a closed port.

Depending on the implementation, the conference server may report session loss to an external component, or notify the signaling and control planes so that they can tear down the connection and free resources.

Player/Recorder

The player/recorder operates under the control of the IVR and VUI. Its purpose is to play audio prompts to the user and record audio, such as the name of a participant or location. It can also record the audio from a meeting and play announcements to the entire conference.

Video Mixer/Compositor

After the control plane has successfully negotiated the video stream characteristics and conference management has determined the type of video presentation required, the video mixer/compositor is responsible for creating the overall video experience. It receives and decodes the incoming streams in various formats and creates the appropriate output streams for the endpoints based on conference policy.

Stream characteristics from the various connected endpoints can be different, depending on the sending and receiving capabilities of the attached devices. In addition, it is possible for devices to send asymmetric streams. For example, a device with a low-resolution camera can transmit a smaller Quarter Common Interchange Format (QCIF), or 176×144, stream, but expect to receive a larger Common Interchange Format (CIF), or 352×288, picture size as the receive stream.

The video mixer must be capable of receiving streams in a wide range of bit rates, picture formats, and compression schemes, and it must be capable of sending streams in formats expected by the other devices. After decoding, the mixer may opt to create an output stream by tiling together smaller versions of the input streams, a mode known as *continuous presence* (CP). Alternatively, it may instead select a specific stream for transmission based on the loudest talker, a mode known as *voice-activated switched* (VAS) *mode*.

There are two common presentation modes: one in which all participants see the active speaker (including the person speaking), and another in which the active speaker instead sees the previous speaker. The mode in which the active speakers see themselves is useful if there is no other indicator that their image has been selected for distribution. The downside to this mode is that some delay usually occurs between the audio and video, and the lag in lip synchronization can be a distraction to the speaker.

A simplified form of a video mixer is a video switch. The video switch operates in image passthrough mode, in which it simply takes incoming video packets from one participant (such as the current speaker) and forwards the packets to the other participants. The video switch does not operate on the video payload, but updates the packet header so that it can be forwarded.

Video Transrater

A video transrater is a device inserted in the path between two endpoints that lowers the video bit rate in one direction. Figure 2-2 shows a topology with several endpoints and a transrater. Video transrating is a key component needed to create an integrated conferencing service that links endpoints from LAN, broadband, and mobile networks.

Figure 2-2   *Video Transrating Network*

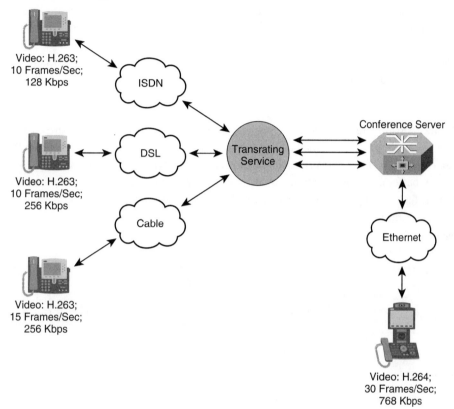

When endpoints negotiate video characteristics for the media streams, they decide on three main attributes:

■ The send/receive bit rate

■ The frame rate

■ The send/receive compression scheme (video codec)

Depending on the network topology, some devices may connect to the conference with high-speed connections, and others may be restricted to lower speeds. Connecting at lower speeds could be a result of link bandwidth limitations or network policy restrictions. The device may also connect at a lower speed if it has processor limitations that limit the rate at which it can receive video data.

For bandwidth-constrained devices to receive a high-bandwidth video stream, the conference server must add a transrater to the video path. The transrater performs rate matching by converting the high-bandwidth stream to a lower-bandwidth stream suitable for the destination endpoint.

Because high-speed video devices on a high-bandwidth network can always accept lower-speed incoming streams, video conferencing network topologies apply transrating in only one direction, from the high-bandwidth endpoint to the low-bandwidth endpoint.

In the opposite direction, the video mixer simply forwards the lower-speed stream without processing. Figure 2-3 shows the block diagram for a transrater. In Figure 2-3, video RTP packets are received from the network. Because packets may arrive out of order, they are first placed into a jitter buffer and reordered based on their RTP sequence number. Packets are then decoded and the media content placed into a raw picture buffer. The raw picture information is then re-encoded at a lower bit rate as required by the device to which the packets will be sent.

Figure 2-3 *Transrating Block*

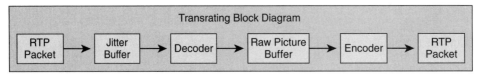

Video Transcoder

Video transcoding converts one stream type into another and changes one or more of the video characteristics. The block diagram of a transcoder is shown in Figure 2-4. A video transcoder may change the encoding format (codec), bit rate, resolution, and frame rate by decoding the incoming stream into a raw video buffer and then re-encoding it. Because the transcoder can easily select the output bit rate, transrating functionality is built in, and therefore, conference topologies do not need a separate transrater.

Figure 2-4 *Video Transcoding Block*

Audio Mixer

Within a conference, the audio mixer is responsible for selecting the input streams and summing these streams into a mixed output stream. This section provides a detailed view into the various modules that comprise it.

The audio mixer is the core component in the media plane. It is responsible for selecting incoming audio streams, summing them, and distributing the summed output back to the participants.

When mixing audio streams in a large conference, the audio mixer selects only a subset of the input streams; typically, the mixer selects three or four of the loudest streams for summation. The reason is because the human ear is capable of differentiating between only three or four distinct talkers. The mixer discards the remaining audio streams.

The mixer may also include an event reporting mechanism, allowing it to communicate internal events to other system components. For example, a conferencing system component might need to display on a web interface which participants are currently speaking. Another event of interest is media streaming failure detection. Media failure events can notify the signaling stack to initiate a call disconnection.

In addition to creating an output stream containing the three or four loudest participants, the audio mixer must also satisfy another requirement: participants who are included in the mix should not hear their own audio in the mix. Some delay occurs in the summation and return of the composite audio, and therefore, participants in the mix could potentially hear a delayed echo of their own streams played back to them, after mixing.

To avoid self-echo, each endpoint that contributes a stream for the audio mix receives a unique output stream, which does not contain audio from the same participant.

This approach is referred to as *N–1 summation*, where *N* is the number of mixed streams, and the stream returned to a conferee is the summation of the mixed streams, minus the stream contributed by that individual.

Figure 2-5, which illustrates the basic components of an audio conferencing system, shows an example in which the mixer has four input streams: stream 1, stream 2, stream 3, and stream 4. Streams 1, 2, and 3 have been selected for summation, but stream 4 has not. Figure 2-5 illustrates how endpoints that have streams selected for summation (mixing) receive a special mix in which the audio from their own stream is omitted. For the device assigned to steam 1, the mixed stream is the summation of stream 2 and steam 3. For stream 2, the mixed stream is the summation of stream 1 and stream 3, and so on. For stream 4, which is not contributing to the mix, the return stream is made up of all three contributing streams (that is, steam 1, stream 2, and stream 3).

Figure 2-5 *Audio Mixer Block Diagram*

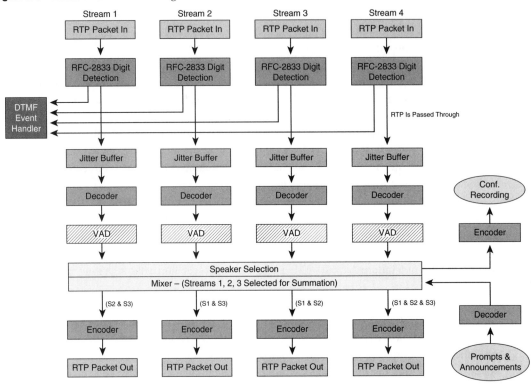

The following sections describe the components of the audio mixer block.

Network (IP/UDP) Module

The User Datagram Protocol (UDP) stack is responsible for sending and receiving RTP packets to and from the remote devices. Each incoming stream requires one socket. An endpoint signals the desired address and port for an incoming stream to the remote endpoint during the initial call setup. For H.323, the endpoint includes this information in the H.245 signaling. For SIP, the endpoint lists this information in the SDP part (offer/answer) of the SIP signaling.

RFC 2833 DTMF Detection and Generation

RFC 2833 is a standard that specifies a method of signaling Dual Tone Multiple Frequency (DTMF) digits using an RTP payload. The RFC 2833 DTMF detection and generation module is used by the audio mixer to detect incoming digits and to generate outgoing digits if directed to do so by media processing. The detector examines the incoming packet header payload type. If the payload type matches the negotiated RFC 2833 value, the packet is further interpreted to determine the DTMF digit it contains. The mixer drops RFC 2833 digit packets before they enter the jitter buffer.

If an RFC 2833 packet arrives, the detector sends the decoded digit event to a DTMF event handler. The event handler usually forwards these events to a voice user interface to invoke some function, such as playing a roll call of participants, entering a breakout session, or possibly muting the ingress stream.

In some situations, it might be necessary for the mixer to receive and then regenerate RFC 2833 packets. This situation arises when a participant wants to bring a voice-mail system and then play a message from the mailbox to other participants in the meeting. After adding the voice-mail system to the meeting, the participant presses digits on the phone, and the mixer forwards those packets to the conference system, allowing the voice-mail system to respond accordingly.

Another situation that requires a mixer to generate DTMF occurs when DTMF is required to manually connect two separate conferences, using an out-dial process.

Compensating for Network Issues: The Jitter Buffer

Receivers must handle three potential anomalies in the input audio stream:

- RTP packets arriving at a receiver may exhibit variability in arrival times (jitter), encountered during transmission over the network.

- Packets may arrive at the mixer in the incorrect order.

- RTP packets can be duplicated in the network, resulting in two or more of the same packet.

However, for the mixer to operate properly, it must receive a stream of packets with uniform interpacket spacing, in the order they were transmitted.

A jitter buffer at the input of the receiver corrects error conditions introduced by the packet network and provides the mixer with a continuous stream of data. For each input stream, the receiver allocates a jitter buffer. As packets arrive, the receiver places the packets in the jitter buffer and then reorders the packets using the RTP sequence number. Duplicate packets are discarded.

A jitter buffer maintains an input buffer level, equal to the amount of data in the buffer, measured in units of time. This input buffer level may have a fixed or dynamic size. If the jitter buffer is a fixed size, it is not changed based on packet arrival characteristics.

In more-advanced implementations, the buffer can have a dynamic size and is referred to as an *adaptive* jitter buffer. In the dynamic or adaptive mode, as packets begin to arrive, the jitter buffer algorithm can recalculate the buffer size needed based on the packet arrival pattern. If the incoming stream exhibits highly variable rates of packet arrival, the algorithm maintains a larger steady-state input buffer level to absorb momentary periods of input buffer starvation. When this occurs, the buffer is unable to provide packets at the real-time audio rate.

A large jitter buffer level provides more protection against jitter buffer starvation. However, if a jitter buffer maintains an input level that is too large, the jitter buffer adds significant delay to the stream, resulting in perceptible audio delay.

If the jitter buffer level is small, the latency is reduced, but the buffer provides less protection against starvation. If the packet experiences a high delay through the network and arrives late, the mixer is forced to play concealed audio in place of the packet. In this case, the jitter buffer discards the packet if it arrives too late to play. The mixer cannot always produce acceptable concealed audio to replace the discarded packet, a situation that can result in audio quality issues, in the form of audible clicks and pops in the output stream.

Generally, an audio jitter buffer should be sized as small as possible to avoid excess latency while avoiding RTP packet starvation.

Send-Side Voice Activity Detection Module

Voice Activity Detection (VAD) is a network optimization that omits packets with a low energy level. If the energy level drops below a certain threshold, RTP packets are no longer transmitted. The use of VAD can significantly reduce the amount of bandwidth consumed by a VoIP call. When VAD is active, the sending side stops transmitting audio RTP packets and instead transmits a special silence packet to the remote device. The silence packet carries a silence detection (SID) payload, indicating that packets are not being sent because VAD is active. The receiving side can then generate a local replacement stream to the listener, referred to as *comfort noise*. This process is known as *comfort noise generation* (CNG). Receipt of a silence packet also notifies the receiver that it can temporarily suspend packet loss calculations.

Receive-Side Voice Activity Detection Module

The receive-side VAD module serves two purposes. It examines the incoming RTP packets for voice content and flushes the jitter buffer if a silence packet is received. The silence packet indicates that the sender is no longer actively sending RTP packets with audio data.

The second purpose is to check the incoming packets to identify whether the packet contains speech from a participant or ambient background noise. If the packet is deemed to be background noise, the receiver does not include the stream in the audio mix.

Speaker Selection Module

The speaker selection module is a critical component of the conferencing system. Its purpose is to examine incoming streams and select the correct streams for inclusion in the set of mixed participants. The speaker selection algorithm should change the current mix of participants in a way that is smooth and imperceptible to the participants. It should also avoid clipping the leading and trailing part of talk spurts.

An example of a stream selection algorithm follows.

For each incoming stream, three criteria are assessed:

- The short-term window value, containing a running average of the voice energy level for a period of less than 50 milliseconds

- The long-term window value, containing a running average voice energy level for a period up to 200 milliseconds

- The currently observed inactivity or silent period, which is the amount of time the speaker has remained silent

After the speaker selection algorithm calculates these values, it then determines which, if any, of these streams are eligible for potentially becoming one of the active speakers.

If the selection algorithm finds a potential candidate, the algorithm compares the preceding parameters with the same parameters associated with participants in the current mixed stream.

Criteria for Determining Whether a Stream Should Be Mixed

The algorithm first determines the number of currently active streams. If the number is less than the maximum allowed (usually three to four), the algorithm includes the next available stream in the mixed stream. Any time the number of current speakers is less than the maximum, the mixer does not invoke the speaker selection algorithm, as long as the stream meets the earlier eligibility criteria.

If the number of active streams exceeds the maximum, the algorithm must determine whether a new stream should replace one of the existing streams. An example of the steps in a speaker selection algorithm follows:

1. Selection Criteria One: Silent Participant Replacement

    The algorithm checks each active participant for voice activity. If some streams have been silent for a period of time, the selection algorithm replaces the one with the longest silent period with the loudest new active stream.

2. Selection Criteria Two: Short Window Comparison

If selection criteria one is not met, the algorithm checks the value for the short window period (< 50 ms) for each active participant.

If the short window power level of a new stream exceeds the power level of an existing stream in the mix (by a threshold T1), the new stream replaces the existing stream.

3. Selection Criteria Three: Long Window Comparison

    If neither of the preceding criteria is met, the algorithm uses the long window power level. If a new stream has a long window power level that exceeds the power level of an existing stream by a threshold T2, the new winner replaces the weakest previous stream.

After the algorithm selects the active streams, it combines them into a set of N composite streams and then forwards the composed streams to the encoder for transmission.

Encoder

The encoding module compresses the mixed stream using the compression algorithm (for example, G.711uLaw, G.729, G.722, and so on) negotiated for this endpoint. After compression, the encoder performs the RTP packetization. The steps in RTP packetization include the following:

■ **Setting the RTP payload type**—The encoder sets the payload type field based on the codec used for compressing the payload. The payload type indicates to the receiver how to decode the arriving packet.

■ **Setting the RTP time stamp field**—Each RTP packet contains a time stamp, which reflects the sampling instant of the first octet in the packet. Initial time stamps are picked randomly. The sampling instant is derived from a sampling clock. For audio streams, RTP time stamps are essentially sample counts. The RTP time stamp between one packet and the next increases by a sample count that corresponds to the packetization period. For example, if the mixer is generating G.711 audio packets, transmitted at 8-kHz mono, with a 20-millisecond sampling period, each packet contains 160 samples of 1 byte each. In this example, the RTP time stamps between successive packets would be seen to increase by 160 samples.

When used with time stamps contained in Real Time Control Protocol (RTCP) sender reports, it is possible for the receiver to synchronize an audio stream with another stream, such as video. Chapter 4, "Media Control and Transport," and Chapter 7, "Lip Synchronization in Video Conferencing," provide much more detail on this topic.

■ **Assigning an RTP sequence number**—Each RTP packet is assigned a 16-bit monotonically increasing sequence number; this field of the RTP packet wraps around after reaching a value of 65535. The receiver uses the RTP sequence number to put arriving packets in order and to detect lost packets.

- **Setting the Synchronization Source field**—The Synchronization Source ID (SSRC) is used to uniquely identify RTP streams from a specific sender. The SSRC is a 32-bit number and is used to label specific streams.

- **Adding the contributing source IDs**—The Contributing Source IDs (CSRC) field contains a list of SSRCs identifying the streams that contributed (were mixed) to create this packet. The CSRC field is optional, and the sender can choose not to include it.

After the RTP packets' headers are populated, the encoder then forwards the completed RTP packet to the UDP stack for transmission.

Conferencing Architectures

Conferencing architectures can be classified into two basic models: centralized and distributed. A centralized architecture provides multiple services to video conferencing endpoints, but one single, standalone device provides each service. This approach is the most common architecture for audio and video conferencing systems. Centralized architecture provides single points for administration and management. Adding new functionality involves simply upgrading one device in the network.

In a distributed architecture, each service provides a logical functionality distributed among multiple physical devices. The constituent devices for each service communicate with each other using various protocols to provide this logical service. An argument in favor of distributed conferencing is the fact that the network load is more distributed, which might provide more flexibility when adding features to endpoints.

The following sections provide a high-level discussion about different aspects of centralized and distributed architectures.

Centralized Architecture

In a centralized model, all the components of a conferencing system are implemented in a single server. Figure 2-6 shows an example of a centralized conferencing system with the necessary software modules. These software modules interact with each other through the interprocess communication methods provided by the operating system running in that server.

Figure 2-6 *Centralized Conferencing System with Software Modules*

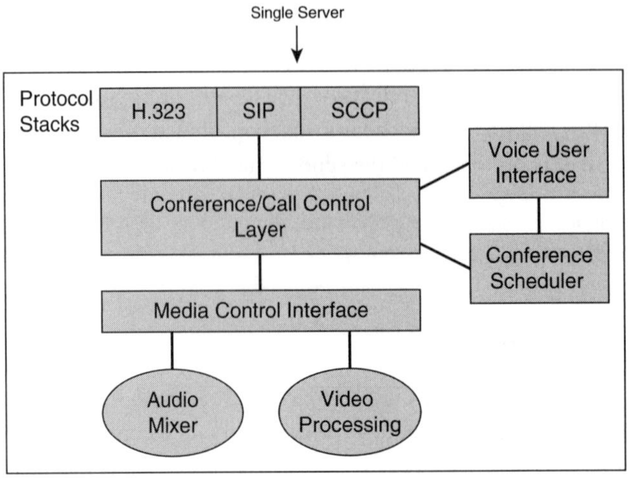

The conference control (also known as call control) module processes the signaling messages, decides whether to admit the incoming request to join a conference, and creates and processes requests to and from other internal components. The VUI and conference scheduler functions were discussed earlier in this chapter. The media control interface provides an application programming interface (API) for the conference control module to access the media services such as audio mixing. The media components send and receive audio and video packets and provide media services such as audio or video mixing. The media components can be software modules or perhaps DSP cards co-located in that server.

Distributed Architecture

To scale a conferencing system to a large number of participants, the conferencing system must be decomposed into many different components, each on a separate hardware platform, which are geographically dispersed across the network. These components must establish signaling relationships to work together as a single system.

The distributed system appears to the end user as a single device, but in fact, it is a network of devices, each providing a specific service. The Session Initiation Protocol (SIP) is especially well suited to supporting such a distributed framework, so the next section describes one example of a distributed conferencing system built on top of SIP. This model consists of several components:

- A conference control entity called the focus

- A conference policy server that defines and controls the conference

- Media policies that run on a media server to process the audio and video streams

Accessing the Focus

The central entity in the distributed architecture is called the *focus*. The focus maintains a signaling relationship with all the endpoints (or participants) in the conference. Conference and participant operations such as creating/maintaining/destroying conferences and adding/deleting participants occur in the focus. Each conference must have a unique address of record (AoR) that corresponds to a focus. A conference server could contain multiple focus instances, and each focus may control a single conference.

A caller joins a conference by connecting to a SIP Uniform Resource Identifier (URI). This SIP URI in the context of a conference is also called a *conference URI*. An example of a SIP URI is SIP:conference1@cisco.com. When a user connects to this conference, the user's endpoint connects to the focus.

Each conference operates under the constraints described by the conference policy. The conference policy describes the operational characteristics of the conference instance.

This governance controls all meeting services, including security aspects such as membership policy and media policy. Membership policy controls such attributes as which endpoints can join the conference, what capabilities they have, how long a meeting should last, and when a conference should remove a participant.

Media policy prescribes the range of stream characteristics for the various streams in the conference. These characteristics include allowable audio and video codecs, the minimum and maximum bandwidth, the maximum number of participants, and so on.

Conference Policy Server

The conference policy server is the repository for the various policies stored in the system. There is only one instance of the conference policy server within the system. No standard protocol exists for communication between the focus and the policy server.

Users join a conference by sending a SIP INVITE to the unique URI of the focus. If the conference policy allows it, the focus connects the participant to the conference. When a participant SIP endpoint wants to leave the conference, the endpoint sends a SIP BYE message to the focus, indicating that it is leaving the conference.

When a conference is to be terminated, the focus sends a BYE message to each endpoint. After all endpoints have been disconnected, the instance of the focus and the conference policy associated with the conference are destroyed. All the resources (audio and video ports) associated with that conference are freed. The focus rejects attempts by endpoints to reconnect to the unique conference URI.

Media Server

The media server establishes a signaling relationship with the focus on the control plane. It provides all the services of an audio mixer and video media processor (MP). The media server terminates all media streams from the endpoints and returns the mixed audio and video streams to each device based on conference policy.

Full-Mesh Networks

Another option for decentralized conferencing is a full-mesh conference, shown in Figure 2-7. This architecture has no centralized audio mixer or MP. Instead, each endpoint contains an MP that performs media mixing, and all endpoints exchange media with all other endpoints in the conference, creating an N-by-N mesh. Endpoints with less-capable MPs provide less mixing functionality. Because each device sends its media to every other device, each one establishes a one-to-one media connection with every other conferenced endpoint.

Figure 2-7   *Full-Mesh Conference Architecture*

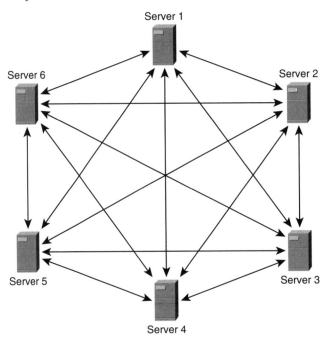

Within this N-by-N mesh, two connected endpoints must be able to negotiate a common codec. However, endpoints may use different codecs for other pairwise connections.

Endpoints that send media with the same characteristics (codec, frame rate) to multiple endpoints may use IP multicasting; in general, however, such support is not widely deployed in corporate networks.

If no centralized signaling server is present, each endpoint must similarly establish a one-to-many signaling connection with all other endpoints in the conference. Endpoints may not use IP multicast for these signaling connections.

In the full-mesh conference topology, each device provides its own media processing, and therefore endpoints do not need to transrate or transcode video streams. Because endpoints negotiate media characteristics between device pairs, it is not necessary to reduce the quality of the entire conference to the "lowest common denominator." In contrast, a nondistributed conference server may implement video mixing by simply passing through video from the loudest endpoint to all other endpoints with no video processing, a mode called *image passthrough*. In this case, the media processor in the conference server must reduce the quality of the single output video stream to the lowest common denominator of quality among the destination endpoints.

Advanced Conferencing Scenarios

Modern conferencing system designs provide more features by integrating the conference control with other collaboration services. For example, a user can join a conference call with a single mouse click instead of dialing a number and going through an authenticating process. This section provides some examples of those advanced features. These scenarios assume that the endpoints have some basic capability such as support for call transfer.

Escalation of Point-to-Point-to-Multipoint Call

In this scenario, a point-to-point call between two participants becomes a conference call with more than two parties. Participant A is in a point-to-point call with participant B and wants to invite a third participant, participant C. Participant A finds a conference server, sets up the conference, gets the URI or meeting ID, and transfers the point-to-point call to the conference server. Participant A then invites participant C into the conference call. Participant A can add participant C using different methods, one of which is a dial-out process. In a dial out, the conference server sends the invite to the endpoint to join a conference.

Lecture Mode Conferences

A lecture mode conference has a lecturer who presents a topic, and the rest of the participants can ask questions. There are two different styles of lecture mode meetings:

- **Open**—Open meetings allow participants to ask questions any time without requesting permission to speak.

- **Controlled**—In a controlled meeting, the meeting administrator or lecturer must give a participant permission to ask questions or speak. If the administrator denies the request from an audience member to ask a question, the audio from that audience member is not mixed, even if that participant is the loudest speaker. In this case, the focus instructs the mixer to exclude video from that participant in the mix.

In lecture mode video conferences, participants see the lecturer, and the lecturer sees the last participant who spoke. If none of the participants has spoken yet, the lecturer might see all the participants in a round-robin mode. In round-robin mode, the lecturer sees each participant for a few seconds.

Lecture-style meetings usually have data streams (web conferencing) associated with them. The participants can see the documents that the lecturer shares in a browser window.

Panel Mode Conference

A panel mode conference is a variation of the lecture mode conference. A panel mode conference has few panelists and more participants. This scenario is similar to having more than one lecturer in a lecture mode conference. Depending on the conference policy, end users can see one or more panelists in a continuous presence mode, in addition to seeing the participant who is speaking or asking a question.

Floor Control

Floor control coordinates simultaneous access to the media resources in a conference. For instance, the meeting organizer or moderator can ensure that all participants hear only one participant. Or, the moderator can allow only certain participants to enter information into a shared document. End users can make floor control requests through a web interface or IVR. In addition, endpoints can provide access to floor control via floor control protocols. Floor control protocols allow the endpoints and conference servers to initiate and exchange floor control commands.

Video Mixing and Switching Scenarios

When a user joins a video conference, the conference server offers the user one of a set of predefined video presentations. The conference server describes each video presentation using a textual description and an image specifying how the presentation will appear on the screen. In this scenario, by choosing a video presentation, the user chooses how many video streams (participants) to view simultaneously and the layout of these video streams on the screen.

Either conference policy or authorized participants may control the contents of each subwindow. Other aspects, such as the number of different mixes in the conference and the format of a custom mix for each user, are similar to audio mixing and use similar server capabilities and authorization methods.

The following is a list of typical video presentations; these are some of the common layouts available today in commercial products:

- **Single view**—This presentation typically shows the video of the loudest speaker. The loudest speaker sees the last speaker. If the last speaker has dropped out of the conference, the video mixer shows the previous last speaker.

- **Dual view**—This presentation shows two streams.

- **Quadrate view**—This presentation shows four streams.

- In multiview presentations, one of the streams shows the loudest speaker.

Summary

This chapter provided an overview and comparison of several conferencing architectures and described the internal components that comprise these systems. It also provided a detailed look at the theory of operation for an audio mixer and described the purpose and operations involved in video composition, transrating, and transcoding.

The chapter closed with a review of the various types of meetings and video mixing scenarios.

References

Even, R. and N. Ismail. IETF RFC 4597, *Conferencing Scenarios*. June 2004.

Rosenberg, J. IETF RFC 4353, *A Framework for Conferencing with the Session Initiation Protocol*. February 2006.

Schulzrinne, H. and S. Petrack. IETF RFC 2833, *RTP Payload for DTMF Digits, Telephone Tones, and Telephony Signals*. May 2000.

Schulzrinne, H., S. Casner, R. Frederick, and V. Jacobson. IETF RFC 3550, *RTP: A Transport Protocol for Real-Time Applications*. July 2003.

This chapter covers the following topics:

- Evaluating video quality, bit rate, and signal-to-noise ratio

- Video source formats

- Basics of video coding

- Hybrid coding

- Scalable layered codecs

- Switching frames

- Video codecs

CHAPTER 3

Fundamentals of Video Compression

This chapter covers the basics of video encoding and decoding and describes most of the algorithms used by standard video codecs. In addition to the encode/decode process, this chapter describes the preprocessing and post-processing used by most endpoints. Left out of this chapter is the Real-time Transport Protocol (RTP) packetization process, which is covered in Chapter 4, "Media Control and Transport."

Evaluating Video Quality, Bit Rate, and Signal-to-Noise Ratio

When evaluating the efficiency of a video codec, there is one primary criterion: the quality at a given bit rate. Most video conferencing endpoints negotiate a maximum channel bit rate before connecting a call, and the endpoints must limit the short-term one-way average bit rate to a level below this negotiated channel bit rate. A higher-efficiency codec can provide a higher-quality decoded video stream at the negotiated bit rate. Quality can be directly measured in two ways:

- By visually inspecting the decoded video

- By using a formula that mathematically compares the decoded video to the original video sequence

Visually inspecting the output of a decoder is a perceptually qualitative process and is generally useful only for side-by-side comparisons between different codecs. The quality level from a subjective standpoint typically ranges from "sub-VHS quality" at the low end to "DVD quality" at the high end. It is important to note that this perceptual quality incorporates the size of the image, the frame rate, and the spatial quality of the video. Business-oriented video conferencing endpoints can achieve VHS quality at 384 kbps, with 352×288 resolution and 30 frames per second (FPS). DVD quality generally requires a higher resolution of 640×480 at a frame rate of 30 FPS and no significant loss of video spatial quality. DVDs use the MPEG-2 codec and are limited to a bit rate of 10 Mbps, whereas VHS tapes encode video in an analog format.

A more objective measure of codec performance is the peak signal-to-noise ratio (PSNR). It is a measure of how much a decoded image with pixel values $P_O(x,y)$ deviates from the original image $P_I(x,y)$. The PSNR is determined by first calculating the mean squared error (MSE) between the two images:

$$MSE = \sum_{x,y}|P_O(x,y) - P_I(x,y)|^2$$

Then, the PSNR is the log ratio of the largest possible pixel value to the MSE, measured in dB:

$$PSNR = 10 \log_{10}\left(\frac{Max^2}{MSE}\right)$$

Although this formula is an objective calculation, it does not necessarily correlate to the quality of an image as perceived by the human visual system. Nonetheless, it is useful as a tool to compare different codecs.

To minimize the end-to-end delay of the video streams, video codecs used for video conferencing must operate in a mode that supports low delay. As a result, these codecs might not be able to take advantage of extended features or special coding methods commonly used when compressing material for one-way viewing, such as the encoding used for DVDs. Three of these features that are not available to video conferencing codecs include B-frames, multipass coding, and offline coding.

B-frames allow a codec to compress a frame using information from a frame in the past and a frame in the future. To compress a B-frame, the encoder must first process the future referenced frame, which requires the encoder to delay the encoding of the B-frame by at least one frame. Because of the one-frame delay, most codecs for video conferencing do not implement B-frames.

Multipass coding is the process of encoding a stream multiple times in succession. After performing the first pass, the encoder analyzes the result and determines how the encoding process can be altered to create the same quality encoded video at a lower bit rate. A multipass codec typically re-encodes a bitstream at least once, and possibly twice. Obviously, this sort of multipass processing is not possible with a codec used for video conferencing.

Offline coding is simply the process of encoding a video sequence in non-real time using computationally intensive offline hardware to achieve a lower bit rate with higher quality. Offline coding can provide a significant boost to codec efficiency, particularly for the more complex codecs such as H.264. However, this method is not available for video conferencing endpoints.

When evaluating a codec to use in a video conferencing product, it is important to observe the quality of a decoded bitstream that was encoded without any of the prior methods. When using encoded/decoded test video sequences for evaluation, make sure that those test sequences were created as follows:

- Without B-frames

- Without multipass coding

- In real time rather than offline

Video Source Formats

When two endpoints establish a video connection, they must negotiate a common supported format. This format includes the codec algorithm and parameters of that algorithm, such as frame rate and bit rate.

Profiles and Levels

Codec specifications generally define a wide breadth of features that can be used to encode a video sequence. Some of the more complex features might require additional resources, such as CPU power and memory. In addition, more CPU power is needed when decoding video with higher frame rates, image sizes, and bit rates.

Therefore, to facilitate decoders with fewer available resources, the codec specifications often define profiles and levels:

- Profiles define a limited subset of features that will be used by the encoder. Fewer features in the bitstream will reduce the resources needed on the decoder, and the decoder complexity. As an example, some codec profiles prohibit B-frames, which normally require additional frame buffer memory and CPU processing.

- Levels define limitations on parameter ranges, such as image size, frame rate, and bit rate.

Frame Rates, Form Factors, and Layouts

Two endpoints in a video conference negotiate a maximum video bit rate before connecting. Video codecs can generate bitstreams ranging from 64 kbps to 8 Mbps and more. Higher bit rates consume more network bandwidth but provide greater video quality and frame rate. A bit rate of 384 kbps is considered "business quality" for conferencing systems. However, as high-definition TV (HDTV) video conferencing becomes more prevalent, the definition of business quality might evolve to mandate HDTV resolution, and higher bit rates approaching 4 Mbps.

After the conference participants choose a video bandwidth, the endpoints choose a nominal frame rate, which is also negotiated between the two sides during call setup. For desktop PC systems with limited CPU power, the nominal frame rate is often 15 FPS, whereas higher-end standalone video conferencing systems can generally support nominal frame rates of 30 FPS. However, during the call, the actual frame rate might change over time, because the encoder must constantly trade off between bit rate, frame rate, and quality. When the video camera on an endpoint captures a high degree of motion, the encoder can maintain the same frame rate and quality by increasing the bit rate. However, because the endpoints have predetermined the maximum allowable bit rate, the encoder must instead keep the bit rate constant and lower the frame rate or quality.

Video codecs generally support a standard-size video frame format called Common Intermediate Format (CIF). The CIF format is 352×288, and other standard sizes include variations of the CIF format, shown in Table 3-1. In addition to CIF, the two other common sizes are Quarter-CIF (QCIF, 176×144) and 4xCIF (4CIF, 704×576). For all CIF variations, each pixel has an aspect ratio (width to height) of 12:11. The codec standards often refer to pixels as pels and may define a pel aspect ratio. For the CIF size of 352×288, the overall aspect ratio of the entire frame is 4:3. The total aspect ratio of a Sub-Quarter CIF (SQCIF) frame is 16:11.

Table 3-1   *Video Formats*

Format	Total Aspect Ratio	Size
SQCIF	16:11	128×96
QCIF	4:3	176×144
CIF (or full CIF)	4:3	352×288
4CIF	4:3	704×576
9CIF	4:3	1056×864
16CIF	4:3	1408×1152

Standard and High Definitions

Chapter 7, "Lip Synchronization in Video Conferencing," describes the formats for standard-definition (SD) and high-definition (HD) video formats. Some high-end video conferencing systems, such as telepresence endpoints, support HD video cameras. These cameras provide video images with a higher resolution than the traditional SD formats (NTSC/PAL/SECAM) allow. SD and HD differ in several aspects:

- **Aspect ratio**—Aspect ratio refers to the ratio of width to height of the video frame. SD typically has a 4:3 aspect ratio, whereas HD has a 16:9 aspect ratio.

- **Resolution**—HD cameras provide a video signal with a resolution as high as 1920×1080 pixels, whereas the maximum resolution of an NTSC SD signal is 704×480.

- **Interlaced or progressive**—HD cameras may provide video signals that are either interlaced or progressive. When specifying the resolution or frame rate of an HD camera, it is common to add a *p* or an *i* at the end of the specification to denote interlaced or progressive. For instance, the format 720p60 corresponds to a video signal with a size of 1280×720 pixels, progressively encoded at 60 FPS. The format 1080i50 is 1920×1080 pixels, interlaced, with 50 fields (or 25 frames) per second. Most often, the frame rate is left out of the notation, in which case it is assumed to be either 50 or 60. Also, a description of an HD signal may specify a frame rate without a resolution. For instance, 24p means 24 progressive frames per second, and 25i means 25 interlaced frames per second.

Much like interlaced processing, support for the higher resolution of HD encoding is limited to certain codecs, and often to specific profiles and levels within each codec.

Color Formats

The color and brightness information for pixels can be represented in one of several data formats. The two common formats are RGB and YCbCr. The RGB format represents each pixel using values for the red (R), green (G), and blue (B) additive color components. The YCbCr format represents each pixel using the brightness value (Y), along with color difference values (Cb and Cr), which together define the saturation and hue (color) of the pixel. The brightness values comprise the luminance channel, and the color difference values comprise the two chrominance channels. The chrominance channels are often referred to as *chroma channels*.

The video codecs discussed in this chapter process images in the YCbCr color format and therefore rely on the video-capture hardware to provide frame buffers with YCbCr data. If the capture hardware provides video data in RGB format, the encoder must convert the RGB frames into YCbCr before beginning the encoder process. This process is called *colorspace conversion*.

Video encoders process data in YCbCr format because this format partitions the most important visual information in the Y channel, with less-important information in the Cb and Cr channels. The human visual system is more sensitive to degradation in the luminance channel (Y) and is less sensitive to degradation in the chrominance channels. Therefore, the data pathways in the encoder can apply high compression to the Cr and Cb channels and still maintain good perceptual quality. Encoders apply lower levels of compression to the Y channel to preserve more visible detail. Codecs process YCbCr data that consists of 8 bits in each channel, but some codecs offer enhanced modes that support higher bit depths.

The first operation of the encoder is to reduce the resolution of the Cr and Cb channels before encoding, a process known as *chroma decimation*. Figure 3-1 shows different formats for chroma decimation.

The original, full-resolution frame of source video from the camera is represented in a format called 4:4:4. Each 4 represents a full-resolution channel, and 4:4:4 corresponds to full resolution of the Y, Cb, and Cr channels. 4:2:2 represents full resolution in the Y channel, with half the resolution in the horizontal direction for Cb and Cr. 4:1:1 represents a video image with a quarter of the resolution in the horizontal direction for Cb and Cr, with full resolution for Y. The codecs discussed in this chapter use a format known as 4:2:0, which departs from the usual nomenclature and represents an image with half the resolution in both horizontal and vertical directions for Cb and Cr, with full resolution for Y.

Figure 3-1 *Chroma Decimation*

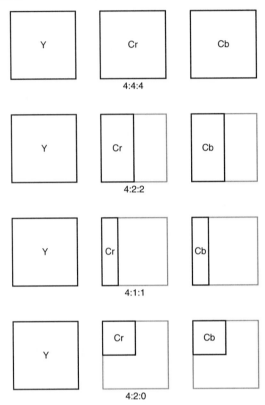

Whereas the 4:2:0 chroma decimation from 4:4:4 to 4:2:0 provides immediate reduction in the source bit rate without a significant degradation in quality, in two instances it is beneficial to retain higher chroma resolution (4:4:4 or 4:2:2):

■ The encoder should retain 4:4:4 or 4:2:2 resolution if the video stream will undergo further processing at a professional studio. Studio processing demands the highest resolution for chroma channels.

■ The original 4:4:4 resolution should be retained if the video signal will be used later for chroma keying. *Chroma keying* is a special effect that replaces a specific color in the video sequence with a different background video signal. A typical chroma key video production places a green screen behind an actor and then later replaces the green color with a different background video. The chroma key replacement operation provides the best results if the chroma channels are available at the highest resolution possible, to perform the pixel-by-pixel replacement in areas with a highly complex pattern of foreground and background pixels, such as areas of fine wispy foreground hair.

To downsample from 4:4:4 to 4:2:0, the encoder creates reduced-resolution channels for Cb and Cr by interpolating values of Cb and Cr at new locations, relative to the original full-resolution Cb and Cr channels. Codecs for video conferencing use one of two variations of this interpolation, as shown in Figure 3-2.

Figure 3-2   *Chrominance Locations for 4:2:0 Interstitial/Co-Sited Interpolation*

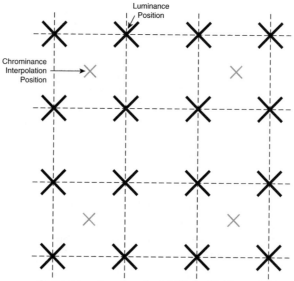

Chrominance Locations for 4:2:0 Interstitial Interpolation

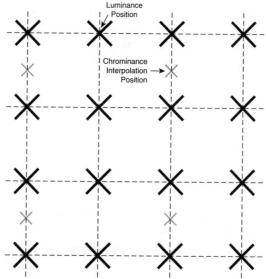

Chrominance Locations for 4:2:0 Interstitial/Co-Sited Interpolation

In the first format, called *4:2:0 interstitial*, the interpolation positions are centered at locations that are halfway between two adjacent full-resolution pixels, both horizontally and vertically. In the second format, called *4:2:0 interstitial/co-sited*, the interpolation locations are halfway between two pixels vertically and are aligned with original pixel locations horizontally. Table 3-2 shows the 4:2:0 variations used by the standard video conferencing codecs.

Table 3-2   *4:2:0 Formats Used by Video Codecs*

Codec Standard	Image Format
H.261	4:2:0 interstitial
H.263	4:2:0 interstitial
MPEG-4 Part 2	4:2:0 interstitial/co-sited
H.264	4:2:0 interstitial/co-sited

In addition, codecs must use a special variation of 4:2:0 when field coding interlaced video data. Figure 3-3 shows this variation.

For each individual field in an interlaced image, the encoder offsets the location of the chroma interpolation point up or down vertically, depending on whether the field is the top field or the bottom field. As a result, the chroma sampling positions are spatially uniform, both within each field and within the entire two-field frame.

Basics of Video Coding

Video coding involves four major steps: preprocessing, encoding, decoding, and post-processing. At the heart of the encoder is a feedback loop that predicts the next frame of video and then transmits the difference between this prediction and the actual frame. Because the encoder uses a recently decoded frame to generate a prediction, the encoder has a decoder embedded within the feedback loop.

Preprocessing

Before an image is handed to the encoder for compression, most video conference endpoints apply a preprocessor to reduce video noise and to remove information that goes undetected by the human visual system.

Noise consists of high-frequency spatial information, which can significantly increase the pixel data content, and therefore increase the number of bits needed to represent the image. One of the simpler methods of noise reduction uses an infinite impulse response (IIR) temporal filter, as shown in Figure 3-4.

Figure 3-3 *Chrominance Locations for Interlaced 4:2:0 Video*

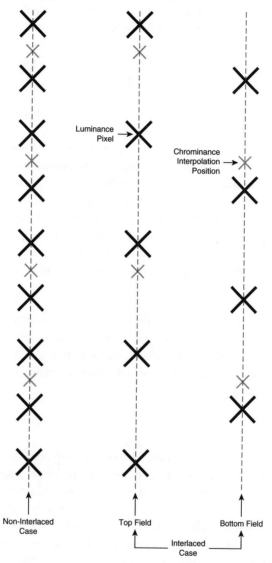

Figure 3-4 *Temporal Filtering Using an Infinite Impulse Response Filter*

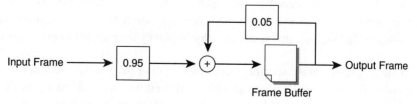

In this scenario, the preprocessor creates a new output frame by adding together two weighted frames. The first weighted frame is the current input frame multiplied by 0.95. The second weighted frame is the previous output of the preprocessor multiplied by 0.05. This process effectively blurs the image slightly in the temporal direction, reducing background noise. When participants use a noisy video source, such as a webcam, the endpoints can apply a stronger temporal filter by increasing the percentage of the previous frame used in each iteration.

A second function of a preprocessor is to remove information that is generally not perceived by the human visual system. As a result, the encoding algorithm produces a smaller bitstream with less information, but without loss of detail. Preprocessing operations often take advantage of the fact that the human visual system perceives less spatial resolution in areas of the image that contain a high degree of motion. To remove this "unseen" information, the preprocessor can use a spatiotemporal filter to blur an area of the image spatially at locations of high motion. The preprocessor performs this operation on a pixel-by-pixel basis by calculating the difference in value between a pixel in the current frame and the corresponding pixel in the previous frame. If this difference is greater than a threshold value, this pixel is deemed to be in an area of high motion, and the preprocessor can apply blurring to that pixel in the current frame, typically using a spatial low-pass filter.

Even though preprocessing is almost always used by video conferencing endpoints, the decoder is unaware of the process. Because codec specifications describe only how a decoder interprets the bitstream, preprocessing is not within the scope of the standards and therefore is never mentioned in codec specifications. However, to achieve high quality, endpoints generally must implement one or more of these preprocessing steps.

Post-Processing

The codecs in this chapter divide the image into 4×4 or 8×8 pixel areas called *blocks* and then encode each of these blocks one at a time. The decoding process is *lossy*, meaning that the decoded image deviates slightly from the original image. After the decoding process, the resulting pixel values deviate from the original pixel values somewhat smoothly within each block. However, the pixel deviations might not match up at the boundaries between two adjacent blocks. Such a mismatch in pixel deviations at a boundary causes a visible discontinuity between adjacent blocks, a phenomenon known as *block artifacting*.

To combat block artifacts, decoders can implement deblocking filters, which detect these block border discontinuities and then modify the border pixels to reduce the perceptual impact of the block artifacts. Deblocking filters can range in complexity from simple to extremely complicated:

- At the simple end of the spectrum, a deblocking filter can simply calculate the difference between two pixels at the border of a block. If the difference is above a preset threshold, the post-processor can apply a blurring operation to the pixels on each side of the border.

- More complicated deblocking filters attempt to discern whether the discontinuity is due to a block artifact or due to the edge of a real object in the scene. In addition, if the deviations at the boundary are great, the blurring filter can modify pixels at the border and pixels one position farther away from the border pixels.

Unlike preprocessing, encoder specifications usually specify the method of post-processing, because the encoder and decoder use the output of the post-processor to encode/decode the next frame. Because the encoder and decoder must remain in lockstep, they must each use an identical reference frame with identical post-processing.

Encoder Overview

Video codecs may apply intracoding or intercoding. An *intraframe*, also called an I-frame, is a frame that is coded using only information from the current frame; an intracoded frame does not depend on data from other frames. In contrast, an interframe may depend on information from other frames in the video sequence.

Figure 3-5 shows an overview of intra-image encoding and decoding. The intra coding model consists of three main processes applied to each frame: transform processing, quantization, and entropy coding. Figure 3-5 also shows the corresponding decoder. The decoder provides the corresponding inverse processes to undo the steps in the encoder to recover the original video frame.

Figure 3-5 *Encoder and Decoder Processes*

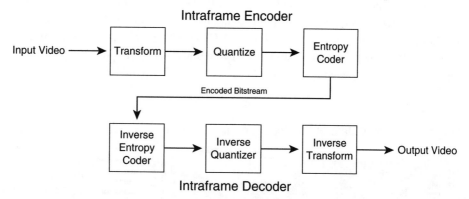

Transform Processing

Each frame of video data at the input to the encoder is considered to be in the spatial domain, where each pixel occupies an (X, Y) location in the original video frame. The transform process in Figure 3-5 converts a video image from the original spatial domain into the frequency domain. The frequency domain representation expresses the image in terms of the two-dimensional frequencies present in the original image. Table 3-3 lists the transform algorithms used by various codecs.

Table 3-3 *Codec Transform Algorithms*

Codec	Transform Type
H.261	8×8 DCT
H.263	8×8 DCT
MPEG-4 Part 2	8×8 DCT
H.264	4×4 integer
H.264 enhanced	8×8 or 4×4 integer

The encoder divides the image into 8×8 or 4×4 blocks and then applies the transform to each block. The output of each transform is an array of the same size as the input block.

There are two types of transforms:

■ Discrete cosine transform (DCT)

■ H.264 integer transform

The DCT requires a high degree of internal computational precision, whereas the integer transform consists of simpler mathematical operations that use shifts and additions, which require less precision. The DCT and integer transforms differ mathematically, but they provide the similar function of decomposing the spatial domain into the frequency domain; this direction is referred to as the *forward DCT*, or FDCT. The inverse DCT (IDCT) performs the reverse transformation, converting frequency-domain values to the spatial domain. Figure 3-6 shows the 8×8 FDCT applied to several original pixel blocks.

Figure 3-6 *Forward DCT*

Original 8×8 Pixel Data at the Top, and the Corresponding FDCT at the Bottom

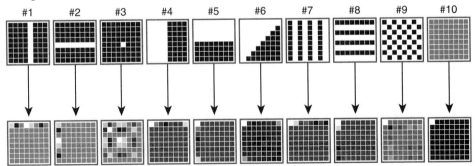

The output DCT values are typically in the range [–2048, 2047]. In Figure 3-6, therefore, the outputs of the DCT are shown normalized so that the lowest value is shown as black and the highest value as white. Image patterns 4, 5, and 6 contain less frequency information, because those patterns consist of a single edge. The DCT can represent these patterns with only a few large-magnitude DCT output values.

Each position in the transform output array actually corresponds to a pattern of pixels. For the 4×4 transform, the original 4×4 pixel block in the spatial domain can be thought of as a weighted sum of 16 different 4×4 pixel image patterns, each corresponding to a different two-dimensional frequency pattern. Each of these patterns is called a *basis function*. At the output of the transform, each value in the 4×4 array corresponds to one of these image patterns, and the value itself provides the weighting value applied to the corresponding pattern. Therefore, the values in the output array of the transform are referred to as *coefficients*. Figure 3-7 shows the frequency pattern corresponding to each coefficient position in the 4×4 transform output array.

Figure 3-7   *16 Basis Functions of the H.264 4×4 Integer Transform*

Frequency Domain Coefficients   Corresponding Spatial Domain Patterns

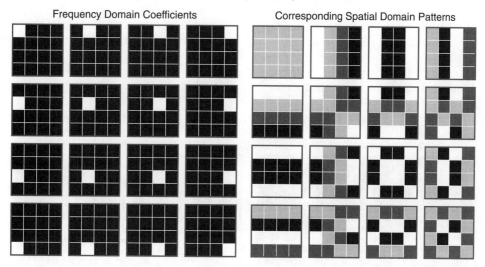

The set of blocks on the left shows each possible coefficient location in the transform output array, and the set of blocks on the right shows the corresponding pixel pattern for each coefficient weighting value. In Figure 3-7, all the basis functions have been normalized so that the lowest-valued pixel in each basis function displays as black, and the highest-valued pixel in each basis function displays as white.

The coefficients correspond to frequency patterns as follows:

■   Coefficients near the upper-left corner of the transform output array correspond to low-frequency patterns; these are patterns that vary slowly over the span of the original input block. In addition, the coefficient at the upper-left corner is referred to as the *DC coefficient* because it represents the amount of zero-frequency information in the block. This zero-frequency information is just a representation of the average value of all pixels in the block. The notation DC refers loosely to the concept of direct current, which yields a constant voltage. The remaining coefficients are called *AC coefficients* because they correspond to varying frequency patterns. The notation AC refers loosely to the concept of alternating current, which yields a constantly changing voltage.

■   Coefficient values near the lower left correspond to frequency patterns containing high vertical frequencies (such as a series of horizontal edges).

■   Coefficient values near the upper right correspond to frequency patterns containing high horizontal frequencies (such as a series of vertical edges).

■   Coefficient values near the lower right correspond to frequency patterns containing high horizontal and vertical frequencies (such as a checkerboard pattern or a pattern of diagonal lines).

Figure 3-8 shows the basis functions for the 8×8 DCT.

Figure 3-8   *64 Basis Functions of the 8×8 DCT Used in H.261, H.263, and MPEG-4 Part 2*

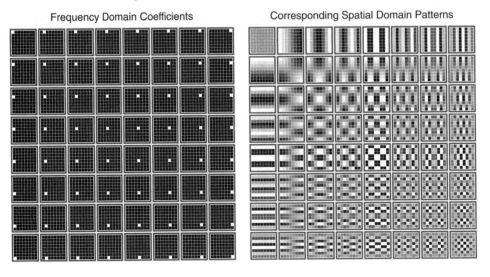

Frequency Domain Coefficients   Corresponding Spatial Domain Patterns

An 8×8 DCT is more efficient when representing large, low-frequency areas, because it needs only a few values from the upper-left corner to represent a larger 8×8 area of slowly varying pixel values. However, the H.264 codec achieves good efficiency with a 4×4 transform.

The transformation from spatial domain to frequency domain facilitates image compression in two ways:

- Images encoded in the frequency domain can be encoded with fewer bits. The reason is because typical images consist of mainly low-frequency information, which can be represented with a small number of values from the upper left of the DCT output array. Typical images have little or no high-frequency information, which means that the output of the transform will have values near the lower-right corner that are either small or zero. As described in the section "Entropy Coding," the number of bits needed to describe this sort of skewed data distribution is less than the number of bits needed to describe the original image in the spatial domain. All codecs in this chapter use this feature.

- In the frequency domain, the human visual system is more sensitive to the low-frequency information, represented by values near the upper-left corner of the transform, and is less sensitive to the high-frequency information, represented by the coefficients in the lower right of the transform. Therefore, the encoder can reduce the precision of coefficients representing the high-frequency information without severely affecting the perceived quality of the encoded video. As a result, all codecs represent the lowest-frequency coefficient (the DC coefficient) with a high degree of precision. In addition, the H.264 and the MPEG-4 Part 2 codecs progressively reduce the precision, and therefore the information content, of the coefficients representing the higher frequencies.

All codecs divide the original image into macroblocks (MB), each of which contains a 16×16 pixel area. The encoder further divides the MBs into 4×4 or 8×8 blocks and then transforms the pixels into frequency domain coefficients. Because the codecs use 4:2:0 chrominance decimation, the pixel area of the Cb and Cr components in an MB will be 8×8 rather than 16×16.

Quantization

The processing unit in Figure 3-5 that performs the quantization step is the quantizer. *Quantization* is the process of reducing the precision of the frequency domain coefficients. In the simplest form, the encoder quantizes each coefficient by simply dividing it by a fixed value and then rounding the result to the nearest integer. For instance, the H.261 specification quantizes the DC coefficient by dividing it by 8. By reducing the precision of coefficients, less information is needed to represent the frequency domain values, and therefore the bit rate of the encoded stream is lower. However, because the quantization process removes precision, some information from the original image is lost. Therefore, this process reduces the quality of the encoded image. As a result, codec schemes that use quantization are considered *lossy* codecs, because the quantization process removes information that cannot be recovered.

Quantization is performed using an input-output transfer function. Figure 3-9 shows an example.

Figure 3-9 *Input/Output Quantization Transfer Function*

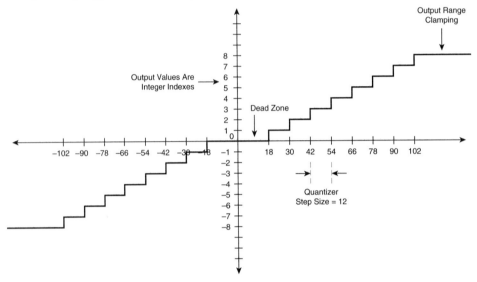

The transfer function demonstrates several aspects of quantization. The transfer function is always a stairstep, and the fewer the steps, the coarser the quantization. The range of each step on the input (x) axis is called the quantization step size. In Figure 3-9, the quantization step size is 12, which means that each step maps 12 different input values to the same output value. The output values are integer indexes, known as *quantization levels*.

In the intraframe pipeline, the quantizer operates on output transform coefficients, which may consist of signed numbers. The one exception is the scenario in which the DCT operates on original pixel values; in this case, the DC coefficient represents the average value of all pixels in the original image block and therefore is always positive. However, the quantization transfer function must accommodate both positive and negative values of DCT coefficients.

One characteristic of the DCT is that most codecs define the precision of the coefficient values to be 4 bits more than the precision of the input values. In the case of an intra coded 8×8 DCT block, the original pixels have 8 bits of precision, corresponding to values in the range [0, 255]. The DCT output values have 12 bits of precision, corresponding to values in the range [−2048, 2047]. This level of output precision is necessary to allow the IDCT to recover the original pixels to a value within ±1. Therefore, 12 bits of precision allows encoders to start with the "maximum" level of information content in the frequency domain and then reduce the precision as needed to achieve compression. Because the raw coefficients from the transform function have higher precision than the original image pixels, the quantizer must accommodate this wider range of input values.

Transfer functions generally apply *clipping*, a process that limits the output of the function to a maximum value. In Figure 3-9, the quantization process clips input values greater than or equal to 102 to an index of 8.

The transfer function might or might not apply a dead zone. Figure 3-9 shows a transfer function with a dead zone, which clamps input values in the vicinity of 0 to 0. This dead zone attempts to eliminate low-level background noise; if a coefficient is close to 0, it is assumed to be background noise and gets clamped to 0.

In some cases, the transfer function can have nonuniform step sizes, as shown in Figure 3-10.

Figure 3-10 *Quantizer with a Nonuniform Step Size*

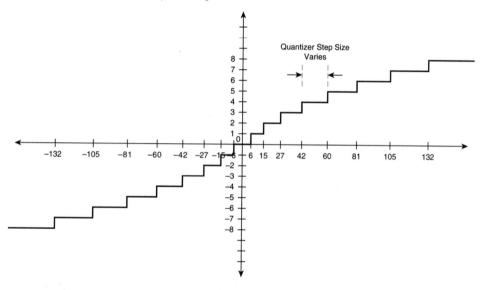

In this approach, the degree of coarseness is proportional to the magnitude of the input value. The principle is that larger input values may be able to suffer a proportionately higher amount of quantization without causing an increase in relative distortion. None of the codecs in this chapter uses nonuniform step sizes; however, the G.711 audio codecs outlined in Chapter 4 uses this method.

Quantization of the transform coefficients may consist of two methods:

- **Constant quantization**—In constant quantization, the encoder uses the same quantization step size constant for each coefficient in the 4×4 or 8×8 pixel area.

- **Matrix quantization**—In contrast, matrix quantization applies a different quantization step size to different coefficients. Typically, the matrix quantization process applies a larger step size to higher-frequency coefficients located near the lower right of the transform, because the human visual system is less sensitive to these frequency patterns. Codecs that use matrix quantization generally assign a single quantization level to a block and then use a matrix of numbers to scale the quantization level to the final step size used for each coefficient. Figure 3-11 shows such a matrix of scale factors applied to 8×8 blocks. H.264 and MPEG-4 Part 2 are video conferencing codecs that use matrix quantization.

Figure 3-11 *Quantization Matrix for Interblocks, Defined in MPEG-4 Part 2*

8	17	18	19	21	23	25	27
17	18	19	21	23	25	27	28
20	21	22	23	24	26	28	30
21	22	23	24	26	28	30	32
22	23	24	26	28	30	32	35
23	24	26	28	30	32	35	38
25	26	28	30	32	35	38	41
27	28	30	32	35	38	41	45

In most codecs, the bitstream does not specify a step size directly; instead, the bitstream contains a quantization value, often denoted by the variable Q. The encoder and decoder then use this Q value to derive the final quantization step size. A high Q value results in a larger step size and more compression.

Entropy Coding

The final stage of the generalized encoder is entropy coding, as shown in Figure 3-5. *Entropy coding* is a lossless codec scheme that seeks to reduce the bit rate by eliminating redundancy in the bitstream. Entropy coding generally operates on a string of one-dimensional data, which means that each two-dimensional quantized coefficient array must be converted into a one-dimensional string.

The entropy of a bitstream is defined as the lowest theoretical average number of bits per symbol needed to represent the information in the bitstream. It also corresponds to the theoretical minimum number of bits per symbol that an ideal entropy coder can achieve. If the bitstream contains n symbols, and the probability of each symbol is P(n), the entropy of the bitstream is calculated using the Shannon entropy formula:

$$H(X) = -\sum_{1}^{N} P_n \log_2 P_n$$

The entropy of a symbol sequence roughly indicates of how well an entropy coder will be able to compress the sequence. Sequences that have lower entropy can be coded using fewer bits per input value. Sequences that have lower entropy are those with a more highly skewed probability distribution, with some input values occurring much more frequently than other values. Such is the case for DTC coefficients, which have probability distributions skewed toward lower values.

Entropy coding generally falls into three categories: run-length coding, variable-length coding, and arithmetic coding.

Run-Length Coding

The simplest form of entropy coding is run-length coding, which achieves compression for streams containing a pattern in which a value in the stream is often repeated several times in a row. When a single value is repeated, it is more efficient for the encoder to specify the value of the repeated number and then specify the number of times the value repeats. A 1-D sequence of quantized DCT coefficients often contains long runs of zeros for the high-frequency coefficients, allowing a run-length coder to achieve a high degree of lossless compression. When the run-length coder specifically codes the number of zeros between nonzero values, this coding scheme is often called a *zero-run-length coder*.

The decoder expands each run and length pair from the encoder into the original uncompressed string of values.

Variable-Length Coding

Another form of entropy coding is variable-length coding (VLC). VLC lowers the number of bits needed to code a sequence of numbers if the sequence of numbers has a nonuniform statistical distribution. Figure 3-12 shows a sample statistical distribution for the magnitudes of AC coefficients.

Figure 3-12 *Skewed Probability Distribution for AC Transform Coefficients*

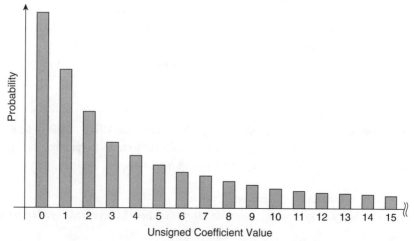

Figure 3-12 shows only the magnitude of the AC coefficient values, because most codecs encode the sign of each AC coefficient separately from the magnitude. The statistical probability distribution is highly skewed, with a much higher probability of encountering lower-valued coefficients.

For these data profiles with skewed probabilities, VLC attempts to represent the high-probability values with shorter bit sequences and the lower-probability values with longer bit sequences. Table 3-4 shows one possible VLC table that can be used in H.264 for AC coefficients. It is a standard table called the *Exp-Golomb-coded syntax*.

Table 3-4   *Exp-Golomb-Coded VLC Table*

Input Value	Encoded VLC Bit Sequence
0	1
1	010
2	011
3	00100
4	00101
5	00110
6	00111
7	0001000
8	0001001
9	0001010
...	

Table 3-4, consisting of input values and output VLC bit sequences, is referred to as a *VLC code table*. After the encoder constructs the code table, it uses the table to look up the variable-length bitstream of each input value. Instead of using a mathematical algorithm, this process uses a mapping method to map a set of input values into a set of variable-length strings. Therefore, the values in the input set are often referred to as *indexes*, or *symbols*, and many of the codec specifications refer to input symbols, rather than input values. Codecs also refer to the VLC table as the symbol code table.

Because the 0 value has the highest probability, it is represented using a single bit, with a bit string of 1. The input symbol 1 is represented using 3 bits, with a bit string of 010. The idea is to use a VLC table that minimizes the average number of bits per symbol, averaged over the entire bitstream, which is calculated using the following formula:

average number of bits per input value =
probability of symbol #1 * number of bits in the VLC code for symbol #1 +

probability of symbol #2 * number of bits in the VLC code for symbol #2 +

probability of symbol #3 * number of bits in the VLC code for symbol #3 +

…

probability of symbol #*n* * number of bits in the VLC code for symbol #*n*

The resulting value is in units of average bits per symbol. The VLC process consists of two phases:

- The encoder creates a VLC table that provides the lowest average bits per input value for the input sequence. Most codecs use precalculated, fixed VLC tables, which are based on typical probability distributions encountered in DCT coefficients of natural images.

- The encoder converts the input values to the variable-length values by looking up the bit sequences in the code table.

To work, the VLC table must exhibit one property: No VLC entry in the code table is permitted to be a prefix of any other entry.

An input stream with a more highly skewed probability distribution can take advantage of a VLC table that results in a VLC output stream with a lower number of average bits per pixel. However, it is possible to modify the input stream to further skew the probability distribution before VLC coding. The encoder performs this modification by coding input symbols jointly. Two or more symbols are coded jointly if they have a higher probability of appearing together, rather than separately. As an example, Figure 3-13 shows an input symbol string with four symbols: A, B, C, and D.

Figure 3-13 *Coding Symbols Jointly in the VLC Table*

Symbols Coded Individually:

A B B D C A B C D D C A C A B D C D B A B C D C A B D A B D A C A B C D

VLC Code Table

A: 9 Entries = 25%   00
B: 9 Entries = 25%   01
C: 9 Entries = 25%   10
D: 9 Entries = 25%   11
    Number of Bits Total = 72

Symbols Coded Jointly:

A B|B|C D|A B|C D|C D|A B|C D|A B|C D|A B|C D|C A B D|A B|A|C D|A B|C D

VLC Code Table

AB: 8 Entries = 22%   10
CD: 8 Entries = 22%   11
 A: 1 Entries = 3%   000
 B: 1 Entries = 3%   001
 C: 1 Entries = 3%   010
 D: 1 Entries = 3%   011
   Number of Bits Total = 44

When considering each symbol individually, the probability distribution is flat, meaning that each symbol on average appears 25 percent of the time. The VLC code table for this distribution would contain codes of the same length, which means that simple VLC coding of these four symbols would not reduce the number of bits per value. However, in this symbol stream, the A symbol is often followed by the B symbol, and the C symbol is often followed by the D symbol. In this case, an improved VLC code table would code the A and B symbols jointly and the C and D symbols jointly by adding two new entries to the VLC code table. When an A symbol is followed by a B symbol in the data stream, this pair is coded with a single variable-length code, and similarly for a C symbol followed by a D symbol. The new input symbol set has a highly skewed probability distribution and can benefit from a VLC.

H.26x codecs achieve a VLC coding with a lower average number of bits per pixel by first applying run-length coding of the AC coefficients and then coding the run and length values jointly. Statistically, certain combinations of run and length occur together with high frequency, further skewing the probability distribution and thus improving the performance of VLC coding.

The VLC decoder uses the code table to perform the mapping operation in reverse. At each stage of the VLC decoding process, the decoder finds the VLC code in the code table that matches the bits that appear next in the bitstream from the encoder.

One of the disadvantages of VLC is that it usually cannot achieve an average number of bits/pixel that is as low as the theoretical entropy of a bitstream.

As you can see in Figure 3-13, with symbols coded individually, the theoretical entropy is 2 bits per pixel, and the VLC table achieves this average number of bits per symbol. When the same stream is coded jointly, the theoretical entropy is 1.92 bits per symbol, but the VLC table achieves an average bit rate of 2.2 bits per symbol. The reason the VLC cannot achieve the theoretical entropy is because the bit length of each symbol is restricted to an integer number of bits per symbol. In general, VLC coding generates an output bitstream with an average number of bits per symbol that is often 5 percent to 10 percent greater than the theoretical entropy. One way to effectively achieve a fractional number of bits per symbol is to use arithmetic coding rather than VLC coding.

Arithmetic Coding

Given an input symbol set, arithmetic coding is an entropy coding mechanism capable of achieving an average number of bits per pixel equal to the entropy of the bitstream by effectively coding each symbol using a noninteger number of bits per pixel. The idea of entropy coding is to convert the entire sequence of input symbols into a single floating-point number. This number is constrained to have a value within a preset range. One sample range is the span between 0.0 and 1.0. The only requirement for this floating-point number is that it must have enough digits of precision to represent the symbol sequence; the longer the symbol sequence, the more digits of precision that are required.

The arithmetic coder follows a series of steps to derive the value of this floating-point number. To set up the encoding process, the encoder establishes a working range by setting the upper level of the range to 1.0 and the lower level of the range to 0.0. As the encoder processes the symbols, it uses an algorithm that causes the upper level to reduce over time and the lower level to increase over time. As a result, the working range narrows after each symbol is coded. After all the symbols have been coded, the encoder calculates a floating-point number with enough precision to fall within the final working range. This floating-point number represents the entire coded bitstream. Figure 3-14 shows the steps needed to determine the final working range.

Figure 3-14 *Arithmetic Coder Range Iteration*

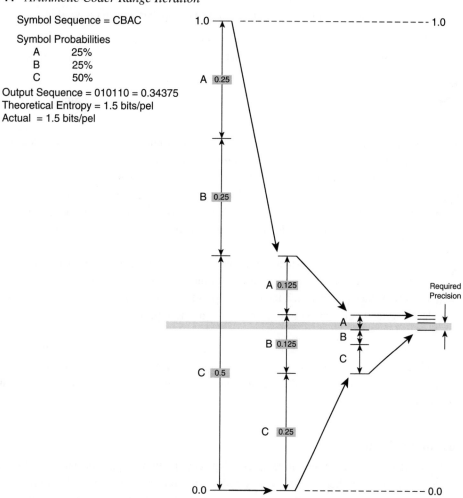

Symbol Sequence = CBAC

Symbol Probabilities
A   25%
B   25%
C   50%

Output Sequence = 010110 = 0.34375
Theoretical Entropy = 1.5 bits/pel
Actual   = 1.5 bits/pel

Figure 3-14 illustrates the method used to code the input stream, which in this example consists of three unique symbols. The process involves three main steps:

Step 1   Divide the working range into spans, as shown in Figure 3-14. Given N possible unique symbols in the bitstream, there will be N spans in the working range, and each span has a distance proportional to the symbol probability. This type of arithmetic coder is often referred to as an *N-arry arithmetic coder* because there are N spans, corresponding to N unique symbols in the input stream. If a symbol has a probability of .1, its corresponding range will be equal to 10 percent of the working range. In this example, the input symbols A, B, and C each have probabilities .25, .25, and .5. It does not matter in what order the spans appear within the working range.

Step 2   The encoder reads a symbol from the input stream and finds the corresponding span in the working range. This span becomes the new working range and defines the new upper level and lower level of the range.

Step 3   Return to Step 1 and repeat, using the new smaller working range, subdivided into spans.

When the final working range is determined, the encoder must calculate a binary floating-point number with enough precision to place the number entirely within the working range. In Figure 3-14, this final binary number is .010110, equal to a decimal value of 0.34375. The final binary number is selected such that it will still fall within the working range after it is extended by an infinite number of 1s. In other words, if the binary number .010110 were extended to .010110111111111 …, this extended number would still fall within the working range.

The decoder derives the original symbol stream from the floating-point number using steps similar to the encoding process. The decoder starts with the same initial working range of 0.0 to 1.0 and then determines the span in which the floating-point number falls to decode the first symbol. The decoder then iteratively narrows the working range and repeats the process.

In practice, an arithmetic coder can create an output stream with an average number of bits per symbol equal to the theoretical entropy of the input stream. As a result, arithmetic coding generates an encoded stream with a bit rate that is typically 5 percent to 10 percent less than a VLC encoded bitstream.

Binary Arithmetic Coders

The arithmetic coder described in the preceding section, with N spans, is called an *N-arry arithmetic coder.* Another type of entropy coder is the binary arithmetic coder. In this case, there are only two spans in the working range, representing a binary decision. Each symbol is encoded as a sequence of binary decisions, where each decision narrows the working range. Figure 3-15 shows an example of a binary decision tree used to code symbols using a binary arithmetic coder.

Figure 3-15 *Sample Decision Tree for a Binary Arithmetic Coder*

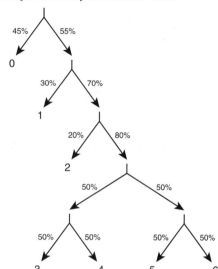

The first decision is whether the symbol is 0 or not 0. For this decision, the spans in the arithmetic coder are sized to reflect the probabilities for this decision. After this decision, the second stage of the decision tree determines whether the symbol is 1 or not 1. For this second decision, the encoder uses a different set of spans, which reflect the probabilities for this decision point. At each binary decision point, the encoder swaps in a new set of spans optimized for the probabilities for that decision point. Of course, the decoder must also use the same set of spans at the same decision points to remain in lockstep with the encoder.

DCT Scanning

Entropy coding operates on one-dimensional data only, which means that the encoder-side processor must convert the two-dimensional array of quantized DCT coefficients into a one-dimensional array. This conversion process uses one of several DCT scanning patterns. Figure 3-16 shows some sample patterns for the 8×8 DCT.

Figure 3-16 *Scanning Methods for 8×8 Transform Coefficients*

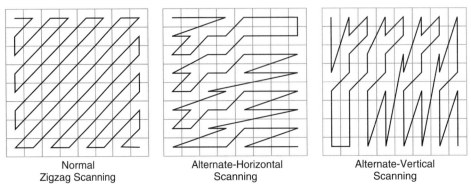

Normal
Zigzag Scanning
      Alternate-Horizontal
Scanning
      Alternate-Vertical
Scanning

The purpose of the DCT scanning pattern is to create a one-dimensional array that maximizes the efficiency of the entropy coder. Maximum efficiency is generally obtained by scanning the largest magnitude coefficient values first and the smallest magnitude coefficient values last. This distribution provides two benefits:

- It skews the probability distribution of possible values for each coefficient, which lowers the theoretical entropy, resulting in fewer bits per value.

- It allows the entropy coder to better estimate the actual probability distribution of possible values for each coefficient, which allows the encoder to optimize the method of entropy coding.

Encoders can specify different scanning patterns to optimize the performance of the entropy coder. The encoder can signal the best scanning pattern either explicitly, or implicitly as a function of previously decoded pixels. The selection of the scanning pattern depends on the frequency content in that block:

- An 8×8 block with no bias toward horizontal or vertical frequencies should use normal zigzag scanning, because most of the nonzero coefficients will be biased in the upper left quadrant of the DCT.

- An 8×8 block with somewhat greater horizontal frequency content (for instance, many vertical lines) should use alternate-horizontal scanning, because most of the nonzero coefficients will be biased in the top half of the DCT.

- An 8×8 block with somewhat greater vertical frequency content (for instance, many horizontal lines) should use alternate-vertical scanning, because most of the nonzero coefficients will be biased in the left half of the DCT.

Adaptive Encoding

Most of the stages in a codec can make use of adaptive coding. Adaptive coding optimizes the performance of a codec by varying the codec algorithm parameters during the encoding process. One common example is adaptive VLC coding, which switches among different VLC symbol code tables from moment to moment in response to changes in the probability distribution of the input data stream. However, with any adaptive scheme, the decoder must be able to figure out how the parameters have changed to remain in lockstep with the encoder. The encoder uses one of two methods to communicate the parameters in use:

■ Explicitly signaling the algorithm parameters in the bitstream. The encoder can inject side information into the bitstream to communicate the most suitable set of parameters to use for an encoding process. The downside of this process is that the side information increases the bit rate of the encoded stream. As an example, codecs explicitly transmit the value of the DCT quantization step size.

■ Implicit parameter selection based on past decoded information. This process is often referred to as *content-adaptive processing*. In this scenario, information that has already been decoded by the decoder (and also observed by the encoder) is used to determine future codec parameters. Both the encoder and decoder must use the same information and the same content-based analysis to calculate the codec algorithm parameters.

The benefit of this method is that no additional side information needs to be transmitted to signal the parameter selection. The downside is that this previously decoded information might not correctly predict the best set of codec parameters to use. One example of content-adaptive coding is from H.263, MPEG-4 Part 2, and H.264. All three codecs have a mode to determine the zigzag DCT scanning pattern for a block, based on whether the block is expected to be dominated by strong vertical or horizontal frequencies. This determination is made by observing the frequency content of previously decoded neighboring blocks.

Content-Adaptive VLC

One type of content-adaptive processing is a content-adaptive VLC processor. In this case, the VLC table changes over time in response to the statistical properties of recently decoded information. One example is the content-adaptive VLC (CAVLC) in H.264, which defines several VLC tables for coding the quantized DCT coefficients.

The selected table is a function of parameters from two previously decoded blocks: the block located to the left of the current block, and the block located above the current block. The content-adaptive algorithm uses several parameters from those blocks, including the number of nonzero DCT coefficients, the type of MB (P, B, and so on), and whether the block used a special intra prediction mode. The decoder mirrors these adaptive algorithms and selects the same VLC table as the encoder on a block-by-block basis to stay in lockstep with the encoder.

Content-Adaptive Arithmetic Coder

Whereas a content-adaptive VLC coder chooses from among several pre-fixed VLC tables, a content-adaptive arithmetic coder incrementally modifies its own span lengths as a function of the statistics of recently decoded information. The goal is to change the span lengths so that they are proportional to the probabilities of the symbols in the input stream. In the case of a binary arithmetic coder, the adaptive coder attempts to make the span lengths proportional to the estimated probabilities of each binary decision.

A common feature of adaptive arithmetic coders is a state machine that attempts to "learn" about the statistical distribution of input symbols over time to make the best guess for the span lengths. Much like the adaptive VLC, both the encoder and the decoder must use the exact same algorithm to determine span lengths so that they both remain in lockstep. One example is the content-adaptive binary arithmetic coder (CABAC) in the H.264 codec.

Hybrid Coding

The previous discussion covered the coding steps taken for intraframes. As discussed in the section "Encoder and Decoder Overview," intraframes are coded using information only from the current frame, and not from other frames in the video sequence. However, other than Motion-JPEG, codecs for video conferencing use a hybrid approach consisting of spatial coding techniques discussed previously, along with temporal compression that takes advantage of frame-to-frame correlation in the time domain. The encoder describes this interframe correlation using motion vectors, which provide an approximation of how objects move from one frame to another.

The next sections discuss the interframe coding process, which uses a feedback loop along with motion estimation to take advantage of frame-to-frame correlation.

Hybrid Decoder

When analyzing a hybrid codec, it is easier to start by analyzing the decoder rather than the encoder, because the encoder has a decoder embedded within it. Figure 3-17 shows the block diagram for the hybrid decoder.

Figure 3-17 *Hybrid Decoder*

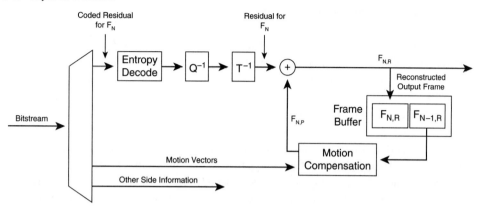

The encoder creates a bitstream for the decoder by starting with an original image, with frame number N, denoted by $F_{N,O}$. Because this frame is the original input to the encoder, it is not shown in the decoder diagram of Figure 3-17. For this image, the output of the encoder consists of two chunks of information in the bitstream: motion vectors and coded image information. The encoder forwards this information to the decoder; it is the input on the left side of Figure 3-17.

The motion vectors describe how the decoder should manipulate the previously decoded image to become an approximation of the current original image $F_{N,O}$. The previously decoded image is referred to as the *reference frame*, denoted by $F_{N-1,R}$, and the approximation for the current frame $F_{N,O}$ is called the *predicted frame*, denoted as $F_{N,P}$

To create the motion vectors, the encoder divides the original image N into blocks of size 4×4, 8×8, or 16×16 (depending on the codec) and then calculates a motion vector for each block. The motion vector points to a pixel area in the previously decoded reference image $F_{N-1,R}$ that most closely resembles the block in the original image $F_{N,O}$.

On the receiver side, the decoder creates $F_{N,P}$ by starting with a blank image and then dividing it into an array of blocks, just like in the encoder. For each block in $F_{N,P}$ the decoder uses the motion vector for that block to extract the corresponding area from the previously decoded reference frame $F_{N-1,R}$. This process is called *motion compensation*.

However, this predicted frame $F_{N,P}$ is usually a crude approximation of the original frame $F_{N,O}$, because motion vectors can describe only simple translational motion of blocks of pixels. Motion vectors cannot describe nonuniform movement of objects in the image or handle cases where overlapping objects move in such a way as to reveal or obscure each other. To enhance this crude predicted frame $F_{N,P}$ the encoder also creates the same $F_{N,P}$ and then sends the difference between the predicted frame $F_{N,P}$ and the original frame $F_{N,O}$. This difference is called the *residual*. The encoder then performs spatial coding on this residual, using the usual sequence of

DCT/quantization/entropy coding, to create the coded residual. The final bitstream created by the encoder consists of the coded residual multiplexed with the motion vectors.

The decoder decodes the coded residual for frame F_N and then adds it to the predicted frame $F_{N,P}$ to create the fully decoded image. The resulting decoded frame is called the *reconstructed image*. The two image buffers in the frame buffer hold both the currently decoded image $F_{N,R}$ and the previously reconstructed image $F_{N-1,R}$. After the decoder finishes creating $F_{N,R}$, this frame is then used as the reference frame for the next image, F_{N+1}.

Note one important thing about this spatiotemporal coding process: The encoder and decoder must create the exact same predicted frame $F_{N,P}$ to remain in lockstep. The decoder creates the predicted frame by manipulating the previous decoded frame $F_{N-1,R}$, which is reconstructed after a lossy encode/decode process. Because $F_{N-1,R}$ is the result of a lossy reconstruction, the encoder must also use the same lossy decoding reconstruction process to derive the same $F_{N-1,R}$. Therefore, the encoder must have a decoder within it to reconstruct the same decoded frame that is reconstructed at the decoder. The encoder then applies the motion vectors to $F_{N-1,R}$, in the same manner as the decoder to derive the predicted frame F_{N-P} If the codec specifies a deblocking filter, the motion compensation is applied after the deblocking filter. As a result, the deblocking filter is inside the feedback loop. When used in this manner, the deblocking filter can reduce the bit rate of the stream slightly, in addition to lowering the perceptual degradation of block artifacts.

P-Frames

An interframe predicted using motion vectors that point to a previous frame is referred to as a *P-frame*, short for predicted frame. However, for some video codecs, a P-frame is not restricted to using the most recent frame in the video sequence. The P-frame may instead refer to one of several frames that have appeared in the recent past. For example, the H.264 codec may include motion vectors that refer to one of several previous frames, and the motion vector must also include an index to designate which frame is used.

Even if a frame is considered a P-frame, it may contain MBs that are intracoded. If the video contains a lot of motion, the motion compensation for that block might not result in pixels that resemble the corresponding pixels in the original image. In this case, the encoder may decide to code a block or MB as an intrablock by applying the transform/quantize/entropy coding pipeline directly to original image pixels.

Hybrid Encoder

Figure 3-18 shows the data flow of the corresponding hybrid encoder.

Figure 3-18 *Hybrid Encoder*

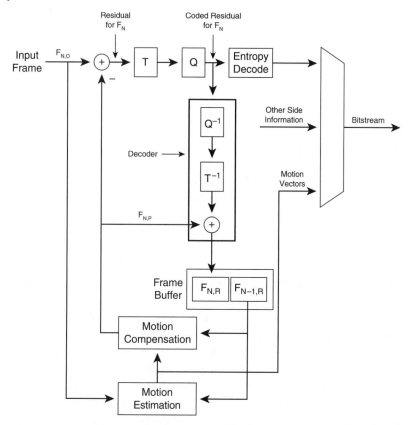

When encoding frame $F_{N,O}$, the first step is performed by the motion estimation unit, which calculates the motion vectors that transform the previously reconstructed image $F_{N-1,R}$ into the current predicted image $F_{N,P}$. However, the motion estimation unit does not directly create the predicted image $F_{N,P}$. Instead, the motion estimation unit sends these motion vectors to the motion compensation unit, which applies the motion vectors to previously decoded frame $F_{N-1,R}$ to create the predicted frame $F_{N,P}$. The motion compensation units in the encoder and decoder are identical. The encoder subtracts the predicted frame $F_{N,P}$ from the original frame $F_{N,O}$, generating residual image data. If the images have a precision of 8 bits per pixel, each pixel, in both the original frame and the reconstructed frame, can range from 0 to 255. As a result, the residual values at the output of the subtraction unit have a possible range of [–255, 255]. The encoder applies the DCT transform to this residual image, followed by quantization and entropy coding, to create a coded residual.

To complete the loop, the encoder must perform the same steps as the decoder by decoding image N to create $F_{N,R}$, which is used to create the prediction $F_{N+1,P}$ for the next encoded frame. To perform this reconstruction, the encoder contains a decoder, as shown in Figure 3-18. This embedded decoder performs inverse quantization and IDCT on the coded residual and then adds the resulting decoded residual to the predicted frame $F_{N,P}$ to obtain the reconstructed image $F_{N,R}$.

However, the embedded decoder needs to perform only the lossy steps of the decoder process, which includes inverse quantization and IDCT. Because the entropy coding is lossless, the embedded decoder can begin with data that emerges from the output of the quantizer and still obtain the same reconstructed image $F_{N,R}$ as in the decoder. Note that any processing block that is inside the encoder loop must be duplicated exactly in the decoder loop so that both encoder and decoder remain in lockstep.

The operation of the decoder is not affected by operations that happen outside of the encoder loop, and therefore these operations are considered outside the scope of the codec standards. The most significant example of a processing step outside the encoder loop is the motion estimator. The method by which the encoder performs motion estimation is not specified in any of the codec standards; the standards leave the method of motion vector selection up to the encoder.

The example in Figure 3-18 made the assumption that all blocks in the interframe are intercoded with motion vectors. However, video codecs typically define interframes to consist of both intercoded blocks and intracoded blocks. The encoder makes this determination on an MB basis, which means that the encoder must also send this per-MB decision as side information inside the bitstream. For each block, the encoder finds the motion vector that provides the best match between adjacent frames; if this best motion vector results in a large residual, however, the encoder may instead code the block as an intrablock, which means the encoder and decoder will not use the feedback loop for that block. When encoding an intrablock, the encoder applies the DCT to original image pixels, which have a range of [0, 255], rather than to the residual values, which have a range of [−255, 255].

Predictor Loop

The prediction-based hybrid codec relies on the fact that the encoder and decoder use the exact same predicted frame. Because the predicted frame is generated from the reconstructed frame, the reconstructed frame $F_{N,R}$ in the encoder should be identical to the reconstructed frame $F_{N,R}$ in the decoder. If the two reconstructed frames deviate, the deviations accumulate with each pass of the feedback loop, and the encoder and decoder drift away from each other over time.

To ensure that the reconstructed frames in the encoder and decoder are the same, the lossy decoding process in the encoder (inverse quantization followed by IDCT) should ideally be mathematically identical to the same process in the decoder. The inverse quantization step is a simple, well-defined process that uses integer math; therefore, this step is naturally identical in the encoder and decoder. However, the same is not always true for the inverse 8×8 DCT. Even when using 32-bit floating-point math, different implementations of the IDCT may result in pixel residuals (for an interblock) that have slight deviations. Codec specifications take these deviations into account in two ways:

■ Codecs typically specify the maximum deviation tolerance for the IDCT. Each pixel output of the IDCT is typically allowed to deviate from the exact theoretical output by no more than a single brightness level out of 255. In addition, codec specifications often limit the sum total deviation of all pixels in the 8×8 block.

■ To prevent these small deviations from accumulating over time, the H.261 and H.263 codecs recommend that each block should be transmitted as an intrablock, with no dependency on the predictor loop, on average once every 132 times the block is coded. This suggestion is referred to as an *informative recommendation* because it is a suggested best practice and is therefore technically outside the scope of the codec standard.

Motion Estimation

Figure 3-19 shows the motion estimation process on the encoder, which is by far the most CPU-intensive step in the encoder/decoder system.

Figure 3-19   *Motion Estimation Process for Motion Vector (M_x, M_y)*

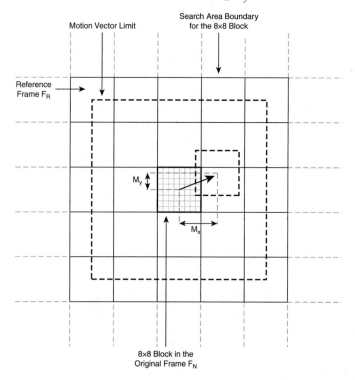

For each block in the original image F_N, the encoder searches the reference frame F_R in the same vicinity to find a reference block most highly correlated to the original. In this example, the block size is 8×8, and the encoder limits the motion vector to a range of ±16 pixels for both X and Y components.

For each block in the original image, the encoder compares candidate motion vectors within the possible motion vector range. For each possible motion vector, the encoder determines the level of correlation between the original block and the candidate reference block by calculating the error between the two blocks. Encoders use different measurements to calculate the error, but a common formula is the sum of absolute differences. In this formula, the encoder computes the absolute difference between corresponding pixels and then adds the results to create the error:

$$\text{Error} = \sum_{x,y} |F_{N,R}(x,y) - F_{N,O}(x,y)|$$

For the encoder to determine the error for a single candidate motion vector using this formula on 8×8 blocks, the encoder must perform 64 subtraction operations followed by 64 additions. In this example, where motion vectors can have integer values in the range [−16, +15], there are a total of 32×32 = 1024 possible candidate motion vectors, including the (0,0) motion vector. For the encoder to find the best motion vector, it must calculate the correlation error for all 1024 candidate motion vectors and then use the one with the minimum error value. This process requires (64+64)×1024 = 131,072 calculations per 8×8 block in the original image. For a CIF video sequence with a format of 352×288 / 15 FPS, the number of calculations for motion estimation alone using this technique will be 131,072 calculations × 1584 blocks per frame × 15 frames per second = 3.1 billion calculations per second.

To reduce the computational load of the motion estimation process, the encoder may test only a subset of candidate motion vectors per block. In addition, the encoder can adopt an iterative approach, as shown in Figure 3-20.

The encoder first tests a sparse set of motion vectors within the search range and uses the vector with the lowest error to narrow the search area for the following iteration. The encoder repeats this process until the last iteration, when the encoder compares candidate motion vectors that point to one of nine offsets in a 3×3 pixel area.

However, special-purpose signal processors can provide an exhaustive motion search for each block in the original image without resorting to this iterative technique. High-end, standalone, room-based systems usually have these special processors; this difference accounts for the higher quality and lower bit rates of room-based video conferencing endpoints compared to PC-based desktop endpoints. The need for high-computation motion estimation in the encoder is also the reason that some PC-based endpoints use dedicated external hardware for the encoding process but use PC-based software for the decoding process.

Figure 3-20 *Iterative Motion Vector Search Method*

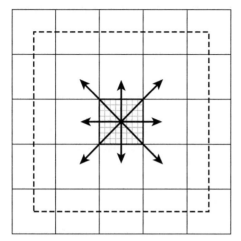

Iteration 1: Evaluate the best of nine
sparse motion vectors.

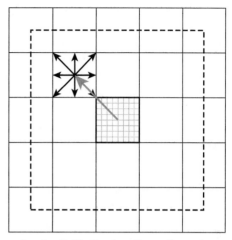

Iteration 2: Starting from the motion vector
chosen in iteration 1, evaluate the best of
nine surrounding motion vectors.

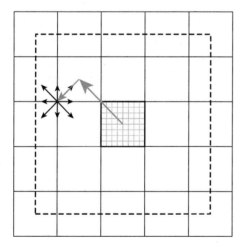

Iteration 3: Repeat, starting from the
motion vector selected in iteration 2.

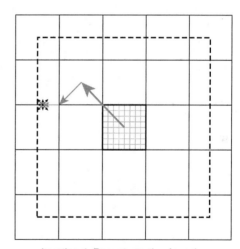

Iteration 4: Repeat, starting from the
motion vector selected in iteration 3.

One important thing to understand about motion vectors is that they point in the opposite direction of the data transfer. In Figure 3-19, the motion vectors chosen by the motion estimation unit point from the current original image F_N to the previous reconstructed image. However, in actuality, the motion compensation unit forms the predicted image by moving data in the opposite direction, from the tip of the arrowhead (in previous reference frame $F_{N-1,R}$) back to the tail (in the current predicted frame $F_{N,P}$). Therefore, a motion vector points to the source rather than to the destination.

The motion estimation process is applied only to the luminance channel: These luminance vectors are divided by a factor of 2 to obtain the motion vectors used for the chrominance channels, which have half the resolution in the 4:2:0 color format.

Different codecs use different variations of motion estimation. Higher-performance codecs allow motion vectors with more precision, down to 1/4 pixel. To further improve the accuracy of a reconstructed image, some codecs offer an advanced mode that varies the actual motion vector over the span of an 8×8 block, described later in section "Overlapped Block Motion Compensation." In addition, codecs can specify that a frame should be motion- compensated based on multiple motion vectors, each pointing to a separate reference frame.

1/2 Pel and 1/4 Pel Motion Estimation

In the motion estimation unit, pixels in the reference frame are considered to be color values located at integer X and Y locations. Motion vectors with single-pixel accuracy will map integer-aligned pixels in the reference frame to integer-aligned pixel locations in the original image frame.

However, some codecs allow motion vectors to have an accuracy of 1/2 pixel or 1/4 pixel (also known as *1/2 pel* or *1/4 pel*), described later in the section "Overlapped Block Motion Compensation". In these cases, each motion vector can point to a source location in the reference frame that represents an array of pixels offset by a fractional pixel distance from the integer-located reference pixels. The decoder must interpolate these in-between pixel values. Figure 3-21 shows the method of interpolating 1/2 pel locations based on a simple two-dimensional bilinear filter.

Figure 3-21 *Subpixel Interpolation for 1/2 Pel Motion Vectors*

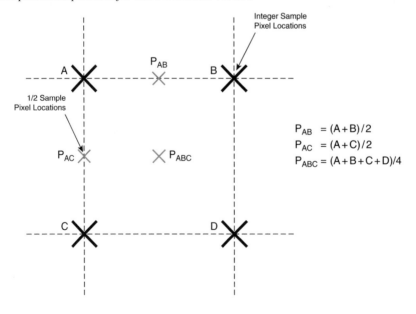

However, 1/4 pel interpolation used in H.264 typically requires an interpolation filter with higher accuracy to effectively make use of the finer 1/4 resolution.

When the motion estimator searches for a motion vector with 1/2 or 1/4 pel accuracy, the encoder first chooses the best motion vector down to single-pel accuracy and then proceeds to find the best 1/2 or 1/4 pel accurate motion vector in close proximity to that integer-pel vector. To find the best 1/2 pel motion vector, the encoder first scales up the candidate area of the reference frame by a factor of 2 in the X and Y direction using the interpolation filter. The encoder then calculates the correlation error for the eight possible surrounding 1/2 pel (x,y) motion vector offsets and chooses the motion vector that results in the lowest error.

Conventions for Motion Estimation

Video codecs define the maximum range of motion vectors. The basic modes of operation for the codecs covered in this chapter use a range of approximately +/– 15 pixels for X and Y motion vector components, but some codecs offer modes that permit the X and Y components to be more than double this basic range.

Another convention of video codecs has to do with restricted and unrestricted motion vectors. A restricted motion vector is a motion vector that must only refer to pixels entirely within the boundaries of the reference frame. However, some codecs have optional modes that allow unrestricted motion vectors, which can refer to regions outside the picture boundaries. For these outer regions, the encoder and decoder fill in the missing pixels by creating a pixel value using the closest edge pixel in the frame.

Overlapped Block Motion Compensation

One advanced motion compensation technique is overlapped block motion compensation (OBMC), illustrated in Figure 3-22.

OBMC allows the motion vector to vary on a per-pixel basis over the span of the block. Each pixel is motion-compensated using motion vectors from the current block and motion vectors from surrounding blocks. The possible surrounding blocks that may provide the additional motion vectors are the four blocks that are horizontally or vertically adjacent, as shown in Figure 3-22. The compensation unit uses motion vectors from two of these four blocks, determined on a per-pixel basis, according to the position of the pixel in the current block: For each pixel, the motion compensator uses the closest horizontally adjacent block and the closest vertically adjacent block. Therefore, the motion compensator uses a different set of motion vectors for pixels in each quadrant of the current block.

Figure 3-22   *Overlapped Block Motion Compensation*

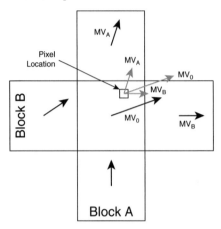

Weighting Factor W_0							
4	5	5	5	5	5	5	4
5	5	5	5	5	5	5	5
5	5	6	6	6	6	5	5
5	5	6	6	6	6	5	5
5	5	6	6	6	6	5	5
5	5	6	6	6	6	5	5
5	5	5	5	5	5	5	5
4	5	5	5	5	5	5	4

Weighting Factor W_A							
2	2	2	2	2	2	2	2
1	1	2	2	2	2	1	1
1	1	1	1	1	1	1	1
1	1	1	1	1	1	1	1
1	1	1	1	1	1	1	1
1	1	1	1	1	1	1	1
1	1	2	2	2	2	1	1
2	2	2	2	2	2	2	2

Weighting Factor W_B							
2	1	1	1	1	1	1	2
2	2	1	1	1	1	2	2
2	2	1	1	1	1	2	2
2	2	1	1	1	1	2	2
2	2	1	1	1	1	2	2
2	2	1	1	1	1	2	2
2	2	1	1	1	1	2	2
2	1	1	1	1	1	1	2

Motion-Compensated Pixel Value = $(W_0 \times MC(MV_0) + W_A \times MC(MV_A) + W_B \times MC(MV_B))/8$

In Figure 3-22, the candidate pixel is closest to the top and right sides of the current block, so the compensator uses motion vectors from the adjacent blocks directly above and to the right of the current block. Based on each motion vector, the decoder first calculates three motion-compensated pixel values. Then the motion-compensation algorithm applies a weighting value to each motion-compensated predicted pixel. The weighting value for each motion vector is a function of the pixel location in the current block and is given by weighting matrices. Figure 3-22 shows the matrices for MPEG-4 Part 2. The weighted prediction values are summed to calculate the final predicted pixel value.

B-Frames

For some codecs, interframes are not restricted to contain only P-frames. Another type of interframe is the B-frame, which uses two frames for prediction. The B-frame references a frame that occurs in the past and a frame that occurs in the future. The term B-frame is short for between-frame.

Figure 3-23 shows a sequence of I-, P-, and B-frames.

Figure 3-23 *Sequence of I-, P-, and B-Frames*

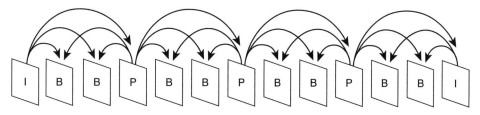

The arrows in Figure 3-23 show the dependencies between frames. The dependency of a frame can be determined by observing the arrows that point to the frame. The source of each arrow represents a dependency. Each P-frame depends on a previous P- or I-frame. Each B-frame depends on the nearest surrounding I- or P-frame.

When encoding a B-frame, the encoder sends two motion vectors for each block. The motion vector that points to a previous reference frame is called the *forward motion vector* because this motion vector extrapolates motion forward in time. The motion vector that points to a future reference frame is called the *backward motion vector* because this motion vector extrapolates motion backward in time.

The encoder and decoder predict each block in a B-frame by extracting the pixel areas referenced by the two motion vectors and then averaging those pixel areas to create the block for the predicted frame $F_{N,P}$. Even though B-frames require additional side information in the bitstream for the extra motion vectors, compressed B-frames are often much smaller than I- or P-frames.

The encoding/decoding of a B-frame is a noncausal process, because the B-frame cannot be processed until after a future frame is processed. To make the decoding process easier, the encoder reorders frames in the encoded bitstream so that the backward-referenced frame appears before the B-frame, as shown in Figure 3-24.

Figure 3-24 *Display Order (Top) and Bitstream Order (Bottom) of Frames*

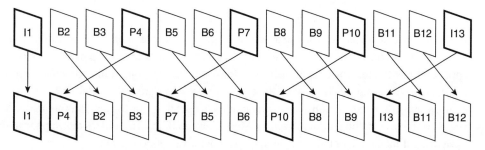

Any frame dependencies required by a B-frame appear in the bitstream before the B-frame. The resulting sequence of frames is called the *bitstream order, transmission order,* or *decoding order.* After decoding, the decoder must reorder the frames to match the original video sequence, and this final order is called the *display order, temporal order,* or *picture number order.*

One additional B-frame mode is called *direct mode.* In this mode, the encoder does not include the usual forward and backward motion vectors with the B-frame. Instead, the B-frame derives its forward and backward motion vectors from the motion vector used by the corresponding block of image data in the next frame.

Figure 3-25 shows the derivation. When a frame is coded with this mode, the corresponding block of data in the next frame must have a motion vector associated with it, even though it may be an intrablock. Therefore, the B-frame direct mode is one example in which an intrablock must still have a motion vector.

Figure 3-25 *B-Frame Direct Mode*

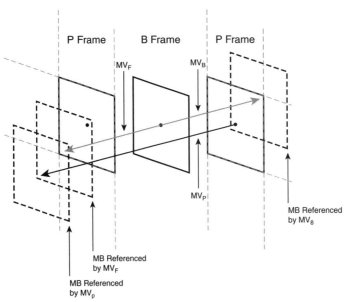

If objects travel at a constant rate, in a straight line, from the previous reference frame to the next P-frame, the decoder can simply use bilinear interpolation to estimate the motion vectors that apply to the B-frame. However, if the motion deviates from a straight line, or deviates from a constant speed during this time span, the encoder may also send a small delta vector that compensates for this deviation. The decoder adds the delta vector to each interpolated motion vector to arrive at the final motion vectors. Most video conferencing codecs that support B-frames have a direct mode, but not all of them include a delta vector correction.

Figure 3-26 shows other possible I-, P-, and B-frame patterns. Patterns of I-, P-, and B-frames are often referred to as *IPB patterns*. Specific patterns are often expressed using a notation that strings together single letter frame types. The first example in Figure 3-26 has an IPB pattern of IBBBB. The second example has an IPB pattern of IBPBPBPB.

Figure 3-26   *Other Possible I, P, and B Patterns*

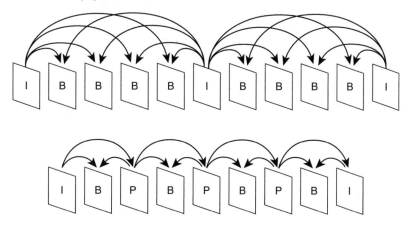

In all sequences, P-frames depend on I-frames or other P-frames, and B-frames depend on P- or I-frames. A disadvantage of using P-frames is that if an I-frame or P-frame is corrupted due to channel errors or packet loss, the error propagates through the frame sequence until the sequence reaches an I-frame.

There is one universal requirement for sequences of I-, P-, and B-frames: No frame may depend on a B-frame as a reference. As a result, a corrupted or lost B-frame will not cause an error to ripple through the sequence. Viewed from another perspective, either the encoder or decoder may discard B-frames to reduce the frame rate, without causing errors in other frames. For example, the encoder may discard B-frames to keep the bitstream from exceeding a predetermined maximum channel bit rate.

Alternatively, the decoder can drop B-frames if it has insufficient CPU power to provide the full frame rate. The capability to gracefully scale down the frame rate in this manner is called *temporal scalability*. An equivalent way of describing this scalability is to say that B-frames are not retained inside the predictor loop of the encoder and are therefore not needed to predict other frames. Because B-frames are not in the feedback loop, post-processing of those B-frames using a deblocking filter is technically out of scope in the codec specifications, even though the deblocking filter is in scope for I- and P-frames.

B-frames pose a significant problem for video conferencing because they add latency to the video bitstream. A sequence consisting of IBBPBBPBBPBBI requires the encoder to add a delay of two frames to its pipeline, because the encoding of the B-frames must be delayed until the next P or I frame is encoded. Typically, this video delay adds an unacceptable latency to the one-way path between two video conferencing endpoints.

Predictor Loops for Parameters

The section "Predictor Loop" explained the predictor loop for a hybrid codec, in which the output of the encoder is a coded residual image based on a motion-compensated predicted frame. This prediction loop forms the outer loop of a hybrid coder. However, this paradigm of coding a residual can be extended to other parts of the codec algorithm and is not limited to motion-compensated prediction of pixel areas. Most codecs use smaller prediction loops in various parts of the bitstream. Like the hybrid coder prediction loop, the encoder and decoder may form a prediction based on information accessible to the decoder. Therefore, the prediction can be based on the following:

- Information in previously decoded frames.

- Information in the current frame that has already been decoded. Because the encoder usually processes MBs in raster-scan order, the previously decoded image information consists of image data to the left of or above the current MB.

However, unlike the outer loop of a hybrid coder, some of these inner loops use only lossless entropy coding to code the residual.

The most common predictor loop specified by video codecs is the coding of motion vectors for a block. In this case, the codec creates a predictor by extracting the motion vectors of surrounding previously decoded blocks in the same frame and then takes the average value of these motion vectors as the predictor for the current MB. The encoder then creates a residual by subtracting the prediction from the actual value of the motion vector. The encoder then codes this residual losslessly. Similar to the outer loop of the hybrid coder, both the encoder and decoder must use the same algorithm to calculate an identical predictor. For motion vectors, this predictor often uses an average of three motion vectors, relative to the current block or MB:

- The motion vector from the block to the left of the current block

- The motion vector from the block above the current block

- The motion vector from the block to the left of and above the current block

However, in a case like this that uses multiple input values, the predictor algorithm may specify either an average of the values or a median of the values. The median is defined as the middle value. The advantage of using a median value is that it tends to reject outward-lying values, which may result from either noise or anomalous corner case conditions.

However, encoders use variations on these prediction algorithms when surrounding information is not available, which may happen in several scenarios:

- 8×8 blocks located at the left edge of the frame do not have a neighboring block to the left.

- 8×8 blocks located at the top edge of the frame do not have a neighboring block above.

- Information in neighboring blocks might not be available. For instance, a neighboring intrablock has no motion vectors; therefore, the prediction algorithm cannot make use of motion vectors from this neighboring block.

In these cases, encoders specify variations of the prediction algorithm to handle these cases. For example, if a neighboring block is either nonexistent or without a motion vector, a prediction algorithm may instead use a motion vector prediction of zero.

As an example of another predictor loop, some codecs predict DCT coefficients for blocks that are intracoded. This process is applied after the DCT, and the DC coefficient is often treated differently from the AC coefficients. Because the DC coefficient represents the block's average value, it is often predicted by averaging the DC coefficients of three adjacent blocks: the block to the left, the block above, and the block to the above left.

Some AC coefficients can also be predicted, but only if the encoder and decoder can detect that the block will have strong vertical frequencies or strong horizontal frequencies. The prediction algorithm can determine whether the block is likely to have strong horizontal or vertical frequencies by observing the frequency content of adjacent blocks, resulting in two scenarios:

- If the block to the left has strong vertical frequencies, corresponding to strong horizontal edges, these edges are likely to continue into the current block that is being decoded. These strong horizontal edges are represented by large values for AC coefficients in the first column of the current DCT, and these values are likely to be the same as corresponding DCT values in the block to the left. Therefore, in this scenario, the prediction for the first column of AC coefficients will be the corresponding column of AC coefficients in the block to the left. The remainder of the AC coefficients are coded separately.

- If the block above has strong horizontal frequencies, corresponding to strong vertical edges, these edges are likely to continue into the current block that is being decoded. These strong vertical edges are represented by large values for AC coefficients in the first row of the current DCT, and these values are likely to be the same as corresponding DCT values in the block above. Therefore, in this scenario, the prediction for the first row of AC coefficients will be the corresponding row of AC coefficients in the block above. The remainder of the AC coefficients are coded separately.

After using this prediction, the residual is entropy-coded.

H.264 has a mode that predicts an intrablock in the spatial domain (before DCT coding) by observing motion vectors from neighboring blocks. Based on these motion vectors and the spatial pixel content of these neighboring blocks, the H.264 algorithm attempts to predict how pixel values from surrounding blocks have entered the current block. After using this prediction, the residual is DCT coded like a typical interblock.

The predictor algorithm can also define circumstances in which a prediction should not be used, in cases where previously decoded data indicates that no good predictor is available. For this case, the predictor specifies a nominal prediction value, such as zero; a zero predictor value is the same as using no prediction. However, nominal prediction values may be nonzero. For example, when an intrablock is coded without using predictions from surrounding blocks, the predictor for the DC coefficient of the intrablock typically uses a value that is the midpoint of its possible range. That is because the DC coefficient represents the average value of all pixels in the original block, and a predictor value equal to the halfway point minimizes the average residual error.

Error Resiliency

If the network drops bitstream packets, decoders may have difficulty resuming the decoding process for several reasons:

- Bitstream parameters may change incrementally from one MB to another. One example is the quantization level: Most codecs allow the bitstream to change the quantization level by a delta amount between MBs. If the network drops a packet, the decoder will not have access to the previous incremental changes in the quantization level and will not be able to determine the current quantization level.

- Bitstream prediction loops may depend on other previously decoded parts of the bitstream. If a packet drops, data in this packet cannot be used as part of the prediction loop in the future.

Video codecs provide error resiliency using several methods:

- Explicit error correction, such as forward error correction (FEC)

- Unique start codes

- Reversible VLCs

- Data dependency isolation

- Redundant slices

- Data prioritization

The following sections describe each.

Error Correction

Forward error correction (FEC) is a process that uses extra bits to detect and correct for errors in the bitstream. When using FEC, the bitstream is first segmented into packets, and then the FEC process is applied to each packet.

Start Codes

Start codes in the bitstream demarcate boundaries between major segments of the bitstream. Each type of start code is assigned a pattern that must not be used by any other bitstream syntax element. If a decoder encounters an error in the bitstream and is unable to determine the alignment of coded parameters, the decoder scans the bitstream until it finds the next start code, and then it resumes parsing the bitstream. In this approach, the decoder cannot use the bitstream between the location of the bit error and the next start code unless the bitstream uses a reversible VLC, discussed next.

Reversible VLCs

Reversible VLCs permit a decoder to parse a bitstream by scanning the bitstream in either a forward or reverse direction. To make use of a reversible VLC, the decoder first decodes the bitstream in the forward direction. If the decoder encounters an error, it scans forward in the bitstream until it finds the next start code, and then the decoder scans backward from the start code and parses the bitstream in reverse, using reversible VLC codes, until it again encounters the bitstream error. Therefore, a reversible VLC allows the decoder to parse as much of the uncorrupted bitstream as possible in the presence of an error.

Table 3-5 shows an example of a reversible VLC table. The value of s codes the sign of the number. In a normal VLC table, no VLC entry is permitted to be a prefix of any other entry. A reversible VLC adds one additional requirement: For the purposes of backward scanning, no VLC entry is permitted to be a suffix of any other entry.

Table 3-5   *Reversible VLC Code Table*

Value	VLC Code
0	1
1 or –1	0s0
2 or –2	001s0
3 or –3	011s0
4 or –4	00101s0
5 or –5	00111s0
6 of –6	01101s0
7 or –7	01111s0

However, a reversible VLC table will not provide error resiliency for packets discarded by the network because of bit errors.

Data Dependency Isolation

Data dependency isolation attempts to minimize the dependencies between segments of the bitstream. Typically, a codec defines a bitstream hierarchy. At the top of the hierarchy is a frame of video. This video frame consists of groups of blocks (GOB) or slices. Each GOB/slice consists of a series of MBs, each of which represents a 16 ×16 pixel array.

Senders usually packetize video bitstream so that each RTP packet contains bitstream from a single GOB/slice. As a result, if an RTP packet is lost on the network, the data loss is confined to a single GOB/slice. To provide error resilience in the presence of packet drop, each GOB/slice should not depend on any other GOB/slice in the frame. This requirement means that all predictor loops in the codec should restrict their prediction algorithms to use information that is within the current GOB/slice only. Motion vectors are often predicted as a function of the motion vectors in surrounding MBs. To provide data dependency isolation, this prediction method should use motion vectors only from blocks in the same GOB/slice. Many codecs offer a mode to provide this data dependency isolation between GOBs/slices.

Redundant Slices

Codecs may send redundant slices, which often have a smaller size and lower quality. The decoder may use these redundant slices in place of corrupted slices.

Data Prioritization

Codecs may provide ways to classify the bitstream by levels of importance and then apply a different quality of service to the different levels:

■   At the MB level, the encoder can classify some MBs in the image to be more important: These MBs generally contain movement and must be decoded correctly to provide good quality at the decoder. One way to provide a higher level of quality for these MBs is to arrange them into one or more slices and then send these slices over the network with a higher quality of service. In H.264, flexible MB ordering (FMO) allows each slice to contain an arbitrary collection of MBs in a frame, allowing the encoder to collect the most important MBs into a single slice.

■   Encoders typically use Arbitrary Slice Ordering (ASO) with FMO. ASO allows slices to be sent in an arbitrary order.

■ The encoder may use slice classification. In this mode, the encoder defines different slice classifications. Slice-based classifications include header information, non-B-frame information, and B-frame information. The encoder may send each type of slice with a different quality of service.

■ The encoder may use data partitioning. Data partitioning reorganizes the data in each slice of the bitstream so that common values are grouped. This approach uses a reversible VLC, and the final arrangement allows better error recovery. H.263 defines the following data partitioning per slice:

— First, the encoder sends the MB headers.

— Then, the encoder sends all motion vectors, in the form of coded differences.

— Then, the encoder sends DCT coefficients.

Scalable Layered Codecs

Scalable codecs offer a way to achieve progressive refinement for a video bitstream. A scalable bitstream is composed of a base layer accompanied by one or more enhancement layers. The base layer provides a base level of quality, and each enhancement layer provides incremental information that adds to the quality of the base layer. These codecs are also called *layered codecs* because they provide layers of enhancement. A video conferencing system can use scalable codecs in several ways:

■ **Capacity limitations at the encoder**—If the encoder lacks the CPU resources to encode all layers, it can selectively suspend coding for some enhancement layers.

■ **Bandwidth limitations at the encoder**—If the instantaneous bandwidth capacity at the network interface of the encoder drops, the encoder can selectively suspend coding for some enhancement layers.

■ **Bit rate control at the encoder**—If the camera captures a high degree of motion, the resulting bit rate of the encoded stream might spike and threaten to exceed the prenegotiated channel bandwidth. To compensate for this sudden increase, the encoder can selectively suspend coding for some enhancement layers.

■ **WAN bandwidth limitations**—If a video stream must pass from a LAN to a WAN, the WAN might not have sufficient bandwidth to accommodate all layers of the scalable bitstream. In this case, either the encoder or a gateway at the LAN/WAN interface can prune selected enhancement layers from the bitstream as the bitstream passes from the LAN to the WAN. The method of pruning depends on the form of the bitstream:

— The encoder may issue a single stream onto the network containing the multiplex of all enhancement layers.

> — The encoder may issue separate streams onto the network, one for each enhancement layer.

Video conferencing systems may then use one of two pruning methods:

■ A smart gateway between the LAN and the WAN can selectively drop enhancement layers, whether the layers are encoded into a single multiplexed bitstream or into individual streams.

■ The encoder can send the enhancement layers on different multicast addresses, and decoders in the WAN can subscribe to a subset of enhancement layers. For this scenario, the encoder must issue enhancement layers in separate network streams. For an enhancement layer to cross the LAN/WAN boundary, at least one endpoint in the WAN must subscribe to the enhancement layer.

Video conferencing systems can leverage scalable codecs to link endpoints with different CPU/ bandwidth capacities. A scenario that illustrates the benefits of scalability is a video conference with high-resolution, LAN-based video endpoints and low-resolution, mobile phone-based endpoints. The encoder issues a single set of layers. The high-resolution endpoint can use all the enhancement layers, whereas the mobile endpoint can use only the base layer. Intermediate endpoints can use the base layer plus a subset of the enhancement layers.

Without a scalable codec, an encoder must use one of two methods to accommodate endpoints with different CPU/bandwidth capacities:

■ The encoder could create separate streams, each optimized for an endpoint with a different CPU/bandwidth capacity. This method consumes additional bandwidth for each type of endpoint that joins the conversation, and consumes extra CPU power on the encoder.

■ The encoder could create a single stream that would accommodate the endpoint with the lowest CPU/bandwidth capacity, thereby sacrificing quality for the high-end endpoints.

For a scalable codec, it is highly desirable for the resulting set of encoded layers to have a total bit rate that does not significantly exceed the bit rate of a corresponding nonlayered stream that produces the same quality as the layered stream with all layers decoded. Past incarnations of scalable codecs have failed to achieve this goal, which is why scalable video has not become widely adopted. However, scalability without an increase in bit rate is now a possibility, using the scalable extension to the H.264 codec, called *H.264-SVC*, which implements a special form of motion-compensated temporal filtering.

Scalable codecs typically offer three types of scalability:

■ SNR (signal-to-noise ratio) scalability

- Spatial scalability

- Temporal scalability

SNR and Spatial Scalability

SNR scalability uses a base layer, providing a lower level of image quality. Each enhancement layer acts much like the residual difference image of a hybrid codec and represents a "correction layer" that is added to the base layer. The addition of each enhancement layer reduces the error between the decoded image and the original image, thus increasing the SNR and the quality.

Spatial scalability uses a base layer consisting of a smaller-size image sequence. The enhancement layers add information to increase the image resolution. There is little difference between spatial scalability and SNR scalability. Encoders commonly use two types of methods for spatial scalability:

- Pyramid coding

- Sub-band filtering

Pyramid coding is similar to SNR coding. First, the decoder increases the size of the base image by applying a scale factor to the image. Then the decoder uses the enhancement layer as a coded residual, which improves the SNR of the scaled base image. In the pyramid coding scheme, each enhancement layer is a residual image with a higher resolution than the preceding layer. As a result, this method generally increases the number of pixels that the encoder must process. In a typical example, the encoder may create a base layer image with a size half the width and height of the original image and then generate an enhancement layer equal in size to the original image. In this case, the encoder must process 1.25 times the number of pixels in the original image.

Sub-band filtering is also known as *wavelet filtering*. In this method, the encoder transforms each image into sub-bands representing different spatial frequencies, as shown in Figure 3-27.

Figure 3-27 *Spatial Sub-Band Analysis*

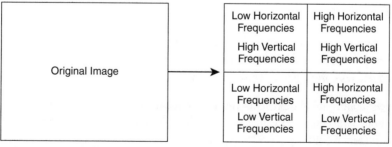

The sub-bands consist of four separate images, each of which represents a different frequency sub-band of the original image. The key aspect of this transformation is that each sub-band image occupies 1/4 the area of the original image, which means that the total size of all sub-bands is equal to the size of the original image. Therefore, unlike pyramid coding, the sub-band coding method does not increase the number of pixels that must be encoded.

Similar to DCT analysis, the location of each sub-band corresponds to the type of frequencies contained in that sub-band. Using the typical convention, the sub-band in the lower left corresponds to low frequencies and is the base layer. This image is simply a scaled-down version of the original image. The remaining sub-bands describe spatial frequencies that are predominantly horizontal (the upper-left sub-band), predominantly vertical (the lower-right sub-band), and both horizontal and vertical (the upper-right sub-band). These three high-frequency sub-bands are typically grouped into a single enhancement layer. This process of transforming an image into sub-bands is called *analysis* and is performed using filters called *analysis filters*.

The decoder may decide to use only the base layer, which is just a scaled-down version of the original image. Alternatively, the decoder may use the base and enhancement layers to reconstruct the full resolution image. This reconstruction process on the decoder is called *synthesis* and is performed using synthesis filters.

The encoder can apply analysis filters recursively on the low-frequency sub-band, creating a new set of enhancement layers, as shown in Figure 3-28.

Figure 3-28 *Recursive Application of Analysis Filters*

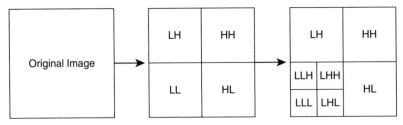

Each sub-band is denoted using a notation that uses *L* to represent a low-frequency component and *H* to represent a high-frequency component. In the case where the original image is decomposed into four sub-bands:

■ The first symbol represents the horizontal frequencies. Low horizontal frequencies correspond to smoothly varying pixel values in the horizontal direction. High horizontal frequencies correspond to vertical edges.

■ The second symbol represents vertical frequencies. Low vertical frequencies correspond to smoothly varying pixel values in the vertical direction. High vertical frequencies correspond to horizontal edges.

In the first decomposition into four quadrants, the upper-left sub-band is denoted LH and represents low-frequency horizontal information and high-frequency vertical information. The LL quadrant can be further decomposed in a recursive manner. The notation extends to the decomposition of this quadrant and uses three symbols. The first symbol is always *L*, to denote that the recursive sub-bands are derived from a low-frequency sub-band.

In this two-stage decomposition, the base layer is represented by LLL. The first enhancement layer is represented by LLH, LHL, and LHH. The second enhancement layer is represented by LH, HL, and HH.

Temporal Scalability

In a bitstream with temporal scalability, the base layer represents a lower frame rate sequence, and the enhancement layer adds information to increase the frame rate. Two methods are commonly used for spatial scalability: B-frames and temporal sub-band filtering.

B-frames offer temporal scalability, because they can be discarded by either the encoder or the decoder. As described previously, no frame in a bitstream relies on information in B-frames, which means that either the encoder or decoder may drop B-frames without impacting the remaining frames:

- The encoder may discard B-frames to keep the bitstream from exceeding a predetermined maximum channel bit rate.

- The decoder can drop B-frames if it has insufficient CPU power to provide the full frame rate.

However, B-frames impose a minimum delay of at least one frame in the encoder, because the future P- or I-frame must be processed before the B-frame can be processed. Because video conferencing systems attempt to minimize delays, B-frame scalability might not be viable for low-delay conferencing applications.

Temporal sub-band filtering, also known as *temporal wavelet filtering*, is a process that transforms a sequence of input frames into two different sequences: a sequence of frames representing the low-frequency temporal information, and a sequence of frames representing the high-frequency temporal information, as shown in Figure 3-29.

Figure 3-29 *Temporal Sub-Band Scalability*

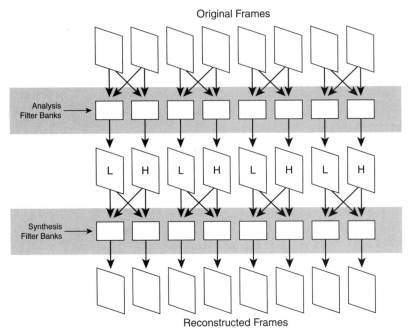

L = Low Frequency Temporal Information
H = High Frequency Temporal Information

Temporal sub-band filtering provides a key benefit: The total number of frames after the transformation remains the same. The low-frequency temporal frames constitute the base layer, and the high-frequency temporal frames constitute an enhancement layer. The base layer has a frame rate that is half the frame rate of the original sequence. If the decoder decides to use only the base layer, this base layer has a frame rate that is half the original frame rate. Just like the spatial sub-band method, the process that converts the original frames into frequency bands is called *analysis* and uses filters called *analysis filters*.

The decoder can use both the base layer and the enhancement layer to reconstruct the original sequence of frames at the full frame rate. This reconstruction process on the decoder is called *synthesis* and uses *synthesis filters*. A new standard for scalable coding, H.264-SVC uses this method of temporal sub-band filtering along with a method to motion-compensate the sub-bands. The resulting method is by far the most promising approach to scalable coding.

Figure 3-29 shows that the analysis filters operate by taking a pair of frames as input and generating a pair of temporal sub-band frames as output. Therefore, analysis filters impose a minimum delay of at least one frame in the encoder. Because video conferencing systems attempt to minimize delays, temporal sub-band scalability might not be viable for low-delay applications.

The encoder can apply analysis filters recursively on the low-frequency sub-band, creating a new set of enhancement layers, as shown in Figure 3-30.

Figure 3-30 *Temporal Scalability, with One Base Layer and Three Enhancement Layers*

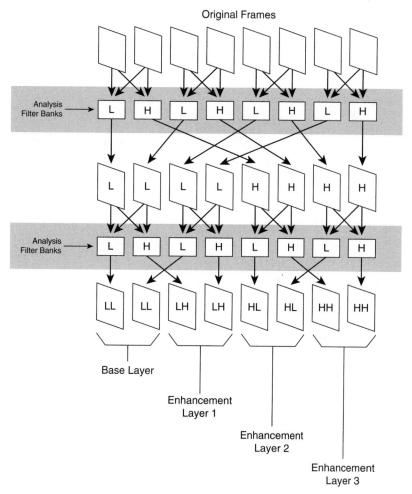

This example shows a base layer and three enhancement layers, as described in Table 3-6. The abbreviations assigned to each frame correspond to the order in which analysis filters are applied:

- The first letter indicates the filter band applied in the first round of analysis filters.

- The second letter indicates the filter band applied in the second round of analysis filters.

Each round of analysis filters separates the original frequency spectrum into two halves: the lower frequencies and the higher frequencies.

Table 3-6   *Layer Assignment for Temporal Sub-Band Scalability*

Layer	Frame Label
Base layer	LL
Enhancement layer 1	LH
Enhancement layer 2	HL
Enhancement layer 3	HH

In this example, the base layer consists of the two LL frames, at 1/4 the original frame rate.

Video bitstreams can make use of both temporal scalability and spatial/SNR scalability, as shown in Figure 3-31.

Figure 3-31   *Scalable Bitstream, with One Base Layer and Two Enhancement Layers*

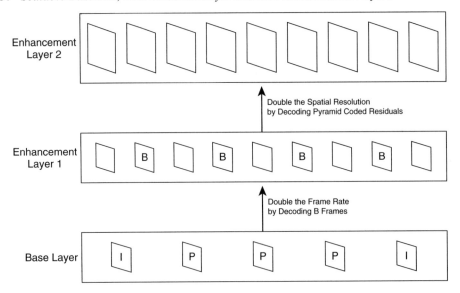

In this example, the base bitstream consists of a low-frame-rate, small-size image sequence. Enhancement layer 1 increases the frame rate by adding B-frames. Enhancement layer 2 adds spatial resolution with pyramid-coded residual information.

Switching Frames

H.264 added two new types of frames: the SI-frame (switching I) and the SP-frame (switching P), which are used for seamless switching between bitstreams and for random-access capability. Figure 3-32 shows the placement of SP-frames for stream switching.

Figure 3-32 *SP-Frames (Switching P)*

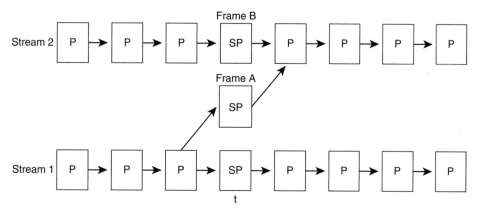

SP-frames are similar to P-frames in that they encode the difference between two frames. At time *t*, SP-frame A and B decode to the exact same image. Therefore, the decoder can switch from stream 1 to stream 2 seamlessly at time *t*. Figure 3-33 shows the use of SI-frames. Similar to I-frames, SI-frames encode an image without depending on other frames. In this figure, whereas I-frames occur infrequently, SI-frames occur more often, allowing a decoder to synchronize to the bitstream faster or to perform fast forward or fast reverse. The result of decoding frame A is identical to the result of decoding frame B. SI-frames are somewhat smaller than I-frames because SI-frames attempt to encode a frame that has already been processed by a lossy encode/decode.

Figure 3-33 *SI-Frames (Switching I)*

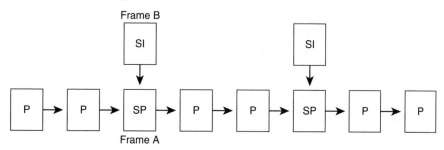

Video Codecs

Based on the codec fundamentals discussed in the first part of this chapter, this section looks into the specifics of standard codecs. This section covers aspects common to codec specifications. Appendix A, "Video Codec Standards," delves into the details of four video codecs: H.261, H.263, H.264, and MPEG-4 Part 2. Most of the codecs share the same specification format: The codecs define a bitstream hierarchy, a method of spatial and temporal compression, and optional features. H.261 is an older legacy codec used only to provide a primitive level of interoperability; however, it is useful to compare this design with the more advanced codecs.

Video Stream Hierarchy

Most codecs organize the bitstream into a hierarchy, as shown in Figure 3-34.

Figure 3-34 *Definition of the Bitstream Hierarchy*

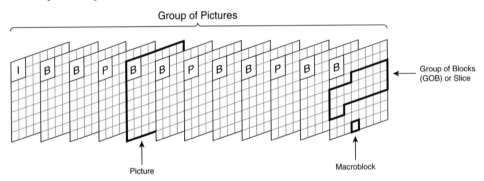

At the top of the hierarchy is a group of pictures (GOP). A GOP often consists of a fixed pattern of I-, P-, or B-frames. One level down in the hierarchy is a picture, consisting of an intra- or interframe. One level further down within this frame is a group of MBs; codecs may refer to this group as either a slice or a GOB. Different codecs provide different levels of flexibility when assigning MBs to GOBs or slices. In the simplest case, H.261 divides each frame into an array of fixed-size rectangular slices, each containing a fixed number of MBs. In contrast, H.264 has a mode called *flexible MB ordering* (FMO), which allows an arbitrary assignment of MBs to slices.

Codecs typically use start codes to define the start of a picture or slice/GOB. Immediately after the start code, each level of the hierarchy may have a header, which establishes parameter values for the upcoming hierarchy layer:

■ The picture start code (PSC) signals the start of a picture and may also signal the start of a GOB.

■ The slice start code or GOB start code signals the start of a slice or GOB.

Macroblocks

For all codecs in this chapter, an MB consists of a 16×16 array of luminance values and two 8×8 arrays of chrominance values in 4:2:0 format, shown in Figure 3-35.

Figure 3-35 *Macroblock Definition*

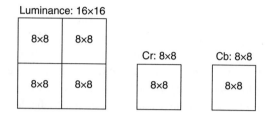

Different codecs may further subdivide the MB in different ways. The H.261 and H.264 codecs show two ends of the spectrum:

- For motion estimation, H.261 applies a motion vector to the entire 16×16 MB. In contrast, H.264 allows a MB to be subdivided in several ways. At the finest level of subdivision, H.264 can divide the 16×16 MB into an array of 4×4 pixel blocks and apply a motion vector to each 4×4 block separately.

- In the transformation process, the H.261 codec divides the MB into 8×8 blocks and applies an 8×8 DCT to each block. In contrast, H.264 can tile the MB into 4×4 or 8×8 pixel areas, and then transform each area with a 4×4 or 8×8 transform.

When coding interlaced video, codecs may switch between frame-based coding and field-based coding on an MB basis, a process called *adaptive frame/field coding*. Different codecs may use different MB formats for field coding versus frame coding. Figure 3-36 shows the field coding format for MPEG-4 Part 2.

Figure 3-36 *Field-Coded Macroblocks in MPEG-4 Part 2*

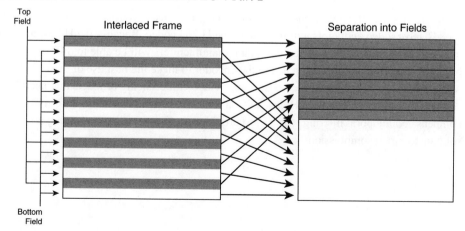

In the case of MPEG-4 Part 2, the top half of each MB contains the top field, and the bottom half of each MB contains the bottom field. In contrast, H.264 codes two fields using an MB pair, where each MB in the pair represents one of the fields.

HD-Capable Codecs

Several codecs support high-definition (HD) video. These codecs include Windows media 9, H.264 baseline profile (level 3.1 or level 4.0 and above), and H.264 Hi profile. H.264 baseline profile does not allow field (interlaced) encoding but does allow frame (progressive) encoding. HD endpoints can still support H.264 baseline profile to encode interlaced video, but this method requires the endpoint to combine the top and bottom field into a single merged frame. H.264 main and Hi profiles support frame encoding, and field coding at higher levels. True HD endpoints need special cameras to support high resolutions. These endpoints are usually used for point-to-point video calls and not for multipoint conferencing.

Summary

All codecs, whether simple or complex, use three fundamental processes in the encoder: transformation, followed by quantization, followed by entropy coding. In addition, encoders use prediction loops to encode the difference between predicted values and actual values. All the encoders discussed in this chapter apply a prediction loop at the image level by predicting an image and creating a residual, which is the difference between the prediction and the actual image. This residual then goes through the three-stage pipeline of transformation, quantization, and entropy coding.

In addition to using a predictor loop at the image level, advanced codecs use smaller, inner predictor loops at various stages of the codec pipeline. These inner loops make use of content-adaptive predictions, which are based on image data previously decoded. More advanced codecs also define highly developed post-processing algorithms, such as deblocking filters.

As future video conferencing endpoints adopt more advanced processors with greater CPU speeds, most video endpoints will migrate to the H.264 codec. Because the H.264 codec offers a high degree of flexibility, video conferencing manufacturers will be able to differentiate their products by adding more intelligence to the encoder to make the best use of the H.264 syntax without brute-force processor methods. Future video conferencing products that need layered compression may evolve to use H.264-SVC, a scalable, layered codec that uses motion-compensated temporal filtering (MCTF) to provide an efficient way of providing a layered solution to video compression.

References

ITU-T Recommendation H.264 / ISO/IEC 14496-10. March 2005. Advanced video coding for generic audiovisual services.

ITU-T Recommendation H.261. March 1993. Video Codec for Audiovisual Services at p x 64 kbits.

ITU-T Recommendation H.263. January 2005. Video coding for low bit rate communication.

MPEG-4 Part 2: ISO/IEC 14496-2: Coding of audio-visual objects - Part 2, Visual, Third Edition. May 2004.

This chapter covers the following topics:

- Overview of RTP

- Overview of RTCP

- RTP devices in conference systems

- Video stream RTP formats

- Detecting stream loss

CHAPTER 4

Media Control and Transport

Endpoints and conferencing systems in an IP network send voice and video packets via Real-time Transport Protocol (RTP). RTP has a companion protocol called RTP Control Protocol (RTCP), which provides information about the RTP streams related to packet statistics, reception quality, network delays, and synchronization. This chapter addresses the following topics:

- Basics of RTP and RTCP and their usage in conferencing systems

- Different RTP devices used in the conferencing architectures

- RTP packetization formats and details for H.263 and H.264 video codecs and I-frame detections for H.263 and H.264 codecs

- Stream loss detection

Overview of RTP

The Audio/Video Transport (AVT) working group of the Internet Engineering Task Force (IETF) developed RTP in 1996 and adopted it as a standard in RFC 1889. Subsequently, the IETF added more refinements to the protocol and republished it as RFC 3550. Always refer to the later RFC for the most current information on RTP. Figure 4-1 shows the relevance of RTP to other protocols used in IP collaboration systems.

Figure 4-1 *RTP in IP Collaboration Systems*

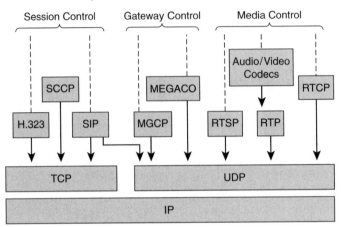

Senders transmit RTP and RTCP packets over UDP, and the endpoints on both sides of the connection negotiate the UDP ports and IP address through the signaling protocols (H.323, Session Initiation Protocol [SIP], or Signaling Connection Control Protocol [SCCP]). The initiator of the connection provides its receive RTP port number and the IP address in the offer (or open logical channel request), and the other endpoint provides its receive RTP port number and IP address in the answer (or open logical channel response), thus establishing two-way packet communication.

Each media stream (audio, video, or data) requires a separate RTP connection on a separate UDP port. There is one minor exception to this rule: if an endpoint must send Dual Tone Multiple Frequency (DTMF) digits using the DTMF RTP payload as defined in RFC 2833. In this case, the same RTP connection can be used to send both DTMF digits and voice packets. Each RTP connection between an endpoint and a conference server is identified by

- RTP *receive* port number of the endpoint

- IP address of the endpoint

- RTP *receive* port number of the conference server

- IP address of the conference server

RTP destination ports on the receiver are always selected with even numbers. The next higher odd port number is used to carry the RTCP traffic for the associated RTP port. The latest revision of the RTP standard, RFC 3550, allows the RTP implementation to use nonadjacent port numbers for RTP and RTCP.

RTP does not provide guaranteed delivery of packets or have a mechanism to handle out-of-order packets. The RTP implementation must address these issues using RTP sequence numbers. The RTP standard comes with a companion *profile* that defines how each field in the RTP packets must be used. However, only one profile is of concern for the discussions in this chapter—the *RTP Profile for Audio and Video Conferences with Minimal Control*, first defined in RFC 1890, and later revised as RFC 3551.

Each RTP packet has three major elements:

■ Fixed header

■ Optional header extension

■ The media payload itself, consisting of an optional payload header, followed by the codec payload

The following subsections describes these elements. "RTP Header" describes various control fields present in the header of the RTP packet. The RTP header includes the fixed header and the optional header extension. The media payload header and the payload itself follow the RTP header.

RTP Header

As stated in RFC 3550, the RTP header has a 12-octet mandatory part followed by an optional header extension. The header has the format illustrated in Figure 4-2.

Figure 4-2 *RTP Header*

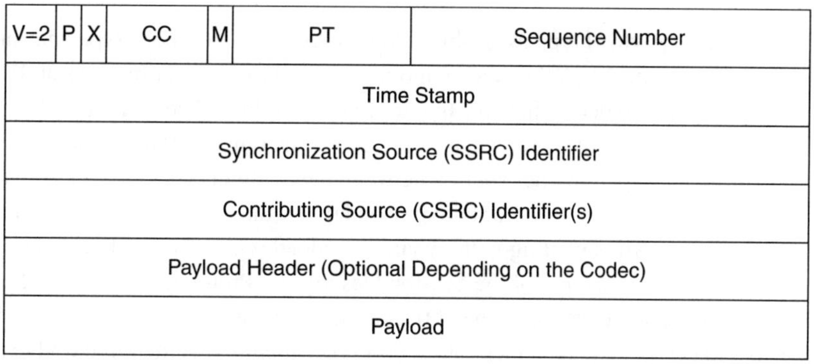

V=2	P	X	CC	M	PT	Sequence Number
Time Stamp						
Synchronization Source (SSRC) Identifier						
Contributing Source (CSRC) Identifier(s)						
Payload Header (Optional Depending on the Codec)						
Payload						

The following sections describe the octets in the RTP header shown in Figure 4-2.

First Octet in the Header

The fields in this first octet of the RTP header are described as follows:

- **Version (V): 2 bits**—This field identifies the version of RTP. The Version field is set to a value of 2 in most RTP implementations to denote the RTP profile defined in RFC 3551.

- **Padding (P): 1 bit**—If the padding bit is set, the packet contains one or more additional padding octets at the end, which are not part of the payload. The last octet of the padding contains a count of how many padding octets should be ignored, including itself. Some encryption algorithms with fixed block sizes might need padding to carry several RTP packets in a lower-layer protocol data unit.

- **Extension (X): 1 bit**—If the extension bit is set, exactly one header extension *must* follow the fixed header.

- **Contributing Source (CSRC) count (CC): 4 bits**—The CSRC count contains the number of CSRC identifiers that follow the fixed header. CSRC is explained in much more detail later in this chapter in the section "Contributing Source Identifiers."

- **Marker (M): 1 bit**—The interpretation of the marker is defined by the RTP profile in use. The M bit is intended to allow significant events such as frame boundaries to be marked in the packet stream. The M bit is helpful in video streams because it allows the endpoint to know that it has received the last packet of the frame so that it may display the full image. Without the M bit, the receiver would need to wait for one additional packet to detect a change to a new frame number.

Payload Type

RFC 3550 defines payload type as a 7-bit field that identifies the codec type and sample rate of media carried in the packet. When the endpoint or conference server receives an RTP packet, it uses the payload type to determine how to interpret the payload. The numeric value of the payload type may be predefined (called static payload types in the range of 0 to 96) or can be dynamically assigned during the capability negotiation between the conference server and the endpoint. There is one important distinction: For the static payload types, the clock rate is specified in the payload format. When using SIP signaling with dynamic payload types, the clock rate should be defined in the appropriate attribute line of the Session Description Protocol (SDP) offer. For example, G.711μ-Law uses a static payload type of 0, and the clock rate is defined in RFC 3551. H.264 is a dynamic payload type, and the clock rate is 90 kHz, which is specified in the SDP as follows:

m = video *rtp port number* RTP/AVP 97
a = rtpmap:97 H.264/**90000**

Sequence Number

The sequence number is a two-octet field that identifies the order in which RTP packets were transmitted. The sequence number allows the receiver to detect packets that were dropped on the network and allows the receiver to handle out-of-order packets. The sender increments the sequence number by 1 for each RTP packet it sends. As defined in RFC 3550, the endpoint or conference server should choose the initial value of the sequence number at random, rather than starting from 0, to prevent known-value encryption attacks.

Time Stamp

The time stamp is a 32-bit integer that increments at the media-dependent rate. As stated in RFC 3550, the time stamp reflects the sampling instance of the first octet of the media data in the RTP packet. As with sequence numbers, senders should choose a random value for the time stamp of the first packet, rather than starting at 0. The time stamp will also wrap around to 0 if it exceeds its maximum 32-bit value. The sender must transmit packets according to the real-time rate of the media, which means that if the sender issues packets with a fixed number of media samples, the delay between RTP packet transmissions should also be fixed. Table 4-1 shows audio sampling rates and their packet sizes.

Table 4-1   *Sampling Rate and Time Stamps*

Sampling Rate	Packet Size in RTP Time-Stamp Units
Audio 10 milliseconds (ms) G.711 at 8000 Hz	80
Audio 20 ms G.711 at 8000 Hz	160
Audio 30 ms G.711 at 8000 Hz	240
Video 30 frames per second at 90,000 Hz	3000 (1130 * 90,000)
Video 25 frames per second at 90,000 Hz	3600 (1/25 * 90,000)

In the case of MPEG bitstreams, which transmit frames out of order, the sender may transmit the RTP packets with out-of-order time stamps, but the sequence numbers will still increase. The receiver must reconstruct the data and play out the media accordingly based on the RTP time stamps. Also, note that a frame of video bitstream may be fragmented across multiple packets, which means that each packet will have the same RTP time stamp, but the sequence numbers will increase.

RTP packetization for audio codecs uses an RTP time-stamp clock that is the same as the sample clock, which means that the sampling clock increases by 1 for each sample. As a result, RTP time stamps for audio are essentially sample indexes. For example, an endpoint uses an audio codec with an 8000-Hz sample rate and an H.261 video codec. Because the sample rate of the audio stream is 8000 Hz, the RTP time stamp uses a sample clock of 8000 samples/second. If an audio stream packet has a size of 20 ms, the number of samples in that packet is 160, and therefore, the size of the packet is 160 RTP time-stamp units. H.261 uses an RTP sample clock of 90 kHz, which means a 29.97 FPS. An H.261 video stream will have a duration between frames of 33.37 ms, and the RTP time-stamp duration will equal 33.37 ms * 90,000 samples/second = 3003 RTP time-stamp units. The sender must assign RTP time stamps based on the absolute position in the source stream, which means that the RTP time-stamp sequence must account for packets not sent because of silence suppression at the sender.

Synchronization Source Identifier

The SSRC is a 32-bit field that serves as a unique identifier for an instance of an RTP stream. The originator of the RTP connection should choose this value at random. No two RTP streams within the same RTP session can have the same SSRC value. If the endpoint or the conference server changes the source IP address, the RTP packet stream must change to use a new SSRC value.

Contributing Source (CSRC) Identifiers

In a conference session, each endpoint transmits audio and video RTP packets to the audio mixer. The audio mixer then picks the top three or four speakers, mixes them, and sends the resulting output stream back to the endpoints. The output RTP packets should include the CSRC field, which is a list of the SSRC values of all participants selected for the mix. The audio mixer sets the CC bit in the first octet of the header to indicate the presence of a CSRC list. Many conferencing systems do not include this CSRC list because the endpoints are not conference-aware.

Payload Header

The RTP packetization method for the media is defined by a payload format definition, which is unique to each codec. A payload format might define a payload header, which resides in each RTP payload. The primary purpose of this header is to convey the state of the encoder to the destination. If the network drops packets, the receiver may use this state information to continue decoding the bitstream after the dropped packets. For instance, Figure 4-3 shows the format of the H.263 RTP packet.

Figure 4-3 *H.263 RTP Packet*

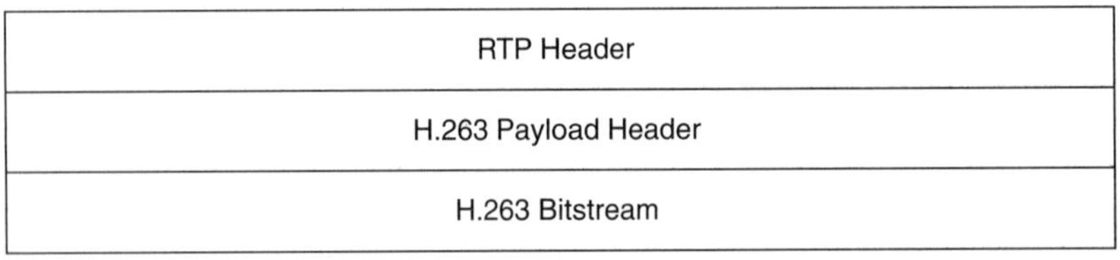

RTP Header
H.263 Payload Header
H.263 Bitstream

The payload header identifies (among other things) the group of blocks (GOB), slice, or macroblock (MB) index for data at the start of the packet. It also indicates whether this packet is part of an I-frame.

Payload

The payload is the actual media data sent and received between endpoints and the conference server. The payload may contain multiple audio frames, which means that the decoder may need to parse the bitstream to determine whether the packet contains more than one frame. RTP packets generally do not contain more than one frame of video; instead, single frames of video typically fragment across multiple RTP packets.

The following shows an example of the RTP header data structure with one CSRC identifier:

```
typedef struct _RTP_HEADER_ {
    u8          v_p_x_cc_m;
    u8          payload_type;
    u16         seq_number;
    u32         time_stamp;
    u32         ssrc;
    u32         csrc[1];
} rtp_header_t;
```

RTP Port Numbers

The send and receive port number may be the same. For instance, the endpoint may choose to send and receive the data in port 16666. Use of the same port numbers is recommended to allow Network Address Translation (NAT) traversal. By default, endpoints use port numbers 5004/5005 (RTP/RTCP), but they can negotiate during the signaling setup to use different port numbers. Many RTP implementers have a general misconception that RTP port numbers should be above 16787, which is not true.

SSRC Collisions

SSRC collision occurs if the endpoint and the conference server choose the same SSRC for their RTP streams. RFC 3550 specifies solutions for how to handle the SSRC collisions. If the conference server finds that both it and the endpoint use the same SSRC for the same session, the conference server should send an RTCP BYE packet, close the connection, and reestablish the connection using another SSRC. RFC 3350 requires that the SSRC identifiers be unique among the devices in the mixer or translator. Because the endpoints typically are not conference aware, the conference server should send the CSRC list to the endpoint so that it can detect SSRC collisions. It is up to the devices to resolve these collisions; most endpoints do not resolve them.

RTP Header Extensions

RFC 3550 provides the flexibility for individual implementations to extend the RTP header to add information. RTP header extensions are most useful in distributed conferencing systems. To extend the RTP header, the sender sets the X bit to 1 in the first octet of the RTP fixed header. Figure 4-4 shows the RTP header extension format.

Figure 4-4   *RTP Header Extension*

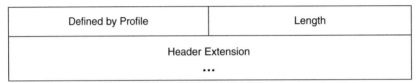

The first 16 bits of the header extension are left open for distinguishing identifiers or parameters. The format of these 16 bits is defined by the application that adds the extension. The header extension contains a 16-bit length field that counts the number of 32-bit words in the extension, excluding the four-octet extension header. (If the RTP implementation is adding just the extension header with no actual extension, the length should be set to 0.) Only a single extension can be appended to the RTP data header.

RTP header extensions are proprietary and specific to each manufacturer. However, conference mixers may use them in ways that supplement the RTP specification to convey more information about the bitstream. For instance, some codecs such as H.263v2 need deep packet inspection to determine whether the packet carries the I-frame. Often, the conference server or the endpoint must scan for I-frames in the incoming RTP packet to render a complete picture. With RTP header extension, the endpoint or the conference server could add a simple marker in the extension to indicate to the other end whether the current frame is an I-frame. The following code snippet adds an extended RTP header to mark a specific packet as a key frame:

```
#define VIDEO_I_FRAME      (0x880)

typedef struct _RTP_HEADER_EXTN_ {
    struct {
        uint16  type;
        uint16  length;
    } header;
    uchar       ext_data[0];
} rtp_header_extension_t;

rtp_header_t  *rtp_hdr;
rtp_header_extension_t *hdr_x;
..............
..............
rtp_hdr -> v_p_x_cc_m |= 0x10;    /* Set the x bit in the header */
hdr_x -> type = VIDEO_I_FRAME;
hdr_x -> length = 0;    /* Since we are not adding actual extension */
```

Overview of RTCP

RTCP is the companion control protocol for RTP. It provides periodic reports that include statistics, quality of reception, and information for synchronizing audio and video streams.

As stated in RFC 3550, RTCP performs two major functions:

■ It provides feedback on the quality of the media distribution. This function is performed by RTCP receiver and sender reports.

■ For each sender, RTCP maps RTP time stamps for each RTP stream to a common sender clock, which allows audio and video synchronization on the receivers.

RTCP carries an identifier called Canonical Name (CNAME) to identify the endpoint name associated with each RTP stream. The RTCP protocol specifies a rate-limiting mechanism for the RTCP packets, allowing RTCP to scale up to a large number of participants within the same RTP session.

Note that a general rule of thumb is that the RTCP bandwidth should not exceed 5 percent of the total RTP bandwidth used in a session.

The following sections describe the structure and functionality of the RTCP packets.

RTCP Packet Headers

RFC 3550 defines five types of RTCP packet formats:

■ Sender report (SR)

■ Receiver report (RR)

■ Source description (SDES)

■ Membership termination (BYE)

■ Application-specific functions (APP)

Each RTCP packet begins with fixed headers, similar to that of RTP data packets, followed by structured elements that may be of variable length according to the packet type but that always end on a 32-bit boundary. Multiple RTCP packets may be grouped to form a compound RTCP packet. Each compound packet is encapsulated in a single UDP/IP packet for transport.

All five RTCP packet types have a fixer header followed by individual packet formats, as shown in Figure 4-5.

Figure 4-5 *Fixed Part of RTCP Packet Format*

V=2	P	IC	PT	Length
Packet Type Specific Information				

The following list describes the packet format:

- **Version (V): 2 bits**—Identifies the version of RTP, which is the same in RTCP packets as in RTP data packets. The version used in most implementations is 2, corresponding to the RTP profile defined in RFC 3551.

- **Padding (P): 1 bit**—If this bit is set, this RTCP packet contains some additional padding octets at the end that are not part of the control information. The last octet of the padding is a count of how many padding octets should be ignored.

- **Item count (IC): 5 bits**—Some RTCP packet formats contain a list of items that are specific to the packet type. This field is used by the individual packet types to indicate the number of items included in this packet.

- **Packet type (PT): 8 bits**—Identifies the RTCP packet type.

- **Length: 16 bits**—Specifies the length of this RTCP packet, excluding this header. A value of 0 is valid and indicates that this packet contains just the fixed header, consisting of the first octet.

RTCP Sender Report

The RTP senders (endpoints or conference server) provide information about their RTP streams through the SR packet type. SRs serve three functions:

- They provide information to synchronize multiple RTP streams.

- They provide overall statistics on the number of packets and bytes sent.

- They provide one half of a two-way handshake that allows endpoints to calculate the network round-trip time between the two endpoints.

Figure 4-6 illustrates the format of the SR.

Figure 4-6 *RTCP Sender Report Format*

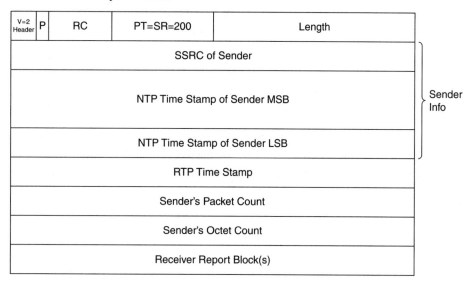

The following list explains the format:

- **Sender report**—The SR is identified by a packet type of 200.

- **NTP time stamp**—The NTP Time Stamp field is a 64-bit value that indicates the time of the RTP time stamp that is included in the report. The format of the NTP packet is a 64-bit number: the top 32 bits indicate the value in seconds, and the bottom 32 bits indicate the fraction of a second.

> **NOTE**   Despite the name, Network Time Protocol (NTP) time stamps are not necessarily derived from, or generated by, an NTP time server; the name only refers to the 64-bit data format, not the NTP time server protocol. The NTP time server protocol specifies that an NTP time stamp "represents counting seconds since January 1, 1900," but that is usually not the case for the NTP value in the RTCP packets. The NTP time stamp represents the wall clock time.

- **RTP time stamp**—The RTP time stamp in the header corresponds to the same instance of time as the NTP time stamp above it, but the RTP time stamp is represented in the same units of the sample clock of the RTP stream. This RTP-to-NTP correspondence allows for audio and video lip synchronization and is discussed extensively in Chapter 7, "Lip Synchronization in Video Conferencing."

- **Sender packet count**—The sender packet count indicates the total number of RTP packets sent since the stream started transmission, until the time this RTCP SR packet is generated. The sender resets the counter if the SSRC changes.

- **Sender octet count**—The sender octet count indicates the number of RTP payload octets sent since the stream started transmission, until the time this SR packet is generated. The sender resets the counter if the SSRC changes. This value can be used to estimate the average payload rate. The sender octet count does not include the length of the header or padding.

- **Receiver report block**—The RR blocks contain zero or more reception report blocks. Each reception report block conveys statistics on the reception of RTP packets from a single synchronization source depending on the number of other sources heard by the sender since the last report.

RTCP Receiver Report

The RTP receivers (endpoints or conference server) provide periodic feedback on the quality of the received media through the RR packet type. An endpoint can use this information to dynamically adjust its transmit rate based on network congestion. For example, if a video endpoint detects high network congestion as a result of packet loss, the endpoint may choose to send at a lower bit rate until the congestion clears.

Figure 4-7 illustrates the format of the RR report, and the following list describes the fields therein.

Figure 4-7 *RTCP Receiver Report Packet Format*

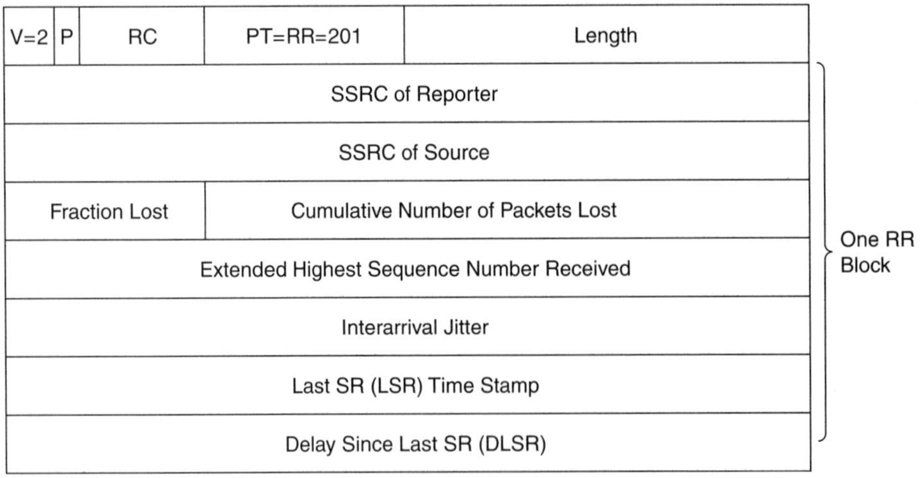

V=2	P	RC	PT=RR=201	Length	
SSRC of Reporter					
SSRC of Source					
Fraction Lost		Cumulative Number of Packets Lost			One RR Block
Extended Highest Sequence Number Received					
Interarrival Jitter					
Last SR (LSR) Time Stamp					
Delay Since Last SR (DLSR)					

- **PT=RR=201**—Indicates that the packet type is set to 201. An RR packet may contain more than one RR block. Each RR block describes the reception quality of a single synchronization source. The RR packet may have up to 31 blocks. Each report block consists of seven fields.

- **SSRC of reporter**—Contains the SSRC of the RR report sender.

- **SSRC of source**—Identifies the SSRC of the source for this report.

- **Fraction lost**—Identifies the fraction of RTP data packets lost since the previous SR or RR packet.

- **Cumulative number of packets lost**—Indicates the total number of RTP data packets from source SSRC that have been lost since the beginning of reception. This number is defined to be the number of packets expected minus the number of packets actually received, where the number of packets received includes any that are late or duplicates. The receiver discards any packets that arrive too late to play through the audio hardware, but these discarded packets are not considered dropped packets.

- **Extended highest sequence number received**—Indicates the highest sequence number observed in the RTP stream.

- **Interarrival jitter**—Estimates the statistical variance in network transit time for the RTP packets sent by the source SSRC.

- **Last sender report (LSR) time stamp**—Indicates the middle 32 bits out of the 64-bit NTP time stamp included in the most recent RTCP SR packet received form the source SSRC. This field is set to 0 if no SR has been received.

- **Delay since last SR (DLSR)**—Indicates the delay, expressed in units of 1/65,536 seconds, between receiving the last SR packet from the source SSRC and sending this RR block. This field is set to 0 if no SR packet has been received.

RTCP Source Description (SDES)

RTCP SDES packets provide participant information and other supplementary details (such as location information, presence, and so on). Figure 4-8 shows the packet format of the RTCP SDES packet.

Figure 4-8 *RTCP SDES Packet Format*

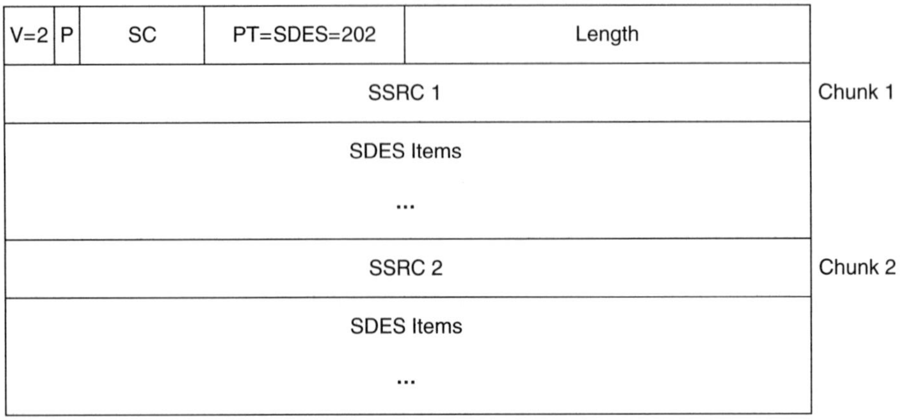

V=2	P	SC	PT=SDES=202	Length	
SSRC 1					Chunk 1
SDES Items					
...					
SSRC 2					Chunk 2
SDES Items					
...					

The following list explains the format:

■ **Payload type**—Is set to 202.

■ **Source count (SC)**—Indicates the number of SSRC/CSRC items included in this packet.

■ **SSRC**—Starts each chunk.

■ **SDES**—Follows the SSRC. A list of SDES items describes that SSRC source. Each of the SDES items is of the format Type (8 bits), Length (8 bits), and Value (text of maximum 255 octets). RFC 3550 specifies several types of SDES values; the one that is more relevant for conferencing applications is CNAME.

CNAME provides a canonical name for each participant that remains constant throughout the session. The CNAME should be unique among all the streams in one RTP session.

RFC 3550 requires that the CNAME be derived algorithmically and not entered manually. For example, the CNAME of an endpoint joining a conference may be ep@10.1.1.1. Figure 4-9 illustrates an RTCP SDES packet from the endpoint (labeled ep in the figure) with a CNAME of ep@10.1.1.1.

Figure 4-9 *RTCP CNAME Packet*

V=2	P	SC	PT=SDES=202	Length=10		
SSRC=765433890000						
Type=1 (CNAME)		Length=10	e	p	@	
10		.	1	.	1	
.						

RTCP BYE

Reception of an RTCP BYE packet indicates that a participant has left a call or conference session. A BYE is also generated when an endpoint or conference server changes its SSRC. For instance, the sender must change the SSRC value in case of an SSRC collision. Figure 4-10 shows the format of the RTCP BYE packet.

Figure 4-10 *RTCP BYE Packet Format*

V=2	P	SC	PT=BYE=203	Length	
SSRC 1					
...					
SSRC *n*					
Length (Opt)			Reason for Leaving (Opt)		

- **Packet type**—Is set to 203.

- **SC**—Indicates the number of SSRC identifiers in the packet. If an endpoint sends multiple streams and leaves the session, the RTCP BYE packet from the endpoint has the SSRC of all the streams sourced by the endpoint. If a conference mixer sends the RTCP BYE packet to the endpoint, the BYE packet contains the CSRCs of the streams that the mixer was mixing.

- **Length**—Optional field identifies the length of the Reason field.

- **Reason**—Optional field indicates the reason for leaving the session.

RTCP APP

The APP packet is application-specific and is intended to be used by applications during the development phase of an RTP application. In a strict sense, RTP does not recommend the use of the APP packet for anything beyond development testing. However, one application of the APP packet is a lip sync mechanism, explained in Chapter 7. Figure 4-11 shows the packet format.

Figure 4-11 *RTCP APP Packet Format*

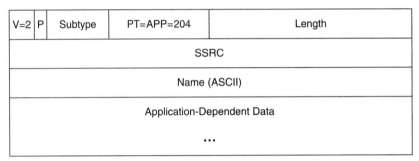

The purpose of the subtype is to group a set of APP packets under one unique name. The packet type is set to 204. The name is a four-octet ASCII string that assigns a unique name for this APP packet. The application-dependent data is a variable-length optional field that is left to the application implementation.

RTP Devices in Conference Systems

The conference server has multiple logical RTP devices, and each of them has different functionalities. This section looks at the functionality of these devices and how they use the RTP/RTCP headers. These devices fall into two categories: RTP translator and RTP mixer.

RTP Translator

Translators have one input stream and one output stream and forward RTP packets with their SSRC identifier intact. If a translator does not change the sample rate of the stream, the translator can pass RTCP packets unchanged. If the translator alters the sample rate, however, the translator must send RTCP packets with new RTP/NTP time stamp pairs. In a conferencing system, translators take different shapes. Examples are media termination point (MTP), transcoder, and transrater.

Media Termination Points

Cisco CallManager MTPs are RTP modules (also called RTP proxies) that serve one function: They terminate and re-originate RTP/RTCP streams without processing the RTP data. Only centralized call agents, like a Cisco CallManager, use these modules. Endpoints always connect directly to CallManager at the signaling level (SIP, H.323, SCCP). However, at the media level,

CallManager may either connect two endpoints directly or may insert an MTP in the media path of the connection. As far as the endpoints are concerned, the MTP appears to be the other endpoint. MTPs provide several features:

- **QoS support**—The RSVP protocol for bandwidth reservation requires endpoints on each side of a connection to send RSVP protocol packets on the same ports that are used for the media. If two endpoints do not support the RSVP protocol for quality of service, CallManager may connect each endpoint to an MTP, and then connect the two MTPs together, and direct each MTP to establish RSVP reservations on the RTP ports.

- **Call control**—MTPs add call control features (such as hold, transfer, and forward) for endpoints that do not natively support these features. Most H.323 endpoints do not support H.450, a standard for call control. As an alternative, CallManager can connect each H.323 endpoint to an MTP and then perform the call control features by rerouting RTP streams among MTPs. In this scenario, each H.323 endpoint experiences one continuous call session, but behind the scenes, CallManager rewires the MTP-to-MTP connections.

- **Topology hiding**—MTPs may provide topology hiding for endpoints or mixers within the private IP space of a protected network. If an external endpoint connects to an endpoint on the trusted side of a firewall, an MTP deployed in the demilitarized zone (DMZ) can terminate the RTP/RTCP media, preventing a direct connection between the external and internal endpoints. However, MTPs do not offer topology hiding for the central call agent, because external endpoints must still connect directly to CallManager to establish H.323, SIP, or SCCP signaling connections.

Conference servers do not need MTPs to handle signaling protocol conversions, such as H.323 to SIP translation, because even though the signaling protocols change, the RTP and RTCP packets remain identical between the two signaling protocols.

MTP devices do not change any of the RTP header parameters or the payload. However, the process of terminating and then reoriginating RTP media packets does consume CPU resources on a call control server. Figure 4-12 shows Cisco CallManager inserting an MTP device into the media path between an endpoint and a conference server.

Figure 4-12 *Media Termination Points*

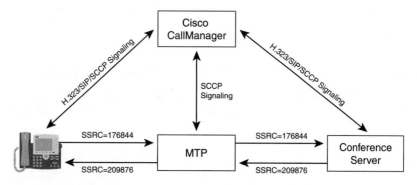

Transcoders and Transraters

Transcoders convert RTP media from one codec to another, and transraters convert RTP media from one bit rate to a lower bit rate. For instance, if an endpoint supports only the Internet Low Bandwidth Codec (ILBC), and the conference server does not support ILBC, an audio transcoder between the endpoint and the conference server can perform the conversion.

In most implementations, audio mixers contain built-in transcoders, because the audio data must be decoded before the summation process. A transcoder is similar to a mixer with one input and one output: Each RTP header is rewritten with a new sequence number, time stamp, and other parameters. However, the SSRC stays the same. In addition, transcoders that change the code type must create new RTCP packets for the output stream.

Video conferencing systems use transraters to lower the bit rate of video or audio RTP streams. For instance, a transrater may convert high-bandwidth 704-kbps H.264 30 frames per second to low-bandwidth 320-kbps H.264 30 frames per second. Transraters handle RTP headers in the same way as RTP transcoders.

Figure 4-13 shows CallManager inserting a transcoder between the endpoint and the conference server to transcode between G.729 and G.711 audio codecs. Figure 4-13 also shows a transrater in the media path between the endpoint and the conference server. Transraters are usually built in to the conference server (or video multipoint control unit [MCU]) and not as a separate device.

Figure 4-13 *Transcoder*

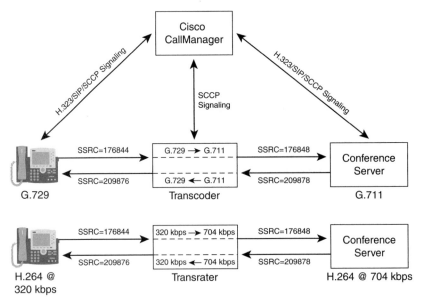

RTP Mixer

An RTP mixer receives RTP packets from one or more RTP sources (such as endpoints), changes the content or format of the RTP packet, generates a new RTP packet, and sends the packet to the RTP sources. There are two models of the RTP mixer. In the first model, the endpoints are aware of being a participant in a multiway (or being in the conference) RTP session. In the second model, the mixer looks just like another endpoint to the endpoints, and the endpoints are not conference-aware. Examples of an RTP mixer include audio mixer, video MCU, and video switcher. The following sections explain the functionality of these devices.

Audio Mixer

The audio mixer is the core of the audio conferencing system. It receives the audio streams from the endpoints, mixes $N + 1$ separate streams, as discussed in Chapter 2, "Conferencing System Design and Architecture," and sends the mixed streams back to the endpoints. Mixers terminate the incoming streams and create new outgoing RTP streams. There is no association between the incoming RTP header parameters (such as SSRC, sequence numbers, and time stamps) and the mixed output stream RTP parameters.

In the model where the endpoints are conference-aware, the mixer should include a CSRC list in each outgoing audio RTP packet and include the SSRC values of each participant in the mix. However, most audio mixer implementations do not add the CSRC identifiers in the outgoing packets. In addition, endpoints without robust RTP implementations might crash when trying to process a CSRC list.

Figure 4-14 shows how the mixer maps the SSRC of the incoming streams into the CSRC list of the outgoing streams.

Figure 4-14   *SSRC/CSRC Handling in the Mixer*

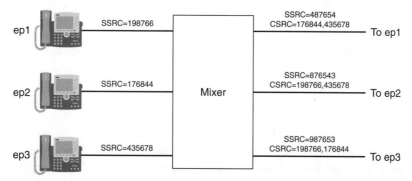

Because each endpoint uses a different crystal clock to derive the RTP sample clock, RTP time stamps of the different incoming RTP streams are not synchronized. The mixer applies timing adjustments, adds the audio streams together, and creates new time stamps and sequence numbers for the outgoing RTP packets.

Video MCU

Video conference systems use video MCUs to mix audio and video streams. The video MCU typically contains tightly integrated video mixers and audio mixers. The audio mixers determine the loudest participants to select which speakers to include in the audio mix. The loudest speaker information drives a speaker selection mechanism, which is a policy that determines which video stream to include in the output mix. The video MCU sends the resulting video and audio mixes back to the participants. Because MCUs terminate and re-create audio and video RTP streams, the MCU creates new RTP headers for the output streams, with new SSRCs. Video MCUs rely on RTCP to reliably perform lip synchronization (explained in Chapter 7).

Figure 4-15 shows an MCU that decodes the video streams from three endpoints, mixes the streams, encodes, and sends back the mixed streams to the endpoints.

Figure 4-15   *Video MCU*

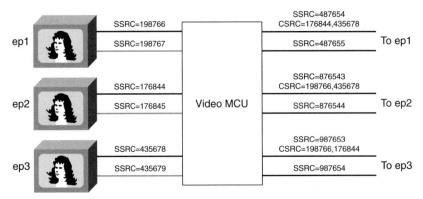

Current MCU implementations include both transcoders and transraters in the MCU, instead of treating them as separate RTP entities.

Video Switcher

The video switcher gets the video streams from the endpoints, applies the conference policy to select one or more of the video streams, and sends the video streams back to the endpoints (with no transcoding, transrating, or composition). The video switcher is implemented either as an appliance that just runs this application or as part of the conference server. The video switcher is also known as a media switcher or video passthrough device.

Video switchers do not change the payload carried in the RTP streams, but rewrite the RTP headers (new SSRC, time stamp, sequence number) for the outbound RTP streams. The reason for rewriting the RTP header is because the RTP stream selected to be sent to the endpoint can be chosen dynamically.

Figure 4-16 illustrates the functionality of a video passthrough mode.

Figure 4-16 *Video Switcher*

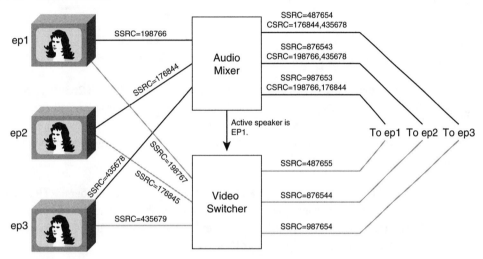

In this example of a voice-activated video conference, the video streams from the video endpoints go to the media switcher, and the audio streams go to the audio mixer. The media switcher communicates with the audio mixer to get the active speaker events. When the active speaker changes, the mixer sends an event message to the switcher, and the switcher sends the stream of that active speaker to all other endpoints in the conference. The switcher maintains the last speaker information and sends the video of the last speaker to the endpoint of the active speaker. As shown in Figure 4-16, the switcher creates a new SSRC for each outgoing video stream, and these SSRCs do not change, regardless of which input stream the switcher has selected. The switcher must not change the SSRC midstream, because endpoints might consider the SSRC change a fatal error.

As with SSRC, the media switcher keeps the time-stamp sequence continuous on the outbound video streams. When the active speaker changes, the switcher uses an input-to-output RTP time-stamp mapping that preserves the continuity of the output stream. However, any time-stamp jump in the input time stamp is reflected on the output stream.

The switcher also maintains the sequence number continuous on the outbound video streams. The only exception is for packets that arrive out of order. The switcher has to make sure that the packets that arrive out of order should also be sent out of order (and let the endpoint handle the out-of-order sequence), as shown in Figure 4-17.

Figure 4-17 *Out-of-Order Packets in Video Passthrough Mode*

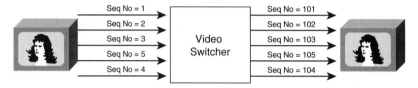

Video Stream RTP Formats

This section describes the RTP payload formats for three video codecs: H.263v1, H.263v2, and H.264. The payload formats describe how the bitstream for a single frame may be fragmented across multiple RTP packets. In addition, each payload format defines a payload header, containing details such as key frame indicators. Because H.263 has largely replaced H.261, this section does not go into the details of H.261 packetization.

As discussed earlier in this chapter, each RTP packet consists of three headers: RTP header, payload header, and codec header. The RTP header and the payload header are per-packet headers, whereas the codec header is not specific to a packet but rather specific to the components of a bitstream, such as picture header, group of blocks, and so on.

H.263

As described in Chapter 3, "Fundamentals of Video Compression," the H.263 codec has three commonly used versions. The RTP payload format for each version differs slightly and is addressed in two different RFCs: RFC 2190 defines the payload format for H.263-1996, and RFC 2429 defines the payload format for H.263-1998 and H.263-2000. Figure 4-18 shows the basic format of an H.263 packet.

Figure 4-18 *H.263 RTP Format*

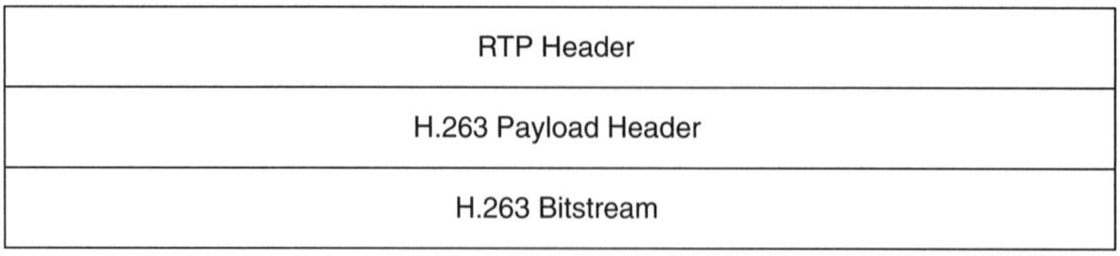

RTP Header
H.263 Payload Header
H.263 Bitstream

The following sections describe H.263-1996, H.263-1998, and H.263-2000 in more detail. You also learn about key frame detection in H.263.

H.263-1996

RFC 2190 defines the payload format for encapsulating H.263-1996 (H.263 or H.263v1) bitstreams in RTP packets. For this version, the payload format defines three modes for the H.263 payload header: mode A, mode B, and mode C. An RTP packet can use one of these three modes, depending on the desired packet size and the encoding options used in the H.263 bitstream. The F and P fields in the payload header determine the mode. The endpoints and the conference servers must be prepared to receive packets in any mode. These modes are *not* negotiated in the SDP offer/ answer.

The next sections describe the three H.263 modes.

Mode A

In mode A, an H.263 payload header of 4 bytes is present before the actual payload, as shown in Figure 4-19. Note that mode A packets always start with a picture code or a GOB start code.

Figure 4-19 *H.263 Mode A Payload Header*

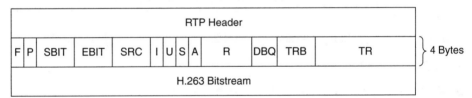

Table 4-2 explains the different bit fields.

Table 4-2 *H.263-1996 Mode A Bit Fields*

Bit Field	Size (in Bits)	Description
F	1	Indicates the mode of the payload header. A value of 0 indicates mode A; a value of 1 indicates mode B or mode C.
P	1	When F=1, a P bit value of 0 indicates mode B, and a value of 1 indicates mode C.
SBIT	3	Start bit position. Specifies the number of most significant bits ignored in the first byte.
EBIT	3	End bit position. Specifies the number of least significant bits ignored in the last data byte.
SRC	3	Specifies the resolution of the current picture.

continues

Table 4-2 *H.263-1996 Mode A Bit Fields (Continued)*

Bit Field	Size (in Bits)	Description
I	1	Set to 0 for an intracoded frame and to 1 for intercoded.
U	1	Set to 1 if the Unrestricted Motion Vector option, bit 10 in PTYPE defined by H.263, was set to 1 in the current picture header otherwise, set to 0.
S	1	Set to 1 if the Syntax-based Arithmetic Coding option, bit 11 in PTYPE defined by H.263, was set to 1 in the current picture header; otherwise, set to 0.
A	1	Set to 1 if the Advanced Prediction option, bit 12 in PTYPE defined by H.263, was set to 1 in the current picture header; otherwise, set to 0.
R	4	Reserved: These bits must be set to 0.
DBQ	2	Differential quantization (DBQ)—the value should be the same as DBQUANT defined by H.263. Set to 0 if the PB-frames option is not used.
TRB	3	Temporal Reference for the B frame as defined by H.263. It is set to 0 if the PB-frames option is not used.
TR	8	Temporal Reference for the P-frame as defined by H.263. It is set to 0 if the PB-frames option is not used.

Example 4-1 shows the Ethereal capture of an H.263v1 mode A frame. Note that the F bit is set to 0.

Example 4-1 *H.263 Ethereal Packet Trace*

```
Frame 4733 (1327 bytes on wire, 1327 bytes captured)
Ethernet II, Src: 00:14:38:be:ec:57, Dst: 00:13:20:12:b5:5d
Internet Protocol, Src Addr: 172.27.75.146 (172.27.75.146), Dst Addr:
  172.27.75.187 (172.27.75.187)
User Datagram Protocol, Src Port: 21468 (21468), Dst Port: 5445 (5445)
Real-Time Transport Protocol
    10.. ....=Version: RFC 1889 Version (2)
    ..0. ....=Padding: False
    ...0 ....=Extension: False
    .... 0000=Contributing source identifiers count: 0
    0... ....=Marker: False
    .010 0010=Payload type: ITU-T H.263 (34)
Sequence number: 59
Timestamp: 117123
Synchronization Source identifier: 2887470011
ITU-T Recommendation H.263 RTP Payload header (RFC2190)
    F: False
```

Example 4-1 *H.263 Ethereal Packet Trace (Continued)*

```
p/b frame: False
Start bit position: 0
End bit position: 0
SRC format: CIF 352x288 (3)
Inter-coded frame: True
Motion vector: False
Syntax-based arithmetic coding: False
Advanced prediction option: False
Reserved field: 0
Differential quantization parameter: 0
Temporal Reference for B frames: 0
Temporal Reference for P frames: 0
H.263 stream: 000081DA0E043FFFFC03958989935EC9AF76C8B3A07FFFFF...
```

Mode B

In mode B, an H.263 bitstream can be fragmented at MB boundaries. Whenever the packet starts at an MB boundary, this mode is used without the PB-frames option. Figure 4-20 shows the mode B payload header.

Figure 4-20 *H.263-1996 Mode B Payload Header*

The fields F, P, SBIT, EBIT, SRC, R, I, U, S, and A are defined as in mode A. The F bit should be set to a value of 1, and the P bit should be set to a value of 0. Table 4-3 explains the remaining fields.

Table 4-3 *H.263-1996 Mode B Fields*

Bit Field	Size	Description
QUANT	5	Quantization value for the first MB coded at the beginning of the packet. Set to 0 if the packet begins with a GOB header.
GOBN	5	GOB number in effect at the start of the packet. GOB numbers are specified differently for different resolutions. Refer to RFC 2190 for details.
MBA	9	Macroblock address (MBA)—the address within the GOB of the first MB in the packet, counting from 0 in scan order. For example, the third MB in any GOB is given MBA = 2.
HMV1	7	Horizontal motion vector predictors for the first MB in this packet.
VMV1	7	Vertical motion vector predictors for the first MB in this packet.

continues

Table 4-3 *H.263-1996 Mode B Fields (Continued)*

Bit Field	Size	Description
HMV2	7	Horizontal motion vector predictors for block number 3 in the first MB in this packet when four motion vectors are used with the advanced prediction option. This information is needed because block number 3 in the MB needs different motion vector predictors than other blocks in the MB. These two fields are not used when the MB has only one motion vector. Refer to RFC 2190 for block organization in an MB.
VMV2	7	Same as HMV2, except that this entry is for vertical motion vector predictors.

Mode C

In mode C, an H.263 bitstream is fragmented at MB boundaries of P-frames if those P-frames have the PB-frames option set. This mode is intended for GOBs whose sizes are larger than the maximum packet size allowed in the underlying protocol when the PB-frames option is used. The F bit is set to 1, and the P bit is set to 1 to indicate mode C. Figure 4-21 shows the mode C payload header.

Figure 4-21 *H.263-1996 Mode C Payload Header*

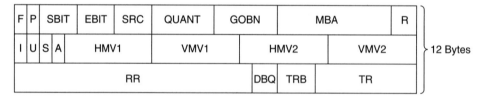

The bit fields are defined the same as in mode A and mode B. The only exception is the 19-bit RR field—these bits are reserved and are set to 0.

Most H.263 endpoint implementations use mode A because of its simplicity and small payload header.

H.263-1998 and H.263-2000

RFC 2429 defines the payload header format for H.263+ (also known as H.263-1998) and H.263++ (also known as H.263-2000) codecs. These codecs are also referred to as *H.263v2*. The payload header consists of a mandatory fixed part of two octets followed by a variable-length optional header. Figure 4-22 shows the packet structure.

Figure 4-22 *H.263v2 Packet Structure*

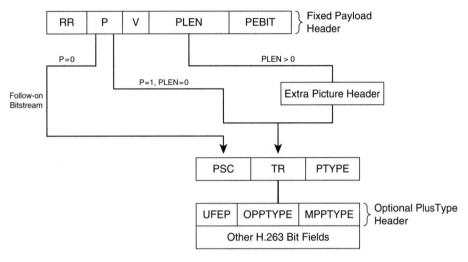

Table 4-4 explains the different bit fields used in the payload header.

Table 4-4 *H.263v2 Payload Header Format*

Bit Field	Number of Bits	Description
RR	5	Reserved—set to 0.
P	1	Indicates a picture start, or a picture segment (GOB/slice) start, or a video sequence end.
V	1	Indicates the presence of a one-octet field containing information for Video Redundancy Coding (VRC).
PLEN	6	Picture header length—length in bytes of the extra picture header. If no extra picture header is attached, PLEN is 0. The length excludes the first two octets of the fixed header.
PEBIT	3	Indicates how many bits are ignored in the last byte of the picture header.

VRC is an optional mechanism intended for error resiliency in packet networks. If V is set to 1, a 1-byte header is attached immediately after the 2-byte fixed payload header.

If P is set to 0, this packet indicates a follow-on stream, meaning that it does not include the start of a picture or a slice. If P is set to 1, this packet contains the start of a picture or a slice. (2 bytes of 0 bits then have to be prefixed to the payload of such a packet to compose a complete picture, GOB, slice, end of sequence [EOS], or end of sub-bit stream [EOSBS] start code.)

The packet may contain an optional extra picture header, which is indicated by a nonzero PLEN value. Encoders add extra picture headers to provide greater error resilience. The value of PLEN indicates the size of the extra picture header.

The actual payload data for each picture consists of an optional picture header, followed by data for a GOB or slices, eventually followed by an optional end-of-sequence code, followed by stuffing bits. As shown in Figure 4-22, the picture header starts with a picture start code (PSC). Table 4-5 explains the fields of the PSC for the H.263v2 codec

Table 4-5   *H.263v2 Picture Header Format*

Bit Field	Number of Bits	Description
PSC	22	Picture start code. If the packet contains the picture or slice, the value is 0000 0000 0000 0000 1 00000. This field should be byte-aligned.
TR	8	Temporal reference. This value increases by 1 for each new frame and then wraps around to 0.
PTYPE	Variable length	Picture type—information about the complete picture.

PTYPE has 13 bits and carries a variety of information. Bit 9 indicates the picture coding type and determines whether the packet carries a key frame (value 0) or P-frame (value 1). If bits 6–8 of the PTYPE field are set to 111, an extended header called a *PlusType header* is added to the payload header. If the PlusType header is added, bit 9 no longer indicates whether the packet carries a key frame, and this I-frame information is instead added to the PlusType header.

The PlusType header consists of the following three fields:

■   Update Full Extended PTYPE (UFEP) of 3 bits.

■   Optional Part of PlusType (OPPTYPE) of 18 bits.

■   Mandatory Part of PlusType (MPPTYPE) of 9 bits. The first 3 bits of MPPTYPE indicate the picture type code (I-frame, P-frame, PB-frame, and so on). If the first 3 bits contain a value of 000, the current frame is an I-frame.

Key Frame Detection in H.263

Video MCUs have a tricky requirement: They must be able to create a seamless output stream for each endpoint, while at the same time switching between multiple input streams based on the loudest speaker floor control policy. The problem is that if the MCU were to switch immediately to a new input stream, endpoints receiving that output stream would detect a discontinuity in the bitstream and would have to wait for a key frame from the new selected stream to resume decoding the stream. To make the output stream appear seamless, the MCU should delay the switch to a new input stream until a key frame arrives from that new input stream. The receiving endpoint detects the discontinuity, but it does not have to wait for a key frame, because the MCU provides a key frame immediately after the switch. The video encoders, depending on the codec and packetization, set bits in the RTP payload header to indicate the presence of an I-frame.

In H.263v1, an I bit in the RTP payload header indicates that the packet belongs to an I-frame. For H.263 mode A, a value of 0 in the twelfth bit from the start of the payload header indicates that the packet belongs to an I-frame. For mode B and mode C, a value of 1 in the thirty-third bit from the start of the payload header indicates that the packet belongs to an I-frame.

With H.263v2, the MCU must resort to deep packet inspection of the codec bitstream to identify the start of an I-frame. The H.263 PSC indicates the I-frame in one of two places, depending on the contents of the PTYPE field:

- **Bits 6–8 of PTYPE != 111**—A value of 0 in bit 9 indicates an I-frame.

- **Bits 6–8 of PTYPE == 111**—A value of 0 in bits 1–3 of the MPPTYPE field indicates an I-frame.

H.264

H.264 is a video codec that delivers visual quality superior to H.263 at the same bit rates. H.264 is also referred to as *Advanced Video Coding* (AVC). H.264 consists of two separate definitions:

- The video coding layer (VCL)

- The network abstraction layer (NAL)

The VCL represents the video content, and the NAL defines the packetization format for transport protocols such as RTP. All data is contained in NAL units. The H.264 bitstream can be of two formats: NAL unit stream and byte stream format. We limit our discussion to the NAL unit stream as specified in RFC 3984.

Basic Packet Structure

Figure 4-23 shows the format of a NAL header, which is the basic structure of an H.264 RTP packet. Per RFC 3984, all H.264 RTP packets contain the 1-byte NAL header field after the RTP header.

Figure 4-23   *NAL Unit Packet Format*

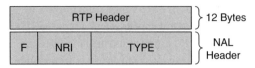

Table 4-6 explains the bit fields.

Table 4-6   *NAL Header Bit Fields*

Bit Field	Size (in Bits)	Description
F	1	Forbidden_zero_bit. A value of 1 indicates that the payload may contain errors or syntax violations. H.264 implementations usually drop packets that have the F bit set to 1. A value of 0 indicates that the payload should not contain any error or syntax violations.
NRI	2	NAL_ref_idc. A value of 00 indicates that the content of the NAL unit does not contain information needed to reconstruct reference pictures for inter-picture prediction. A value of greater than 00 indicates that the receiver must decode the NAL unit to reconstruct other inter-codec pictures.
TYPE	5	This field identifies the type of the NAL unit carried by the packet. A value of 0 is undefined.

The Type field defines the packetization mode, as shown in Table 4-7.

Table 4-7   *NAL Header Type Field Values*

Type	Packet	Description
0	Undefined	—
1–23	NAL unit	Single NAL unit packet.
24	STAP-A	Single-time aggregation packet
25	STAP-B	Single-time aggregation packet
26	MTAP-16	Multi-time aggregation packet
27	MTAP-24	Multi-time aggregation packet
28	FU-A	Fragmentation unit
29	FU-B	Fragmentation unit

The NAL unit type field indicates the type of the packet (and thus the structure of the RTP packet). There are three possible types:

■ **Single NAL unit (SNALU)**—This packet type contains only a single NAL unit as indicated by the type value of 1-23. The H.264 codec specification describes each type value in detail.

■ **Aggregation packet**—This packet type aggregates multiple NAL units into a single RTP payload. There are four versions of this packet, corresponding to type values 24-27.

■ **Fragmentation unit (FU)**—This packet type fragments a NAL unit over multiple RTP packets. There are two versions of this packet (type values 28 and 29).

Figure 4-24 shows the three possible H.264 packet types.

Figure 4-24 *H.264 Packet Type Formats*

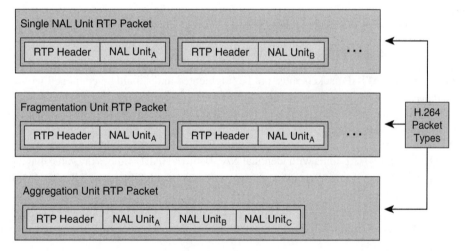

The following sections describe the three NAL unit packet types in more detail.

SNALU

The SNALU payload type contains only a single NAL unit in the payload. Figure 4-25 shows the format of the SNALU. It contains a 1-byte header (the fields are explained in Table 4-6 in the preceding section). The value of the Type field is in the range of 1 to 23.

Figure 4-25 *Format of the SNALU RTP Packet*

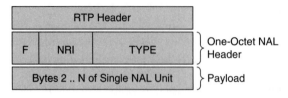

NAL units must be transmitted in the same order as their NAL unit decoding order, and the RTP sequence number should reflect this transmission order.

Aggregation Packet

RFC 3984 defines two basic types of aggregation packets:

- Single-time aggregation packet (STAP)

- Multi-time aggregation packet (MTAP)

The STAP and MTAP packets must not be fragmented and should be contained within a single RTP packet. MTAP is not commonly used for video conferencing.

STAP

STAP aggregates NAL units with identical NALU-time. NALU-time is the value that the RTP time stamp would have if that NAL were transported in its own RTP packet. RFC 3984 defines two types of STAP packets:

- **STAP-A**—NAL units in the aggregation packet share the same time stamp and appear in valid decoding order.

- **STAP-B**—NAL units in the aggregation packet share the same time stamp and may not be in the correct decoding order.

Figure 4-26 shows the packet format of the STAP-A packet. The value of the Type field in the NAL header is set to 24. The Size field (two octets) indicates the size of the NAL unit in bytes, which includes the NAL unit header plus data.

Figure 4-27 shows the format of the STAP-B packet. The type field is set to a value of 25. The STAP-B packet consists of a two-octet decoding order number (DON) that indicates the NAL unit decoding order. The DON is required because the transmission order and the decoding order might differ, and the DON indicates the decoding order.

Figure 4-26 *H.264 STAP-A Packet Format*

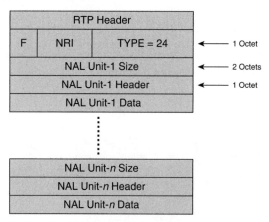

Figure 4-27 *H.264 STAP-B Packet Format*

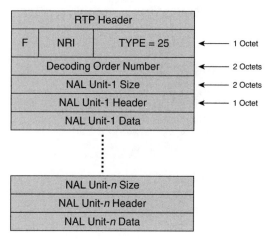

MTAP

MTAP aggregates NAL units with potentially different NALU times. RFC 3984 defines two types of MTAP packets:

- MTAP-16 (16-bit time-stamp offset)

- MTAP-24 (24-bit time-stamp offset)

Figure 4-28 shows the packet format of MTAP-16.

■ The Type field is set to a value of 27.

■ The payload header contains a two-octet decoding order number base (DONB). The MTAP packet contains multiple NAL units. The DONB contains the value of DON for the first NAL unit in the MTAP packet.

Figure 4-28 *H.264 MTAP-16 Packet Format*

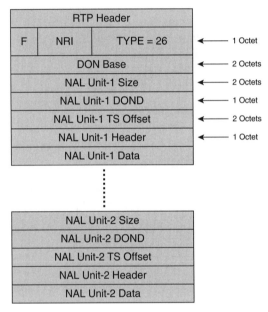

Figure 4-29 shows the packet format of MTAP-16. The Type field is set to a value of 27.

The choice between MTAP-16 and MTAP-24 is application-dependent. The only difference between the two packet formats is the length of the time-stamp offset field.

Fragmentation Unit Packet

The fragmentation unit (FU) allows a sender to fragment a single NAL unit into several RTP packets. The sender of the FU packet must send the fragments in consecutive order with ascending RTP sequence numbers. The receiver should reassemble the NAL unit according to the same RTP sequence number. The RTP time stamp of an RTP packet carrying an FU is set to the NALU time of the fragmented unit.

Figure 4-29 *H.264 MTAP-24 Packet Format*

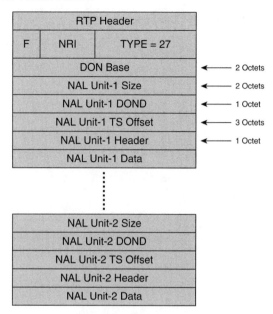

RFC 3984 defines two types of fragmentation unit packets. Figure 4-30 shows the FU-A packet format, which consists of a one-octet NAL header, followed by a one-octet FU header, followed by FU payload.

Figure 4-30 *H.264 FU-A Packet Format*

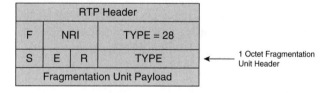

Table 4-8 summarizes the Fragmentation Unit header fields.

Table 4-8 *H.264 Fragmentation Unit Packet Header Fields*

Bit Field	Size (in Bits)	Description
S (start)	1	The Start bit indicates the start of the fragmented NAL unit payload. When the following FU payload is not the start of a fragmented NAL unit payload, this bit is set to 0.
E (end)	1	The End bit indicates the end of a fragmented NAL unit. This bit is set to 0 otherwise.
R (reserved)	1	The sender must set this bit to 0, and the receiver must ignore this bit.
Type	5	The value should be set according to Table 7-1 of the H.264 ITU spec.

Figure 4-31 shows the packet format of the FU-B packet. The packet structure of an FU-B packet is similar to that of an FU-A packet, except for the presence of a DON field.

Figure 4-31 *H.264 FU-B Packet Format*

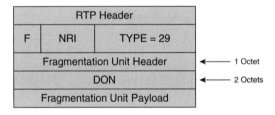

If a NAL unit can fit into a single FU, the NAL unit should be fragmented. In other words, the fragmented NAL unit must not be transmitted in one FU, which means that the Start and End bit of the FU header cannot be set to 1 in the same FU packet. If a fragmentation unit is lost, the receiver should discard all remaining FUs of that NAL unit.

Key Frame Detection in H.264

Key frame detection with H.264 packets is straightforward. Table 4-9 summarizes the steps to detect a key frame for each packet type.

Table 4-9 *H.264 Key Frame Detection for Different Packet Types*

Packet Type (as Indicated by the Type Field in the NAL Header)	Steps to Detect the Key Frame in the NAL Header
SNALU (type value between 1 and 23)	The packet contains a key frame if the Type field within the NAL header contains a value of 5 (coded slice of an IDR picture).

Table 4-9   *H.264 Key Frame Detection for Different Packet Types (Continued)*

Packet Type (as Indicated by the Type Field in the NAL Header)	Steps to Detect the Key Frame in the NAL Header
STAP-A	If (type == 24), skip the next 3 bytes (NAL header and size) and go to the NAL unit header. If the Type field of the NAL unit header contains a value of 5, the packet carries a key frame.
STAP-B	If (type == 25), skip the next 5 bytes (NAL header, DON, and size) and go to the NAL unit header. If the Type field of the NAL unit header contains a value of 5, the packet carries a key frame.
MTAP-16	If (type == 26), skip the next 8 bytes (NAL header, DON base, size, DOND, and TS offset) and go to the NAL unit header. If the Type field of the NAL unit header contains a value of 5, the packet carries a key frame.
MTAP-24	If (type == 27), skip the next 9 bytes (NAL header, DON base, size, DOND, and TS offset) and go to the NAL unit header. If the Type field of the NAL unit header contains a value of 5, the packet carries a key frame.
FU-A	If (type == 28), skip the next 3 bytes and go to the NAL unit header. If the Type field of the NAL unit header contains a value of 5, the packet carries a key frame.
FU-B	If (type == 29), skip the next 1 byte and go to the FU unit header. If the Type field of the FU header contains a value of 5, the packet carries a key frame.

Detecting Stream Loss

Conference server components must handle endpoint failures properly. Signaling protocols might provide some failure information, such as the SIP session-expires header. However, the media plane of the entire conferencing architecture must ensure that a backup mechanism detects and handles an endpoint failure in mid-session. The two common mechanisms to handle such scenarios are Internet Control Message Protocol (ICMP) unreachable messages and RTP inactivity timeout messages.

If the application in the endpoint fails (for example, the endpoint closes the RTP port it is listening to), the conference server might get ICMP unreachable messages from the endpoint IP stack for the packets it is sending to the endpoint. Upon detecting that, the conference server can close the RTP/RTCP channels and initiate the termination of the signaling relationship with the endpoint and recover the audio and video ports. Using ICMP to detect the endpoint failure is not a reliable method, because firewalls sometimes filter out all ICMP packets.

Some implementations use RTP timeouts to handle the cases of endpoint crashes or failures. The conference server starts an RTP inactivity timer for each RTP session to the endpoint. If the server receives any RTP packets while the timer is running, the server restarts the timer. If the timer expires, the server assumes that the endpoint is dead. However, server implementations must consider whether some endpoints may be in receive-only mode, or whether an endpoint has silence suppression activated. Both of these scenarios inhibit RTP packet transmission.

If endpoints support RTCP, reception of an RTCP packet might indicate that the endpoint is still alive.

Summary

This chapter has described the fundamentals of RTP/RTCP protocol formats and their application to conferencing systems. The chapter covered the different types of RTP devices used in conferencing systems and their functionalities. The chapter also discussed the payload formats, packet types, and key frame detections for common video codecs. The chapter concluded with a brief explanation of stream loss detection with ICMP unreachable messages and RTP inactivity timeout messages.

References

Bormann, C., J. Ott, G. Sullivan, S. Wenger, C. Zhu, L. Cline, G. Deisher, T. Gardos, D. Newell, and C. Maciocco. IETF RFC 2429, *RTP Payload Format for the 1998 Version of ITU-T Rec. H.263 Video (H.263+)*. October 1998.

ITU-T Recommendation H.264, Series-H audio visual and multimedia system, May 2003.

Schulzrinne, H., S. Casner, R. Frederick, and V. Jacobson. IETF RFC 3550, *RTP: A Transport Protocol for Real-Time Applications*. July 2003.

Wenger, S., M. M. Hannuksela, T. Stockhammer, M. Westerlund, and D. Singer. IETF RFC 3984, *RTP Payload Format for H.264 Video*. February 2005.

Zhu, C. IETF RFC 2190, *RTP Payload Format for H.263 Video Streams*. September 1997.

This chapter covers the following topics:

- SIP overview

- SIP transactions and dialogs

- SIP messages

- SIP record routing

- Event subscription and notification

- Session Description Protocol

- SIP conferencing models

- Ad hoc audio conferencing

- Ad hoc video conferencing

- Scheduled conferences

- RSVP/QoS support in conferencing flows

CHAPTER 5

Signaling Protocols: Conferencing Using SIP

Session Initiation Protocol (SIP) is a signaling protocol used for establishing media (audio, video, and instant messaging) sessions as part of audio/video conferencing, telephony, and other IP collaboration systems. SIP can also be used for presence and event notifications. SIP is defined in RFC 3261. This chapter addresses the following topics:

■ Overview of SIP, including different elements of the protocol and message structures.

■ Overview of Session Description Protocol (SDP) and its different parameters.

■ Introduction to conferencing support in SIP.

■ Ad hoc and scheduled conferencing operations, including specific aspects of SIP with respect to supporting video conferencing with call diagrams and examples. Technical notes are added to provide implementation-specific details.

■ Video codec extensions and RSVP support.

SIP Overview

A SIP network consists of four types of elements:

■ User agent

■ Proxy server

■ Redirect server

■ Registrar

Each element performs specific functions and is independent of the others. These can be hosted on one server or run individually across the network. Each of these SIP elements is addressed using Uniform Resource Identifier (URI).

User Agent

User agents are audio/video endpoints and call control servers in a SIP network. These endpoints have a client element, the user agent client (UAC), and a server element called the user agent server (UAS). A SIP user agent (UA) has both a client and a server. The client initiates the requests, and the server initiates the responses.

A SIP conference server is sometimes also referred to as *Back-2-Back UA* (B2BUA). It is a SIP element that has two UAs working back to back and thus can control the SIP dialogs as they go through it. Note that the endpoints are not considered B2BUAs. Figure 5-1 shows a SIP UA (video phone) initiating a SIP call to another user agent.

Figure 5-1 *SIP UAs in a SIP Session*

Proxy Server

A proxy server receives SIP requests, determines where to send them, and passes them to the next server (the next server could be a user agent). The proxy server can provide functions such as authentication, authorization, routing of messages, security, and so on.

There are two types of proxy servers: stateful and stateless. A stateful proxy server stores incoming requests it receives, along with the responses it sends back and the outgoing requests it sends to other UAs and proxies. A stateless proxy server maintains no proxy information after it services a request. A stateful proxy server can keep track of active sessions, which allows it to load-balance the sessions across multiple SIP control servers.

Figure 5-2 shows two UAs (IP phones) involved in a SIP session through a single proxy server. Both phones are registered with the proxy server. IPP1 sends a SIP INVITE message to the proxy. The proxy finds the location of the called party (IPP2) and forwards the INVITE. The proxy forwards all responses (100 Trying/200 OK) from IPP2 to the calling party (IPP1). In this example, the ACK response goes directly from IPP2 to IPP1. This can happen if the proxy does not insert a Record-Route SIP header in the SIP messages. Record-Route headers are explained in detail in the section "SIP Record Routing."

Figure 5-2 *SIP Session Through Proxy Server*

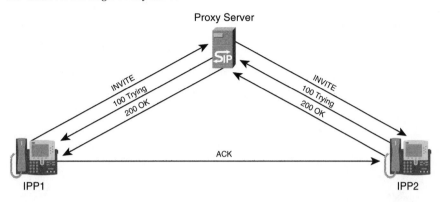

Redirect Server

A redirect server accepts a SIP request directed toward a particular UA and returns an alternate address to the initiating UA, thus providing forwarding services.

Figure 5-3 shows a SIP redirection of a call initiation.

Figure 5-3 *SIP Redirect Server*

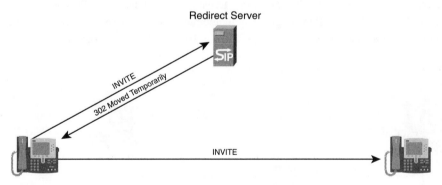

Registrar

A registrar processes the registration requests from UACs. The registration request contains the current location (typically, IP addresses) of the UA. The registrar maintains a location database to associate SIP URIs to IP addresses. Note that the location could also be a different phone number or URL that is used by the UA for receiving calls. Registrars are usually colocated with the proxy servers.

Figure 5-4 shows an example of SIP registration from a UA to a registrar.

Figure 5-4 *Registration Sequence*

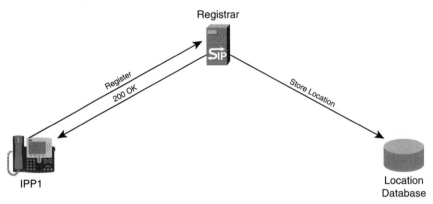

SIP Transactions and Dialogs

A transaction is defined by a request/response sequence: A SIP client sends requests to a SIP server, and the SIP server returns responses to the client. In Figure 5-5, a SIP UA sends an INVITE to another SIP UA and receives the responses (100 Trying/200 OK). The initial INVITE and the responses are considered to be part of one transaction. In general, ACK is not considered part of the transaction. Later SIP messages may include the disconnect request, known as the BYE message; these later messages are considered to be part of another transaction.

Figure 5-5 *SIP Transactions and Dialogs*

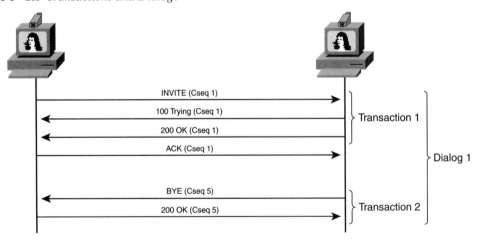

Each SIP message contains a 32-bit CSeq header value, which identifies each transaction.

As defined in RFC 3261, a dialog represents a peer-to-peer SIP relationship between two UAs. Dialogs facilitate proper sequencing and routing of messages between SIP endpoints.

Dialogs are uniquely identified using three fields:

- The SIP header Call-ID

- The SIP header From tag

- The SIP header To tag

Messages that use the same values for these identifiers belong to the same dialog. In Figure 5-5, for example, transaction 1 and transaction 2 form a dialog.

SIP Messages

SIP signaling comprises a series of requests (also called *methods*) and responses. A request consists of the following:

- Request line (identifies the type of the method)

- Headers

- Message body (optional)

A SIP response message consists of the following:

- Status line (identifies the status code of the request)

- Headers

- Message body (optional)

SIP Requests

The following are the different types of SIP requests:

- **INVITE**—Invites an endpoint to join the call

- **BYE**—Terminates the dialog between two UAs

- **OPTIONS**—Requests information on the capabilities of the remote UA

- **MESSAGE**—Sends instant messages (not part of a dialog)

- **ACK**—Confirms that a UA has received a final response to an INVITE method

- **REGISTER**—Provides the registration of the location

- **CANCEL**—Terminates the last pending request

- **INFO**—A mid-session method to pass the informational elements

- **PRACK**—Reliable provisional acknowledgment that confirms that a UA has received a provisional response, such as "180 Ringing"

- **UPDATE**—Updates the SIP session

- **SUBSCRIBE**—Requests notification of an event or a set of events from an UA

- **NOTIFY**—Sends an event notification to the subscribed SIP UA

- **REFER**—Indicates that the receiver should contact a third party using the contact information provided in the request

Example 5-1 shows a SIP request message.

Example 5-1 *SIP Request Message*

```
!The following line is the request line
INVITE sip:meetingplace@172.27.14.53 SIP/2.0
!The following lines are the SIP headers
Via: SIP/2.0/UDP 172.27.14.4:5070;branch=8dJXAX9MDw

Max-Forwards: 70
To: <sip:meetingplace@172.27.14.53>
From: <sip:8764@172.27.14.4>;tag=ds17aa9bd4
Call-ID: 11022705439144@172.27.14.4
CSeq: 1 INVITE
Content-Length: 251
Content-Type: application/sdp

!The following lines are the SDP body


v=0
o=Sam 1549546120 0 IN IP4 10.10.10.26
s=-
c=IN IP4 10.10.10.26
t=0 0
m=audio 49220 RTP/AVP 0
a=rtpmap:0 PCMU/8000
```

The following sections describe the different components of the SIP request message.

Request Line

The request line is the first line in the SIP request. It indicates the SIP method and the device to which this message is addressed. The last part of the request line is the version number, as indicated by SIP/2.0 in Example 5-1.

Request Headers

Example 5-1 shows the following headers:

- **Via**—The Via header indicates the transport to be used and carries the address and the port number to where the responses need to be sent. When this message passes through the SIP proxies, each proxy adds a Via header to the SIP request before forwarding it. This mechanism helps in detecting loops in routing.

  The last part of the Via header is a branch parameter. It is used to identify the transaction created by the request and can also be used to distinguish between two versions of SIP RFC (RFC 2543 and RFC 3261). SIP devices that are compliant only with RFC 2543 do not insert the branch parameter into the Via header. RFC 2543 defines the basic SIP protocol, and RFC 3261 adds refinements to that. RFC 3261 obsoletes RFC 2543.

- **Max-Forwards**—The Max-Forwards header is used to detect loops in the forwarding path. Each proxy that received the SIP request decrements this counter by 1 before forwarding it. If a proxy receives a SIP request with a Max-Forwards value of 0, it sends an error back to the originator of the request.

- **To**—The To header identifies the recipient (or called party) device.

- **From**—The From header identifies the originator (or caller) of the request. The From header can optionally carry a display name (such as From: "Sam" <sip: 8764@172.27.14.4> tag=ds17aa9bd4). An anonymous request is indicated by the keyword Anonymous (for example, From: Anonymous <........>). The Tag parameter to used to identify the SIP dialog.

- **Call-ID**—The Call-ID header provides a globally unique identification to a SIP call.

- **CSeq**—The command sequence (CSeq) is an identifier that matches the request and responses of a transaction. It carries a value and the method name. The value can be an arbitrary number. The responses to the request should carry the same CSeq header as that of the request.

SIP Responses

SIP responses are associated with a SIP request. Example 5-2 shows a typical response message.

Example 5-2   *SIP Response Message*

```
SIP/2.0 200 OK
Via: SIP/2.0/UDP
172.27.14.4:5070; branch=z9hG4bKhWn9PFlB2yaZbsvp36
From: <sip:dallas-1@172.27.14.4>;tag=ds15cee408
To: <sip:meetintplace@172.27.14.53>;tag=E2CE8-87E
Date: Fri, 01 Mar 2002 00:15:28 GMT
Call-ID: 11021984836447@172.27.14.4
Server: Cisco-conferenceserver
CSeq: 1 INVITE
Allow: INVITE, OPTIONS, BYE, CANCEL, ACK, PRACK, UPDATE, REFER, SUBSCRIBE, NOTIFY, INFO,
REGISTER, PUBLISH
Contact: <sip:meetingplace@172.27.14.53:5060>
Reason: Q.850; cause=47
Content-Length: 0
```

The first line of the response contains the protocol version (SIP/2.0) and the status code (such as 200), along with a text description (such as OK). The status code is an integer from 100 to 699. RFC 3261 defines the following classes of responses:

- **1xx responses**—1xx responses are called *provisional* or *informational responses.* A recipient of a SIP message can send a provisional response to indicate that the request was received and is being processed. RFC 3261 states that a provisional response may contain message bodies such as SDP or XML (Extensible Markup Language). Examples of provisional responses are "100 Trying," "180 Ringing," and "183 Session Progress."

- **2xx responses**—A 2xx response is the last response message sent by the recipient for the associated request. Therefore, 2xx messages are always considered to be "final" messages. An example of a 2xx response is "200 OK."

- **3xx responses**—3xx responses give information about the user's new location or an alternative service that the caller might use to satisfy the call. For example, if a proxy server receives an INVITE and cannot locate the recipient, it may send back a 3xx response to the sender requesting the caller to try a new address (and the new addresses is indicated in the header of the 3xx response). An example of a 3xx response is "301 Moved Permanently."

- **4xx responses**—4xx responses indicate failure and mean that the recipient could not process the request. The reason for the failure is indicated in the response itself. An example of a 4xx response is "400 Bad Request."

- **5*xx* responses**—5*xx* responses indicate failure due to an error encountered in the server. An example of a 5*xx* response is "500 Internal Server Error."

- **6*xx* responses**—6*xx* responses indicate that the server has definitive information about the recipient. For example, if the recipient does not want to take the call, the server or UA sends a "603 Decline."

Table 5-1 summarizes the commonly used response codes.

Table 5-1 *SIP Response Codes*

SIP Response Code	Reason
100	Trying
180	Ringing
200	OK
301	Moved permanently
302	Moved temporarily
400	Bad request
600	Busy
603	Decline
604	Does not exist

The request to which a particular response belongs is identified using the CSeq header field. This header field contains the sequence number and the method of the corresponding request. In Example 5-2, it is an INVITE request.

SIP Record Routing

When establishing a SIP call, the INVITE flows through one or more SIP proxies (if the caller does not know the address of the recipient) to the recipient. The subsequent SIP messages are sent back and forth between the caller and recipient directly, without the proxy getting involved in the signaling. However, in some cases, the proxy server may need to be present in the SIP signaling path to see all the messaging between the endpoints for the duration of the call. One example is the scenario in which the proxy is connected to a billing server and needs to report how long the call is active for billing purposes. The method by which a proxy indicates that it wants to stay in the path is called *record routing*.

Right before forwarding the initial INVITE, the proxy adds a Record-Route header that contains the URI of the proxy itself. This header makes sure that all subsequent requests belonging to the dialog are forwarded through the SIP elements that have record routed.

Event Subscription and Notification

RFC 3265 extends the SIP specification, RFC 3261, to support a general mechanism allowing subscription to asynchronous events. Such events can include statistics, alarms, and so on.

The two types of event subscriptions are in-dialog and out-of-dialog. A subscription that uses the Call-ID of an existing dialog is an in-dialog subscription, whereas the out-of-dialog subscription carries a Call-ID that is not part of the existing ongoing dialogs. Figure 5-6 shows an example of out-of-dialog subscription.

Figure 5-6 *Subscribe and Notify*

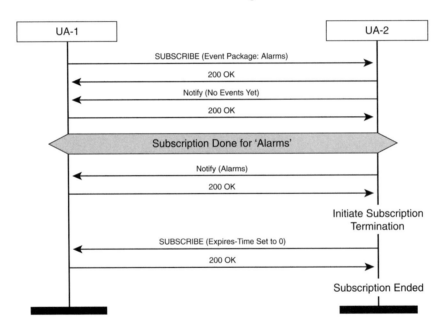

In Example 5-3, UA-1 is sending a SUBSCRIBE to UA-2 and subscribes for an event package called *alarms*. Event packages are implementation-dependent and are not defined in the specifications.

Example 5-3 *SUBSCRIBE from UA-1 to UA-2*

```
SUBSCRIBE sip:ua-1@172.27.14.53 SIP/2.0
Via: SIP/2.0/UDP 172.27.14.4:5070; branch=z9hG4bKhWn9PFlB2yaZbsvppn2Xlw~~34
Max-Forwards: 70
To: <sip:ua-1@172.27.14.53>
From: <sip:ua-2@172.27.14.4>;tag=ds7c86cbb5
```

Example 5-3 *SUBSCRIBE from UA-1 to UA-2 (Continued)*

```
Call-ID: 1bbd7b2:1009fdd37c1:-7f7e@172.27.14.4
CSeq: 1 SUBSCRIBE
Content-Length: 0
Contact: <sip:ua-2@172.27.14.4:5070>
Content-Type:
Expires: 600
Event: alarms
```

A UA interested in event notification sends a SUBSCRIBE message to a SIP server (a SIP server could be just another SIP UA but provides additional services). The SUBSCRIBE message establishes a dialog, and the server immediately replies to this message using the 200 OK response. At this point, the dialog is established. The server sends a NOTIFY request to the user every time the event to which the user subscribed changes. NOTIFY messages are sent within the dialog established by the SUBSCRIBE. The NOTIFY messages usually carry an XML body that describes the event.

As part of the message exchange to establish a subscription, the server sends a NOTIFY message to the client with an indication of no events. Subscriptions have a limited life span (note the Expires header set in Example 5-3) and therefore must be periodically refreshed. A SUBSCRIBE with an Expires value of 0 indicates unsubscription.

Session Description Protocol

SIP uses SDP (defined in RFC 2327), which defines a syntax to describe the media sessions. The SDP is carried as an application body (Content-Type: application/SDP) in the SIP messages. SDP consists of text messages using the ISO 10646 character set in UTF-8 encoding. A SDP consists of a session-level description (details that apply to the whole session and all media streams) and optionally several media-level descriptions (details that apply to a single media stream). Table 5-2 describes the session-level SDP parameters as defined by RFC 2327.

Table 5-2 *Session-Level SDP Parameters*

Field Type	Mandatory/ Optional	Description	Example
v=	Mandatory	Protocol version	v=0
o=	Mandatory	Owner/creator or session identifier	o=Sam 154954610 0 IN IP4 10.10.10.26
s=	Mandatory	Session name	s=conference call
i=	Optional	Session information	i=conference call to Cisco Unified MeetingPlace Express

continues

Table 5-2 *Session-Level SDP Parameters (Continued)*

Field Type	Mandatory/ Optional	Description	Example
u=	Optional	URI of description	u=http://www.cisco.com/sdp
e=	Optional	E-mail address	e=example@xyz.com
p=	Optional	Phone number	p=+91-44-510623456
c=	Optional	Connection information; not required if it is included in the media level	c=IN IP4 10.10.10.22
b=	Optional	Bandwidth information; not required if it is included in the session level	b=CT:128
k=	Optional	Encryption key; not required if it is included in the media level	k=base64:7658339339
t=	Optional	Time the session is active	t=7776543 987656

Table 5-3 shows the syntax and examples of media-level SDP parameters.

Table 5-3 *Media-Level SDP Parameters*

Field Type	Mandatory/ Optional	Description	Example
m=	Mandatory	Media name and transport address	m=video RTP/AVP 31
i=	Optional	Media title	i=conference call to Cisco Unified MeetingPlace Express
c=	Mandatory	Connection information; optional if it is included in the session level	c=IN IP4 10.10.10.22
b=	Mandatory	Bandwidth information; optional if it is included in the session level	b=CT:128
k=	Optional	Encryption key	k=base64:7658339339
a=	Optional	Attribute lines	a=rtpmap:0 PCMU/8000

Real-time Transport Protocol RTP specifies how media streams should be packetized. The headers of RTP packets include a payload type (ptype) that defines the type of data packet. RTP payload types can be static or dynamic. Static payload types are fully defined in the audio/video profile.

Payload numbers 0 through 96 are static payload types. In the following example, payload number 0 is a static payload type for PCMU (G.711 μ-law):

```
m=audio 49000 RTP/AVP 0
a=rtpmap:0 PCMU/8000
```

Dynamic payload types are defined during the session setup and are identified using payload numbers above 96. In the following example, the originator assigns 121 to identify codec G.722.1 during the SDP offer:

```
m=audio 49000 RTP/AVP 121
a=rtpmap:121 G7221/16000
```

SIP Conferencing Models

There are two basic models for supporting multipoint conferencing through SIP:

- A centralized model in which all the participants establish a two-way communication to a conference server. Conference servers could be cascaded, but this topology is transparent to the endpoint. As discussed in Chapter 2, "Conferencing System Design and Architecture," IETF documents label this conference server the *focus*.

- A distributed model in which the control plane (conference control and signaling) resides in the conference server, and the media processing is moved to separate devices. The following sections focus on the centralized model because it is widely developed and deployed.

A conference server controls the signaling plane of the conference, including creation, maintenance, and termination of the conference; adding and removing users; and managing Interactive Voice Response (IVR) sessions. The following sections discuss the basic elements of SIP conferencing, including the conference URI, early and delayed offer messages, and Dual Tone Multiple Frequency (DTMF) support.

Conference URI

A conference in a SIP framework is identified through a conference URI. The conference URI is the destination where all the SIP requests are sent and created/managed by the conference server. An example of the conference URI is sip:meetingplace@cisco.com. Users can enter these URIs manually in their SIP client to dial into the conference system. Alternatively, the conference system embeds this in a web link and sends the link to the user through e-mail or instant messenger. If the user dials in from the public switched telephone network (PSTN), the PSTN gateway determines the destination conference URI, typically by prompting the user to enter touch tones on the telephone pad. This prompting functionality is provided by the IVR system. The gateway is configured to either forward signaling to a conference URI or forward these DTMF tones to the conference server, which looks up the conference URI and instructs the gateway to forward the call.

Early and Delayed Offer

Endpoints establish connections on the media plane by first negotiating media properties such as codec types, packetization periods, media IP address/RTP port numbers, and so on. This information is transmitted with SIP messages using SDP. An endpoint may use two methods of exchanging SDP information:

- **Early offer**—In the early offer, the endpoint sends the media SDP in the initial INVITE and receives an answer from the conference server.

- **Delayed offer**—In a delayed offer, the endpoint sends an empty INVITE (INVITE with no SDP offer), receives an SDP offer from the conference server, and then sends back the final answer.

Figure 5-7 shows examples of early and delayed offers. A delayed offer is typically used by call control entities that do protocol translation (for example, an H.323 endpoint dialing into a call agent that has a SIP trunk to the conference server). In this case, the call agent may send a delayed offer INVITE to the conference server as soon as it receives an H.323 SETUP from the endpoint. The endpoint media capabilities are not known to the call agent until the H.245 OLC/OLC-ACK is done.

Figure 5-7 *Early and Delayed Offer*

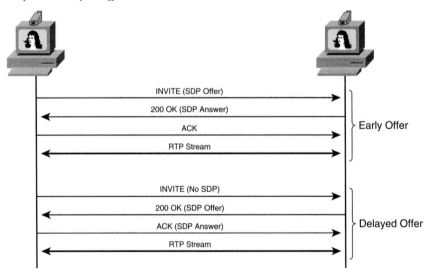

DTMF Support

Endpoints that connect to a conference server via a PSTN gateway often must navigate through an IVR using DTMF tones, and therefore DTMF support in the endpoints and the conference server is important to the conferencing support. Endpoints can use three methods to send DTMF digits:

- Voice-band

- In-band

- Out-of-band

Voice-band DTMF tones are modulated as actual tones in the media. Endpoints that dial into a PSTN gateway must play DTMF tones in the media stream so that the PSTN gateway can "hear" the tones. Endpoints connecting via an IP network send DTMF information in-band or out-of-band. RFC 2833 is a special way of sending DTMF in-band, and Key Press Markup Language (KPML) provides a way for the endpoints to send DTMF out-of-band.

RFC 2833

RFC 2833 defines RTP payload types for carrying DTMF digits in-band in the media stream. This capability is specified as MIME type telephone-event in the SDP offer. Consider the following SDP offer, which is sent from a SIP endpoint to the conference server:

```
m=audio 19008 RTP/AVP 0 8 116
a=rtpmap:0 PCMU/8000
a=rtpmap:8 PCMA/8000
a=rtpmap:116 telephone-event/8000
```

The endpoint is indicating that it is capable of supporting RFC 2833 through the MIME type telephone-event (dynamic payload type 116). The conference server then can include the same in the SDP answer. When the user presses a digit, the endpoint sends an encoded RTP packet with the payload type of 116 (as negotiated in the preceding example).

KPML

KPML is an out-of-band mechanism to collect DTMF digits. A KPML flow is established using SUBSCRIBE/NOTIFY. An endpoint can advertise that it supports KPML by including the string kpml in the Allow-Events header in the initial offer message. Similarly, the conference server may indicate the same in the response. The conference server then sends a SUBSCRIBE to the endpoint with the event package kpml. If the subscription succeeds, the digits are sent in the NOTIFY messages. Figure 5-8 shows the KPML subscription between an endpoint and the conference server.

Figure 5-8 *KPML Sequence*

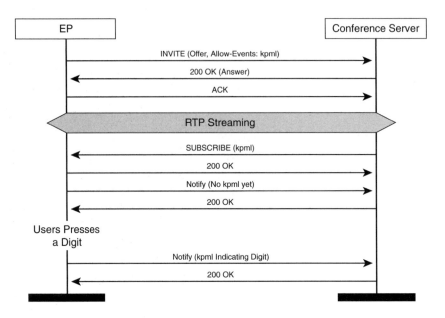

Ad Hoc Audio Conferencing

Conferences are often referred to as either ad hoc or scheduled, based on the method by which they are invoked. Ad hoc conferences are created on-the-fly, without any prearranged scheduling. Scheduled conferences are "booked" in advance. The difference has to do with resource allocation: The conference server has limited resources to perform video and audio mixing. If a conference is scheduled in advance, the conference server is guaranteed to be able to allocate the required audio and video mixing resources. The signaling flow of an ad hoc audio and video conference is the same except for the presence of video media description in the SDP.

Because ad hoc conferences are created on-the-fly, the conference server cannot always guarantee that resources will be available at the time the conference is created. The conference server creates an ad hoc conference when the first participant connects to a URI associated with a conference that does not currently exist. Figure 5-9 shows an example of a conference started with an early offer.

Figure 5-9 *Basic Ad Hoc Conference Flow*

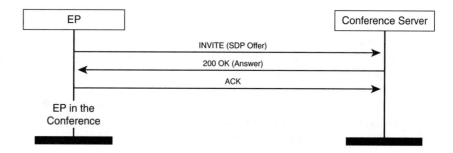

The following explains the flow illustrated in Figure 5-9:

1. The endpoint dials into the conference. Assume that this URI represents ad hoc conferences in the system. The endpoint sends the INVITE to the conference server with the SDP offer as follows:

    ```
    v=0
    o=san 1549546120 0 IN IP4 10.10.10.26
    s=-
    c=IN IP4 10.10.10.26
    m=audio 49220 RTP/AVP 0 8
    ```

    The conference server checks whether the mixer resources are available and creates a conference instance.

2. The conference server sends a 200 OK response with the SDP answer as follows:

    ```
    v=0
    o=CiscoSystemsSIP-GW-UserAgent 3402 403 IN IP4 10.10.10.2
    s=SIP Call
    c=IN IP4 10.10.10.54
    m=audio 20000 RTP/AVP 0
    ```

    Note that some SIP endpoints and conference servers may send an optional 100 TRYING message before sending 200 OK.

3. The endpoint completes the transaction by sending the final ACK.

The following notes provide some insight into the message flow from an implementation point of view:

■   Static payload types such as PCMU (G.711 µ-law)/PCMA (G.711 A-law) do not require rtpmap attributes in the SDP offer/answer. The rtpmap attribute is used to map the RTP payload type number to a media encoding name that identifies the payload format. An example is payload type number 34, which maps to payload format H.263.

■   The conference server can choose any payload type from the offer. Typically, the payload type is determined through a conference-wide policy. In the absence of such a policy, the conference server selects a payload type by giving preference to those appearing at the top of the list.

■   After the endpoint is in the conference, any change in the media property is communicated through the RE-INVITE message (also called *mid-call INVITE*). A RE-INVITE can be sent by either the conference server or the endpoint.

■   The default direction of the media stream is duplex (send and receive). If the endpoint just wants to receive the stream (examples include listen-only mode), it should include a=recvonly/a=sendonly in the SDP offer/answer.

■   A session-level attribute is applied to all the media in the SDP offer/answer. However, a media-level attribute (if present) overrides a session-level attribute.

■   The endpoint may add a session-expires header with a value in the initial INVITE to indicate how long this session is valid. The conference server can respond by adding the Session-Expires header back in the response. If the conference server does not support session expiry, it can respond in two ways:

    — The conference server can omit the Session-Expires header in the response.

    — The conference server can set a value of 0 in the Session-Expires header to indicate infinite session duration.

The endpoint starts an active session timer and sends a RE-INVITE or UPDATE message to extend the session upon each instance of session timer expiry. The absence of the Session-Expires header implies no expiration. Note that if the conference server does not set the Session-Expires header in response to a RE-INVITE or UPDATE, the endpoint should disable the session timer and assume an infinite session duration.

An endpoint can leave a conferencing session by sending a BYE. Alternatively, the administrator or conference chairman can disconnect a participant from a conference, in which case the conference server sends a BYE to the endpoint. The conference server deletes the ad hoc conference instance when the last endpoint drops out of the conference.

In some cases, the endpoint may initiate a delayed-offer INVITE. In that case, the conference server sends an SDP offer in the 200 OK response, and the endpoint sends the answer in the final ACK.

Ad Hoc Video Conferencing

A video-enabled endpoint uses the same procedure to join a conference but offers additional parameters in the SDP offer to describe the properties of the video media stream.

Example 5-4 shows an SDP offer, in which endpoint A sends an INVITE to the conference server.

Example 5-4 *SDP Offer from an Endpoint for Joining Ad Hoc Video Conference*

```
v=0
o=san 1549546120 0 IN IP4 10.10.10.26
s=-
c=IN IP4 10.10.10.26
m=audio 49220 RTP/AVP 0 8
m=video 49222 RTP/AVP 109 34 96 31
a=rtpmap:109 H264/90000
a=fmtp:109 profile-level-id=42800c max-mbps=10000
a=rtpmap:34 H263/90000
a=rtpmap:96 H263-1998/90000
a=fmtp:96 SQCIF=1 QCIF=1 CIF=1 CIF4=2
a=rtpmap:31 H261/90000
a=fmtp:31 CIF=1 QCIF=1
```

The conference server chooses audio codec 0 (G.711µlaw) and video codec 34 (H.263) and responds with the SDP answer shown in Example 5-5.

Example 5-5 *SDP Answer from a Conference Server for Ad Hoc Video Conference*

```
v=0
o=CiscoSystemsSIP-GW-UserAgent 3402 403 IN IP4 10.10.10.2
s=SIP Call
c=IN IP4 10.10.10.54
m=audio 20000 RTP/AVP 0
c=IN IP4 10.10.10.54
m=video 22786 RTP/AVP 34
c=IN IP4 10.10.10.54
a=rtpmap:34 H263/90000
```

The following sections describe the video SDP parameters that are sent in the SDP offer/answer.

Video SDP Extensions

The common video codecs used in video conferencing are H.261, H.263, and H.264. This section explains the syntax and semantics for describing parameters related to video codecs. Currently, no standard method exists to specify certain video-related parameters in the SDP offer/answer. These parameters include the following:

- Frame rate

- Video annexes

- Maximum bit rate

- Frame resolution (also called *form factor*) (Resolution means size, like 320×240.)

Video endpoints and conference servers use the a=fmtp attribute to carry codec-specific parameters. Note that SDP extensions for supporting video are still going through the standards process, and many endpoints and conference servers are using proprietary attributes in the SDP offer/answer. These variations might lead to interoperability issues between endpoints/conference systems.

H.261 Codec Attributes

SDP may contain ftmp parameters, which are media-level attributes that endpoints can use to define product-specific codec parameters not defined as part of the SDP specification. Some examples for H.261 are represented in the following syntax:

```
a = fmtp:<rtp payload type> <options>
<rtp payload type> = 31
<options> = "Size ¦ Annex" where
  Size = "QCIF = MPI" or "CIF = MPI"
  MPI = 1 or 2
  Annex = D
```

Size indicates both a picture size and a frame rate. MPI stands for maximum picture interval. MPI=1 means that maximum (decodable) picture rate per second is about 30, and MPI=2 implies that the maximum picture rate per second is about 15. H.261 defines two resolutions: Common Interchange Format (CIF) and Quarter CIF (QCIF). Example 5-6 shows H.261 SDP syntax.

Example 5-6   *Example of an H.261 SDP*

```
m=video 49222 RTP/AVP 31
a=rtpmap:31 H261/90000
a=fmtp:31 CIF=1 QCIF=1
```

H.263 Codec Attributes

The H.263 draft defines three MIME types:

- H.263

- H.263-1998

- H.263-2000

The attributes defined here can be used with any of these three MIME types:

```
a = fmtp:<rtp payload type> <options>
```

The <rtp payload type> for H.263 is a static payload type of 34. H.263-1998/H.263-2000 uses dynamic payload types.

The syntax for specifying the picture size is as follows:

```
<options> = size ¦ annex
Size = "SQCIF=MPI" or "QCIF=MPI" or "CIF=MPI" or "CIF4=MPI" or "CIF16=MPI" or
"XMAX=xmax, ymax,mpi"
MPI = 1 or 2
Annex = F/J/T
```

Size indicates both the picture size and the MPI. H.263 defines multiple resolutions: SQCIF, QCIF, CIF, CIF4, CIF16, and CUSTOM. The annex values in the preceding example are just a representation rather than the comprehensive list of annexes that can be supported. The dimension of the custom picture size is defined by X and Y values. Example 5-7 shows a representation of H.263 codec parameters in the SDP offer.

Example 5-7 *Example of H.263 Optional Codec Parameters*

```
m=video 22334 RTP/AVP 96
a=rtpmap:96 H263-1998/90000
a=fmtp:96 QCIF=1 SQCIF=1 CIF=2 CIF4=2 CUSTOM=352,240,1
```

The SDP offer in Example 5-7 indicates that the sender supports H.263-1998 at a clock rate of 90 kHz. The fmtp indicates that the sender hopes to receive QCIF picture size with a maximum packet interval (MPI) of 1. If QCIF is not possible, the sender prefers to receive SQCIF with an MPI of 1 followed by CIF with an MPI of 2. Most encoders support at least QCIF and CIF resolutions.

The optional parameters discussed in Example 5-7 are applicable for H.263-1998 only. For H.263-2000, these options (picture size, MPI) are specified through profiles and levels. Example 5-8 shows an SDP offer for H.263-2000. H.263-1998 does not support profiles and levels.

Example 5-8 *Example of H.263-2000 Optional Codec Parameters*

```
m=video 22334 RTP/AVP 96
a=rtpmap:96 H263-2000/90000
a=fmtp:96 profile=0; level= 10;
```

NOTE There are three versions of H.263: H.263, H.263-1998, and H.263-2000. If no fmtp parameters are present in the SDP offer for an H.263 codec, it is safe to assume a form factor of QCIF at 30 frames per second (FPS). For H.263-2000, if no fmtp parameters are present, the default is profile=0 and level=10.

The sender can indicate the supported H.263 annexes in the fmtp attribute. H.263 annexes are enhancements to the core H.263 algorithm (H.263 baseline) that achieve improved performance and increased functionality. Additional supplemental information may also be included in the bitstream for enhanced display capability and external usage. In total, there are 16 negotiable annexes, named C to T, as explained in Appendix A. Example 5-9 shows an SDP offer that indicates the support of annexes F, J, and T.

Example 5-9 *H.323 Annex in the SDP*

```
m=video 49198 RTP/AVP 96
a=fmtp:96 SQCIF=1 QCIF=1 CIF=1 CIF4=2 CUSTOM=352,240,1 CUSTOM=704,480,2 F J T
a=rtpmap:96 H263-1998/90000
```

H.264 Codec Attributes

H.264 uses a dynamic payload type. The encoding name in the rtpmap is H264, and the clock rate must be set to 90000. The optional H.264 parameters profile-level-id, max-mbps, max-dpb, max-br, parameters-sets, packetization-mode, interleaving-depth, deint-buf-size, init-buf-time, and max-dcon-diff, if any, must be included in the a=ftmp line. These parameters are expressed in MIME type strings.

H.264 media format is specified through the parameters profile-level-id *and* packetization-mode. The stream properties of H.264 streams are specified through the parameters sprop-parameter-sets, sprop-deint-buf-req, sprop-interleaving-depth, sprop-max-don-diff, and sprop-init-buf-time. The capability parameters are specified through max-mbps, max-fs, max-cpb, max-dpb, max-br, redundant-pic-cap, and max-rcd-nalu-size.

These parameters are used for declaring receiver capabilities and in general set the upper limit for what the receiver can support. Thus, a sender may select to set its encoder using lesser or equal values of these parameters.

The profile-level-id has three subcomponents:

■ **Profile-idc** (one octet)—Indicates whether this entry represents an H.264 profile. A decimal value of 42 indicates that this entry is an H.264 profile. Baseline profile is used for video conferencing.

■ **Constraint** (one octet)—The first 3 bits indicate whether this is a Main profile, Baseline profile, or Extended profile. The last 5 bits are reserved.

■ **Level** (one octet)—Indicates the capability. Valid levels are 1, 1.1, 1.2, 1.3, 2, 2.1, 2.2, 3, 3.1, 3.2, 4, 4.1, 4.2, 5, and 5.1. For instance, level 3.0 is 4CIF at 25 FPS. Refer to the ITU-T H.264 codec specification for complete details on each of these levels.

Example 5-10 shows an SDP offer from a video endpoint.

Example 5-10 *H.264 Video SDP*

```
m=video 6010 RTP/AVP 96
b=AS:768
a=fmtp:96 CIF=1 QCIF=1/MaxBR=7680 profile-level-id=428014
a=framerate:25.0
a=rtpmap:96 H264/90000
a=sendrecv
```

In Example 5-10, a profile-level-id value of 428014 indicates the following:

- **42**—Represents an H.264 profile.

- **80 (10100000)**—Baseline and Extended profiles are supported.

- **14 (decimal 20)**—Level 2.0.

Example 5-11 shows an SDP offer from another SIP video endpoint. Note that max-mbps is an optional parameter. If present, this parameter should replace maxBR.

Example 5-11 *H.264 Video SDP*

```
m=video 49222 RTP/AVP 109 31
b=TIAS:128000
a=rtpmap:109 H264/90000
a=fmtp:109 profile-level-id=42800c max-mbps=10000
a=rtpmap:31 H261/90000
a=fmtp:31 CIF=1 QCIF=1
```

Bandwidth Information in the SDP

Bandwidth usage is specified with the attribute b: *<modifier> <bandwidth value>*. *Modifier* should be application-specific (AS), conference type (CT), or transport-independent application-specific (TIAS), as defined in RFC 3890. The AS bandwidth includes the bandwidth that the RTP data traffic will consume, including the lower layers, down to the IP layer. Therefore, the bandwidth is in most cases calculated by considering the entire IP packet, which includes RTP payload, RTP header, UDP header, and IP header. TIAS indicates the actual bandwidth in bits per second without the lower-layer overhead. If present at the session level, this entry indicates the bandwidth for all the media lines in the SDP offer/answer.

Although a session-level AS parameter should indicate the bandwidth needed for all the media lines in the SDP offer/answer (including audio), you might find that some of the endpoint implementations indicate just the video bandwidth needed.

Some endpoints may send a session-level AS parameter in addition to media-level TIAS to maintain backward compatibility with endpoints that do not support TIAS. In those cases, the session-level AS indicates the transport-independent rate for the call, and the TIAS parameter in the video session is the maximum bit rate that the endpoint can receive. Example 5-12 shows the presence of the bandwidth attribute in the SDP.

Example 5-12   *Bandwidth Attribute in Video SDP*

```
a=video 18664 96
b=TIAS:320000
a=rtpmap:96 H263-1998/90000
a=fmtp:96 QCIF=1 SQCIF=1 CIF=4
```

The b= parameter indicates that the endpoint expects to receive 320 kbps of video, which represents only the H.263 payload without the protocol headers. Upon receiving this SDP information, the conference server allocates CPU resources, and possibly network resources, to accommodate this bandwidth.

Multiple Stream Support and Grouping of Media Lines

Advanced video endpoints may ask the conference server to send multiple video streams. The initial INVITE has one audio m-line (media line) and multiple video m-lines. Multiple video stream capability requires the ability to group the media lines so that the conference server knows which audio stream and video streams are tied together for lip-sync purposes. RFC 3388 defines some attributes (group) for the grouping. The syntax is as follows:

```
a=group:LS
a=mid:<identification tag>
```

> **NOTE**   In this example, LS stands for lip synchronization.

Consider Example 5-13.

Example 5-13   *Media Line Grouping*

```
v=0
o=Ron 276544 2887654 IN IP4 10.10.10.18
t=0 0
c=IN IP4 10.10.10.18
a=group:LS 1 2
m=audio 20000 RTP/AVP 0
a=mid:1
m=video 20002 RTP/AVP 31
a=mid:2
m=video 20004 RTP/AVP 34
a=mid:3
```

The sender of this SDP offer would like to receive three media streams: one audio stream (identified as mid:1) and two video streams (mid:2 and mid:3). Audio stream 1 and video stream 2 are grouped, which indicates that these need to be lip-synced. RFC 3388 mandates that all media streams have a prefix of mid, whether or not they are included in the group, which is why the third stream has a prefix of mid even though it is not included in the group.

Escalation and De-escalation

Escalation is a process that allows a video-capable endpoint to join the conference in the audio-only mode and later establish a video stream. This process occurs in response to one of two scenarios:

- End users begin a call in audio-only mode and then decide to add a video connection, either through inserting the camera or enabling video in their video phone.

- An end user turns on a video camera while in an audio-only call, causing the endpoint to automatically establish a video connection. An escalation occurs through RE-INVITE from the endpoint, as illustrated in Figure 5-10.

Figure 5-10 *Escalation to Video*

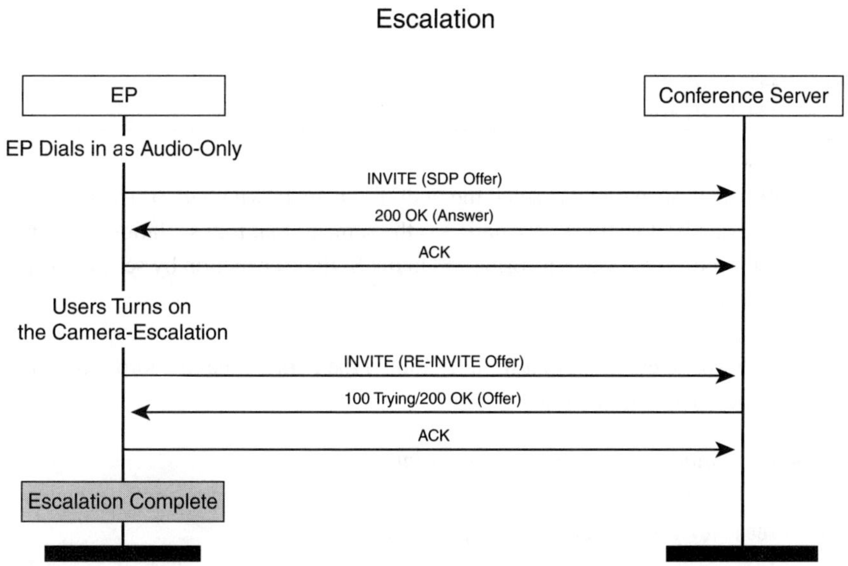

In the RE-INVITE, the endpoint uses the previous SDP offer/answer information but adds another m-line that includes the video properties. Note that the endpoint can take this opportunity to renegotiate the audio properties, but this type of renegotiation is uncommon.

In Example 5-14, an endpoint sends a RE-INVITE to the conference server to add video to the existing audio session.

Example 5-14 *Escalation Request from an Endpoint*

```
v=0
o=bob 2808844564 2808844564 IN IP4 ep.xyz.com
s=
c=IN IP4 ep.xyz.com
t=0 0
m=audio 49172 RTP/AVP 0
a=rtpmap:0 PCMU/8000
m=video 44172 RTP/AVP 31
a=rtpmap:34 H261/90000
```

In Example 5-15, the conference server responds with the SDP answer confirming that video will be streamed to the endpoint.

Example 5-15 *Escalation Response from the Conference Server*

```
v=0
o=alice 2890844526 2890844526 IN IP4 meetings.xyz.com
s=
c=IN IP4 meetings.xyz.com
t=0 0
m=audio 49174 RTP/AVP 0
a=rtpmap:0 PCMU/8000
m=video 44172 RTP/AVP 31
a=rtpmap:34 H261/90000
```

De-escalations are scenarios in which the endpoint tears down a video stream in an audio/video conference. The SIP flow for de-escalation is the same as that for escalation. The endpoint repeats the offer but removes the video information in the SDP offer section by setting the port number of the video stream to 0.

In Example 5-16, an endpoint that initially joined the conference in audio/video mode is now removing video from the session.

Example 5-16 *De-escalation Request from an Endpoint*

```
v=0
o=bob 2808844564 2808844564 IN IP4 ep.xyz.com
s=
c=IN IP4 ep.xyz.com
t=0 0
m=audio 49172 RTP/AVP 0
a=rtpmap:0 PCMU/8000
m=video 0 RTP/AVP 31
a=rtpmap:34 H261/90000
```

In Example 5-17, the conference server sends the answer SDP, acknowledging the removal of video for the endpoint.

Example 5-17   *De-escalation Response from the Conference Server*

```
v=0
o=alice 2890844526 2890844526 IN IP4 meetings.xyz.com
s=
c=IN IP4 meetings.xyz.com
t=0 0
m=audio 49174 RTP/AVP 0
a=rtpmap:0 PCMU/8000
m=video 0 RTP/AVP 31
a=rtpmap:34 H261/90000
```

The following describes the implementation details of the escalation and de-escalation scenarios:

■ If a SIP UA wants to reject a specific media line in the offer, it should set the RTP port m-line to 0 in the answer.

■ In de-escalation, the endpoint should set the RTP port number to 0 in the video m-line when sending the RE-INVITE.

■ In responding to the RE-INVITE offer, the SIP UA (either the conference server or endpoint) should keep the version number, defined in the o= line, the same as that of the previous answer if there is no change in the SDP offer. Incrementing the version for every offer/answer poses interoperability issues.

Escalation and de-escalation present resource-allocation challenges to the conference server. When the endpoint sends the initial INVITE to the conference server to set up an audio-only connection, there is no standard way to indicate in the SIP header or in the SDP offer that this endpoint is video-capable. Therefore, the conference server cannot know at this point whether it needs to allocate a video port to handle a possible escalation. There are a few possible solutions to address this issue:

■ Do not reserve video ports for endpoints that request an audio-only stream. As a result, the conference server will reject an escalation to video if video ports are not available.

■ Reserve the ports based on the conference policy. The conference system should let the administrator choose a resource management policy. Examples of such a policy include always reserving audio and video ports for all the ad hoc conferences.

Media Control Support

Two primary video-specific media control operations need to be supported on video conferences:

- Video fast update (VFU; also called *fast video update* [FVU])

- Video freeze picture

An endpoint issues a VFU if its decoder requires an I-frame to continue decoding the video stream. When the encoder receives the VFU, it encodes the next frame as an I-frame. The decoder can request a full update or can ask the encoder to update only a part of the frame. The frame is divided into smaller parts, each called a group of blocks (GOB). GOBs are further subdivided into smaller units called macroblocks (MB). An endpoint can specify a video refresh for certain GOBs or MBs. However, endpoints typically request full frames.

Video freeze picture is sent from an encoder to a decoder. In case the encoder is aware of a change in the transmitted picture that would cause loss of synchronization, it requests the decoding side to freeze the picture—that is, to stop presenting the changes until a new stable image is encoded and transmitted. When an endpoint receives the video freeze picture request, it stops decoding the video until it receives a release signal that is part of the video bitstream. This release signal is sent by the encoder when it generates a new I-frame. A typical conferencing application of picture freeze occurs when the active speaker in a multipoint video conference changes. In this case, the conference server can send picture freeze to the endpoints and then send a release signal (the I-frame from the active speaker).

SIP currently has no standard method to support these operations, and competing proposals have emerged for adding these capabilities. However, most of the SIP endpoints and conference servers use the SIP INFO message with an XML document to communicate the codec control primitives. The XML body is carried in an INFO message and is sent by either the endpoint or the conference server. Example 5-18 shows an XML description of an I-frame request sent from a conference server to an endpoint.

Example 5-18 *Video Fast Update Request*

```
INFO sip:endpoint@10.10.10.5:5060 SIP/2.0
Via: SIP/2.0/UDP 10.10.10.2:5060;branch=z9hG4bK123F
From: confserver <sip:msi-vsw-006000@10.10.10.2>;tag=1F144-1EEF
To: endpoint <sip:endpoint@10.10.10.5>;tag=50a0a0a-13c4-418c31c9-5cb8215-d53
Date: Sun, 08 Jan 2006 00:02:08 GMT
Call-ID: 1c7b7a8-50a0a0a-13c4-418c31c9-5cb8215-338d@10.10.10.5
User-Agent: Cisco-meetingplaceexpress
Max-Forwards: 70
Timestamp: 1014941016
CSeq: 101 INFO
Contact: <sip:confserver@10.10.10.2:5060>
Content-Type: application/media_control+xml
```

Example 5-18 *Video Fast Update Request (Continued)*

```
Content-Length: 168

<?xml version="1.0" encoding="utf-8"?>
<media_control>
    <vc_primitive>
        <to_encoder>
        <picture_fast_update>
        </picture_fast_update>
        </to_encoder>
    </vc_primitive>
</media_control>
```

Note that the Content-Type header is set to application/media_control+xml.

Even though using INFO for FVU is commonly supported among the video endpoints and conference server vendors, the solution is not approved by the IETF for a number of reasons:

■ It may incur too much overhead.

■ It may incur excessive delay.

■ It is not generic for video, because it does not work with other signaling protocols such as Real Time Streaming Protocol (RTSP).

IETF is currently defining a standard for codec control. It is not SIP-based but rather RTCP-based.

Scheduled Conferences

Scheduled conferences add complexity to the SIP flows. A SIP endpoint dialing into a scheduled conference takes the following steps:

1. Endpoints typically connect to an IVR before joining a conference. The IVR is either part of the conference server or tightly controlled by the conference server. The IVR terminates the endpoint signaling and authenticates the user. Authentication may include asking the user to enter the meeting ID of the conference.

2. After the user has been authenticated, the IVR typically prompts the user for a recorded name, generally with a message such as "At the tone, please say your name. When finished, press the pound key." The IVR records the user's name.

3. The conference server connects the endpoint to the conference and then issues an announcement, often including the recorded name of the new participant.

In addition, a conference server may supply a rich set of in-conference features for scheduled conferences, such as conference chairman controls. Chairman controls allow the meeting administrators to eject a participant from the meeting, mute participants, and so on.

The following sections discuss the SIP flows for different aspects of scheduled conferencing, such as IVR operation and in-conference features.

Entry IVR

In the centralized conferencing model, the conference server is the central entity and terminates all the SIP signaling. After the media has been connected, the conference server performs IVR functionality, including DTMF collection, in the media plane, without further actions on the signaling plane, as shown in Figure 5-11.

Figure 5-11 *Initial IVR Session*

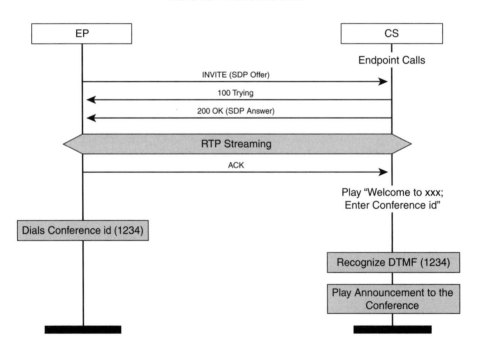

Initial IVR Session to Determine the Conference
the User Wishes to Join

In a distributed conferencing model, however, one central, logical conference server is composed of many individual servers. An endpoint might need to be moved from one physical server to another.

In Figure 5-12, endpoint EP dials into the entry IVR associated with the conference server, enters the meeting ID, and goes through the name-recording process. Centralized logic then moves the endpoint to another entity in the conference server that hosts the conference itself. Note that the name recording could be done after the endpoint moves to the conference.

Figure 5-12   *Conference Join Through REFER*

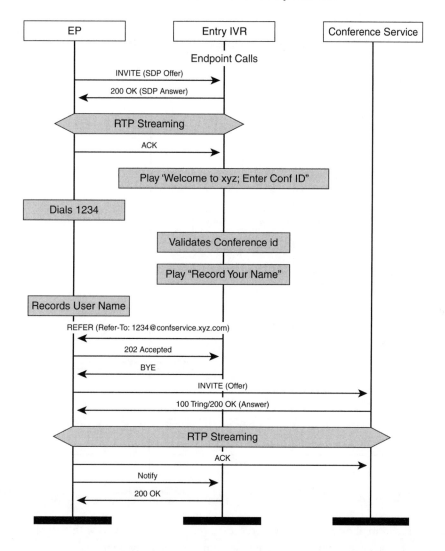

The entry IVR uses the REFER method to redirect the endpoint to the conference service component. The Refer-To header in the REFER provides the contact URI of the conference server.

The endpoint then sends an INVITE to that URI. The entry IVR sends a BYE to the endpoint immediately after the REFER message, because the INVITE dialog between the entry IVR and the endpoint is no longer meaningful.

Some implementations use INVITE with the Replaces header rather than REFER, as defined in RFC 3891 and as shown in Figure 5-13. The Replaces header is used to logically replace an existing SIP dialog with a new dialog.

Figure 5-13   *Conference Through INVITE with the Replaces Header*

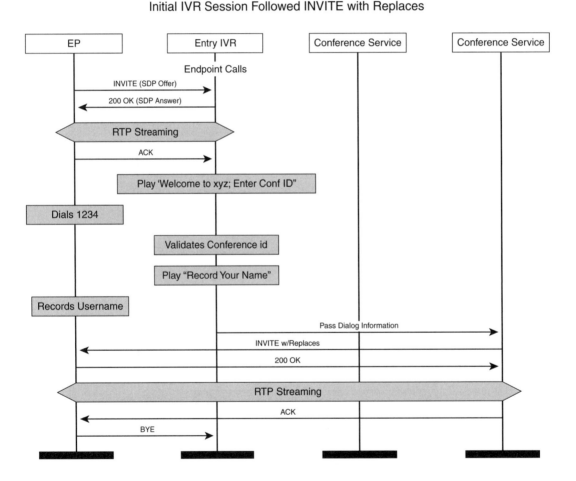

In this scenario, the destination conference server sends an INVITE with a Replaces header directly to the endpoint, while the endpoint still has a connection to the IVR. The IVR must provide the conference server with the information it may need from the IVR dialog. This information can be exchanged between the conference service and initial IVR through some out-of-band mechanism.

The rationale behind using INVITE with Replaces over REFER has to do with security considerations. The endpoint is authenticated by the conference system when it establishes a dialog relationship with the initial IVR. If the endpoint has to send another INVITE to the conference service (as a result of the REFER), it needs to be authenticated again by the conference service. With INVITE with Replaces, because the INVITE is initiated by the conference system, the conference system can reuse the credentials already established for the endpoint.

In-Conference Features

While in a conference, the endpoint can initiate a number of in-conference features. These features include roll call request, mute, unmute, hold/resume the call, transfer, and so on. The following sections address some of the most common features briefly.

Roll Call

A roll call as shown in Figure 5-14, asks the conference system to announce the names of all users in the conference. The announcement can be a public announcement, played to all participants in a conference, or it can be a private announcement, played to only a single participant. An end user who requests a private roll call enters the request by pressing a special digit (typically, the pound sign followed by a digit). The conference server detects the DTMF digit(s) and plays the names of all the callers in the system. During a private announcement, the conference server mutes the requesting endpoint while it plays the recorded names of participants. In Figure 5-14, the key sequence #4 notifies the conference server that the endpoint wants a roll call.

Figure 5-14 *Roll Call*

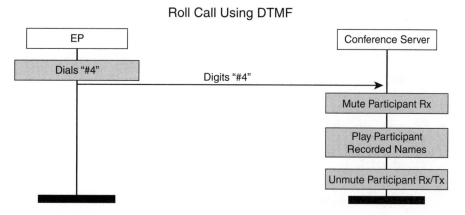

The conference servers get the DTMF digits and play the prerecorded participant names to the endpoint. Note that the conference server mutes and unmutes the receive side of the stream before playing the names.

Hold and Resume

The user presses the Hold button on the phone to place the conference call on hold. The endpoint initiates a RE-INVITE and puts the audio stream in sendonly mode, as shown in Figure 5-15.

Figure 5-15 *Call Hold*

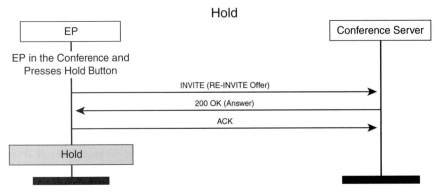

In the following SDP offer/answer exchange, note that the endpoint adds the attribute line a=sendonly, causing audio to flow only from the EP to the conference server. The conference server responds with a=recvonly.

The EP sends RE-INVITE with the offer shown in Example 5-19.

Example 5-19 *RE-INVITE with SDP Offer for Call Hold*

```
v=0
o=bob 2808844564 2808844564 IN IP4 ep.xyz.com
s=
c=IN IP4 ep.xyz.com
t=0 0
m=audio 49172 RTP/AVP 0
a=rtpmap:0 PCMU/8000
a=sendonly
```

The conference server responds with the answer shown in Example 5-20.

Example 5-20 *RE-INVITE with SDP Answer for Call Hold*

```
v=0
o=alice 2890844526 2890844526 IN IP4 meetings.xyz.com
s=
c=IN IP4 meetings.xyz.com
t=0 0
m=audio 49174 RTP/AVP 0
a=rtpmap:0 PCMU/8000
a=recvonly
```

When the user resumes the conference call, the endpoint sends a RE-INVITE again with the SDP offer a=sendrecv, and the conference server responds with the same.

Mute and Unmute

An endpoint can mute itself using one of two methods:

- The endpoint can halt transmission of audio/video media packets to the conference server.

- The endpoint can request that the conference server ignore packets from the endpoint.

An endpoint can instruct a conference server to ignore audio or video media packets by sending proper DTMF tones. In Figure 5-16, the key sequence #5 notifies the conference server that the endpoint wants to be muted. In response, the conference server plays an announcement to the endpoint and proceeds to mute the participant. Unmute works the same way as described for mute.

Figure 5-16 *Participant Mute*

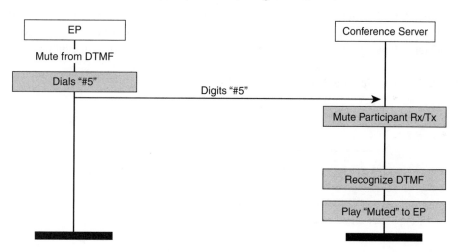

Inconf Control Using DTMF

Outdial

Some conference systems can dial out to a participant when the conference is about to start. The conference server obtains the participant outdial information from a directory through Lightweight Directory Access Protocol (LDAP) or from a presence server. Regardless, after the conference server knows the SIP URL of the participant, it initiates an INVITE with the SDP offer. In Figure 5-17 the conference server initiates outdial to a participant. The conference server sends an early offer in the INVITE and gets back an answer SDP in the "200 OK" response message.

Figure 5-17 *Outdial from the Conference Server*

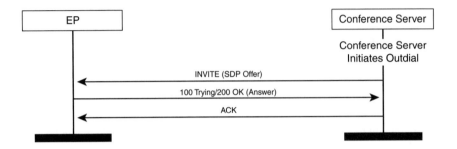

RSVP/QoS Support in Conferencing Flows

Bandwidth reservation is important for the audio and video streams, and RFC 3312 provides the resource-reservation support in SIP. Audio streams should have a higher quality of service (QoS) than video streams because video tolerates delays better than audio. The endpoint may include a successful bandwidth reservation as a precondition of joining the conference. Or, the endpoint can make the reservation optional. Figure 5-18 shows a Resource Reservation Protocol (RSVP) conference flow where the endpoint indicates RSVP as a precondition in the initial INVITE.

Figure 5-18 *RSVP Flow Between Endpoint and Conference Server*

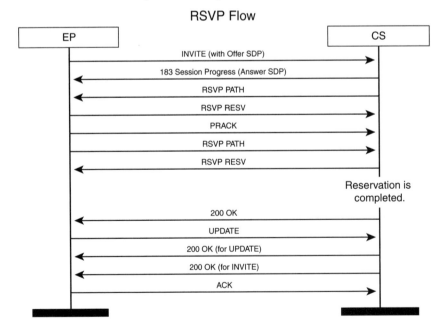

The following steps explain the flow shown in Figure 5-18:

1. The endpoint sends an INVITE and includes the following QoS attributes in the SDP offer:

   ```
   m=audio 20000 RTP/AVP 0
   c=IN IP4 10.10.10.2
   a=curr:qos e2e none
   a=des:qos mandatory e2e sendrecv
   ```

   des is the desired status; it indicates that the session establishment should stop until this criterion is met.

   curr is the current status of the network resources of the media stream.

   In the preceding example, the SDP offer from the endpoint indicates that the current QoS status for the audio stream is none (no reservations are made), and the desired status is an end-to-end (indicated by e2e) reservation in both directions. This criterion is a mandatory precondition (indicated by the MIME string mandatory).

2. If the conference server supports RSVP, it knows when resources in its "send" direction (from the conference server to the endpoint) are available, because it receives RESV messages from the network. However, it does not know the status of the reservations in the other direction. The conference server sends a "183 session progress" message and requests confirmation by specifying conf:qos for resource reservations in its recv direction, as shown in the following example:

   ```
   m=audio 30000 RTP/AVP 0
   c=IN IP4 10.10.10.25
   a=curr:qos e2e none
   a=des:qos mandatory e2e sendrecv
   a=conf:qos e2e recv
   ```

3. After sending the answer, the conference server starts reserving network resources for the media stream. When the endpoint receives this answer, it starts reserving network resources, too. The conference server sends PATH messages toward the endpoint, and the endpoint sends PATH messages toward the conference server.

4. Eventually, the conference server receives RESV messages confirming the reservation. However, it waits until resources in the other direction are reserved, too, because it did not receive any confirmation, and the preconditions still have not been met.

5. The endpoint sends a Provisional ACK (PRACK) message introduced in RFC 3262 in response to "183 session progress." The PRACK message does not contain SDP offer/answer body.

6. When the endpoint receives RESV messages, it sends an updated offer (in UPDATE) to the conference server, as shown in the following example:

   ```
   m=audio 20000 RTP/AVP 0
   c=IN IP4 10.10.10.2
   ```

```
a=curr:qos e2e send
a=des:qos mandatory e2e sendrecv
```

7. The conference server responds with an answer SDP ("200 OK" in response to UPDATE) that contains the current status of the resource reservation (that is, sendrecv), as shown in the following example:

```
m=audio 30000 RTP/AVP 0
c=IN IP4 10.10.10.25
a=curr:qos e2e sendrecv
a=des:qos mandatory e2e sendrecv
```

8. At this point, preconditions are met, allowing session establishment to resume. The conference server returns a "200 OK" response.

9. The session establishment ends with the endpoint sending a final ACK to the conference server.

Any mid-session changes to the media properties, such as IP address changes, result in a RE-INVITE from either direction.

Summary

This chapter has reviewed the fundamentals of SIP and its implementation on the conferencing systems. SIP support for video conferencing is evolving but may gain dominance and provide industry-wide interoperability if the IETF can resolve several open issues discussed in this chapter.

References

Camarillo, G., G. Eriksson, and H. Schulzrinne. IETF RFC 3388, *Grouping of Media Lines in the Session Description Protocol*. December 2002.

Camarillo, G. (ed.), W. Marshall (ed.), and J. Rosenberg. IETF RFC 3312, *Integration of Resource Management and Session Initiation Protocol*. October 2002.

Handley, M., and V. Jacobson. IETF RFC 2327, *SDP: Session Description Protocol*. April 1998.

Handley, M., H. Schulzrinne, E. Schooler, and J. Rosenberg. IETF RFC 2543 (obsolete), *SIP: Session Initiation Protocol*. March 1999.

Mahy, R., B. Biggs, and R. Dean. IETF RFC 3891, *The Session Initiation Protocol (SIP) "Replaces" Header*. September 2004.

Roach, A. B., IETF RFC 3265, *Session Initiation Protocol—Specific Event Notification*. June 2002.

Rosenberg, J., and H. Schulzrinne. IETF RFC 3262, *Reliability of Provisional Responses in Session Initiation Protocol*. June 2002.

Rosenberg, J., H. Schulzrinne, G. Camarillo, A. Johnston, J. Peterson, R. Sparks, M. Handley, and E. Schooler. IETF RFC 3261, *SIP: Session Initiation Protocol*. June 2002.

Schulzrinne, H., and S. Petrack. IETF RFC 2429, *RTP Payload Format for the 1998 Version of ITU-T Rec. H.263 Video (H.263+)*. October 1998.

Schulzrinne, H., and S. Petrack. IETF RFC 2833, *RTP Payload for DTMF Digits, Telephony Tones and Telephony Signals*. May 2000.

Westerlund, M. IETF RFC 3890, *A Transport Independent Bandwidth Modifier for the Session Description Protocol*. September 2004.

This chapter covers the following topics:

- H.323 overview

- H.323 endpoint aliasing

- H.225 call signaling

- H.245 control protocol

- H.323 Empty Capability Set

- H.323 device types

- H.323 gatekeeper services

- Using service prefixes with MCUs

CHAPTER 6

Signaling Protocols: Conferencing Using H.323

Although multimedia conferencing is migrating toward SIP signaling, as described in Chapter 5, "Signaling Protocols: Conferencing Using SIP," many organizations continue to have a significant investment in legacy H.323 endpoints. This chapter provides a general overview of basic H.323 signaling concepts.

H.323 Overview

H.323 is a widely deployed International Telecommunication Union (ITU) standard, originally established in 1996. It is part of the H.32x series of protocols and describes a mechanism for providing real-time multimedia communication (audio, video, and data) over an IP network. In this chapter, the intent is to familiarize you with some of the basic concepts involved in the H.323 architecture and signaling models, with an emphasis on voice and video conferencing. It does not attempt to cover all aspects of H.323 networking.

Additional standards referenced under the H.323 umbrella include H.225.0, Q.931, H.245, and Real-time Transport Protocol / RTP Control Protocol (RTP/RTCP). The ITU standards for H.225 and H.245 describe the H.323 session and media control signaling, which are reviewed in this chapter.

Components of an H.323 network include media-terminating devices such as phones, video conferencing terminals, gateways, and multipoint conferencing units (MCU, for hosting meetings). Devices in this group are categorized as endpoints in the H.323 network. Other components include gatekeepers and H.323 border elements. Gatekeepers provide services such as a network dial plan and bandwidth management for endpoints. The H.323 border element connects two H.323 networks to provide call routing and authorization between the networks. Because this chapter focuses on voice and video conferencing, the emphasis is primarily on endpoints.

In the following section, the individual components comprising an H.323 stack are reviewed. Figure 6-1 shows the basic components of the H.323 signaling stack.

Figure 6-1 *H.323 Signaling Stack*

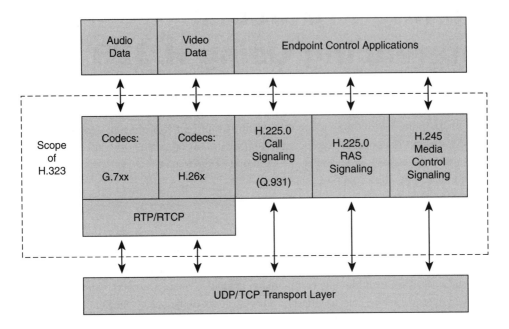

H.323 stack components can be separated into two main categories: signaling and media.

Signaling components include the following:

- **H.225.0 call signaling**—H.225.0 provides a mechanism for initiating calls between devices.

- **H.225.0 RAS**—Registration, Admission, and Status (RAS) provides controls on bandwidth utilization and endpoint location.

- **H.245 media control**—H.245 provides a mechanism for negotiating media types and characteristics between endpoints.

H.323 media components include the following:

- **Audio and video codecs**—Codecs provide the method for encoding and decoding media streams.

- **RTP and RTCP stacks**—RTP and RTCP provide a mechanism for transporting and managing media packet data over an IP network. Chapter 4, "Media Control and Transport," discusses this topic in depth.

The following sections provide details about H.323 endpoint addressing and call establishment.

H.323 Endpoint Aliasing

When making calls between devices using H.323, a calling device can specify the called party using a number of schemes. H.323 provides several methods for addressing and identifying endpoints, including the following:

- E.164 Dialed Digits

- H.323 ID

- URL ID

- MobileUIM

- E-mail ID

- Transport address

The E.164 Dialed Digits addressing scheme assigns a dialed digit string to each device and is one of the more familiar modes of endpoint aliasing. The dialed digit string is based on the ITU-T E.164 standard, which describes the numbering plan for international public telecommunications. E.164 numbers may include any digits between 0 and 9 and have a recommended maximum of 17 digits. H.323 network administrators assign numbers according to a dial plan. The dial plan establishes the dialing pattern to reach specific endpoints in the network. An endpoint that wants to call another endpoint does so by calling the assigned destination number of the other party.

The H.323 ID is a string-based alias assigned to the endpoint, such as conferenceroom222 or johnsmith. These types of IDs are useful only locally and typically are used between endpoints and gatekeepers. The role of an H.323 gatekeeper is explained later in this chapter.

The H.323 URL ID has the format h323:*user@hostname*, where the *user* field identifies the service or user and the *hostname* contains either an IP address or DNS hostname. Examples include h323:confhost@172.19.136.146, h323:user6@gk1.enterprise.com, and so on. This format of endpoint identification provides a mechanism for web-based, clickable dialing and eliminates specific dial plan routing issues.

The MobileUIM field is used with wireless networks. It permits interworking between devices, as described in ITU-T standard H.246 Annex E.1.

H.323 calls may be placed using an e-mail ID as the called endpoint address. The e-mail ID is an RFC 822–compliant address.

Endpoints connected to a gatekeeper may use the gatekeeper to translate E.164 dialed digits into a transport address.

The H.323 standard also describes other less frequently used methods for identifying an endpoint.

H.225 Call Signaling

The H.225 recommendation describes the protocol for H.323 session control, including call initiation and connection management. It fully describes how an H.323 call is initiated, established, and disconnected. H.225 is derived from the Q.931 ISDN signaling standard, after modification for packet networks. It is based on Abstract Syntax Notation 1 (ASN.1) encoding. This section reviews common H.225 message types and content.

H.225 uses a reliable TCP connection between devices on the IP network. The device initiating the call opens a TCP connection to the called device, which is listening on TCP port 1720.

H.225 Message Format

H.225 protocol data units follow the same format as Q.931 messages. Figure 6-2 illustrates the header used by H.225 messages.

Figure 6-2 *H.225 Message Structure*

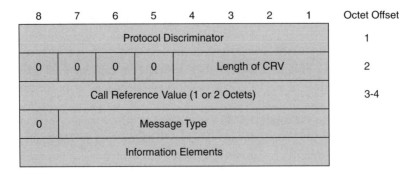

The following list describes the H.225 message header:

■ **Protocol Discriminator (one octet)**—The Protocol Discriminator identifies the Layer 3 protocol. For Q.931 messages, this value is always 8. It distinguishes user-network call control from other messages.

■ **Call Reference Value (one octet)**—This value contains the length of the Call Reference Value (CRV) field, which follows it. The value may indicate a 1- or 2-byte CRV.

- **Call Reference Value (one or two octets)**—The CRV is used to uniquely identify each active call in progress. The value is assigned at the beginning of the call. Other subsequent requests and responses associated with this call instance carry the same CRV value.

- **Message Type (one octet)**—The Message Type field identifies the message (for example, Setup, Connect, Call Alerting, and so on). The message type determines what additional information is allowed in the next field, Information Elements.

- **Information Elements**—The contents of this variable-length field depend on the preceding field, Message Type. The two types of information elements (IE) are single-octet elements and variable-length elements. The IEs carry information related to the message type, such as calling and called number, bearer capability, and so on.

Common H.225 Message Types Used in H.323 Signaling

This section describes some of the protocol data units (PDU) used in initiating, establishing, and disconnecting H.323 calls. The PDUs are transmitted over the H.225 signaling channel, and each packet is sent as a whole message. The message is defined using a structure defined by a *Transport Protocol Data Unit Packet* (TPKT). A TPKT format is defined by IETF RFC 2006 and is used to delimit individual messages within the TCP stream. The TPKT contains a one-octet version ID, followed by a one-octet Reserved field, followed by a two-octet PDU Length field, followed by the PDU itself.

Setup Message

The Setup message is used to initiate a call to a remote device. When an H.323 endpoint initiates a call to a remote device, it first establishes a TCP connection. After the TCP connection has been established, the originating endpoint sends a setup request.

After sending a Setup message, the originating endpoint starts the setup timer. If the terminating endpoint fails to respond within the timer interval, the originating endpoint may retry the setup request or terminate the call.

Mandatory fields in the Setup message include the following:

- Protocol Discriminator

- Message Type

- CRV

- Bearer Capability

- User-User Information Element (UUIE)

The Bearer Capability field of the Setup message is used to tell the receiver about the nature of the call, such as whether the call is audio only or whether it will be an audiovisual call. The subfield Information Transfer Capability is set to Unrestricted Digital Information for calls that include video data. The Bearer Capability information element is required in the Setup message. It is optional in other messages.

The Setup message may optionally contain fields such as the E.164 number of the called party, the calling party name/number, a fast-start IE, and other information. Fast Connect operations are discussed in a later section of this chapter.

If the receiving device is a Voice over IP to public switched telephone network (VoIP-PSTN) gateway, it examines the called number and may ring a locally attached phone, or it could initiate an outgoing trunk call to the PSTN. In the case of IP-IP gateways, the call is terminated locally by the gateway and reoriginated using H.323 or Session Initiation Protocol (SIP) signaling toward the destination device.

Call Proceeding

The Call Proceeding message is sent by the called endpoint as an indication that the call is in the process of being established and that no more Call Establishment messages will be accepted for this call instance. Call proceeding is an optional message.

After the called party receives a notification of the incoming call (for example, a phone is ringing), the called party returns an Alerting message.

Alerting

The Alerting message is an optional status message issued by the called endpoint to the caller. This message confirms that the called endpoint has initiated an indication of the incoming call to the called user (that is, the phone is ringing).

Setup ACK

The called device sends a Setup ACK message to the calling endpoint as an acknowledgment of a Setup message.

Connect

The Connect message is sent from the called party to the calling party to inform the caller that the call has been answered. The Connect message usually initiates the start of any toll charge accounting. The H.225 connection is complete when the Connect message has been transmitted.

Notify

The Notify message allows endpoints to exchange information during the life of the call. One such use is for the called endpoint to return details on its bearer capabilities after the call connects.

Cisco Unified CallManager uses H.225 Notify messages during call transfer to indicate the transferee name and number information to the calling party. That is, when A calls B, and B transfers the call to C, the information about C is sent to A using the H.225 Notify message. In this way, party A can know to whom he or she is speaking.

Release Complete

The Release Complete message may be sent by either endpoint. It indicates that the sender has terminated the call and that the CRV is reusable. No further H.225 signaling is possible for this call after Release Complete is received, and any allocated resources should be released. The Release Complete message contains a return code indicating the reason for call termination. The ITU-T H.225.0 Recommendation contains a full list of call termination cause codes.

Figure 6-3 illustrates the basic call flow for establishing an H.225 connection between endpoints. When the call has reached the Connect state, H.245 media negotiations can begin.

Figure 6-3 *Basic H.225 Call Connection Sequence*

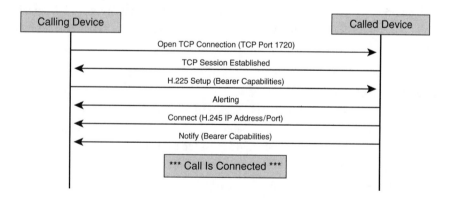

The next section describes H.245 signaling in detail, which is used for negotiating media streams between endpoints.

H.245 Control Protocol

The H.245 recommendation provides the mechanism for the negotiation of media types and RTP channel establishment between endpoints. Using the H.245 control protocol, endpoints exchange details about the audio and video decoding capability each device supports. H.245 also describes how logical channels are opened so that media may be transmitted. Like H.225, H.245 messages are encoded using ASN.1 notation.

The H.245 session information is conveyed to the calling device during the H.225 exchange. After the Setup message has been transmitted, the called device can use any one of the Alerting, Call Proceeding, or Connect messages to return the IP address and port to be used for the H.245 control session. When the calling endpoint receives the information, it immediately initiates a TCP connection with the specified IP address, and H.245 negotiations start.

Although media can be established before the H.225 Connect message is received, Cisco IOS PSTN gateways do not complete bridging between the IP and the telephony side until the call is fully connected. This prevents two-way audio communication before billing can be started.

The following section describes some of the more important H.245 messages used in media negotiation and control.

H.245 Messages

This section describes some of the H.245 PDUs frequently used in establishing H.323 media connections. The messages include PDUs for exchanging endpoint decoding capability, determining how endpoints should behave when conflicts arise, and for opening and closing logical channels. Logical channels are opened and closed depending on the decoding capability and requirements of the endpoints. Each H.245 logical channel is numbered. Logical channel 0 is used for the control channel, and it is always assumed to be open as long as endpoints remain connected.

Terminal Capability Set

The Terminal Capability Set (TCS) message contains the media and feature capability of the sender. After the H.245 connection is established, each side sends a TCS message to the remote device. The TCS message is the first H.245 message exchanged between connecting endpoints. The receiving endpoint uses this information to determine its options for initiating media streams to the TCS message sender.

The TCS message includes the following:

- A list of audio codecs supported, including packetization periods and payload types.

- A list of video codecs supported. Video codecs include H.261, H.263 and associated annexes, H.264 (including profiles and levels), picture formats/resolution, maximum bit rates, minimum picture interval (MPI) corresponding to the frame rate, and so on.

- The Dual Tone Multiple Frequency (DTMF) relay type supported. Common DTMF relay types include H.245 alphanumeric, H.245 signal, and voice band. Many video endpoints support only voice-band mode. In this mode, DTMF signals are played directly into the audio stream as tones.

- Whether the sender supports features such as T.38 fax mode, RFC 2833 DTMF signaling (encoding DTMF digits in an RTP payload format), and the far-end camera control (FECC).

- Alternate capability set.

The alternate capability set is a grouping of the individual modes (for example, G.711, G.722, CIF H.263, and so on) that the endpoint is capable of supporting. These alternate capability sets are then grouped into the simultaneous capability set.

Simultaneous Capability Set

As described in the preceding section, H.323 devices use the TCS message to provide a complete list of their receive capabilities. The simultaneous capability set is a subsection within the TCS message, allowing the sender to describe which of the listed capabilities can be used concurrently. The devices specify this in terms of groups of alternate capability sets. For example, an endpoint may have listed some compute-intensive audio and video codecs as receive capabilities, but it may not support using both of them at the same time (because of processor constraints). In such a case, the sender uses the simultaneous capability set to list which combinations are allowed.

For example, an endpoint might have indicated support for H.263 video streams and G.711 and G.723 audio streams. For this example system, when H.263 video is active, only G.711 audio may be used. The simultaneous capability set would then carry a combination of H.263 video and G.711 audio and another with G.723 audio only.

H.245 User Input Indications

The User Input Indication is used to transmit local digit and hookflash events to the remote endpoint. Depending on the DTMF relay session parameters negotiated during the TCS exchange (alphanumeric versus signal), these indications may contain just the digit itself or the digit and the period of time the digit was pressed (digit duration).

Indicating DTMF Relay Support in the TCS Message

Endpoints supporting out-of-band DTMF relay indicate this support in the receiveUserInputCapability TCS element. The three frequently used values are

- Hookflash

- DTMF

- basicString

The values are Boolean, and when true, indicate that the signaling type is supported. If both the local and remote devices support one or more of these, they may send H.245 User Input Indication messages to convey events when the local endpoint wants to signal a digit or hookflash.

The basicString Boolean value indicates support for DTMF relay for characters 0 through 9, *, and #. The DTMF Boolean value is a superset of basicString. Through the use of Signal and Signal Update messages, the endpoint additionally conveys the time duration the digit was pressed (and the digit itself). If hookflash support is also set to true, the hookflash event is sent with the Signal message.

As an alternative to H.245 DTMF relay, digit events may also be transmitted using RFC 2833 packets in the media stream. RFC 2833 packets are interleaved with media packets, unlike out-of-band DTMF relay, which involves the transmission of User Input Indication messages over the H.245 signaling channel. Because media packets have a higher transport priority, RFC 2833 DTMF signaling is often the preferred digit transport mechanism if intermediate signaling proxies are involved.

Another option used by many video endpoints is to play DTMF tones within the audio stream itself. In this mode, the audio decoder detects the tones and reports them as digits to the control layer.

Master-Slave Determination

The Master-Slave Determination (MSD) exchange uses two values to determine which side shall be master and which side shall be slave. After an endpoint sends its TCS, it sends the MSD message.

Endpoints use the result of the MSD exchange to establish roles between each device for the purpose of managing logical channels and to determine how conflicts should be handled. For example, the master has the role of assigning session IDs for logical channels and for generating the key when media encryption is used. The decision as to the master-slave role is returned in the MSD ACK message.

The MSD message contains values for Terminal Type and a randomly chosen Status Determination Number. Each endpoint compares the values received against its own value. The side that has the higher Terminal Type value becomes the master. If both sides have the same value for Terminal Type, the one with the higher Status Determination Number becomes the master. If by coincidence both sides select the same value again, the MSD is rejected and the negotiation retried. When an endpoint connects to a conference server, the conference server is always the master.

Open Logical Channel Requests

In H.323, a logical channel represents a communication path used for media or data transmission. Endpoints use the H.245 OpenLogicalChannel (OLC) messages to create these pathways.

The OLC request can be transmitted after the sender receives a TCS and has completed the MSD exchange. When opening a unidirectional logical channel, the device that will be transmitting data on the channel sends the OLC request. An endpoint sends OLC requests to open audio, video, or other streams, such as those used for FECC. For media, the OLC request carries information such as the codec to be used and the payload type that will be used in the RTP packets.

The specific content of the OLC request depends on the type of stream being opened. For audio streams, the OLC request contains information such as the codec, packetization period, dynamic payload type, logical channel number, whether silence suppression will be used, and RTCP port information. The OLC request is acknowledged using an OLC ACK response. The OLC ACK contains the remote IP address and port to which packets should be transmitted.

After the OLC ACK has been received, RTP streaming may start, and the RTCP channel is opened. The RTCP channel may be used for exchanging RTCP messages, such as the sender and receiver reports. RTCP channels are bidirectional.

Logical Channel Numbers

Each OLC request includes the forward logical channel number (LCN). The LCN identifies a specific channel and is used as a reference in OLC responses (OLC Acknowledgment or OLC Reject) and when the channel is closed in the Close Logical Channel request.

Open Logical Channel for Audio Streams

Figure 6-4 shows an OLC example for an audio stream.

In this example, the request is to open a 64-kbps G.722 audio channel with a 20-millisecond (ms) packetization period. The local IP address for RTCP is 128.107.138.232, and the UDP port is 6001. The forward LCN is 2.

Open Logical Channel for Video: H.261 and H.263 Streams

This section provides some details about the video-specific characteristics found in the OLC request for video streams. The OLC request for video streams includes elements such as the video codec, RTP payload type, maximum transmit bit rate, the resolution and frame rate, and the RTCP channel information.

Figure 6-5 shows a typical OLC request for an H.263 video stream. The next section examines the elements contained within the request in detail.

Figure 6-4 *Example of an audio OLC Request*

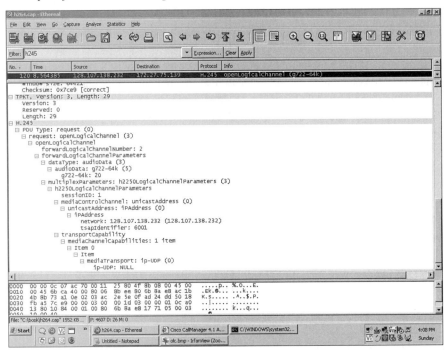

Figure 6-5 *H.245 OLC Request for an H.263-1996 Video Stream*

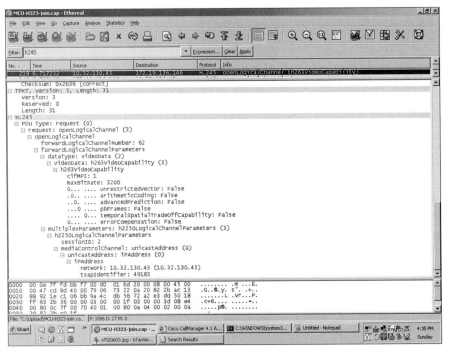

Payload Types and Formats

For H.261 and H.263-1996 video encoding, the payload types are static and are specified in RFC 3551 (H.261 uses payload type 0x31, and H.263-1996 uses type 0x34). Newer video codecs such as H.263-1998, H.263-2000, and H.264 use dynamic payload types. In Figure 6-5, an OLC request is shown with h263VideoCapability listed in the Video Data field, along with a bitmap indicating any supported annexes.

The next sections provide additional details about the video elements found in the OLC request shown in Figure 6-5.

Maximum Bit Rate

The Maximum Bit Rate (maxBit rate) field of the OLC request is specified in units of 100 bits per second. In Figure 6-5, the maximum transmit video bit rate is 3200, or 320 kbps. The OLC receiver must be able to accept an incoming video data rate up to the maximum specified in maxBit rate. This rate must be lower than or equal to the value indicated by the receiver in the TCS it sent earlier. The value refers only to the video streaming rate and does not take into account any overhead from transport headers.

Video Resolution (Picture Format) and Minimum Picture Interval

H.263 video supports a number of picture sizes and frame rates. The five standardized picture formats, from smallest to largest, are sub-QCIF, QCIF, CIF, 4CIF, and 16CIF. It is also possible to negotiate custom picture formats.

The specific video picture size and frame rate to be used in a transmission are included in the OLC request. The h263VideoCapability resolution and Minimum Picture Interval (MPI) value, such as qcifMPI=x or cifMPI=x, indicate an image size and the rate at which frames will be transmitted for that size. The value for x is calculated by the following formula:

$$MPI = 30 \text{ / frame rate}$$

The MPI value indicates the expected frame rate at which the sender will transmit video. For example, an MPI of 2 indicates a frame rate of 15 frames per second (FPS), and an MPI of 3 indicates a frame rate of 7.5 FPS.

In Figure 6-5, the h263VideoCapability field indicates cifMPI=1. This informs the receiver that the sender will be transmitting a picture format with Common Interchange Format (CIF) resolution, with a frame rate of 30 FPS.

The h263VideoCapability section of the OLC is also used to indicate special encoding capabilities, listed in terms of annexes. In Figure 6-5, these are shown to be a bitmap, with a value of 1 indicating that the encoder supports the annex, and a value of 0 when it does not.

Open Logical Channel for H.264 Streams

The OLC request for H.264 streams carries similar information to the H.263 streams but is encoded differently. The transmitting endpoint encodes information about stream characteristics using a Generic Video Capability structure. This same structure may be found in the TCS message. Information carried in the structure includes a maximum transmit bit rate and media encoding characteristics, expressed in terms of an H.264 Profile and Level indication.

H.264 streams carry a dynamic payload type with values in the range of 96 to 127. The value selected is indicated in the dynamicRTPPayloadType field. The valve specified indicates to the receiver that the transmitter will use this designated value for its RTP payload type in all H.264 RTP packets sent on this channel.

H.264 Profile and Level

The H.264 Profile value describes the characteristics of the video encoding that will be used in the transmitted media stream. The Level value indicates the maximum bit rate and frame rate and the number of macroblocks (MB) per second that will be transmitted. MBs represent fundamental regions within picture transmissions.

Figure 6-6 provides an example of an OLC request for an H.264 video stream. The Generic Video Capability structure carries the maximum bit rate in units of 100 bps. It is shown here as 3840, or 384 kbps. It also contains the H.264 Profile and Level values in an encoded format.

Figure 6-6 *H.264 OLC Request*

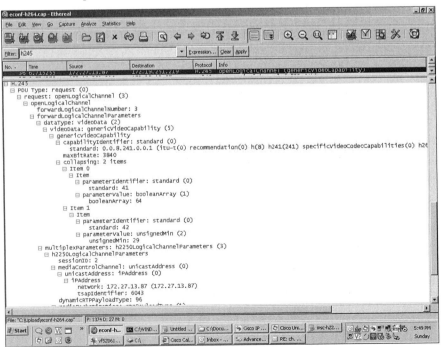

In Figure 6-6, after the maximum bit rate, the next structures of interest are the two parameter identifier/value pairs. The first parameter identifier of 41 indicates that the parameter value content is describing the H.264 profile. The next parameter identifier/value pair describes the H.264 level used for this media stream.

This combination is indicated by a parameter identifier of 42, followed by a parameter value of 29. The parameter identifier 42 indicates that the parameter value describes the H.264 level parameter.

The ITU-T H.241 specification fully describes the profile and level assignments. The profile is a Boolean array, which allows an endpoint to indicate support for one or more of the Baseline (bit 2), Main (bit 3), or Extended (bit 4) profile types. The Baseline profile requires the least computing resources and is frequently used for video conferencing systems.

As described earlier, Figure 6-6 shows a profile value of 64 and a level of 29. Using Table 6-1 and Table 6-2, the Boolean array with value 64 is interpreted as the Baseline profile, and the parameter value of 29 correlates to level 1.2. Table 6-1 and Table 6-2 are excerpts from the ITU-T Specification H.241 (07/2003) and provide details on interpreting the profile and level values.

Table 6-1 describes how to decode the Generic Video Capability parameter found in the OLC request to determine the H.264 profile. The profile defines the encoding complexity and compression characteristics for the video stream.

Table 6-1   *H.241–H.264 Capability Parameter: Profile*

Parameter Name	Profile
Parameter description	This parameter is a Boolean array.
	If bit 2 (value 64) is 1, this value indicates the Baseline profile.
	If bit 3 (value 32) is 1, this value indicates the Main profile.
	If bit 4 (value 16) is 1, this value indicates the Extended profile.
	All other bits are reserved, shall be set to 0, and shall be ignored by receivers.
	In a decoder capability, each bit set to 1 means that the terminal is capable of decoding the indicated profile(s) using the level and other optional parameters in this Generic Capability.
	In an OLC message, each bit set to 1 means that the logical channel contents obey all constraints of the indicated profile(s).
Parameter identifier value	41.
Parameter status	Mandatory. This parameter appears exactly once in each Generic Capability.
Parameter type	booleanArray.
Supersedes	This field is not included.

Table 6-2 shows the correlation between the level parameter as set in the Generic Video Capability structure and the H.264 level number. The level number provides information about the video transmission in terms of the maximum bit rate, number of MBs per second, and frame size.

Table 6-2   *H.241: Level Parameter Values*

Level Parameter Value	H.264 Level Number
15	1
22	1.1
29	1.2
36	1.3
43	2
50	2.1
57	2.2
64	3
71	3.1
78	3.2
85	4
92	4.1
99	4.2
106	5
113	5.1

Open Logical Channel Acknowledgment

When a device receives an OLC request, it examines the details of the incoming request and allocates the required resources. Resources may include a digital signal processor (DSP) channel and UDP ports for the RTP and RTCP sessions. After associating the resources with the logical channel, the endpoint returns an OLC ACK to the sender over the H.245 session.

The OLC ACK message contains the RTP and RTCP IP address and port details (to which RTP should be transmitted), along with the LCN associating the OLC ACK with the OLC request.

Close Logical Channel

When an endpoint wants to close a channel it has opened, it sends a Close Logical Channel (CLC) message to the remote device. The receiver of CLC responds with a Close Logical Channel Acknowledgment (CLC ACK) response.

Close Logical Channel Acknowledgment

The CLC ACK is transmitted in response to a CLC request. It is not possible for a device to stop a peer from closing its own channels.

Request Channel Close

The Request Channel Close message requests that the remote side close a previously opened logical channel. The request includes the LCN and a reason code indicating why the sender requests that the channel be closed.

There are two possible responses to Request Channel Close messages. The recipient may return a Request Channel Close Acknowledgment, indicating the channel will be closed, or it may reject the request. When rejecting the request, the endpoint sends a Request Channel Close Reject, with a cause code field. Figure 6-7 illustrates the Request Channel Close PDU.

Figure 6-7   *Request Channel Close*

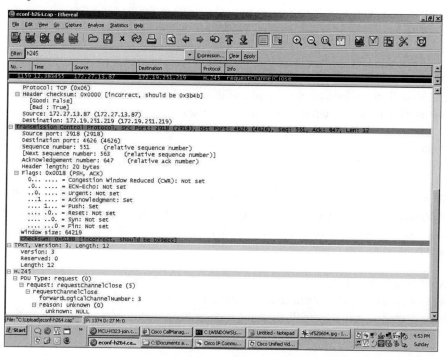

H.245 EndSession Command

The EndSession command indicates the end of the H.245 session. After an endpoint has sent the EndSession command, it does not send any more H.245 messages. There is no acknowledgment for EndSession.

Video-Specific H.245 Messages

This section describes H.245 messages used specifically for video sessions. These commands may be initiated from either side after the video session has been established. These include commands for requesting a device change its video transmission rate, to stop and start video decoding, and to request that a sender transmit an intraframe.

H.245 Flow Control Command

The Flow Control command is a directive from the decoder of the receiving side to the encoder of the transmitting side. The decoder sends the Flow Control message to request that the encoder adjust its maximum transmit bit rate. The two parameters for the Flow Control command include the LCN and a new maximum bit rate. The bit rate is specified in units of 100 bps.

H.245 Miscellaneous Indication

The Miscellaneous Indication message carries several types of indications between video endpoints. This section outlines some common uses.

When an endpoint is muting or unmuting its video transmit stream, the muting endpoint may inform the remote device by sending a Miscellaneous Indication message.

To indicate that a video stream is muted, the Miscellaneous Indication carries an indication type of logicalChannelInactive. When normal transmission begins or resumes, the Miscellaneous Indication type of logicalChannelActive is sent. The Miscellaneous Indication carries the LCN to which the operation applies.

Another indication type is VideoTemporalSpatialTradeoff. This indication is sent to an encoder to request a change in the stream characteristics. The function provided by VideoTemporalSpatialTradeoff signaling is described in detail in the following section.

H.245 Miscellaneous Command

The Miscellaneous command transports mid-call video requests. The Miscellaneous command may be sent at any time after the logical channel has been established, and it does not receive an acknowledgment.

There are two classes of Miscellaneous command messages:

- Encoder control commands

- Decoder control commands

The Miscellaneous command carries an LCN identifying the video channel to which the request applies. A partial list of Miscellaneous command request types follows:

- **VideoFreezePicture**—This command instructs the decoder on the receiver to complete the assembly of the current video image and then display it without further change until the sending side releases it. The release occurs when the transmitter sends an intraframe video bitstream with the Freeze Picture Release bit set to true. After the release has been received, the decoder resumes decoding and displaying.

- **VideoFastUpdatePicture**—This command is sent by an endpoint receiving a video stream. It instructs the encoder at the sender to complete the encoding of the current frame and then to generate and transmit a full intraframe as soon as possible. VideoFastUpdatePicture is sent whenever an endpoint needs to receive a full reference frame to continue decoding.

- **VideoFastUpdateGOB**—VideoFastUpdateGOB instructs the encoder to update one or more group of blocks (GOB). A GOB is a subset of a picture frame and consists of a group of MBs in scan order.

- **VideoTemporalSpatialTradeoff**—VideoTemporalSpatialTradeoff is sent by an endpoint receiving a video stream and requests that the encoder change its trade-off between temporal and spatial resolution. It uses an index from 0 to 31, with higher numbers requesting a higher frame rate.

If the encoding device supports VideoTemporalSpatialTradeoff, it sets the corresponding bit in the forwardLogicalParameters field of the OLC request. Upon receipt of the OLC ACK, the encoder transmits a VideoTemporalSpatialTradeoff indication with its initial value. The decoding side may request a new value by sending a request to the encoder.

In Figure 6-8 (taken from an Ethereal trace), the sender has requested a VideoFastUpdatePicture for LCN 3. When this message arrives at the remote device, its encoder generates an intraframe (I-frame) and transmits it to the requesting device over the RTP stream corresponding to LCN 3.

Figure 6-8 *H.245 Miscellaneous Command Example*

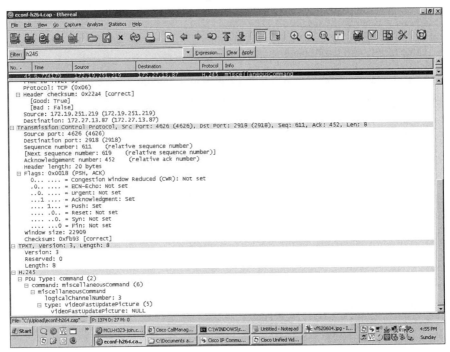

When the H.225 session is connected, the H.245 media negotiations can begin. The message sequence chart in Figure 6-9 illustrates the end-to-end H.245 negotiations required to establish bidirectional audio and video streams. In this example, a two-way H.264 video call is established.

H.323 Fast Connect Mode

The H.323 Fast Connect feature is an optimization added as part of H.323 Version 2. Fast Connect signaling can establish media streams in a point-to-point call with one round-trip message exchange, enabling immediate media exchange after the call has been connected. When Fast Connect mode is not used, the media connect is established using standard H.225 and H.245 signaling, called *Slow Start mode*.

Users with endpoints that use H.323 Slow Start signaling may experience audio clipping because of the delay caused by the additional H.245 message exchanges after the connect. In these cases, the initial speech of the called party can be lost, because the media may not be fully established by the time the called party begins speaking. In Fast Connect mode, this scenario is minimized because the media channels are established with significantly fewer message exchanges.

Figure 6-9 *H.245 Negotiations for Audio/Video Media Establishment*

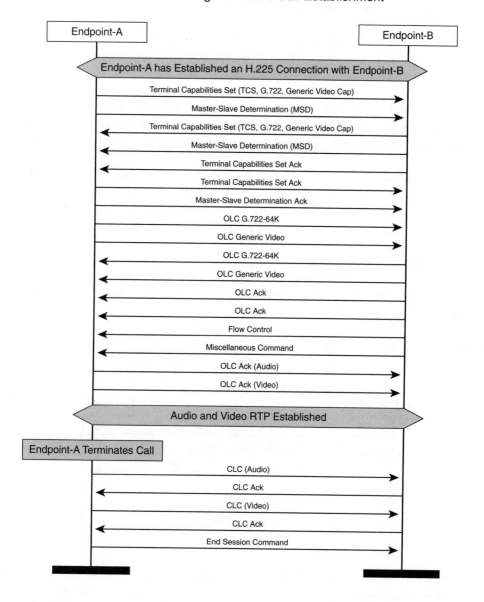

H.245 Exchange for Video Call Establishment

Other improvements include tunneling H.245 messages over the same TCP connection used for H.225 signaling, and Early H.245 mode, in which the H.245 channel is opened as early in the H.225 call sequence as possible.

When an endpoint is using Fast Connect mode, the Fast Start element is added to the H.225 Setup message. The Fast Start element carries an embedded OLC request, a suggested codec, and a set of reverse logical channel parameters.

The reverse logical channel parameters carry the codec, IP address, and port numbers for RTP and RTCP sessions for the calling endpoint. If the called endpoint also supports Fast Connect and accepts the codec, it may immediately start an RTP stream toward the calling endpoint.

The called device responds by placing a similar Fast Start element in the H.225 Connect message, which contains an embedded OLC, along with its set of reverse logical parameters. After these have been exchanged, each side has sufficient information to establish a two-way media exchange.

The H.245 session is still required for other mid-call H.245 messages, such as User Input Indication, CLC, and so on, but it can be established later after the media connects or use the tunneling mechanism over the H.225 session. For a Fast Connect call, the TCS messages are exchanged after the Fast Connect response is received and after media establishment.

H.323 video devices do not generally support H.323 Fast Start mode.

Figure 6-10 shows the messages exchanged for a basic Fast Connect call, without early H.245 mode or H.245 tunneling.

Figure 6-10 *Fast Connect Media Establishment*

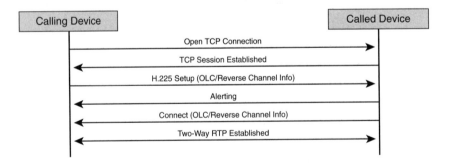

Basic H.323 Fast Connect Signaling

The next section describes the H.245 signaling used to implement simple call hold, resume, and transfer operations.

Using the Empty Capability Set

Basic phone features include the ability to transfer a call to another party and to place a call on hold and resume it later. Calls are placed on hold or transferred by means of the hold and transfer buttons on the phone. As part of the hold and transfer operations, the RTP media channels are closed and reopened again. In the case of hold/resume, the channels are opened to the same phone; for transfer, media resumes with a new device. The next section describes how the Empty Capability Set (ECS) message can be used to provide both of these services. H.323 also includes support for hold, resume, and transfer by means of the H.450.x protocol, but that is beyond the scope of this chapter.

Call Hold Signaling with the Empty Capability Set

To indicate to the remote device that a hold operation is in progress, the endpoint initiating the hold operation sends a special form of the TCS, known as the *ECS message*, sometimes referred to as *TCS=0*.

The ECS is a TCS with all capability fields set to null and support for it is a mandatory part of H.323 Version 2 and later. It does not disconnect the call, but simply informs the remote side that the sender does not currently have any decoding capability. As a result, the remote side closes all logical channels toward the sender. The side going on hold does likewise, media terminates, and the call is placed on hold.

When the call is resumed, the resuming device sends a new TCS message with all supported codecs listed. The normal H.245 negotiations occur, and the call is reestablished.

Call Transfer with the Empty Capability Set

Call transfer using ECS requires that the phones involved use a common H.323 signaling agent. When a call is connected and the transfer button is pressed, the H.323 call signaling agent in the transferring phone sends ECS to the remote device, and media is closed. When the party to which the call was transferred answers, then the transfer button is pressed again and the H.323 call signaling agent sends a new TCS and negotiates media on behalf of the phone to which the call was transferred.

For instance, suppose that phone A is connected to phone B, and the user of phone A wants to transfer the call to phone C. The user at phone A presses the transfer button, dials the number of phone C, and then presses transfer again. Phone C starts ringing, and the H.323 call signaling agent waits for the user at phone C to answer. When phone C is answered, the H.323 call agent sends a new TCS with the terminal capability of phone C. When phone B receives the new TCS, the logical channels are reopened, and the media is connected between phone B and phone C.

H.323 Device Types

H.323 devices include terminals, gateways, multipoint control units (MCU), and gatekeepers. In the next section, the functions and features provided by each of these common network elements are reviewed in detail.

H.323 Terminals

Terminals are end-user devices and may communicate with other terminals on the network, or with gateways when calling devices on other network types. Terminals include phones and phone systems running the H.323 protocol stack, desktop and room conferencing systems, and personal computers running an H.323 multimedia communications program such as Microsoft NetMeeting. Basic devices provide audio support and can optionally include video or data features, such as a whiteboard or application sharing modes.

H.323 Gateways

H.323 gateways allow interworking between devices on the IP network and devices on other network types, such as the PSTN. The gateway provides transparent signaling and media conversion between packet-and circuit-switched networks, allowing endpoints to communicate with remote devices without regard for the signaling methodology used by those devices.

Figure 6-11 shows an H.323 gateway interconnecting the H.323 and PSTN networks.

Figure 6-11 *Interfacing Between the H.323 and PSTN Networks*

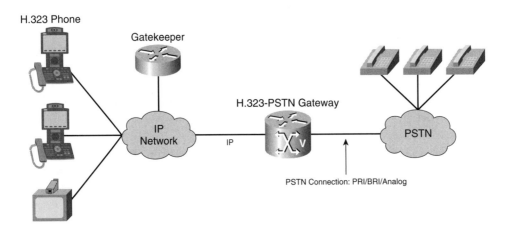

H.323 to PSTN Interconnection

H.323 Multipoint Control Units

MCUs are conferencing systems allowing three or more participants into an audio or video conference call. The MCU manages conferences and provides audio and video mixing services for the meeting participants. Chapter 2, "Conferencing System Design and Architecture," covers the architecture and features provided by the MCU in detail.

H.323 Gatekeepers

A gatekeeper is an optional H.323 component on the network. When present, it provides important services for terminals, gateways, and MCUs under the control of a system administrator. These services include allowing endpoints to call one another using a dial plan and providing access and bandwidth control. The next section provides details about gatekeeper services.

Endpoints, gateways, and MCUs can be configured to use the services of a gatekeeper. These devices use the RAS protocol for gatekeeper communication. Basics of the RAS protocol are discussed later, in the section "Gatekeeper RAS Signaling."

H.323 Gatekeeper Services

The H.323 gatekeeper provides many features, including access control, address translation, bandwidth management, dial plans, and other services that improve scalability of the H.323 network. This section provides an overview of some common gatekeeper features. Endpoints and gatekeepers communicate using the RAS protocol.

Required H.323 Gatekeeper Features

The H.323 gatekeeper provides administrative control over an H.323 network. The features provided by a gatekeeper can be separated into two groups: mandatory and optional.

The four mandatory features of an H.323 gatekeeper are as follows:

- **Address translation**—This feature provides name translation services.

- **Bandwidth control**—The gatekeeper can grant or deny bandwidth requests between calling and called endpoints.

- **Admission control**—This service allows the administrator to impose restrictions on endpoint admission to the H.323 network.

- **Zone management**—Zone management is used for communication with other gatekeepers in the network.

Address Translation

This gatekeeper service translates E.164 numbers and H.323 IDs into endpoint IP addresses. This capability enables an H.323 endpoint to call another endpoint without knowing the IP address of the called device.

Because an H.323 endpoint may make a direct point-to-point call if the caller knows the DNS name or IP address of the remote device, gatekeepers are not required for a basic call. However, allowing calls to be placed between endpoints using symbolic aliases simplifies H.323 client administration. If endpoints use Dynamic Host Configuration Protocol (DHCP), the IP address assigned to the endpoint can change over time, but the alias name remains the same.

Bandwidth Control

Bandwidth control allows the network administrator to configure limits on bandwidth usage for calls initiated by H.323 endpoints. At a minimum, the gatekeeper must have support for the RAS messages: Bandwidth Request (BRQ), Bandwidth Confirm (BCF), and Bandwidth Reject (BRJ).

Admission Control

This service allows the network administrator to control which devices gain access to the H.323 network. Gatekeepers maintain call admission policy and may grant or deny network access based on the system configuration. Admission control is accomplished by using H.225 RAS signaling.

Zone Management

A zone is composed of the devices actively registered with a single gatekeeper and includes terminals, gateways, and MCUs. Each endpoint belongs to only one zone. Large networks may contain multiple zones and gatekeepers. A gatekeeper can communicate with other gatekeepers for purposes of routing calls between devices in different zones. Networks with multiple gatekeepers can be organized in either peer-to-peer or hierarchical configurations.

Optional H.323 Gatekeeper Features

Some of the optional gatekeeper services include advanced bandwidth management, special call authorization and routing features, and routing of H.225 and H.245 signaling messages.

A partial list of optional gatekeeper features follows:

- **Call authorization**—Administrative control via access rules

- **Call management**—Provides services such as call forwarding

- **Bandwidth management**—More advanced control over network resource consumption

- **Call control signaling**—Direct and gatekeeper routed signaling

Call Authorization

When an H.323 terminal or gateway initiates a call to another endpoint, the gatekeeper can reject the call request based on administrative criteria. These include disallowing calls based on time of day or access rules, such as between certain devices.

Call Management

The call management feature keeps track of active call information for all endpoints in the zone. This feature allows call rerouting for purposes of redirection, busy call forwarding, and load balancing.

Bandwidth Management

Audio and video traffic on an H.323 network can consume network capacity quickly. The bandwidth management feature allows the gatekeeper to reject call admission requests when the requested bandwidth is not available.

Bandwidth management can control network utilization based on traffic coming into the zone (interzone), out of the zone (remote), or within the zone. Other advanced management criteria include limiting the amount of bandwidth available to specific applications.

Gatekeeper Signaling Options

There are two signaling modes in a gatekeeper-controlled H.323 network:

- Direct endpoint signaling

- Gatekeeper routed call signaling (GKRCS)

Direct Endpoint Signaling

When the gatekeeper is configured for direct endpoint signaling, the calling and called endpoints exchange RAS admission control messages with the gatekeeper, but the H.225 and H.245 messages are exchanged directly between the calling and called endpoints, without gatekeeper involvement.

Figure 6-12 shows the signaling path for direct endpoint signaling.

Figure 6-12 *Direct Endpoint Signaling*

Directed Call Signaling

Gatekeeper Routed Call Signaling

In GKRCS, H.225 and H.245 messages are routed through the gatekeeper rather than directly between endpoints. The gatekeeper acts as a signaling intermediary between the calling and called device. The gatekeeper has the most control when configured for GKRCS in terms of system policy administration.

Figure 6-13 shows the signaling path for gatekeeper routed signaling.

Figure 6-13 *Gatekeeper Routed Call Signaling*

GK Routed Signaling (GRS)

Gatekeeper RAS Signaling

Gatekeepers communicate with endpoints, gateways, and MCUs using the RAS protocol. The following sections provide an overview of the basic concepts and messages used in RAS signaling but do not encompass the entire RAS message set.

RAS signaling channels are the first to be opened between the gatekeeper and gatekeeper-managed devices and are separate from the call establishment and media channels.

RAS signaling uses UDP port 1719 for H.225 messages and UDP port 1718 for multicast gatekeeper discovery.

RAS Gatekeeper Discovery

RAS signaling messages fall into two categories: gatekeeper discovery and call admission control.

Devices can discover the gatekeeper for their zone in two ways. Devices configured with the IP address of the gatekeeper can use unicast discovery mode, in which they directly send a Gatekeeper Request (GRQ) message to the gatekeeper and register immediately. One GRQ message is sent per logical endpoint, so an MCU or gateway can potentially send many GRQ messages to the gatekeeper.

If the device has not been configured with the IP address of the gatekeeper, it can use multicast discovery mode, in which it sends the GRQ message to the default UDP multicast address 224.0.1.41 and UDP port 1718.

For each GRQ received, the gatekeeper replies with either a Gatekeeper Confirm (GCF) or a Gatekeeper Reject (GRJ) response. The GCF includes the transport address that the gatekeeper uses for registration and status messages.

Endpoints not receiving a response to GRQ retransmit the request periodically.

RAS Messages

This section describes the basic RAS messages used by an H.323 device when operating in gatekeeper-controlled mode.

Registration Request

Devices begin the gatekeeper registration process by sending the Registration Request (RRQ) message to the gatekeeper. This request may include a significant amount of information about the registering device, such as manufacturer, product ID, and version IDs. For use with call routing, the RRQ includes the call signaling and RAS IP address and port of the endpoint and the terminal alias. The terminal alias can be in the form of the H.323 ID (a symbolic name) or an E.164 number (a series of dialed digits). The gatekeeper may respond with RCF (Registration Confirm) or RRJ (Registration Reject).

After the device has registered with the gatekeeper, other devices may call the endpoint with either the E.164 number or the H.323 ID.

Registration Confirm

If the registration is successful, the gatekeeper sends the RCF response to the endpoint. The RCF response includes a text string with the gatekeeper name.

Registration Reject

A gatekeeper can reject the registration request by sending an RRJ response. The RRJ contains a reject reason code indicating why the request failed.

Admission Request

When a gatekeeper-controlled endpoint calls another device on the H.323 network, the calling endpoint first sends an Admission Request (ARQ) message to the gatekeeper. The ARQ message carries the amount of bandwidth requested and an identifier of the calling and called party, such as a dialed digits (E.164) number.

Admission Confirm

The gatekeeper returns an Admission Confirm (ACF) message when granting an admission request. Included in the ACF message is the bandwidth value, the gatekeeper call routing model, and the IP address of the called device to be used for establishing the H.225 signaling channel.

Admission Reject

If the gatekeeper cannot grant an admission request, it responds with an Admission Reject (ARJ) message. The ARJ message includes a reason code indicating why the ARQ request was rejected.

Mid-Call Bandwidth Requests

When a device needs to modify the session bandwidth during a call, it sends a bandwidth request message to the gatekeeper. For instance, an endpoint might need to request additional bandwidth when it adds video streams to an existing call. Endpoints adjust the bandwidth by sending a Bandwidth Request (BRQ) message to the gatekeeper with the new bandwidth requirement. If the bandwidth is available, the gatekeeper grants the request, signaled via the Bandwidth Confirm (BCF) message.

If the bandwidth requested exceeds the amount available, the gatekeeper responds with a Bandwidth Reject (BRJ) message and reason code.

Disengage Request

A device sends the Disengage Request (DRQ) to inform the gatekeeper that the endpoint is being dropped. DRQ is transmitted immediately after the H.225 Release Complete message. DRQ may also be sent from the gatekeeper to the device and forces the call to be dropped.

Disengage Confirm

The gatekeeper sends the Disengage Confirm (DCF) response to the device after successfully processing a DRQ. When the endpoint receives the DCF, it can reregister with the gatekeeper using the RRQ request.

Configuring a Gatekeeper in Cisco Unified CallManager

Cisco Unified CallManager (CUCM) supports H.323 gatekeepers, which may be configured using the CUCM configuration web page, as shown in Figure 6-14. In addition, a separate H.225 gatekeeper-controlled trunk definition is required, as shown in Figure 6-15.

Cisco Unified CallManager can also interwork with H.323 devices directly, without a gatekeeper. Any device that calls Cisco Unified CallManager resources directly (without a gatekeeper) must have its DNS name or IP address preconfigured in CallManager; otherwise, calls from the device are not accepted. H.323 gateways can access CallManager resources (for example, phone, PSTN gateways and trunks, and so on) by either having a specific H.323 gateway definition in CallManager, or by means of an H.225 gatekeeper controlled trunk.

Figure 6-14 shows a part of the web-based configuration page associated with the gatekeeper definition (as shown in the next section). Note that the technology prefix value configured in the CallManager trunk definition must match the value specified in the gw-type-prefix of the Cisco IOS-based gatekeeper.

Figure 6-15 shows a subsection of the CUCM configuration page for the gatekeeper-controlled trunk definition. The definitions correspond to the Cisco IOS gatekeeper configuration elements discussed in the next section.

Figure 6-14 *Sample Gatekeeper Definition in Cisco CallManager*

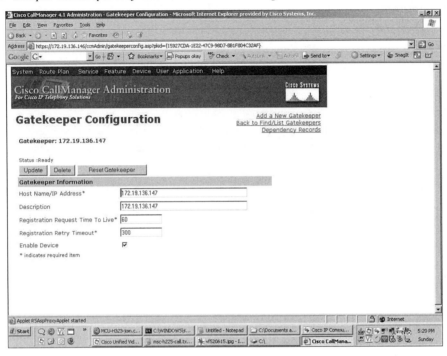

Figure 6-15 *Section of the Cisco CallManager Configuration Page for an H.225 Gatekeeper-Controlled Trunk*

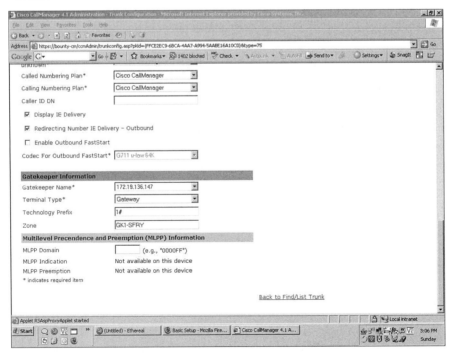

Configuring Gatekeeper Support in a Cisco IOS Router

Example 6-1 illustrates a sample H.323 gatekeeper configuration in a Cisco IOS router.

Example 6-1 *Sample Cisco IOS Gatekeeper Configuration*

```
gatekeeper
 zone local GK1-SFRY cisco.com
 zone prefix GK1-SFRY 23..
 gw-type-prefix 1#* default-technology
 no shutdown
```

In this simple example, the network has only one gatekeeper. The configuration also shows the following:

■ The **zone local** statement identifies the local zone name and defines the domain name for endpoints registering with an e-mail address.

■ The **zone prefix** statement identifies local endpoints and in-zone calls.

■ The **gw-type-prefix** statement specifies the type prefix string (which must match the corresponding values in the Cisco CallManager trunk configuration).

■ The **default-technology** statement routes all calls to the CallManager trunk.

■ Gatekeeper configuration statements are configured under the gatekeeper sub-config mode.

H.225 Call Setup for Video Devices Using a Gatekeeper

The message sequence chart shown in Figure 6-16 illustrates two endpoints registering with a gatekeeper. The call flow shows endpoint A initiating a video call to endpoint B. In the diagram, both endpoints first register with the H.323 gatekeeper. After registration, Endpoint A initiates a call to Endpoint B using the gatekeeper direct endpoint signaling model.

Figure 6-16 *H.225 Connection Establishment with a Gatekeeper*

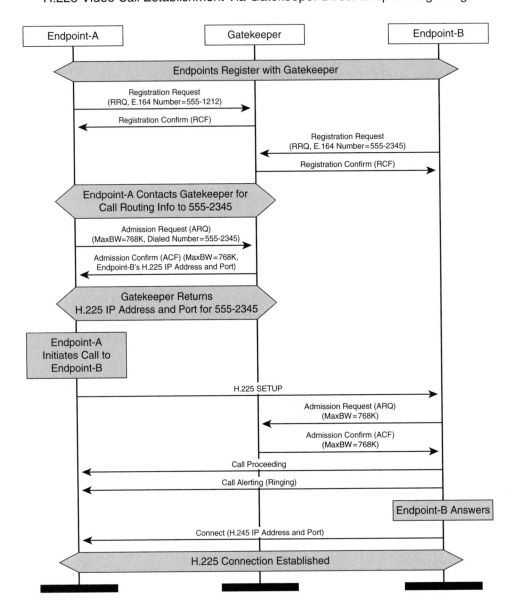

H.225 Video Call Establishment Via Gatekeeper Direct Endpoint Signaling

Using Service Prefixes with MCUs

MCUs can host multiple conferences simultaneously, and a single conference may have multiple video layouts or video presentation modes.

Predefined service prefix codes allow MCUs to associate network services and video layouts with specific patterns within E.164 access numbers. Users can call different numbers to access the same meeting, but with different bit rates and different video layouts. For example, a user could start a conference by dialing the following digit sequence:

Service prefix+Conference ID number

In Table 6-3, access number 851234 contains the service prefix for continuous presence conferencing with a 384-kbps rate (85) and a conference ID of 1234. The MCU establishes the conference 1234 as soon as the first call is connected.

Table 6-3   *Sample Service Prefix Association with Conference Characteristics*

Conference Type	Display Format	Service Prefix	Comments
Voice activated, H.263, 384 kbps		81	The display shows the current active speaker.
Continuous presence, four endpoints, H.263, 768 kbps		85	The display shows the last four speakers.
Continuous presence, seven endpoints		87	The display shows up to seven endpoints.

Other participants wanting the same screen layout as the first caller would join by dialing the same pattern, 851234.

If the participants want a different layout for the conference—perhaps voice-activated mode, for example—they dial a different service prefix specifying the desired presentation mode (for example, 811234).

Service prefixes can be used to describe other meeting attributes, such as bit rate, port reservation size, maximum number of participants, picture format (CIF, QCIF, and so on), the maximum frames sent per second, and whether data sharing is supported.

Summary

This chapter described the basics of H.323 signaling for audio and video and how it is used in conferencing systems. It explored the underlying protocols used for connection establishment and media negotiations and described some of the techniques, services, and components used for endpoint-to-endpoint communications.

References

International Telecommunication Union (ITU-T). H.225.0: Infrastructure of audiovisual services—Transmission multiplexing and synchronization. 2006.

International Telecommunication Union (ITU-T). H.241: Extended video procedures and control signals for H.300-series terminals. 2003.

International Telecommunication Union (ITU-T). H.245: Control protocol for multimedia communications. 2006.

Schulzrinne, H., S. Casner, R. Frederick, and V. Jacobson. IETF RFC 3550, *RTP: A Transport Protocol for Real-Time Applications*. 2003.

This chapter covers the following topics:

- Understanding lip sync skew

- Lip sync approaches

- Understanding the sender side

- Understanding the receive side

- Real-time Transport Protocol

- Correlating time bases using RTCP

Lip Synchronization in Video Conferencing

Chapter 3, "Fundamentals of Video Compression," went into detail about how audio and video streams are encoded and decoded in a video conferencing system. However, the last processing step in the end-to-end chain involves ensuring that the decoded audio and video streams play with perfect synchronization. This chapter focuses on audio and video; however, video conferencing systems can synchronize any type of media to any other type of media, including sequences of still images or 3D animation. Two issues complicate the process of achieving synchronization:

■ Real-time Transport Protocol (RTP)-based video conferencing systems separate audio and video into different RTP streams on the network.

■ Video conferencing systems also typically have separate processing pipelines for audio and video within the sender and receiver endpoints.

This chapter covers the process of realigning those streams at the receiver.

Understanding Lip Sync Skew

Lip sync is the general term for audio/video synchronization, and literally refers to the fact that visual lip movements of a speaker must match the sound of the spoken words. If the video and audio displayed at the receiving endpoint are not in sync, the misalignment between audio and video is referred to as *skew*. Without a mechanism to ensure lip sync, audio often plays ahead of video, because the latencies involved in processing and sending video frames are greater than the latencies for audio.

Human Perceptions

User-perceived objection to unsynchronized media streams varies with the amount of skew—for instance, a misalignment of audio and video of less than 20 milliseconds (ms) is considered imperceptible. As the skew approaches 50 ms, some viewers will begin to notice the audio/video mismatch but will be unable to determine whether video is leading or lagging audio. As the skew increases, viewers detect that video and audio are out of sync and can also determine whether video is leading or lagging audio. At this point, the video/audio offset distracts users from the video conference. When the skew approaches one second, the video signal provides no benefit—viewers will ignore the video and focus on the audio.

Human sensitivity to skew differs greatly from person to person. For the same audio/video skew, one person might be able to detect that one stream is clearly leading another stream, whereas another person might not be able to detect any skew at all.

A research paper published by the IEEE reveals that most viewers are more sensitive to audio/video misalignment when audio plays before the corresponding video, because hearing the spoken word before seeing the lips move is more "unnatural" to a viewer (Blakowski and Steinmetz 1996).

Sensitivity to skew is also determined by the frame rate and resolution: Viewers are more sensitive to skew when watching higher video resolution or higher frame rate.

Report IS-191 issued by the Advanced Television Systems Committee (ATSC) recommends guidelines for maximum skew tolerances for broadcast systems to achieve acceptable quality. The guidelines model the end-to-end path by assuming that a single encoder at the distribution center receives both audio and video streams, digitizes the streams, assigns time stamps, encodes the streams, and then sends the encoded data over a network to a receiver. The guidelines specify that on the sending side, at the input to the encoder, the audio should not lead the video by more than 15 ms and should not lag the video by more than 45 ms. This possible lead or lag might arise from uncertainty in the latencies through the digitizing/capture hardware and occurs before the encoder assigns time stamps to the digitized media streams.

At the receiving side, the receiver plays the audio and video streams according to time stamps assigned by the encoder. But again, there is an uncertainty in the latency of each stream through the playout hardware. The guidelines stipulate that for each stream, this uncertainty should not exceed ±15 ms; this tolerance is an absolute tolerance that applies to each stream. Based on these guidelines, two requirements emerge for acceptable lip sync tolerance:

- **Criterion for leading audio**—In the worst-case-permitted scenario, audio leads video at the input to the encoder by 15 ms. The receiver plays the audio stream too far ahead by 15 ms while playing the video stream too far behind by 15 ms. As a result, the maximum amount by which audio may lead video at the presentation device of the receiver is 15 ms + 15 ms + 15 ms = 45 ms.

■ **Criterion for lagging audio**—In the worst-case-permitted scenario, audio lags video at the input to the encoder by 45 ms. The receiver plays the audio stream too far behind by 15 ms while playing the video stream too far ahead by 15 ms. As a result, the maximum amount by which audio may lag video at the presentation device of the receiver is 45 ms + 15 ms + 15 ms = 75 ms.

> **NOTE**   When designing a video conferencing product, you will find it beneficial to find a "skew test person" who is highly sensitive to audio/video misalignment, to provide the worst-case subjective opinion on skew tolerance.

Measuring Skew

Audio/video skew is measured on the output device at presentation time. The output device is also called the *presentation device*. The definition of presentation time depends on the output device:

■ For video displays, the presentation time of a frame in a video sequence is the moment that the image flashes on the screen.

■ For audio devices, the presentation time for a sample of audio is the moment that the endpoint speakers emit the audio sample.

The presentation times of the audio and video streams on the output devices must match the capture times at the input devices. These input devices (camera, microphone) are also called *capture devices*. The method of determining the capture time depends on the media:

■ For a video camera, the capture time for a video frame is the moment that the charge-coupled device (CCD) in the camera captures the image.

■ For a microphone, the capture time for a sample of audio is the moment that the microphone transducer records the sample.

For each type of media, the entire path from capture device on the sender to presentation device on the receiver is called the *end-to-end path*.

A lip sync mechanism must ensure that the skew at the presentation device on the receiver is as close as possible to zero. In other words, the relationship between audio and video at presentation time, on the presentation device, must match the relationship between audio and video at capture time, on the capture device, even in the presence of numerous delays in the entire end-to-end path, which might differ between video and audio.

Figure 7-1 provides another way of looking at media synchronization. This diagram shows the timing of multiple streams playing out the presentation devices of a receiver, without synchronization.

Figure 7-1 *Receive-Side Stream Skews Without Synchronization*

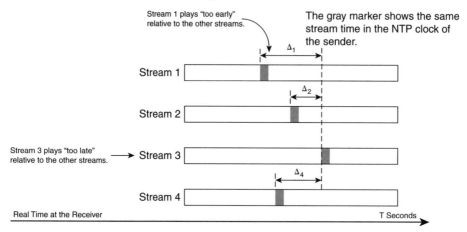

Each stream could be a video or audio stream. The gray marker in each stream corresponds to the same time at the sender, referenced to a clock on the sender that is common to all inputs. This common reference clock is also referred to as a *common reference timebase*. For these streams to play in a synchronized manner, the gray markers must line up; that is, the samples at the gray markers must emerge from the playout devices simultaneously. The goal is to add delay to the streams that play "too early" (streams 1, 2, and 4) so that they play in sync with stream 3, which is the stream that arrives "too late."

Delay Accumulation

Skew between audio and video might accumulate over time for either the video or audio path. Each stage of the video conferencing path injects delay, and these delays fall under three main categories:

- **Delays at the transmitter**—The capture, encoding, and packetization delay of the endpoint hardware devices

- **Delays in the network**—The network delay, including gateways and transcoders

- **Delays at the receiver**—The input buffer delay, the decoder delay, and the playout delay on the endpoint hardware devices

However, most of these delays are unknown and difficult to measure and change over time. This means that the mechanism for achieving lip sync should not attempt to measure and account for each individual delay in the end-to-end media path. Instead, the mechanism must work in the presence of variable, unknown path delays.

Most video conferencing equipment transmits audio and video over a network using RTP, which multiplexes audio and video into separate network streams. This method is in contrast to the format for DVDs, which multiplex the audio and video streams into a single stream called an *MPEG2 program stream*. Because the audio and video streams of a video conference remain separated through the network from endpoint to endpoint, each stream might experience different network delays.

Figure 7-2 shows how differing delays in the end-to-end audio and video paths can accumulate over time, causing the skew between audio and video to increase at each stage of the media path.

Figure 7-2   *Audio and Video Skew Accumulation*

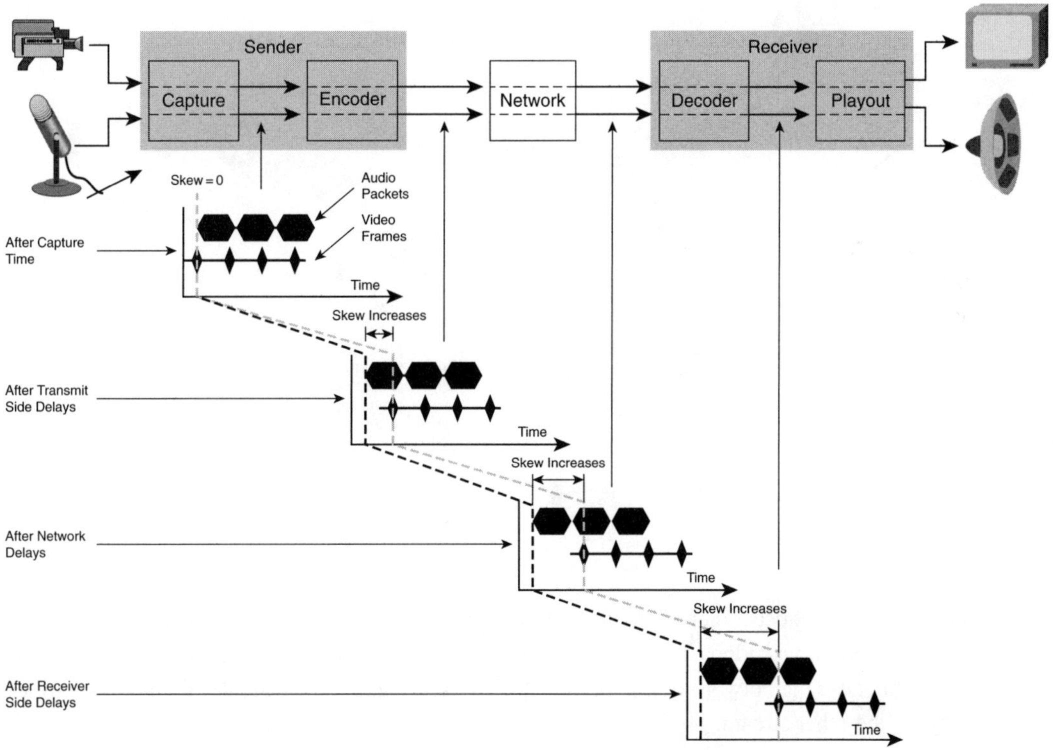

The first graph at the upper left shows the original relationship between video and audio. The graph represents audio as a sequence of packets forming a continuous stream. Each audio packet spans a duration of time corresponding to the audio data it contains. In contrast, the graph represents video as a sequence of frames, where each frame exists for a single instant of time. The figure shows a scenario in which the skew between audio and video increases at three stages of the end-to-end path from sender to receiver: after the sender-side delays, after the network delays, and after the receiver-side delays. To understand how delays creep into each stage, it is necessary to look at how each stage processes data, starting with the network path.

Delays in the Network Path

A lip sync solution must work in the presence of many delays in the end-to-end path, both in the endpoints themselves and in the network. Figure 7-3 shows the sources of delay in the network between the sender and the receiver. The network-related elements consist of routers, switches, and the WAN.

Figure 7-3 *End-to-End Delays in a Video Conferencing System*

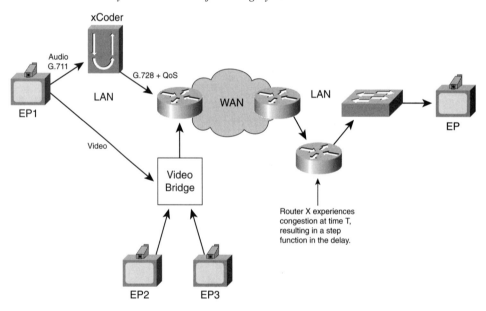

The network also hosts other elements that may process media streams: conference bridges, transraters, and transcoders. These devices might add considerable delay to one or both streams and might cause the network delay for one stream to be significantly greater than the network delay for the other stream.

Bridges combine video/audio streams from multiple endpoints to facilitate a multipoint conference. The process of mixing or combining streams imposes an end-to-end delay.

Transraters re-encode a video stream into a lower bit rate to send the bitstream through a lower-bandwidth network or to a lower-bandwidth endpoint. Transraters typically apply only to video streams.

Transcoders may exist in the network to change the codec type and may apply to either audio or video streams. Figure 7-3 shows a transcoder that translates from G.711 to G.728. A video conferencing network configuration might require transcoders for two reasons:

- **To reduce the bit rate**—Figure 7-3 shows a scenario in which an audio transcoder converts a high-bandwidth audio stream into a low-bandwidth stream. In this case, the high-bandwidth G.711 stream arrives at the transcoder on a high-bandwidth LAN, and the bridge must transcode the audio stream into a lower-bandwidth G.728 version suitable for a low-bandwidth WAN. When a bridge uses a transcoder for the sole purpose of changing the bit rate, it is still called a transcoder, even if the end effect is that of a transrater.

- **To bridge two endpoints with different codec capabilities**—One example for audio is the process of converting from an H.320-centric G.729 codec to an H.323-centric G.723 codec. An example for video is the process of converting from an H.323-centric H.263 codec to an H.320-centric H.261 codec.

Delays for audio and video on some segments of the network might differ due to different quality of service (QoS) levels. Figure 7-3 shows a router configured with QoS to provide lower latency for audio than for video. This difference in quality might be continuous or might arise only when the router suffers heavier-than-normal network congestion.

The congestion level of routers might cause the delays for either audio or video to fluctuate over time. In the figure, router X temporarily experiences a heavy load at time T, causing it to momentarily increase the delay of packets through its queue.

In addition to these short-term events, the long-term, steady-state network path taken by either stream might abruptly change as a result of a change in the dynamic IP routing. Any change in IP routing results in new steady-state end-to-end delays.

Lip Sync Approaches

Video conferencing endpoints generally take two approaches to achieve lip sync:

- **Poor Man's lip sync**—This method assumes that delays in the end-to-end media paths are known and constant. It relies on packet arrival times for synchronization.

- **Common Reference lip sync**—This method assumes that delays in the end-to-end media paths are not easily known and might vary. It relies on a common reference timebase for both audio and video streams.

Poor Man's Lip Sync

The simplest incarnation of a lip sync algorithm is known as *Poor Man's lip sync*. In this method, the receiver uses one criterion to synchronize audio and video: Packets of audio and video that arrive simultaneously at the network interface of the receiver are considered to be synchronized to each other. This approach is fundamentally flawed because delays in the end-to-end path vary both in space (at different points of the path) and time (fluctuations in delay from one moment to the next). In addition, trying to measure, predict, and compensate for these variable delays in the end-to-end path is a futile effort.

When using Poor Man's lip sync, the conferencing system must make several assumptions about the sender, receiver, and network infrastructure:

- **Sender**—For Poor Man's lip sync, the sender generally assumes that the network delay to the receiver is the same for both audio and video streams. However, scenarios might arise in which the delays differ. For instance, a transcoder might be present in the audio path but not the video path. Or, the network might assign a higher QoS to one path, resulting in lower delay for that stream.

- **Receiver**—When operating with Poor Man's lip sync, the receiver must derive a relationship between the time stamps of the two streams by observing the relationship between the packet arrival times and timestamps for each individual stream, and then using that information to derive a relationship between the packet timestamps of the two streams. However, the receiver might have difficulty deriving an accurate relationship, because packet arrival times vary because of arrival-time jitter.

- **Network infrastructure**—Poor Man's lip sync makes the following invalid assumptions:

  — The average network delay remains constant over the long term.

  — The instantaneous network delay remains constant over the short term.

When you are using Poor Man's lip sync, if the sender cannot compensate for network delays, specialized video conferencing network infrastructure might be necessary between the two endpoints. This infrastructure readjusts the synchronization of audio and video streams by adding delay to one stream or another.

An unfortunate byproduct of Poor Man's lip sync is that it often results in the sender or the network infrastructure delaying one or more streams to attempt synchronization at the receiver. However, for maximum flexibility, delays should be introduced only at the receivers, which leads to one of the corollaries of robust lip sync:

Only the receiver should delay media streams to achieve lip sync.

This corollary is necessary for two reasons:

- If the end-to-end audio delay is already significant, the receiver might prefer to avoid adding more delay to the audio stream and forego lip sync. Instead, the receiver might want to go without audio and video synchronization to maintain the lowest audio end-to-end delay for the best interaction between conference participants. The end user makes this decision via the user interface (UI) of the receiver endpoint. Therefore, other entities on the network should not overrule this decision.

- The process of delaying one stream to achieve lip sync should be left to the receiver, because the receiver can take into account its own internal delays in each media path at the same time that it delays one stream or the other to synchronize media. For instance, if audio arrives at the receiver ahead of video, normally the receiver must delay the audio stream to achieve lip sync with the video. However, an input buffer in the receiver might already provide some or all of this delay.

The Offset Slider of Doom

A device commonly used as a sidekick to Poor Man's lip sync is the offset slider of doom. In older PC-based video conferencing and streaming systems, the input devices often had considerable delay in the capture pipeline. In addition, these devices generally did not provide a way of correlating captured samples with real time. To make matters worse, different capture devices had different delays. The sender would make a guess as to the capture pipeline delay for audio and video but would require user input to fine-tune these guesses by means of an *offset slider*, which consisted of a slider bar in the configuration options of the user interface.

With the slider in the middle of its range, the sender would use its nominal guesses for audio and video pipeline latency. The end user could move the slider to the right, which would increase the guess for the audio capture pipeline delay, while keeping the video pipeline delay the same. Or, the user could move the slider to the left, which would increase the guess for the video capture pipeline delay, while keeping the audio pipeline delay the same. Of course, this end-user tuning is the worst violation of the first corollary of lip sync: "A method of lip synchronization must *not* use a mechanism that attempts to measure and compensate for individual delays in the end-to-end path." Instead of compensating for individual delays, the best way to obtain lip sync is with absolute time bases.

Common Reference Lip Sync

The goal of lip sync is to preserve the relationship between audio and video in the presence of fluctuating end-to-end delays in both the network and the endpoints themselves. Therefore, the most important restriction to keep in mind when discussing lip sync for video conferencing is the following:

> Video conferencing systems cannot accurately measure or predict all delays in the end-to-end path for either the audio or video stream.

This restriction leads to the most important corollary of lip sync:

> *A method of lip synchronization must not use a mechanism that attempts to measure and compensate for individual delays in the end-to-end path.*

The second corollary addresses the method that systems should use to achieve lip sync:

> *A method of lip synchronization must use timestamps that can be correlated to a common timebase.*

Before considering a robust method of synchronization using a common reference, it is necessary to cover the data path inside the sender and receiver of a video conference.

> **NOTE**   *Kiosk-quality* lip sync is a term that describes the ability of a video conferencing system to maintain lip sync over a period of several days. A kiosk that provides a continuous video conference should not require a stop/start, disconnect/connect, or reboot to resynchronize audio and video that have drifted out of sync.

Understanding the Sender Side

Figure 7-4 shows the video and audio transmit subsection of a video conferencing endpoint. The microphone and camera on the left provide analog signals to the capture hardware, which converts those signals into digital form. The sender encodes both audio and video streams and then packetizes the encoded data for transport over the network.

Figure 7-4 *Sender-Side Processing*

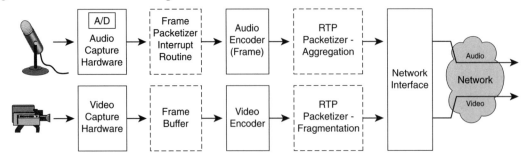

Sender Audio Path

This section focuses on the audio path, which uses an analog-to-digital (A/D) converter to capture analog audio samples and convert them into digital streams. For the purposes of synchronization, it is necessary to understand how each of the processing elements adds delay to the media stream.

The delays in the audio transmission path consist of several components:

- **Audio capture packetization delay**—Typically, audio capture hardware provides audio in packets, consisting of a fixed number of samples. These packets are often called *audio device packets*. Most computer-based hosts, and all professional audio interfaces, offer configurable packet sizes. The packet sizes are typically specified to have units of samples, with pro audio interfaces offering packetization delay as low as 64 samples. At 44.1 kHz/stereo (44,100 samples/second), 64 samples corresponds to a time latency of

$$\frac{64 \text{ samples}}{44100 \text{ samples/second}} = 1.5 \text{ ms}$$

  In this example, the audio card issues 689 packets per second. If each audio sample is 16 bits, with left and right channels, each packet contains

  64 samples $\times$ 2 bytes/sample $\times$ 2 channels = 256 bytes

  These packets are in the form of raw bytes and contain no special packet headers. In both standalone endpoints and PC-based endpoints, the audio capture hardware typically issues an interrupt to the main processor to indicate that a new audio packet is available.

- **Encoder packetization latency**—Audio codecs often use an algorithm that takes fixed-sized chunks of input data, known as *audio frames*, and produces encoded output audio frames. These frames are not to be confused with frames of video. For instance, the G.723 audio codec specifies an input frame size of 30 ms. For 8-kHz mono audio, 30 ms corresponds to 240 bytes. Because codecs must take fixed-sized frames of raw data as input, it is the responsibility of the conferencing firmware to collect packets from the audio card and assemble them into frames of the proper length for the codec. Because the sender must collect multiple audio packets to assemble an audio frame, this type of packetization is considered an aggregation process. Aggregation always imposes a delay, because the packetizer must wait for multiple input packets to arrive.

- **Encoder processing latency**—Encoders process each frame of audio and must complete the processing before the next frame of audio arrives. The G.711 codec uses a simple algorithm that can process audio frames with almost no delay. In contrast, the G.723 codec is more complex and might involve a longer delay. However, for any codec, in no case will the delay exceed one frame time; otherwise, the codec would not be able to keep up with the data rate.

- **RTP packetization delay**—The RTP packetizer collects one or more audio frames from the encoder, composes them into an RTP packet with RTP headers, and sends the RTP packet out through a network interface. The packetization delay is the delay from the time the packetizer begins to receive data for the RTP packet until the time the RTP packetizer has collected enough audio frames to constitute a complete RTP packet. When an RTP packet is complete, the RTP packetizer forwards the packet to the network interface.

Both the packet size of encoded audio frames and the packet size of RTP packets impact delays on the sender side, for two reasons:

- **Whole-packet processing**—Advanced audio codecs such as G.728 require access to the entire input frame of audio data before they can begin the encoding process. If a frame requires data from multiple audio device packets from the capture device, the audio codec must wait for a frame packetizer to assemble audio device packets into a frame before the encoder may begin the encode process. Lower-complexity codecs such as G.711 process audio in frames but do not need to wait for the entire frame of input data to arrive. Because the G.711 codec can operate on single audio samples at a time, it has a very low latency of only one sample.

- **RTP packetization delay**—Even for encoders such as G.711 that have very low latency, RTP packetization specifies that encoded audio frames must not be fragmented across RTP packets. In addition, for more efficiency, an RTP packet may contain multiple frames of encoded audio. Because the RTP packetizer performs an aggregation step, it imposes a packetization delay.

The final stage in the audio sender pipeline is the network interface, which receives packets from the RTP packetization stage and forwards them onto the network. The latency of the network interface is low compared to the other stages. To better show the delays in the transmit portion of the audio path, Figure 7-5 shows a timeline of individual delays.

Time is on the x-axis. In addition, the length of each packet in Figure 7-5 indicates the time duration of the data in the packet. In this figure, the entire packet or frame is available to the next processor in the chain as soon as the leading edge of that packet appears in the diagram. Figure 7-5 shows a common scenario in which successive processing steps perform packetization, increasing the packet size in later stages of the pipeline.

Figure 7-5 *Audio Delays*

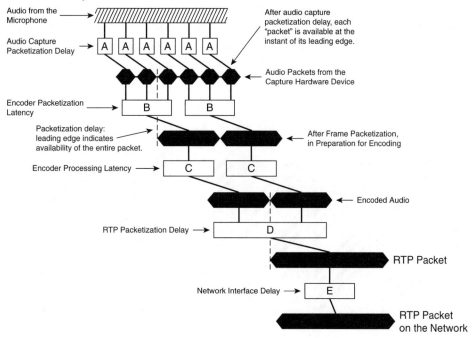

Video Source Format

Most video conferencing endpoints can accept analog video signals from a standard-definition video camera. Three video formats exist:

■ National Television Systems Committee (NTSC), used primarily in North America and Japan

■ Phase-Alternating Line (PAL), used primarily in Europe

■ Séquentiel couleur à mémoire (SECAM), used primarily in France

Many video endpoints can accept either NTSC or PAL formats, whereas SECAM is less well supported. Table 7-1 shows the maximum possible resolution of each format and the frame rate of each.

Table 7-1 *Video Formats*

Format	Usable Video Resolution	Frame Rate
NTSC	640×480	29.97
PAL	720×576	25
SECAM	720×576	25

The vertical resolution of a video frame is measured in *lines of video*, and the horizontal resolution is measured in pixels. Even though the NTSC video signal has a frame rate of 29.97 frames per second, the frame rate is often referred to as *30 FPS* (frames per second). Each of these formats uses a scanning process called *interlacing*, which means that each frame is actually composed of two interlaced fields. Figure 7-6 shows a sequence of interlaced frames for NTSC video.

Figure 7-6   *Interlaced Video Sequence*

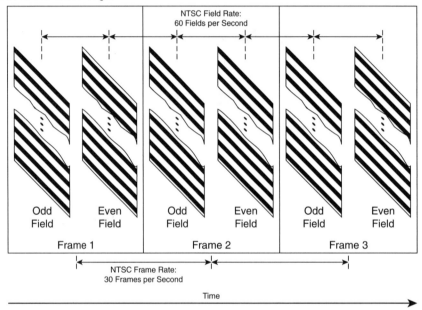

In the sequence, each frame consists of two consecutive fields: The odd field is the first field, and the even field is the second field. The odd field captures every other line of video starting with the first line. The even field captures every other line of video starting with the second line. The field rate is double the frame rate; in this example, the field rate is 60 fields per second. The field that starts with the top line of video in the interlaced frame is often called the top field. The field that ends with the bottom line of video in the interlaced frame is often called the bottom field.

It is important to note that even though a frame is often considered a single entity, it is actually composed of two fields, captured at different points in time, separated by one-sixtieth of a second. When a television displays the video signal, it preserves the one-sixtieth-of-a-second field separation.

Interlacing was adopted as the television standard to satisfy two requirements:

■ The television display must be refreshed faster than 40 times per second to avoid the perception of flicker. This requirement is accomplished with the NTSC field rate of 60 fields per second.

- Bandwidth must be conserved. This requirement is satisfied by transmitting only half the frame content (every other line of video) for each refresh of the television display.

A video endpoint can process standard video for low-resolution or high-resolution conferencing, but the approach taken for each differs significantly.

Low-Resolution Video Input

If the video endpoint is configured to send low-resolution video, the endpoint typically starts with a full-resolution interlaced video sequence and then discards every other field. The resulting video has full resolution in the horizontal direction but half the resolution in the vertical direction, as shown in Table 7-2.

Table 7-2   *Video Formats: Field Sizes*

Format	Usable Field Resolution
NTSC	640×240
PAL	720×288
SECAM	720×288

When capturing from a typical interlaced camera and using only one of the fields, the encoder must always use the same type of field; that is, it must stick to either even fields or odd fields. In the case of NTSC video input, discarding every other field results in video with a resolution of 640×240, at 30 (noninterlaced) FPS. The video endpoint typically scales the video down by a factor of 2 in the horizontal direction to obtain an image with the desired aspect ratio. The resulting video image is considered a frame of video, even though it was derived from a single field.

Alternatively, low-end, PC-based endpoints may use a video signal from a consumer-grade webcam, which might supply a lower-resolution, noninterlaced video signal directly. A common webcam resolution is 320×240 at 15 FPS.

High-Resolution Video Input

Endpoints that intend to use the full resolution available from a standard video camera must use video data from both fields of each frame and therefore must use a video codec that handles interlaced video. When you are using video from an NTSC camera, endpoints that have an interlace-capable codec can support resolutions up to 640×480 at 60 fields per second.

NOTE   Interlaced video can be de-interlaced using complex algorithms that attempt to expand each field into a full-resolution frame. The result is 60 noninterlaced frames per second of full-resolution video. However, this process is not advisable for a video conferencing endpoint because the de-interlacing process doubles the raw video data rate and, therefore, increases the bit rate of the encoded stream. In addition, effective de-interlacing algorithms are highly complex and must intelligently interpolate the values of missing pixels. If the algorithm interpolates new values that do not blend seamlessly with the original pixels, end users will see visual errors or inaccuracies in the display, typically in the form of jagged edges around moving objects. These visual errors are called *artifacts*, and the encoder will have difficulty creating an efficient compressed bitstream.

Sender Video Path

Video capture hardware digitizes each image from the video camera and stores the resulting fields of video in a set of circular frame buffers in memory, as shown in Figure 7-7.

Figure 7-7   *Video Capture Buffering*

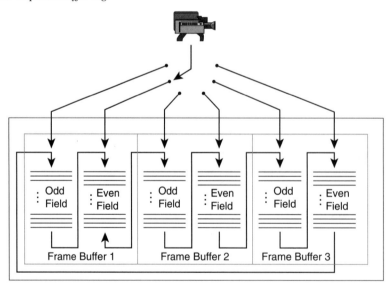

The capture hardware fills the frame buffers in order until it reaches the last buffer, and then it loops back to frame 1, overwriting the data in frame buffer 1. Notice that each frame buffer contains two fields: an odd field and an even field, corresponding to the odd and even field of each frame of interlaced video.

To reduce the capture-to-encode delay, a video encoder may be able to start encoding a new field of video before the capture hardware writes the entire field into memory. Figure 7-8 shows two possible scenarios for sender-side video capture delays.

Figure 7-8   *Sender-Side Video Capture-to-Encode Delays*

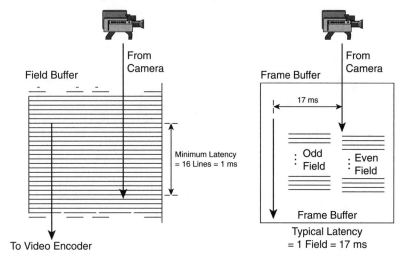

Most video encoders operate on chunks of video data consisting of 16 lines at a time. Therefore, the encoder can provide lower capture-to-encode latency by processing video data after the capture hardware has written 16 lines (of a field) to the frame buffer, corresponding to a latency of 1 ms. However, some video encoders may wait for an entire field of video to fill a frame buffer before beginning the encoding process for that field. In this case, the video capture delay is 1 field of video, corresponding to 17 ms.

A video encoder may encode at a lower resolution and frame rate than the capture hardware. Figure 7-9 shows an encoder that operates at 320×240 resolution, at a nominal frame rate of 30 FPS, by extracting every odd field and scaling it from 640×240 to 320×240; the /2 boxes denote the horizontal scaling.

Figure 7-9 *Encode Process for 30-FPS Video*

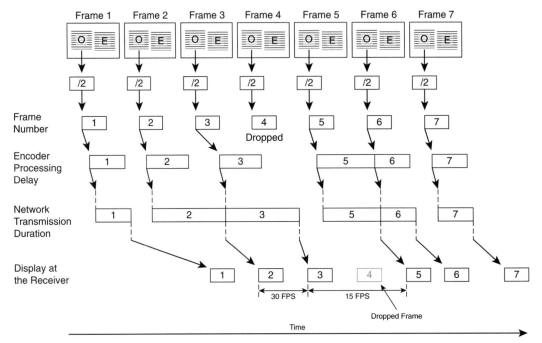

In this scenario, the encoder normally encodes every odd field to achieve 30 FPS. However, if the content of the video changes by a large amount as a result of excessive motion in the video stream, the encoder might fall behind for two reasons:

- The CPU requirements of the encoder might increase, resulting in higher per-frame encoding latency, which might force the encoder to reduce the frame rate.

- The extra motion in the input video might cause the size of the encoded frames to temporarily increase. Larger encoded frames take longer to stream at a constant bit rate, and therefore, the sender might fall behind when attempting to transmit encoded frames onto the network at the real-time rate. In response, the encoder might decide to skip frames to reduce the frame rate. Temporarily pausing the encoding process allows the encoded video bitstream to "drain" out the network interface.

Figure 7-9 shows an example in which larger encoded video frames might cause the bitstream on the network to fall behind the real-time rate. Typically, encoders track the delay from the capture time to the network transmission time; if this delay exceeds a threshold, the encoder begins dropping frames to catch up. Figure 7-9 shows an example in which the encoder falls behind and decides to catch up by dropping the fourth output frame. Encoders routinely trade off between frame rate, quality, and bit rate in this manner.

Two delays exist in the video path on the capture side:

- **Video encoding delay**—The encoding delay is the delay from the time that all data for a frame is captured until the time that the video encoder generates all encoded data for that frame. Video that contains large areas of motion might take longer to encode. In Figure 7-9, the latency of the encoder changes over time. However, despite the time-varying latency of the video encoder, the video stream is reconstructed on the receiver side with original uniform spacing.

- **RTP packetization delay**—The RTP specification determines how the video bitstream must be spliced into RTP packets. Typically, video codecs divide the input image into sections, called *slices,* or groups of block (GOB). The RTP packetization process must splice the encoded bitstream at these boundary points. Therefore, the RTP video packetization must wait for a certain number of whole sections of the video bitstream to arrive to populate an RTP packet. The packetization delay is the time necessary for the packetizer to collect all data necessary to compose an RTP packet.

Understanding the Receive Side

Figure 7-10 shows the receiver-side processing. The audio path consists of the jitter buffer, followed by the audio decoder, followed by the digital-to-analog (D/A) converter. The video path consists of a video decoder, a video buffer, and a video playout device.

Figure 7-10 *Receiver-Side Processing*

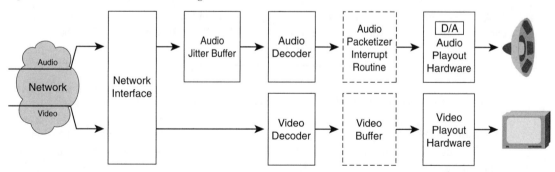

Audio Receiver Path

The receiver requires the jitter buffer in the audio path because packets arriving at the receiver do not have uniform arrival times. The sending endpoint typically sends fixed-sized RTP packets onto the network at uniform intervals, generating a stream with a constant audio bit rate. However, jitter in the network due to transient delays causes nonuniform spacing between packet arrival times at the receiver. If the network imposes a temporary delay on a sequence of several packets, those packets arrive late, causing the jitter buffer on the receive side to decrease. The jitter buffer must be large enough to prevent the buffer from dropping to the point where it underflows. If the jitter buffer underflows, the audio device has no data to play out the audio speakers, and the user hears a glitch.

This scenario, in which the jitter buffer runs out of data for the audio playout device, is called *audio starvation*. Conversely, if the network then transfers these delayed packets in quick succession, the burst of packets causes the jitter buffer to rise back to its normal level quickly.

The jitter buffer absorbs these arrival-time variations; however, the jitter buffer imposes an additional delay in the end-to-end audio pipeline. This delay is equal to the average level of the jitter buffer, measured in milliseconds. Therefore, the goal of the receive endpoint is to establish a jitter buffer with the smallest average latency, which can minimize the probability of an audio packet dropout. The endpoint typically adapts the level of the jitter buffer over time by observing the recent history of jitter and increasing the average buffer level if necessary. In fact, if the jitter buffer underflows and results in a dropped packet, the receiver immediately reestablishes a new jitter buffer with a higher average level to accommodate greater variance.

When the jitter buffer underflows, the audio decoder must come to the rescue and supply a replacement for the missing audio packet. This replacement packet may contain audio silence, or it may contain audio that attempts to conceal the lost packet. Packet loss concealment (PLC) is the process of mitigating the loss of quality resulting from a lost packet. One common form of PLC is to just replay the most recent packet received from the network.

The series of audio processing units—including the input buffer, decoder, and playout device—can be considered a data pipeline, each with its own delay. To establish the initial jitter buffer level, the receiver must "fill the pipe" by filling the entire pipeline on the receive side until the audio "backs up" the pipeline to the input buffers and achieves the desired input buffer level.

In addition, the jitter buffer can provide the delay necessary to re-sort out-of-order packets.

The audio decode delay is analogous to the corresponding audio encoding delay on the sending side. The audio hardware playout delay on the receiver is analogous to the audio hardware capture delay on the sender.

Figure 7-11 shows a graphical depiction of the delays on the receive side. When the receiver depacketizes a large packet into smaller packets, no delay results. The reason is because the receiver does not need to wait for successive packets of data to arrive, because depacketization does not perform an aggregation process. Such is the typical case when the receiver depacketizes the RTP packet into audio frames, and again when the decoded audio goes through the depacketization process to be sliced into yet smaller audio device packets for the audio hardware device.

Figure 7-11 *Receive-Side Audio Processing Delays*

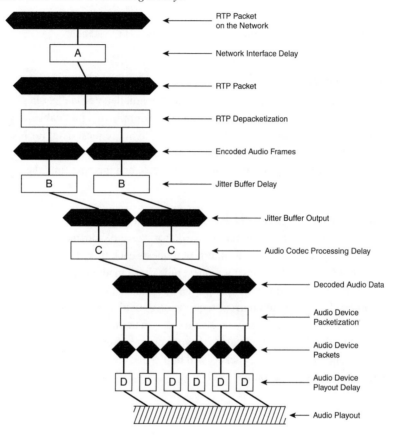

Receiver Video Path

The receiver has several delays in the video path:

■ **The packetization delay**—This latency might be required if the video decoder needs access to more than one slice (or group of blocks) to start the decoding process. However, video conferencing endpoints typically use a low-latency bitstream that allows endpoints to decode a slice without needing to use information from other slices. In this case, the input video packetization process simply reformats the video packet and does not perform any type of packet aggregation, and therefore, this packetization process imposes no delay on the video path.

- **The decode delay**—Analogous to the audio decode delay, it reconstructs slices of the video frame.

- **The synchronization delay**—If necessary, the receiver may impose a delay on the video frames to achieve synchronization.

- **The playout delay**—After the endpoint writes a new decoded video frame into memory, the playout delay is the time until that frame displays on the screen.

Types of Playout Devices

Playout devices come in two types: malleable and nonmalleable. Malleable playout devices can play a media sample on command, at any time. An example of a malleable playout device is a video display monitor. Typically, malleable devices do not request data; for instance, a receiver can send a video frame directly to the display device, and the device immediately writes the frame into video memory. The video frame appears on the screen the next time the TV raster scans the screen.

In contrast, nonmalleable devices always consume data at a constant rate. The audio playout device is an example: The receiver must move data to the audio device at exactly the real-time rate. Nonmalleable devices typically issue interrupt requests each time they must receive new data, and the receiver must service the interrupt request quickly to maintain a constant data rate to the device. After the receiver sends the first packet of audio to the audio device, the audio device typically proceeds to generate interrupt requests on a regular basis to acquire a constant stream of audio data. Audio devices generally receive fixed-size audio device packets of data at each interrupt, and professional audio interfaces can support buffer sizes as low as 64 samples. At 44.1 kHz and a 64-sample buffer size, packets will be 1.5 ms, and the audio device will generate about 689 interrupt requests per second.

RTP

The RTP specification RFC 3550 describes how senders can packetize and transmit media to receivers over the network. Using RTP packets alone, receivers can reconstruct and play audio and video streams from a sender and maintain continuous, glitch-free playback. However, to synchronize separate streams, senders and receivers must use RTCP packets, too. This section covers RTP packets for the purposes of unsynchronized stream playback, and the next section covers RTCP packets for the purposes of adding lip sync.

Canonical RTP Model

Figure 7-12 shows the canonical RTP/RTCP model for a video/audio sender and receiver.

Figure 7-12   *Canonical RTP/RTCP Model*

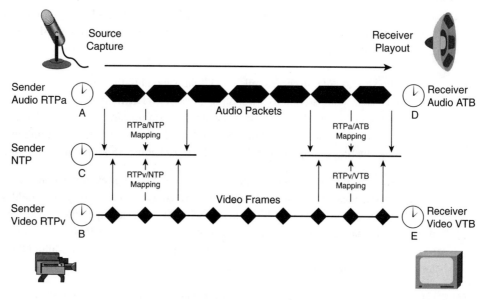

Figure 7-12 shows five different clocks.

At the sender

■   Clock A, used by the audio capture hardware to sample audio data

■   Clock B, used by the video capture hardware to sample video data

■   Clock C, the "common timebase" clock at the sender, used for the purposes of stream synchronization with RTCP packets

At the receiver

■   Clock D, the clock used by the audio playout hardware to play audio data

■   Clock E, the clock used by the video display hardware to display video data

A separate crystal oscillator drives each clock, which means that none of the clocks are synchronized to each other. In most video conferencing systems, the sender audio clock also provides the common timebase clock; however, this example considers the most general case, in which they differ.

RTP Time Stamps

Each capture device (microphone and video capture hardware) has a clock that provides the RTP time stamps for its media stream. The units for the RTP time stamps depend on whether the media stream is audio or video:

- For the audio stream, RTP uses a sample clock that is equal to the audio sample rate. For example, an 8-kHz audio stream uses a sample clock of 8 kHz. In this case, RTP time stamps for audio are actually *sample stamps*, because the time stamp can be considered a sample index. If an RTP packet has a time stamp of 0 and contains 300 samples, assuming the audio is continuous, the time stamp of the following RTP packet has an RTP time stamp of 300.

- For video streams, RTP uses a sample clock equal to 90 kHz. For example, consider an endpoint that encodes a 25-FPS video sequence, derived by encoding every other field of PAL video: If a video frame consists of RTP packets with RTP time stamp 0, the next video frame consists of RTP packets with an RTP time stamp of $1/25 \times 90000 = 3600$. The sender may split a large encoded video frame into multiple RTP packets, in which case all RTP packets belonging to the same frame have the same RTP time stamp.

Remember that the RTP time stamps for the video stream and the audio stream are not related to each other. In particular, keep the following in mind:

- The video and audio RTP time stamps do not begin transmission with the same RTP time stamp. According to the RTP specification, the sender must use a randomly selected beginning RTP time stamp for each stream to avoid known-value decryption attacks in case the endpoints encrypt the streams.

- The crystal clocks on the audio capture hardware and video capture hardware are different (and therefore, unsynchronized).

Because the crystal clocks used for audio and video may differ, these clocks might drift past each other. Crystal clocks typically have an accuracy of ± 100 parts per million (ppm). As an example of clock drift, consider the following worst-case scenario:

- If the audio clock is running at a frequency –100 ppm away from its nominal frequency, it is running .1 percent too slowly.

- If the video clock is running at a frequency +100 ppm away from its nominal frequency, it is running .1 percent too fast.

In this example, the timebase of the video clock is fast relative to the timebase of the audio. Figure 7-13 shows how the timebases will crawl past each other over time.

Figure 7-13   *Clock Crawl for Nonsynchronized Clocks*

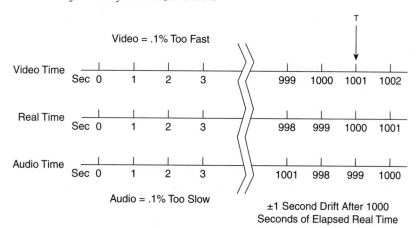

In Figure 7-13, time T corresponds to a real-world time span of 1000 seconds. At this point in time, the audio timebase provides a reading of 999 seconds, and the video timebase provides a reading of 1001 seconds. Although a drift of ± 0.1 percent might not seem like much, it can grow over time; if this drift is not taken into account, these streams will play 2 seconds out of sync on the receive endpoint after a duration of 1000 seconds. A robust conferencing system must ensure long-term lip sync, ideally with a skew of <20 ms between audio and video presentation times.

Because RTP time stamps in the video and audio streams are not directly related to each other, a receiver cannot determine how to synchronize RTP audio and video streams by looking at RTP packets alone.

To provide the receiver with enough information to synchronize audio and video, the receiver must be able to map the RTP time stamps from each stream into a common timebase. The RTCP protocol (discussed later) provides this functionality.

Using RTP for Buffer-Level Management

Using only RTP packets without RTCP packets, receivers can establish buffer-level management. Receivers must establish an audio jitter buffer level that corresponds to the minimum level required to absorb network jitter to prevent a nonmalleable device from starving. Then, during the video conference, receivers must monitor the short-term average jitter buffer level to ensure that it is large enough to absorb arrival-time variations of the currently observed network jitter. In addition to short-term swings, the average buffer level may slowly rise or fall over a long period of time because of differences in the exact frequencies of crystal clocks at the sender and receiver, in which case the receiver must intervene. Buffer-level management is the process of maintaining a relatively constant average jitter buffer level in the face of both short-term variance in the packet arrival times and long-term drift from mismatched sender and receiver clocks.

To achieve buffer-level management, receivers first establish a relationship between incoming RTP packets and the audio device timebase of the receiver as follows:

$$ATBout = RTPin + Krl$$

RTPin represents the RTP time stamp of the incoming packet, and ATBout represents the time stamp in the audio device timebase of the receiver. The audio device timebase of the receiver is defined by the audio device playout clock. Krl is an offset, chosen by the receiver, that maps one timebase into another. Both the RTP time stamp and the audio device timebase are in the same units, equal to the sample rate of the audio stream.

The audio playout device on the receiver typically operates using a pull model: After the receiver activates the audio device, the audio device starts issuing continual interrupt requests for data. The receiver responds to each interrupt by transferring data to the audio device. In this model, the audio playout device generates an interrupt to ask for audio and specifies the audio device time ATBout at which the audio must play. The receiver then uses Krl to calculate the corresponding RTPin RTP time stamp. The receiver must supply this data by retrieving it from the decoder, which in turn retrieves it from the jitter buffer. The value of Krl therefore enforces a mapping from RTP time stamp to audio device timebase, and the receiver must comply with this mapping.

The receiver establishes the value of Krl when the first RTP packet arrives. At this time, the receiver assigns a preliminary mapping from the RTP time stamp of the packet to the audio device timebase (ATB) of the receiver. This mapping achieves buffer management but not synchronization; the receiver must add delay to either the video or audio streams (discussed later) to achieve lip sync.

The receiver establishes the minimum Krl offset needed to satisfy jitter buffer level requirements. After the receiver selects Krl, it can set in motion the data pipeline for the audio stream.

The equation to calculate Krl uses several delay values, all of which are in units of the audio sample rate:

■ The current level of the jitter buffer is A. A will be nonzero if RTP packets have arrived before the receiver decides on a value of Krl.

■ The required nominal jitter buffer level is B.

■ The playout hardware delay is C.

■ The current audio device timebase time is D.

■ The RTP time stamp of the first RTP packet is RTPin1.

The RTP time stamp RTPin1 of the first RTP packet should be mapped to an audio device time ATB1 of

$$ATB1 = D + (B - A) + C$$

In other words, starting from the time right now, the stream must wait until its input buffer rises from its current level A to the desired nominal jitter buffer level B, which takes $(B - A)$ units. The number of audio samples $(B - A)$ represents the time during which the receiver "primes the input pipe" by filling the jitter buffer, which feeds the audio playout device. The $(B - A)$ offset is required because the receive endpoint should not start playing audio through the audio playout device until the jitter buffer has achieved its nominal level. Alternatively, the receiver can supply initial silence audio to the audio playout device to quickly set the jitter buffer to its nominal level.

The receive endpoint estimates a desired value for B, based on the expected characteristics of the network packet jitter. A higher level of network jitter requires a larger input jitter buffer.

If more data has arrived than is needed to fill the jitter buffer to the required level, $(B - A)$ will be negative. A negative value for $(B - A)$ means that a portion of audio data at the beginning of the transmission must be discarded to reduce the jitter buffer to its nominal value.

The receiver logic must also take into account a delay of C through the playout hardware. For the audio playout device, the delay consists of the latency from the time the receiver passes a media packet to the playout hardware until the time the playout hardware passes the data to the D/A converter.

The preliminary offset Krl used for this mapping is as follows:

$$Krl = ATB1 - RTPin1 =$$
$$D + (B - A) + C - RTPin1$$

The receiver now uses this value of Krl to map input RTP time stamps to time stamps in the audio device timebase. The receiver might need to change the level of the input buffer over time by changing the value of Krl. However, changing Krl causes the audio stream going to the playout device to be discontinuous. If the receiver increases Krl, the result is a gap in the audio stream, because the next packet plays at a later-than-normal time, and an intervening gap occurs; by default, the audio playout device is likely to fill this gap with silence. If the receiver decreases Krl, the result is an overlap in samples between the previous and next packet, which requires duplicate samples to be discarded. Gaps or discarded samples result in a glitch in the audio stream. However, the receiver can use two methods to change Krl while preventing an objectionable glitch:

■   The receiver can scale (stretch) the incoming audio data up or down by a small amount so that listeners will not notice the change. When decoded data is scaled up, the data rate entering the receiver effectively increases, and the jitter buffer level increases over time. The opposite effect occurs if the receiver scales down the input data. This method can be used to slowly change the jitter buffer level.

- The receiver can wait for a duration of silence in the audio stream and then change Krl, which has the effect of increasing or decreasing the duration of silence. Listeners will not notice this change in the silence interval. This method can be used to abruptly change the jitter buffer level.

If the receiver does not require media synchronization, the only task left for the receiver is to manage the buffer level over time. The receiver can create a similar pipeline for video and perform the same type of buffer management. However, the video stream has the benefit of being a malleable medium, so the value of Krl can be changed on-the-fly without an objectionable glitch in the output. Another difference between the audio and video paths is this: The receiver typically measures the local video device timebase in units of seconds, instead of the RTP sample rate of 90 kHz.

Correlating Timebases Using RTCP

The RTCP protocol specifies the use of RTCP packets to provide information that allows the sender to map the RTP domain of each stream into a common reference timebase on the sender, called the Network Time Protocol (NTP) time. NTP time is also referred to as *wall clock time* because it is the common timebase used for all media transmitted by a sending endpoint. NTP is just a clock measured in seconds.

RTCP uses a separate wall clock because the sender may synchronize any combination of media streams, and therefore it might be inconvenient to favor any one stream as the reference timebase. For instance, a sender might transmit three video streams, all of which must be synchronized, but with no accompanying audio stream. In practice, most video conferencing endpoints send a single audio and video stream and often reuse the audio sample clock to derive the NTP wall clock. However, this generalized discussion assumes that the wall clock is separate from the capture clocks.

NTP

The wall clock, which provides the master reference for the streams on the sender endpoint, is in units of NTP time. However, it is important to bear in mind what NTP time *is* and what NTP time *is not*:

- NTP time as defined in the RTP specification is nothing more than a data format consisting of a 64-bit double word: The top 32 bits represent seconds, and the bottom 32 bits represent fractions of a second. The NTP time stamp can therefore represent time values to an accuracy of ± 0.1 nanoseconds (ns).

- The most widespread misconception related to the RTCP protocol is that it requires the use of an NTP time server to generate the NTP clock of the sender. An NTP time server provides a service over the network that allows clients to synchronize their clocks to the time server.

The time server specifies that NTP time should measure the number of seconds that have elapsed since January 1, 1970. However, NTP time as defined in the RTP spec does not require the use of an NTP time server. It is possible for RTP implementations to use an NTP time server to provide a reference timebase, but this usage is not necessary and is out of scope of the RTP specification. Indeed, most video conferencing implementations do not use an NTP time server as the source of the NTP wall clock.

> **NOTE**   In the RTP/RTCP protocol, the "NTP time" does not need to come from an NTP time server; the sender can generate it directly from any reference clock. Often, the sender reuses the audio capture clock as the basis for the NTP time.

Forming RTCP Packets

Each RTP stream has an associated RTCP packet stream, and the sender transmits an RTCP packet once every few seconds, according to a formula given in RFC 3550. As a result, RTCP packets consume a small amount of bandwidth compared to the RTP media stream.

For each RTP stream, the sender issues RTCP packets at regular intervals, and those packets contain a pair of time stamps: an NTP time stamp, and the corresponding RTP time stamp associated with that RTP stream. This pair of time stamps communicates the relationship between the NTP time and RTP time for each media stream. The sender calculates the relationship between its NTP timebase and the RTP media stream by observing the value of the RTP media capture clock and the NTP wall clock in real time. The clocks have both an offset and a scale relationship, according to the following equation:

$$\text{RTP}/(\text{RTP sample rate}) = (\text{NTP} + \text{offset}) \times \text{scale}$$

After determining this relationship by calculating the offset and scale values, the sender creates the RTCP packet in two steps:

1. The sender first selects an NTP time stamp for the RTCP packet. The sender must calculate this time stamp carefully, because the time stamp must correspond to the real-time value of the NTP clock when the RTCP packet appears on the network. In other words, the sender must predict the precise time at which the RTCP packet will appear on the network and then use the corresponding NTP clock time as the value that will appear inside the RTCP packet. To perform this calculation, the sender must anticipate the network interface delay.

2. After the sender determines the NTP time stamp for the RTCP packet, the sender calculates the corresponding RTP time stamp from the preceding relationship as follows:

$$\text{RTP} = ((\text{NTP} + \text{offset}) \times \text{scale}) \times \text{sample\_rate}$$

The sender can now transmit the RTCP packet with the proper NTP and RTP time stamps.

Determining the values of offset and scale is nontrivial because the sender must figure out the NTP and RTP time stamps at the moment the capture sensor (microphone or camera) captures the data. For instance, to determine the exact point in time when the capture device samples the audio, the sender might need to take into account delays in the capture hardware. Typically, the audio capture device makes a new packet of audio data available to the main processor and then triggers an interrupt to allow the processor to retrieve the packet. When the sender processes an interrupt, the sender must calculate the NTP time of the first sample in each audio packet, corresponding to the moment in time when the sample entered the microphone. One method of calculating this time is by observing the time of the NTP wall clock and then subtracting the predicted latency through the audio capture hardware. However, a better way to map the captured samples to NTP time is for the capture device to provide two features:

■ A way for the sender to read the device clock of the capture device in real time, and therefore correlate the capture device clock to NTP wall clock time.

■ A way for the sender to correlate samples in the captured data to the capture device clock. The capture device can provide this functionality by adding its own capture device time stamp to each chunk of audio data.

From these two features, the sender can correlate audio samples to NTP wall clock time. The sender can then establish the relationship between NTP time and RTP time stamps by assigning RTP time stamps to the data.

The same principles apply to the video capture device. The sender must correlate a frame of video to the NTP time at which the camera CCD imager captures each field. The sender establishes the RTP/NTP mapping for the video stream by assigning RTP values to the video frames.

NOTE The Microsoft DirectX streaming technology used for capture devices defines *source filters*, which are capture drivers that generate packets of captured data, along with time stamps. Hardware vendors write source filters for their capture hardware. Applications that use these source filters rely entirely on the source filters to provide data with accurate time stamps. If a source filter provides output streams for audio and video, it is critical that the source filter use kernel-level routines to ensure that the time stamps on the packets accurately reflect the time at which the hardware samples the media.

Using RTCP for Media Synchronization

The method of synchronizing audio and video is to consider the audio stream the master and to delay the video as necessary to achieve lip sync. However, this scheme has one wrinkle: If video arrives later than audio, the audio stream, not the video stream, must be delayed. In this case, audio is still considered the master; however, the receiver must first add latency to the audio jitter buffer to make the audio "the most delayed stream" and to ensure that synchronization can be achieved by delaying video, not audio.

In addition, the receiver must determine a relationship between the local audio device timebase ATB and the local video device timebase VTB on the receiver by calculating an offset AtoV:

$$VTB = ATB/(\text{audio sample rate}) + AtoV$$

This equation converts the local audio device timebase ATB into units of seconds by dividing the audio device time stamp by the audio sample rate. The receiver determines the offset AtoV by simultaneously observing Vtime, the value of the real-time video device clock, and Atime, the value of the real-time audio device clock. Then

$$AtoV = Vtime - ATime/(\text{audio sample rate})$$

Now that the receiver knows AtoV, it can establish the final mapping for synchronization.

NOTE The Microsoft DirectX streaming technology used for playout devices defines *render filters*, which are essentially playback drivers that accept packets of data with time stamps that are relative to a global system time. The render filters play the media at the time indicated on the time stamp. Hardware vendors write filters for their playout hardware. Applications that use these render filters rely entirely on the render filters to play data accurately, based on the time stamps. A DirectX streaming render filter provides input connections in the form of input pins. If a render filter provides input pins for audio and video, it is critical that the render filter use kernel-level procedures to ensure that the time at which the hardware displays the media is accurately reflected by the time stamp on the packet.

To establish this mapping, two criteria must be met:

■ At least one RTP packet must arrive from each stream.

■ The receiver must receive at least one RTCP packet for each stream, to associate each RTP timebase with the common NTP timebase of the sender.

For this method, the audio is the master stream, and the video is the slave stream. The general approach is for the receiver to maintain buffer-level management for the audio stream and to adapt the playout of the video stream by transforming the video RTP time stamp to a video device time stamp that properly slaves to the audio stream.

When a video frame arrives at the receiver with an RTP time stamp RTPv, the receiver maps the RTP time stamp RTPv to the video device time stamp VTB using four steps, as illustrated in Figure 7-14.

Figure 7-14 *Audio and Video Synchronization*

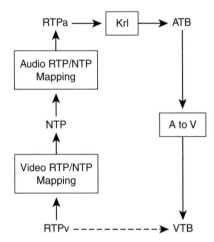

This sequence of steps maps the RTP video time stamp into the audio RTP timebase and then back into the video device timebase. The receiver follows these steps in order:

1. Map the video RTP time stamp RTPv into the sender NTP time domain, using the mapping established by the RTP/NTP time stamp pairs in the video RTCP packets.

2. From this NTP time stamp, calculate the corresponding audio RTP time stamp from the sender using the mapping established by the RTP/NTP time stamp pairs in the audio RTCP packets. At this point, the video RTP time stamp is mapped into the audio RTP timebase.

3. From this audio RTP time stamp, calculate the corresponding time stamp in the audio device timebase by using the Krl offset. The result is a time stamp in the audio device timebase ATB.

4. From ATB, calculate the corresponding time stamp in the video device timebase VTB using the offset AtoV.

The receiver now ensures that the video frame with RTP time stamp RTPv will play on the video presentation device at the calculated local video device timebase VTB.

Lip Sync Policy

The receiver may decide not to attempt to achieve lip sync for synchronized audio and video streams in certain circumstances, even if lip sync is possible. There are two scenarios in which this situation might occur:

■ **Excessive audio delay**—If the receiver must delay audio to establish lip sync, the receiver might instead choose to achieve the lower audio latency of unsynchronized streams. The reason is because lower end-to-end audio latency achieves the best real-time interaction. The receiver can make this determination after it achieves buffer management for both audio and video streams. If the audio stream is the most-delayed stream, the receiver can opt to delay the video stream to achieve lip sync; if the video stream is the most-delayed stream, however, the receiver might opt to avoid delaying audio to achieve lip sync.

- **Excessive video delay**—If the receiver must delay video by a significant duration to achieve lip sync, on the order of a second or more, the receiver might need to store a large amount of video bitstream in a delay buffer. For high bit rate video streams, the amount of memory required to store this video data might exceed the available memory in the receiver. In this case, the receiver may opt to set an upper limit on the maximum delay of the video stream to accommodate the limited memory or forego video delay altogether.

Summary

This chapter covered several fundamental elements of a system that accurately achieves lip sync. The most important concept is this: The lip sync algorithm must depend on an absolute timebase instead of compensating for individual delays in the end-to-end path. To effectively use the NTP timebase as an absolute reference, the sender must establish accurate mappings between the NTP time and RTP media time stamps by sending RTCP packets for each media stream. The operation of the receiver consists of two phases: first, establishing buffer-level management for audio and video streams using only RTP time stamps, and then using NTP time to achieve synchronization. By maintaining absolute time references at both sender and receiver, audio and video remain in sync, even in the presence of variable delays in the end-to-end path.

References

ATSC Implementation Subcommittee Finding: "Relative Timing of Sound and Vision for Broadcast Operations," Document IS-191 of the ATSC (Advanced Television Systems Committee), June 2003. www.atsc.org/standards/is_191.pdf

Blakowski and Steinmetz, "A Media Synchronization Survey: Reference Model, Specification, and Case Studies," *IEEE Journal on Selected Areas in Communications*, Vol. 14, No. 1, January 1996.

Schulzrinne, H., S. Casner, R. Frederick, and V. Jacobson. IETF RFC 3550, *RTP: A Transport Protocol for Real-Time Applications*. July 2003.

This chapter covers the following topics:

- Security fundamentals

- Threats

- Configuring basic security

- Port usage

- NAT and PAT

- Encryption basics

- IPsec and TLS for secure signaling

- Media encryption

- H.323 encryption: H.235

- SIP encryption

CHAPTER **8**

Security Design in Conferencing

This chapter identifies security threats affecting video conferencing deployments and then recommends methods of protecting video communication from these attacks. To be most effective, a video deployment requires several layers of security to protect against internal and external threats.

However, some layers of the security infrastructure can interfere with video conferencing protocols and prevent those protocols from establishing a connection to endpoints in other enterprises over the public Internet. This chapter describes this issue, known as *Network Address Translation (NAT)/firewall traversal.*

Finally, the last part of the chapter describes how video endpoints may use standard methods of cryptography to prevent eavesdropping.

Security Fundamentals

When the term *security* comes up, most people think of encryption. However, security encompasses several important areas of protection. These areas of protection roughly comprise six groups:

- Confidentiality

- Availability

- Authentication

- Identity

- Authorization

- Integrity

Confidentiality between a sender and a receiver means that only the sender and receiver can interpret the data. Two endpoints achieve confidentiality using encryption. To establish an encrypted link, the sender and receiver exchange a cryptographic key in a secure manner, and then each side uses the key to encrypt or decrypt the data stream.

Availability ensures that infrastructure resources are protected from resource depletion from an attacker. Availability requires protection against denial-of-service (DoS) attacks.

Authentication and identity often describe the same concept and may mean two things:

- An endpoint can authenticate data to prove that the data is valid. An endpoint can authenticate data without authenticating identity. A section later in this chapter reveals how cryptographic hashes can authenticate data.

- An endpoint can authenticate its identity by presenting cryptographic credentials that prove its identity. As explained later in this chapter, the participants in the connection use either preshared secrets or cryptographic certificates to establish identity.

Authorization is not to be confused with authentication. Authorization maps the authenticated identity (an endpoint or user) to a set of permissions or capabilities allowed for that user. Secure video conferencing systems often implement authentication and authorization with an AAA (authentication, authorization, and accounting) server such as RADIUS.

Integrity allows a receiver to detect whether an attacker has tampered with data while in transit on the network. One of the ways for an endpoint to provide integrity for a data packet is to authenticate the contents of the entire data packet.

Threats

Without measures to ensure the six fundamental security protections, the network infrastructure and endpoints are open to threats from attackers. This section describes several types of threats and actions you can take to mitigate those threats.

Confidentiality Attacks

Without confidentiality, an attacker can listen to the audio and video streams between two endpoints. Hacker tools are available on the Internet for eavesdropping on voice packet data. One of these tools is called *VOMIT* (Voice Over Misconfigured IP Telephony). VOMIT processes a stream of captured voice packets and plays the audio.

Solution: Apply encryption to the media packets. Vendors of conferencing products are universally adopting the Advanced Encryption Standard (AES) to encrypt media streams. In IP networks, Voice over IP (VoIP) gear typically uses the Real-time Transport Protocol (RTP) to transmit media streams. Secure Real-time Transport Protocol (SRTP) is an extension of RTP that encrypts media streams, defined in IETF standard RFC 3711. See the "Media Encryption" section later in this chapter for details.

Denial-of-Service Attacks

Attacks on availability are called *denial-of-service* (DoS) *attacks*. A DoS attack is any attack that disrupts the availability of service to legitimate users and can take several forms:

- Depletion of network bandwidth

- Depletion of server resources

- Replay attacks

- Malware

- Connection hijacking

- RTP hijacking

The following sections describe each of these DoS attacks in more detail.

Depletion of Network Bandwidth

Depletion of network bandwidth attacks involve flooding the host network with enough data to clog the ingress/egress points in the enterprise network. These attacks appear primarily as a flood of UDP packets. Often, these attacks are launched from a large number of external endpoints on the public Internet, in which case they are referred to as *distributed denial-of-service* (DDoS) *attacks*.

Solution 1: When a flood attack overwhelms the bandwidth of the connection that links a service provider to an enterprise, the only way to stop the attack is to discard attack packets in the service provider. Service providers typically perform this type of packet shunning with an anomaly detector device and a guard device. The anomaly detector identifies potential attack traffic and instructs the guard to scrub the traffic. The guard pinpoints and discards attack packets before they reach the enterprise network. The Cisco Anomaly Detector product and Cisco Guard product are examples of these devices.

Solution 2: Routers and switches can implement bandwidth rate limiting. Cisco routers and switches offer a feature called *microflow policing* to limit the bandwidth of data from an attacker. Enterprises use microflow policing to protect server infrastructure, such as a scheduling server, H.323 gatekeeper, Session Initiation Protocol (SIP) proxy, or CallManager. However, this bandwidth-limiting protection is most effective if it is deployed with two strategies:

- Place a router with microflow policing close to the attacker, such as at the edge of a network. At this location, it is easier for the policing feature to identify attackers.

■ Distribute the microflow policing at several ingress points of the network. A distributed deployment can more easily block a high-bandwidth attack, while at the same time allowing legitimate users to gain access to the resource.

Depletion of Server Resources

DoS attacks do not always involve depleting the bandwidth on a link; instead, DoS attacks can attempt to deplete resources inside a server or endpoint. In certain cases, servers allocate resources when they receive a packet from the network, and the attacker might seek to exhaust these resources by sending a flood of packets to the victim machine. The classic resource depletion attack is the SYN attack, which exploits the TCP protocol. In the TCP protocol, an endpoint requests a TCP connection with a target server by first sending a SYN (synchronize) packet to the server, as shown in Figure 8-1.

Figure 8-1 *Normal TCP Connection Establishment*

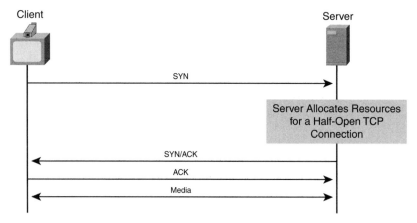

The server allocates resources for the TCP connection and then attempts to complete the TCP protocol by sending a response in the opposite direction, consisting of a SYN/ACK packet. The SYN/ACK packet requests a connection with the endpoint and acknowledges receiving the SYN packet. Normally, the client responds with an ACK packet, which acknowledges the SYN/ACK from the server, and the TCP connection can proceed. However, in a SYN attack, the attacking endpoint does not respond with the final ACK, and the connection at the server eventually times out. However, by sending a flood of SYN packets, the attacking endpoint can overload the target machine with resources allocated for these half-open TCP connections.

Solution: A firewall placed in front of the server can implement SYN cookies, as shown in Figure 8-2.

Figure 8-2   *DoS Protection with a SYN Cookie Firewall*

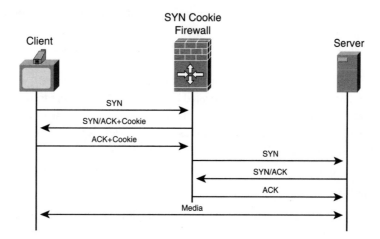

The firewall intercepts the SYN packet and replies directly with a response containing a cookie value. If the originator is valid, the originator sends a final response back to the firewall, along with the cookie. This mechanism is also called *TCP intercept* because the firewall intercepts the TCP setup messages. The firewall does not retain any state for the half-open connection; instead, the firewall uses the cookie to validate the parameters that arrive in the response from the originating endpoint. When the firewall receives the ACK from the client, the firewall validates the cookie and then allows the connection. The firewall then replays the TCP connection handshake sequence to the server. Using this method, the firewall and the protected server do not store state information about half-open TCP connections. Firewalls or intrusion prevention systems typically implement this functionality; however, hosts may implement SYN cookies directly, too.

Replay Attacks

Another attack that can cause disruption is the replay attack. The attacker begins by sniffing and recording the packets flowing on the network between two entities during a legitimate connection. The attacker then replays these packets to one of the endpoints. The target endpoint may consider this replayed stream to be legitimate and attempt to process the data, resulting in excessive resource consumption.

Solution: Endpoints thwart a replay attack by using cryptographic authentication, along with a time stamp or sequence number. The receiver verifies the authentication and then verifies that the time stamp or sequence number is valid.

Malware

Malware is any type of data that can compromise an endpoint or server. A worm is a type of malware that consists of network packets that cause a server to execute a program. When the worm is running on the machine, the worm can take over the server and cause it to fail.

Solution: Endpoints or servers can use an intrusion prevention system (IPS), which is a standalone network device that identifies malware located in packets and then discards the packets before they reach a host. A host-based IPS (HIPS) is a software-based IPS that resides on the server itself, usually at the kernel level. The HIPS identities malware packets and discards them before a running process receives them.

Connection Hijacking

After two video conferencing endpoints establish a legitimate connection, an attacker might attempt to hijack the connection by impersonating one of the participants by issuing signaling commands to take over the conversation. The attacker might also use this type of spoofing to cause the connection to fail, in which case the attack is also considered a DoS attack.

Solution: Endpoints can thwart connection hijacking by authenticating the signaling messages.

RTP Hijacking

Whereas connection hijacking is a method that attempts to take over the signaling layer of a conversation, RTP hijacking operates at the media layer and is an attempt by an intruder to inject RTP media packets into a conversation. The intruder essentially becomes an additional, unwanted participant.

Solution: Endpoints can thwart RTP hijacking by authenticating the media packets.

Authentication and Identity Attacks

Attackers may compromise authentication or identity to exploit theft of service or man-in-the-middle (MitM) attacks.

Theft of Service

By compromising identity, attackers can perpetrate theft of service or toll fraud. As you learned in the "Connection Hijacking" section, an attacker can impersonate another user and then take over an existing connection. An attacker may also steal services by spoofing another endpoint directly and then attempting a direct connection.

Solution: Authenticate signaling packets and use cryptographic identity.

Man-in-the-Middle Attacks

A MitM attack occurs when an attacker inserts a rogue device between two connected endpoints. The MitM can then listen to packets that flow between the endpoints and can modify packets in transit. The MitM is invisible to the two endpoints, which are unaware of the attack. One way for an attacker to become a MitM is to spoof the identity of each endpoint to the other. Figure 8-3 shows this scenario.

Figure 8-3   *A Man-in-the-Middle Attack Between Two Endpoints*

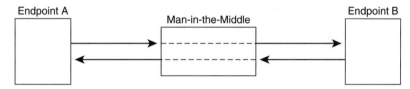

The attacker connects to endpoint A and pretends to be endpoint B, and then connects to endpoint B and pretends to be endpoint A. The MitM acts as a router and can observe packets flowing between endpoints A and B, without either endpoint knowing about the attack. This attack can also work if both endpoints use encryption, without authentication; in this case, the MitM sets up an encrypted link with each endpoint. The MitM can decrypt and then re-encrypt each packet that passes through it. The MitM can also inject data into the media stream or change the media stream.

Solution: Use authentication and integrity for each signaling message and media packet.

Network Infrastructure Attacks

In a video conferencing deployment, security of the underlying network infrastructure is just as important as the security applied to the upper-layer conferencing protocols. Network security protects against several attacks, including the following:

- Reconnaissance

- Layer 2 attacks

- Content-addressable memory (CAM) table flooding

- Address Resolution Protocol (ARP) cache poisoning

- Dynamic Host Configuration Protocol (DHCP) exhaustion

- Rogue DHCP servers

The following sections describe each of these network infrastructure attacks.

Reconnaissance

One vulnerability often overlooked is reconnaissance. Before an attacker attempts to compromise a network, the attacker often gathers as much information about the network as possible. Attackers can attempt to use network-scanning tools to obtain the following information:

- The network topology

- The list of services running on each server

- The ports on each server that are open and active

- The model of hardware running each server

- The version of software running on each server

Solution: Firewalls prevent attackers on the outside of the firewall from using network-scanning tools to probe the infrastructure on the inside of the firewall.

Layer 2 Attacks

Several attacks are possible at Layer 2, the Ethernet link layer. These attacks often require the attacker to have direct access to the internal network. Layer 2 attacks are extremely virulent because after an attacker compromises Layer 2, all layers above Layer 2 might not detect the attack.

Solution: Add security at Layer 2 within the network. A deployment that implements Layer 2 protection inside the network and Layer 3 firewall protections at the edge achieves layered security. An enterprise that has only firewalls at the edge is considered to be "crunchy on the outside, soft on the inside." This weakness means that an attacker who penetrates beyond the firewalls at the edge can easily compromise targets inside the network. Layer 2 protections inside the network result in security that is "crunchy on the inside."

CAM Table Flooding

One Layer 2 exploit is a content-addressable memory (CAM) table flood, which allows an attacker to make a switch act like a hub. A hub forwards all packets to all ports. A switch learns about Ethernet MAC addresses at each of its ports so that it can forward packets only to the port that provides a link to the destination address of the packet. In a heavily switched environment, an attacker receives only packets destined for the attacker. By exploiting a CAM table flood, the attacker can cause the switch to forward all packets to all destinations, allowing the attacker to sniff all traffic.

The mapping of each MAC address to each physical port is contained in the CAM table within the switch. However, the CAM table has a limited number of entries, which means an attacker can cause the table to overflow by sending the switch a flood of Ethernet packets containing random spoofed source addresses. As a result, the switch might discard old, but valid, entries from the table to accommodate the flood of new mappings from the hacker. In this attack mode, the hacker causes the switch to "push out" valid CAM table entries. When a switch attempts to forward a packet, if the MAC address of the packet is not in the CAM table, the switch acts like a hub and forwards the packet to all ports on the switch. Attackers can use CAM table flooding to force a switch to act like a hub, allowing the attacker to sniff packets that would normally go only to a different port.

Solution: Port security is a feature on Cisco switches that limits the number of allowable source MAC addresses per port. Port security can statically assign a list of MAC addresses per port, or it can limit the total number of MAC addresses allowed per port.

ARP Cache Poisoning

When a host attempts to send a packet to an IP address on the same subnet, the originating host must discover the Ethernet MAC address corresponding to the destination IP address. The originating host learns about this mapping by issuing an ARP request packet, which requests the MAC address used by the destination IP address. The destination machine receives this request and responds with an ARP reply that contains the MAC address. The originating host caches this IP-to-MAC address mapping into its local ARP cache. All hosts listen to all ARP reply messages to build up a table of IP/MAC addresses over time. However, at any time, an attacker can issue a gratuitous ARP reply. A *gratuitous ARP reply* is an ARP reply without an originating ARP request. Machines on the subnet often store the IP-to-MAC mapping for this gratuitous ARP reply in their ARP cache. As a result, an attacker can issue a gratuitous ARP reply that maps the IP address of a victim to the MAC address of the attacker, which causes any packets intended for the victim to instead go to the attacker. The attacker can then become a MitM by forwarding this packet traffic to the victim.

Solution: Cisco switches implement a feature called *Dynamic ARP Inspection* (DAI). DAI drops ARP replies if the MAC address in the ARP reply does not match the IP address assigned earlier via DHCP. This feature relies on the capability of Cisco switches to snoop DHCP requests and therefore protects only endpoints that obtain an IP address via DHCP.

DHCP Exhaustion

DHCP exhaustion is a Layer 2 attack that also implements a DoS. An attacker sends a flood of DHCP request packets to the DHCP server, each requesting an IP address for a random MAC address. Eventually, the DHCP server runs out of available IP addresses and stops issuing DHCP bindings. This failure means that other hosts on the network cannot obtain a DHCP lease, which causes a DoS.

Solution: Cisco switches implement a feature called *DHCP snooping*, which places a rate limit on DHCP requests.

Rogue DHCP Servers

DHCP servers can provide not only addresses, but also a wide range of information that endpoints may use. This information includes default DNS servers and a default gateway. An attacker can set up a rogue DHCP server on a subnet to provide bad configuration information to an endpoint. Thus, by using a rogue DHCP server, the attacker can virtually reconfigure endpoints that use DHCP parameters.

Solution: Cisco DHCP snooping also provides a feature that drops DHCP request packets sent to unauthorized DHCP servers, which prevents rogue DHCP servers from issuing DHCP leases.

Endpoint Infrastructure Attacks

Video conferencing endpoints are directly vulnerable to several attacks:

- Desktop endpoint attacks

- Firmware attacks

- Rogue configuration file attacks

The next sections describe each of these attacks.

Desktop Endpoint Attacks

Desktop video conferencing systems that run on PCs are vulnerable to operating system–based exploits:

- As mentioned in the section "Malware," a worm can execute a program on a vulnerable machine, causing a DoS attack.

- As mentioned in the section "Denial of Service," an attacker can attempt to flood a PC with packets that consume resources.

Solution: A HIPS running on the PC can mitigate operating system vulnerabilities.

Firmware Attacks

Some appliance-based video conferencing endpoints run firmware that users can upgrade. Whenever this upgrade feature is present, there is always a possibility that an attacker could attempt to load a rogue firmware image onto the endpoint. For example, an attacker could attempt to download an older firmware image onto the endpoint that does not have newer security protections.

Solution: Endpoints should load only cryptographically signed firmware, which the endpoint vendor authenticates using a cryptographic hash. The "Secure Hashes" section later in this chapter discusses cryptographic hashes.

Rogue Configuration Files

In addition to firmware upgrades, endpoints may also be vulnerable to rogue configuration files. For example, when a Cisco IP phone boots up, it downloads a configuration file from a TFTP server. This configuration file points the IP phone to a list of trusted CallManagers. By compromising this file, an attacker can direct an IP phone to use a rogue CallManager server.

Solution: The endpoint should use only cryptographically signed configuration files. For instance, the configuration file downloaded by a Cisco IP phone is cryptographically signed to prevent forgery.

Server Attacks

Within a video conferencing deployment, servers may run on PCs. These servers may consist of video conference schedulers, H.323 gatekeepers, SIP proxies, video switches, or CallManager servers. Much like the PC-based endpoints, the operating system on these servers is vulnerable to attack. In addition, these servers often represent a single point of failure, which makes them targets for DoS attacks.

General Port-Based Attacks

Much like PC-based endpoints, servers require protection to thwart network port-based attacks such as malware and DoS attacks.

Solution: You can mitigate against port-based attacks as follows:

- Use HIPS to detect attacks on the machine.

- Install a virus scanner on the server.

- Place a firewall in front of the server. In addition to typical firewall access control lists (ACLs), the administrator can configure the firewall to allow only call control traffic to the servers. Typically, UDP-oriented media traffic does not flow to the servers; that traffic flows only from endpoint to endpoint.

■ Activate rate limiting and microflow policing on the routers and switches that connect to the servers. These rate-limiting features are more effective when placed near potential attackers, such as at the edges of the network; this placement allows legitimate users to connect to the servers, even in the presence of a high-bandwidth DoS attack.

Web Server Vulnerabilities

Video conferencing servers, such as H.323 gatekeepers and SIP proxy servers, often host a web server to provide a user interface. This user interface typically provides two important functions:

■ It allows the administrator to configure the device.

■ It allows users to join conferences and view the status of conferences in progress.

However, web servers in general have a higher level of susceptibility to attack than other services, for two reasons. For the web server to operate properly, firewalls allow external users to send high-bandwidth packet streams to the web server on port 80. Hackers can leverage this open port to take advantage of newly discovered flaws that compromise security.

Also, server machines often use two popular web services: Apache and Microsoft Internet Information Service (IIS). Because these web servers are so common, hackers target these services in an attempt to find new vulnerabilities that might not be detected by a firewall or HIPS.

Solution: The web server should offer strong confidentiality and authentication. The HTTPS protocol provides this mechanism by verifying identity, typically using digital certificates (discussed in the "Public Key Cryptography" section later in the chapter) and by encrypting the communications. Two weaker alternatives exist for authentication:

■ **Basic authentication**—This method challenges the user with a username and password. However, basic authentication requires the user to send a password unencrypted, and therefore it is inherently insecure. Basic authentication does not encrypt the communications.

■ **HTTP-Digest**—This method challenges the user with a username and password and protects the password using a hashing mechanism (discussed in the "Secure Hashes" section of this chapter). This method is more secure than basic authentication. HTTP-Digest only provides authentication; it does not encrypt the communication link.

Unneeded Services and Insecure Services

The operating system of the server may run additional services, such as an FTP server, Telnet server, TFTP server, and so on. Each of these services opens an active port on the machine. Every active open port represents an additional threat because it provides yet another way for an attacker to compromise the machine.

In addition, some services such as FTP and Telnet are inherently insecure because they send passwords over the network unencrypted, in the clear.

Solution: Harden the operating system by turning off unneeded services that might open ports on the server machine. In particular, enterprise networks should adopt a policy of disallowing inherently insecure services such as FTP and Telnet.

Configuring Basic Security

Figure 8-4 shows a general configuration for video conferencing security. This configuration involves layers of security, with protection both at the edges of the network and inside the network.

Figure 8-4   *Basic Configuration for Video Conferencing Security*

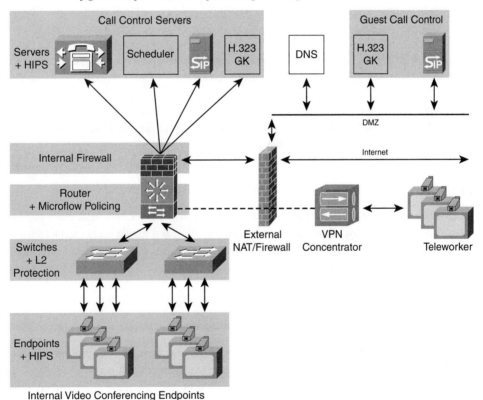

This topology shows a three-legged firewall. The firewall has connections for the enterprise, the Internet, and a demilitarized zone (DMZ). The DMZ contains servers that are accessible by both the internal network and the public Internet. These servers consist of authoritative DNS servers and call control servers that allow endpoints on the public Internet to connect to endpoints inside the enterprise. The firewall has a relatively loose set of rules to allow internal and external endpoints to connect to servers in the DMZ, but it has a stricter set of rules that protects the interior of the enterprise network from both the DMZ and the public Internet.

In addition, the firewall connection for the inner enterprise network also runs a Network Address Translation (NAT) device. The NAT translates private IP addresses inside the enterprise to public addresses routable on the public Internet. The ability for endpoints inside the network to connect to endpoints outside the network through the NAT and firewall is called *NAT/firewall traversal*, often abbreviated as NAT/FW. NAT/FW traversal can pose a problem for video conferencing protocols, as you learn later in the "NAT/FW Traversal" section.

The enterprise also has a VPN concentrator that allows remote workers or small remote branch offices to connect through a firewall. Tunneling authenticated virtual private network (VPN) streams from teleworkers through a firewall requires a simple firewall configuration and is highly secure.

Also shown in Figure 8-4 is Layer 2 protection in the form of port security, dynamic ARP inspection, and DHCP snooping, all of which are features of Cisco switches.

The configuration shows three layers of protection for the call control servers: firewalls to allow only call control traffic, microflow policing on the routers to prevent DoS attacks, and a HIPS located on each of the servers to further protect against malware.

Port Usage

Firewalls are designed to block unsolicited signaling and media packets from the outside network. However, firewalls must allow traffic on certain signaling and media ports used by video conferencing gear, and administrators must configure firewalls to open these ports. Therefore, this section covers the ports used by the protocols H.323, SIP, and Skinny Client Control Protocol (SCCP).

H.323 Port Usage

H.323 is a complex protocol that has evolved over time to allow several variations of connection establishment; these variations use different message sequences and ports. In addition, some messages can use either UDP or TCP ports. Certain messages use fixed ports, and other messages may use arbitrary ports negotiated between the endpoints.

H.323 Call Flow

Figure 8-5 shows the call flows for H.323. This diagram shows the original simple call flow specified in H.323v1.

Figure 8-5   *Call Flows for H.323v1*

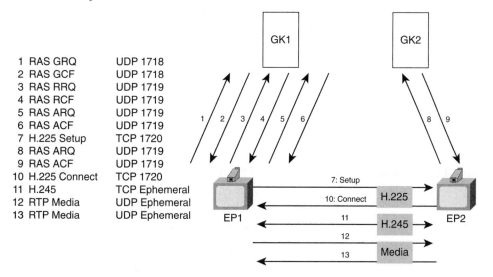

1	RAS GRQ	UDP 1718
2	RAS GCF	UDP 1718
3	RAS RRQ	UDP 1719
4	RAS RCF	UDP 1719
5	RAS ARQ	UDP 1719
6	RAS ACF	UDP 1719
7	H.225 Setup	TCP 1720
8	RAS ARQ	UDP 1719
9	RAS ACF	UDP 1719
10	H.225 Connect	TCP 1720
11	H.245	TCP Ephemeral
12	RTP Media	UDP Ephemeral
13	RTP Media	UDP Ephemeral

The basic H.323v1 case includes the following call flow:

1. EP1 and the gatekeeper use the Registration, Admission, Status (RAS) protocol to pass high-level connection commands. To discover a gatekeeper on the network, endpoints send the RAS Gatekeeper Request Message (GRQ) to UDP multicast address 224.0.1.41, on port 1718. In the process of defining the H.323 specification, the H.323 standards committee registered port 1718 with the Internet Assigned Numbers Authority (IANA) to be the default port for gatekeeper discovery.

2. Gatekeepers respond by sending a Gatekeeper Confirm (GCF) message to UDP port 1718. After the endpoint locates a gatekeeper, all further RAS messages switch over to use the IANA-registered UDP port 1719.

3. The endpoint EP1 registers with its gatekeeper GK1 by sending the RAS Registration Request (RRQ) message to the gatekeeper.

4. The gatekeeper responds with a RAS Registration Confirm (RCF) message.

5. When endpoint EP1 initiates a call, it sends a RAS Admission Request (ARQ) message to the gatekeeper to ask permission to connect to a remote endpoint.

6. Based on locally configured policy, GK1 responds with a RAS Admission Confirm (ACF) message.

7. EP1 establishes an H.225 connection to EP2 using TCP port 1720. Two endpoints use H.225 to establish a control signaling connection. Because EP1 and EP2 establish direct H.225 links, this mode of H.323 signaling is known as the *direct signaling mode*. EP1 sends an H.225 Setup message to EP2, requesting a connection.

8. Before EP2 can complete the connection with a response, it must obtain permission to connect to EP1 by sending a RAS Admission Request (ARQ) message to its local gatekeeper GK2.

9. If GK2 allows the connection based on locally configured policy, it replies with an ACF message.

10. EP2 then replies to EP1 by sending EP1 an H.225 Connect message to confirm the connection. In addition, EP1 and EP2 use H.225 to negotiate a port for a new H.245 connection. Because the endpoints negotiate this port at connection time, the port is referred to as an *ephemeral port* and may have a value in the range 1024–65,535.

11. EP1 and EP2 then establish an H.245 TCP connection, which they use for low-level signaling. H.245 has no default port and may use any port between 1024 and 65,535, negotiated using the previous H.225 exchange. EP1 and EP2 then exchange H.245 messages, which in turn negotiate the UDP ports to use for RTP and RTCP traffic. RTP and RTCP have no default ports and may use any ephemeral port number between 1024 and 65,535. The endpoints may send additional H.225 or H.245 messages.

12. EP1 may now send RTP media to EP2.

13. EP2 may now send RTP media to EP1.

Figure 8-6 shows a more advanced call flow from H.323v4 that permits some of the signaling to use a single port.

Figure 8-6 *Call Flows for H.323v4*

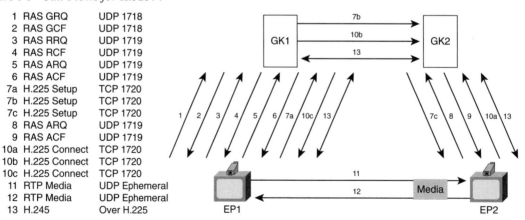

H.323v4 simplifies the firewall configuration for H.323 endpoint communication by offering a variation of H.323 that tunnels H.245 over an existing open connection:

■   Instead of using the direct signaling mode, this call model uses the Gatekeeper-Routed Call Signaling (GKRCS) mode. In this mode, the H.225 messages pass through the gatekeepers, instead of going directly between EP1 and EP2.

■   If endpoints use GKRCS, they may still create direct H.245 connections. However, this example shows a capability of H.323v4 called the *Fast Connect method*. Fast Connect sends H.245 information within the H.225 Setup and Connect messages.

■   Even if the endpoints use Fast Connect, they may still establish direct H.245 connections. However, Figure 8-6 shows a mode known as *H.245 tunneling*: After the initial connection setup is complete, the endpoints tunnel future H.245 messages over the H.225 connection.

H.323 Port Summary

Based on the port usage of H.323, Tables 8-1 and 8-2 list the port configurations needed for a simple firewall configuration for H.323.

Table 8-1 shows the port usage necessary to support four major data streams: RAS, H.225, H.245, and RTP/RTCP.

Table 8-1   *H.323v1 Port Usage*

Function	Port	Transport Type
Gatekeeper discovery	Port 1718	UDP
Gatekeeper RAS	Port 1719	UDP
H.225	Port 1720	TCP
H.245	Ephemeral port: 1024–65,535	UDP
RTP and RTCP	Ephemeral port: 1024–65,535	UDP

Table 8-2 shows the port usage necessary to support Fast Connect with three major data streams: RAS, H.225, and RTP/RTCP. In this scenario, endpoints tunnel H.245 messages over the H.225 connection.

Table 8-2 *H.323v4 Port Usage: Fast Connect + H.245 Tunneling*

Function	Port	Transport Type
Gatekeeper discovery	Port 1718	UDP
Gatekeeper RAS	Port 1719	UDP
H.225	Port 1720	TCP
RTP and RTCP	Ephemeral port: 1024–65,535	UDP

Tables 8-1 and 8-2 present a significant problem: A firewall must keep a large range of UDP ports open for the RTP, RTCP, and H.245 packets, which negates the purpose of a firewall. Instead, most firewalls implement a feature called *Application Layer Gateway* (ALG). In this mode, the firewall inspects the H.323 signaling, snoops the negotiated ephemeral ports, and opens pinholes in the firewall for ephemeral ports used by H.245 (when not tunneled) and RTP/RTCP data. The firewall is stateful because it keeps track of the status of the connection: As soon as the signaling channel (H.225) closes the connection, the firewall closes the pinholes for the other ephemeral ports.

The firewall also implements a timeout: If no media or signaling traverses the firewall for a time period longer than a timeout value, the firewall closes the pinholes.

The firewall must understand all variations of a signaling protocol and must receive updates each time the standard protocol changes or adds new capabilities. Because the firewall is designed to work with any type of H.323 endpoint, the firewall must be constantly tested with many different H.323 endpoint brands, models, and versions. In addition, the firewall must be tested with conference bridges, which use the same signaling as endpoints.

If an ALG firewall is in place, and endpoints use the GKRCS and tunneled mode of H.323, administrators need to statically open only UDP ports 1718, 1719, and 1720; the ALG snoops the signaling and opens other ephemeral ports as needed. In addition, the administrator must statically open port 1718 only between the endpoint and the GK; not between the two endpoints.

H.323 endpoints offering encryption almost always use the H.235 standard. The simpler, more widely adopted version of H.235 encrypts the media packets, but not the signaling. Because the signaling is still in the clear, the firewall can snoop the signaling and open pinholes as necessary.

In cases in which a firewall cannot implement an H.323 ALG, a simpler firewall setup may be used, called a *UDP ALG firewall*, or simply a *stateful firewall*. In this mode of operation, the administrator statically opens the fixed signaling ports and lets the firewall dynamically open media ports as needed. One side of the firewall is considered trusted; the other side is considered untrusted. When a device on the trusted side of the firewall sends a UDP media packet to a destination address and port on the untrusted side, the firewall automatically opens a pinhole for UDP media to flow in the reverse direction; this open port is often referred to as a *reverse pinhole*. The destination port number of this newly opened reverse pinhole is always the same as the source port number of the original outgoing connection. Because endpoints typically set the source port equal to the destination port, the reverse pinhole is also the same as the destination port of the outgoing message.

This constraint means that the return flow of packets from the untrusted side of the firewall to the trusted side must use a destination port number that is the same as the source port number used by the sender on the trusted side of the firewall.

This type of firewall ALG is often called a *symmetric pinhole* or a *bidirectional pinhole*. When both endpoints in a video conference use identical port values, the endpoints are said to use symmetric ports. H.323 does not mandate the use of symmetric ports, but most H.323 endpoints follow this convention to traverse UDP ALG firewalls. One of the downsides of using a UDP ALG is that RTP media from the untrusted endpoint are not permitted through the firewall until the trusted endpoint sends RTP media out through the firewall. If the trusted endpoint delays sending RTP media, the inbound media might be clipped if the firewall drops early inbound packets. To facilitate firewall traversal, the endpoint on the trusted side should immediately send media packets to open the reverse pinhole for the external endpoint.

For TCP connections, the firewall allows bidirectional TCP connections that originate from the endpoint on the trusted side of the firewall.

SIP Port Usage

Firewall configuration for SIP is rather simple: Port 5060 (UDP or TCP) carries the SIP signaling. The SIP signaling protocol negotiates the media ports for RTP and RTCP, which are UDP ports in the range of 1024 to 65,535. A firewall with a SIP ALG snoops the signaling and opens the media ports.

However, a SIP ALG does not work with secure SIP. Secure SIP establishes an encrypted signaling channel using Transport Layer Security (TLS) over TCP port 5061. When two endpoints connect using encrypted signaling, the firewall cannot snoop the signaling and must rely on the UDP ALG trusted/untrusted model to open bidirectional reverse pinholes for the UDP media packets.

SCCP Port Usage

SCCP signaling is similar to SIP: The Cisco SCCP protocol uses port 2000 for signaling, and the signaling messages negotiate the media ports for RTP. Cisco firewalls provide ALGs for SCCP. For RTP media, Cisco IP phones use ephemeral UDP ports ranging from 16,384 to 32,768.

The secure SCCP protocol sends signaling messages over an encrypted TLS tunnel on port 2443. In this case, the firewall must use a UDP ALG to open bidirectional reverse pinholes for RTP media.

Preset Port Numbers

Some video conferencing endpoints allow preset port values, which allow the user/administrator to configure the endpoints to use only a small set of fixed port numbers to carry the RTP media. Endpoints often make this feature available in the advanced section of the endpoint user interface. The endpoints use this set of ports when negotiating the ephemeral port number. The administrator can then configure the firewall to permanently allow traffic on this small set of static ports. However, this approach leaves the network open to vulnerabilities if attackers exploit the permanently open ports.

NAT and PAT

Firewalls at the edges of an enterprise often include functionality called *Network Address Translation* (NAT). One variant of NAT is Port Address Translation (PAT); however, both functions are often generically lumped together as NATP or simply NAT.

The NAT functionality is often part of the firewall and is therefore sometimes referred to as a NAT/FW. The NAT device translates the private IP addresses inside the enterprise into public IP addresses visible on the public Internet. Endpoints inside the enterprise are internal endpoints, and endpoints in the public Internet are external endpoints. For example, devices inside the enterprise might have private IP addresses in the form 10.0.x.x. When a device inside the enterprise connects out through the NAT, the NAT dynamically assigns a public IP address in the form 128.56.74.x. This public IP address is referred to as the *public mapped address* or the *reflexive transport address*. When the NAT forwards this packet to a device on the public Internet, the packet appears to come from 128.56.74.x. When external devices send packets back to the NAT at address 128.56.74.x, the NAT translates the IP addresses back to the internal private addresses and then forwards the packet to the internal network.

PAT is a variant of NAT. In this scenario, the NAT reuses the same external mapped address for multiple internal endpoints but varies the source port to differentiate among the data streams. PAT has the same considerations as NAT.

NATs offer several capabilities:

- NATs map a large set of internal, private IP addresses into a smaller set of external, public IP addresses. The current public IPv4 address space is limited, and until IPv6 emerges as a ubiquitous protocol, most enterprises will have a limited number of IPv4 public addresses available. The NAT allows an enterprise with a large number of endpoints to make use of a small pool of public IP addresses. The NAT implements this functionality by dynamically mapping an internal IP address to an external IP address at the time an internal endpoint makes a connection out through the NAT. Each of these mappings is called a *NAT binding*.

■ NATs provide topology hiding. Because of the address mapping, entities on the public Internet are unaware of the internal, private IP addresses inside the enterprise; external endpoints see only the public mapped source address of a packet.

■ In addition, some NATs can use a different mapping each time a device inside the enterprise makes an outgoing connection to a different external endpoint. In this case, the NAT may provide a different public-to-private mapping for the duration of the new connection, which means that an internal endpoint appears to have two different public IP addresses at the same time, one for each external endpoint. Such obfuscation helps thwart attackers trying to perform reconnaissance.

In addition, a NAT has a notion of trusted and untrusted interfaces, much like a firewall: The NAT creates a binding only if a device on the inside of the enterprise sends a packet to an address on the public Internet. After the NAT creates this binding, it opens a reverse pinhole that allows the device on the public Internet to send packets back to the device on the inside of the NAT. The binding times out after the internal endpoint discontinues sending data for a certain period of time. The binding remains open only if the device on the inside of the NAT continually sends packet out through the NAT to the external endpoint on the public Internet.

NAT Classifications

A NAT is classified by two attributes:

■ **Mapping characteristics**—How the NAT allocates a new external mapped address/port for an internal private address/port

■ **Filtering characteristics**—How the NAT determines whether to forward a packet from the public address space to the private address space after the NAT creates a binding

For any of these mapping characteristics and filtering modes, the following sequence of events occurs to create a NAT binding:

1. An internal endpoint with source address Ai uses a source port Pi to send a packet to an external endpoint. The combination of source address and port is denoted using the notation Ai:Pi.

2. In response to this packet, the NAT sets up a binding and creates an external public mapped address Am and source port Pm for the internal endpoint. This combination of mapped address and port is denoted using the notation Am:Pm.

3. For each UDP or TCP packet, the NAT replaces the private source address Ai:Pi in the packet with the mapped address Am:Pm before forwarding the packet to the external destination.

NAT Mapping Characteristics

The mapping characteristic of a NAT describes how the NAT allocates external addresses Am:Pm, based on the internal source address Ai:Pi. The NAT may implement two main types of mapping:

■ Endpoint-independent mapping

■ Endpoint-dependent mapping

The internal endpoint may send packets with source address Ai:Pi to multiple external endpoints, each with different addresses.

Figure 8-7 shows a NAT that implements endpoint-independent mapping. In this case, the NAT uses the same external mapped address Am:Pm for packets destined for different external endpoints.

Figure 8-7 *Endpoint-Independent Mapping*

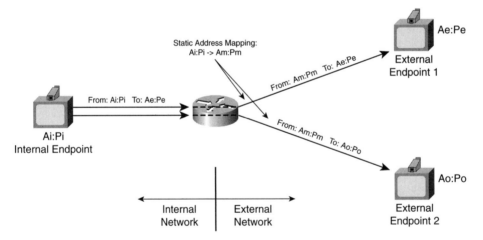

In contrast, Figure 8-8 shows a NAT that implements endpoint-dependent mapping; the NAT allocates different addresses Am1:Pm1 and Am2:Pm2 for different destination endpoints.

Figure 8-8 *Endpoint-Dependent Mapping*

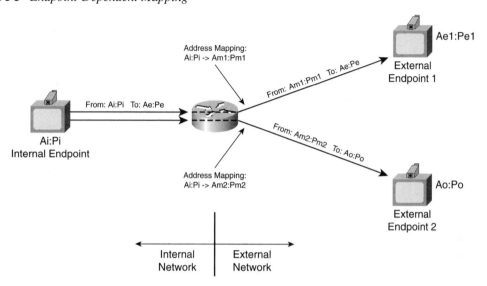

NATs that implement endpoint-independent mapping have an advantage in a video conferencing environment. A later section in the chapter, "STUN," describes how an internal endpoint can determine its public mapped address by communicating with a special server in the public address space called a *STUN server*. After discovering this public address, the internal endpoint can use it when communicating with other public endpoints, but only if the NAT implements endpoint-independent mapping.

NAT Filtering Characteristics

In addition to the mapping characteristics of a NAT, the other quality is the filtering mechanism, which determines whether a NAT allows an inbound packet to traverse the NAT. NATs may display three main types of filtering characteristics:

■ Endpoint-independent filtering

■ Address-dependent filtering

■ Address- and port-dependent filtering

Endpoint-Independent Filtering

Figure 8-9 shows a NAT that uses endpoint-independent filtering.

Figure 8-9 *Endpoint-Independent Filtering*

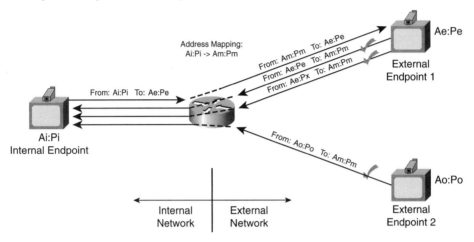

Figure 8-9 includes the following addresses that appear on the internal private network:

- **Ai:Pi**—The source address:port of packets from the internal endpoint

- **Ae:Pe**—The destination address:port of packets from the internal endpoint

Figure 8-9 also includes the following addresses that appear on the public network:

- **Am:Pm**—The source address:port of packets from the NAT to endpoints on the public Internet.

- **Ae:Pe**—The source address:port of packets from the external Endpoint 1 to the NAT. This source address:port uses a port Pe that is the same as the port Pe used as the destination for packets from the NAT to external Endpoint 1.

- **Ae:Px**—The source address:port of packets from the external Endpoint 1 to the NAT. This source address:port uses a port Px that differs from the port Pe used as the destination for packets from the NAT to external Endpoint 1.

- **Ao:Po**—The source address:port of packets from the external Endpoint 2 to the NAT.

When the NAT receives a packet with source address:port Ai:Pi and destination address:port Ae:Pe, the NAT creates a public mapped address Am:Pm. The NAT uses Am:Pm as the source address for the packets forwarded through the NAT to the public address space. After the NAT creates the binding, it forwards a packet from the external network to the internal network if the packet meets one condition: The destination address:port of the packet must be Am:Pm.

This mode has the fewest restrictions. After an internal endpoint sends a packet out through the NAT, any external endpoint can use that binding, because the return packet using that binding may have any source address:port.

Address-Dependent Filtering

Figure 8-10 shows a NAT that implements address-dependent filtering. This type of NAT is also referred to simply as a *restricted NAT*. Figure 8-10 uses the same address:port examples as Figure 8-9.

Figure 8-10 *Address-Dependent Filtering*

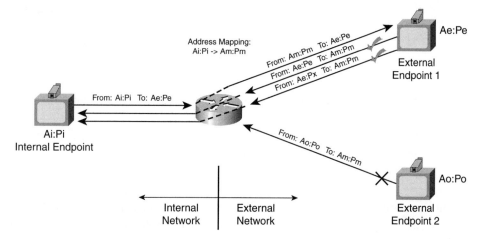

The internal endpoint with source address Ai:Pi sends a packet to an external endpoint with destination address Ae:Pe. The NAT creates a public mapped address Am:Pm. In addition, after the NAT creates this binding, the NAT forwards a packet from the external network to the internal network if

■   The source address of the packet is Ae. However, the source port can be any port.

■   The destination address:port of the packet is Am:Pm.

In this mode, only the external endpoint that received an outbound packet may send a packet back to the internal endpoint. However, the external endpoint can send a packet from any of its source ports.

Address- and Port-Dependent Filtering

Figure 8-11 shows a NAT that implements address- and port-dependent filtering.

Figure 8-11 *Address- and Port-Dependent Filtering*

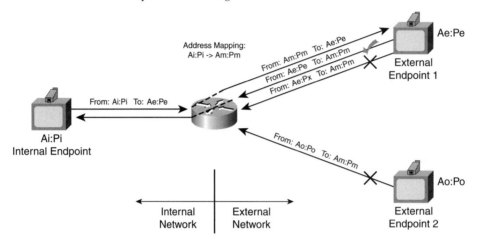

After the NAT creates the binding, it forwards a packet from the external network to the internal network if

■ The source address:port of the packet is Ae:Pe

■ The destination address:port of the packet is Am:Pm

In this case, only the endpoint that received the packet can send a packet back to the internal network, and the packet must have a source port equal to the destination port of the external endpoint.

The Symmetric NAT

A symmetric NAT implements a particular combination of mapping and filtering: endpoint-dependent mapping, along with address- and port-dependent filtering. Figure 8-12 shows a symmetric NAT.

Figure 8-12 *Symmetric NAT*

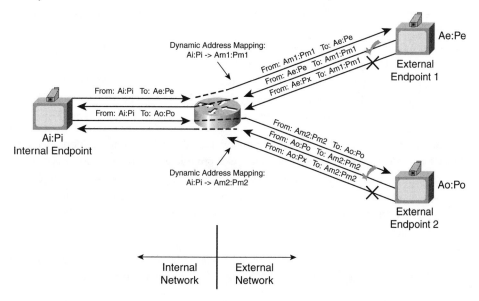

Instead of allocating a static mapped address:port for each unique internal endpoint, the NAT allocates a unique Am:Pm for bindings created by packets with different external destination addresses, even when the packets come from the same internal endpoint. In the figure, the two external mapped address consist of the following:

■ **Am1:Pm1**—The source address:port of packets from the NAT to Endpoint 1 on the public Internet

■ **Am2:Pm2**—The source address:port of packets from the NAT to Endpoint 2 on the public Internet

In addition, the NAT forwards a packet from external to internal networks only if it meets the following criteria:

■ The source address:port of the packet is the same as the original destination of the packet that created the binding.

■ The destination address:port of the packet is the public mapped address associated with the external endpoint.

Most large businesses use symmetric NATs, which have the most restrictive policy.

NAT Complications for VoIP Protocols

NAT presents multiple problems for video conferencing and VoIP protocols, such as the following:

■ External endpoints cannot connect to an internal endpoint in the private address space until the internal endpoint creates a NAT binding by sending packets to the external endpoint. In other words, internal endpoints may not receive unsolicited connections. Of course, this restriction may be considered a security feature. However, one of the goals of NAT traversal is to allow authorized external endpoints to connect to internal endpoints.

■ Several of the video conferencing protocols include source addresses/ports in the protocol signaling messages. These source addresses provide the destination addresses that remote endpoints should use for return packets. However, internal endpoints use addresses from the private address space, and a NAT without an ALG does not alter these internal addresses. When the remote endpoint receives a message, it cannot route packets to the private IP address in the message.

■ NAT bindings time out when the internal endpoint fails to send a packet through the NAT before the NAT timeout expires. Some NATs enforce timeouts as short as one minute.

■ NATs allow secure TLS signaling to traverse through them. However, NATs may have problems with IPsec. IPsec is a protocol that encrypts packets at the IP layer. Native IPsec tunnels cannot traverse a NAT because IPsec requires IP addresses and ports in the IP header to stay the same. To allow IPsec to traverse a NAT, endpoints must tunnel the IPsec packets over UDP. This method of NAT traversal is NAT-T (NAT-Traversal in the IKE). RFC 3947 defines the key exchange method, and RFC 3948 defines the method of UDP encapsulation. Administrators can configure this mode of NAT tunneling, but it requires more configuration management overhead.

■ If two endpoints are behind the same NAT, most commercially available NATs do not allow each endpoint to make a hairpin connection out the NAT and then back into the NAT to the other endpoint. In this scenario, the endpoints must recognize that they are on the same private LAN and use private addresses to establish a direct connection, instead of connecting out the NAT and using public addresses.

In addition, when two endpoints in different enterprises are each behind their own NAT, unusual corner cases may result. Figure 8-13 shows a scenario in which each endpoint has the same private IP address of 10.0.1.1. If these endpoints were to exchange messages containing internal private addresses, they would each attempt to use a remote destination address equal to their own address.

Figure 8-13   *Two Endpoints in Different Enterprises, Each Behind a NAT*

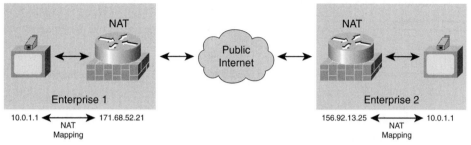

NAT ALGs

In addition to mapping the IP addresses in the IP packet headers, NATs may use ALGs to inspect IP addresses/ports inside the protocol headers of signaling messages, and map them as well. A NAT ALG is similar to a firewall ALG, but a NAT ALG actually changes (maps) the addresses/ports in the signaling messages. This address rewrite is called a *fixup* or a *deep-packet rewrite*. Much like firewall ALGs, NAT ALGs suffer from the following problems:

■   The administrator must be sure to upgrade the NAT firmware to understand the latest version of video conferencing protocols.

■   The NAT cannot inspect the contents of encrypted signaling messages. Whereas a firewall can use a UDP ALG as a workaround for encrypted signaling, a NAT that attempts to pass encrypted signaling has no similar workaround. Because the NAT cannot rewrite the addresses in the protocol message, the signaling protocol breaks. One way around this problem is discussed later, in a scenario in which each endpoint discovers its public mapped address and performs the fixup directly.

NAT/FW Traversal Solutions

NAT/FW traversal refers to the capability of video conferencing endpoints to connect to each other across NATs and firewalls. Because firewalls often include NAT capability, the term *firewall traversal* also applies to NAT/FW traversal. Solutions for firewall traversal should ideally satisfy several requirements:

■   One requirement of a firewall traversal solution is simplicity. If a traversal solution requires a special firewall configuration, the firewall configuration must be as simple as possible. Ideally, any special firewall configuration should be limited to opening only a single port on the firewall. Complex firewall configurations for firewall traversal are difficult to manage and do not scale.

- The traversal solution should allow authorized endpoints on the public Internet to make unsolicited calls to endpoints in the private address space inside the network.

- A NAT/FW traversal scheme should work for symmetric NATs, the most restrictive type of NAT.

- The solution should work for NAT/FWs configured with short timeouts for NAT bindings and ALG pinhole lifetimes.

- If endpoints do not encrypt the call control signaling, the firewall should inspect the signaling to provide two features:

    — By inspecting the signaling, the firewall can implement an ALG. The firewall ALG opens pinholes for the media ports.

    — Many enterprises insist that a firewall should be able to inspect any signaling protocols that pass into or out of the organization to apply security policy to the packets. If a firewall cannot inspect data in a packet, the packet is said to contain opaque data. Opaque data includes protocols the firewall does not understand, as well as encrypted data. Every opaque or encrypted data stream that tunnels out through the firewall is a potential security risk because advanced attack tools that infiltrate an enterprise may use encrypted tunnels to transfer information between the public Internet and the internal network.

- If video conferencing endpoints use encrypted signaling, the firewall cannot inspect the signaling, and the firewall traversal scheme must work in the absence of a protocol-specific ALG.

- Ideally, firewall traversal should not require modification to existing endpoints. Modifications to endpoints may be acceptable in the long term if vendors widely adopt them as standards.

- Ideally, the firewall traversal scheme should not require proxy devices to act as signaling or media gateways, because each proxy server adds another hop to the signaling or media path, which in turn adds more end-to-end delay.

- In addition, proxies located in the DMZ, outside the internal firewall, have less protection from the public Internet. These servers potentially represent a single point of failure. In addition, these servers can present a possible threat. If a hacker takes control of the server, the attacker might have unfettered access to the enterprise, because the internal network trusts the devices in the DMZ.

- The solution should not require proprietary modifications to call control servers such as SIP proxies or gatekeepers.

The following sections describe several firewall traversal solutions.

VPN

Administrators can easily configure a firewall to allow an IPsec VPN tunnel through it to allow remote teleworkers to connect to a VPN concentrator in the enterprise. A VPN tunnel can also allow branch offices to connect seamlessly to the campus network. Because the VPN infrastructure enforces authentication and authorization of the remote entities, firewall inspection of the traffic is not necessary. VPN basically avoids the firewall traversal problem.

The downside of the VPN solution is that it only provides a solution for teleworkers or remote offices that can authenticate to the VPN subsystem. This means that administrators must explicitly grant authorization to these endpoints. The VPN approach does not allow connections to or from other endpoints in the public Internet.

ISDN Gateway

In the early days of IP video conferencing, the only practical way to allow NAT/FW traversal between enterprises was to circumvent the problem by using H.320 ISDN gateways to connect two endpoints over the public switched telephone network (PSTN). Figure 8-14 shows the topology for interenterprise H.323 connectivity, in which two endpoints connect over the PSTN WAN.

Figure 8-14 *Using ISDN to Circumvent the NAT/FW Traversal Problem*

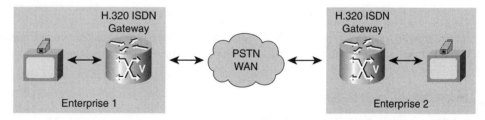

The major downside of this approach is the added delay of converting H.323 to H.320 and then back again. The additional delay reduces the usability of the connection by degrading real-time interaction. In addition, the presence of a gateway complicates the dial plan: Users must dial the gateway, then dial an ISDN phone number, then connect to an Interactive Voice Response (IVR), and then dial the extension of the remote endpoint. In addition, some ISDN gateways may not be compatible with all H.323 endpoints or all modes of H.323.

Universal Plug-and-Play

Universal Plug-and-Play (UPnP) is a standard protocol that allows endpoints to communicate with NAT/FW devices. UPnP allows endpoints to do the following:

- Request the NAT/FW to allocate a public mapped address

- Determine the public mapped address assigned to an endpoint

- Request the NAT/FW to open a pinhole for data arriving at the mapped address

When endpoints use UPnP, they use the mapped addresses directly in all protocol messages, instead of allowing the NAT to perform the fixups. Therefore, the administrator must disable ALG fixups on the NAT. However, UPnP has several downsides:

- The endpoint client must be modified to use UPnP, and the NAT/FW must implement it, which means there exists a chicken-and-egg problem: Only a handful of NAT/FW routers support UPnP; mostly consumer-level devices and only a few endpoints support the protocol. However, Windows XP provides built-in support for UPnP, which means that desktop-based video conferencing endpoints can be easily enhanced to make use of it.

- UPnP does not solve the situation in which both endpoints are behind the same NAT.

- The UPnP discovery mechanism is based on multicast IP addresses; in enterprises, multicast packets are often limited to local subnets. Therefore, the protocol is best for small environments, such as a home office, rather than an enterprise.

UPnP presents a possible security risk because a hacker who has infiltrated an enterprise can use UPnP to open many pinholes on a NAT, making the enterprise vulnerable to attack.

IP-IP Gateway Inside the Firewall

Figure 8-15 shows a solution for NAT/FW traversal using an IP-IP media gateway.

Figure 8-15   *NAT/FW Traversal with an IP-IP Gateway Inside the Firewall*

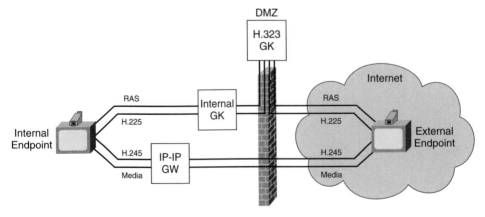

In this approach, all media streams coming from or going to internal endpoints flow through the gateway. In addition, this topology has two gatekeepers:

■ An internal gatekeeper to facilitate connections between internal endpoints

■ A gatekeeper in the DMZ to allow external endpoints to dial into the network

The IP-IP gateway is analogous to an HTTP proxy; users can configure a web browser to use an HTTP proxy, which acts as a gateway between the internal and external network.

The internal GK and IP-IP gateway must have static IP addresses, and the administrator must configure the NAT to assign static public mapped IP addresses to those devices, with bindings that do not time out.

The firewall must implement an H.323 ALG and snoop the signaling to open pinholes for the media in both directions. In addition, the NAT must implement an ALG to rewrite IP addresses in the protocol headers.

Administrators typically use the following firewall configuration for this topology:

■ The firewall permanently opens pinholes to allow UDP RAS traffic on port 1719 to flow between the internal and external GK.

■ The firewall permanently opens pinholes to allow H.225 traffic on port 1720 to flow between the internal and external GK. This topology generally requires endpoints to use GKRCS so that H.225 signaling does not need to pass between external endpoints and the internal IP-IP gateway.

■ For ease of firewall configuration, the administrator can activate an ALG to facilitate H.245 connection establishment: The firewall ALG opens pinholes to allow H.245 traffic to flow directly between external endpoints and the IP-IP gateway, in case endpoints establish H.245 connections but do not tunnel the connections over H.225.

■ The firewall uses an H.323 ALG to open media pinholes.

H.460

Another solution for NAT/FW traversal is to place an IP-IP gateway outside the firewall. Many Session Border Controllers (SBC) commonly implement this feature. SBCs are available from various vendors and perform additional tasks such as adding quality of service (QoS) or call admission control (CAC).

However, an SBC-centric approach gaining traction in the H.323 video conferencing space is the H.460 standard. The standard consists of three major protocols:

- **H.460.17**—NAT/FW traversal of H.323 signaling

- **H.460.18**—NAT/FW traversal of H.323 signaling

- **H.460.19**—NAT/FW traversal of H.323 media

A NAT/FW traversal solution may use either H.460.17 or H.460.18 for signaling and then use H.460.19 for media.

H.460.17 simplifies the firewall traversal somewhat by allowing all H.323 signaling to occur over a single port, whereas H.460.18 still requires multiple ports.

These protocols allow NAT/FW traversal with no additional NAT or firewall configuration and do not use firewall ALGs or NAT ALGs. In fact, administrators must disable the ALG capabilities of the NAT/FW to use these protocols. In addition, these protocols allow traversal of authenticated signaling and encrypted media. However, the H.460 solution requires that endpoints and gatekeepers implement additional signaling inside the H.323 signaling protocols. If an endpoint does not support the additional signaling, a proxy gateway located in the internal network must implement this signaling for the endpoint.

H.460.17

Figure 8-16 illustrates NAT/FW traversal with H.460.17.

Figure 8-16 *H.460.17*

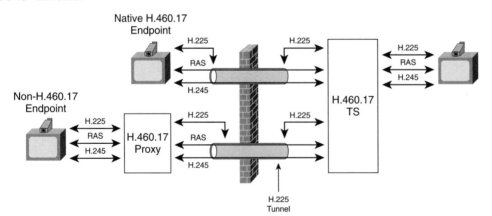

The DMZ contains a traversal server (TS) consisting of a modified gatekeeper. The DMZ GK operates only in GKRCS mode. Inside the enterprise, the diagram shows two types of endpoints: those that support H.460.17 natively, and those that rely on a gateway proxy to incorporate the additional H.323 signaling required by the traversal protocol.

The only firewall configuration necessary requires stateful bidirectional pinholes: When a signaling packet flows from inside the firewall to outside the firewall, the firewall must open a pinhole for packets to flow from outside to inside on the same port. Therefore, endpoints must also use symmetric ports. However, the firewall can achieve an additional level of security by allowing outgoing port 1720 traffic to flow only to the TS.

The H.450.17 protocol requires the endpoints, or endpoint proxies, to send keepalive packets out through the firewall at frequent regular intervals on the signaling ports to preserve the NAT binding. By using the keepalive mechanism, internal endpoints maintain a persistent bidirectional link to the TS. The endpoints may generate keepalive packets by sending either lightweight RAS RRQ re-registrations or empty H.225 TPKT data (Transport Protocol Data Unit Packets) containing no-op messages.

H.460.17 requires one significant modification to the H.323 standard: Instead of sending RAS packets to the TS, an internal H.460.17 endpoint first establishes a long-lived H.225 connection to the TS. The endpoint then sends RAS messages within this H.225 connection. This approach is referred to as *RAS tunneling*. The TS observes the public-mapped address assigned by the NAT for this endpoint and uses this address as the destination for protocol signaling directed back at the internal endpoint.

H.460.17 requires the use of H.245 tunneling, which means that all signaling—RAS, H.225, and H.245—is transmitted over H.225 TCP port 1720.

The primary feature of H.460.17 is the long-lived H.225 connection established between the internal endpoint and the TS, and the keepalive mechanism that preserves the NAT bindings to allow the DMZ TS to complete an unsolicited connection to an internal endpoint.

H.460.18

H.460.18 specifies an alternative method of NAT/FW traversal for H.323 signaling. It uses some of the same mechanisms as H.460.17, including the following:

- H.460.18 requires additional signaling messages inside H.323. If the endpoints do not implement this modification, gateway proxies inside the enterprise must provide this functionality.

- It requires internal endpoints to send keepalive messages to the TS to preserve NAT bindings.

- The TS operates in GKRCS mode only.

- The NAT/FW must open symmetric bidirectional pinholes for the signaling.

Unlike H.460.17, which sends all signaling over an H.225 connection, H.460.18 allows the NAT to open separate ports for RAS, H.225, and H.245. Figure 8-17 shows the topology.

Figure 8-17 *H.460.18*

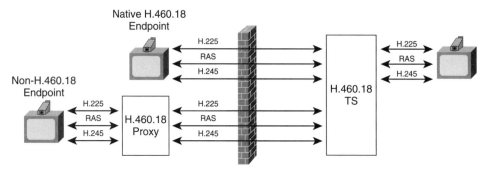

The principal element of H.460.18 is the ability of the TS GK to send a special RAS message to the internal endpoint, which instructs the endpoint to send a packet out the NAT to open a corresponding inbound pinhole. The TS GK uses the H.323 RAS Service Control Indication (SCI) message to communicate this special command to the endpoint. H.323 SCI messages allow either the endpoint or the gatekeeper to invoke new custom-defined services. After an internal endpoint responds to the SCI message and opens a NAT/FW pinhole, the endpoint must keep the NAT binding active by sending frequent periodic keepalive messages out the NAT/FW. The endpoint may use three different keepalive mechanisms, depending on the signaling channel:

- **RAS**—Lightweight RRQ re-registration messages

- **H.225**—Empty TPKT packets

- **H.245**—Empty TPKT packets

The internal endpoint registers with the TS by sending a RAS message. The TS observes the source address of this message to determine the public mapped address for the endpoint. The internal endpoint then maintains the NAT binding for the RAS channel by issuing keepalive messages.

When an external endpoint wants to connect to an internal endpoint, the external endpoint sends a setup message to the TS, and the TS creates a RAS SCI packet that requests that the internal endpoint send an empty H.225 packet out through the NAT to the TS to open a reverse pinhole for the incoming setup message. The RAS SCI message provides the port number on the TS, which is 1720 for H.225 connections, or an ephemeral port for H.245 connections. Upon receiving this RAS SCI packet, the internal endpoint sends a packet to open the reverse pinhole and then sends keepalive packets to preserve the NAT binding. The TS again observes the source address of the packet to determine the public mapped address for the internal endpoint. The TS then forwards the setup message from the external endpoint through the reverse pinhole. If two endpoints attempt to create a direct H.245 connection via H.225 messages, the TS translates the H.245 addresses in the H.225 messages so that both internal and external endpoints terminate their H.245 connections on the TS.

The administrator can add greater security by writing firewall rules to restrict outgoing RAS, H.225, and H.245 messages to flow only to the TS.

H.460.19

H.460.17 and H.460.18 only provide NAT/FW traversal for signaling. Figure 8-18 shows the approach of H.460.19, which provides NAT/FW traversal for media packets that flow between two endpoints located on either side of a NAT/FW.

Figure 8-18   *H.460.19*

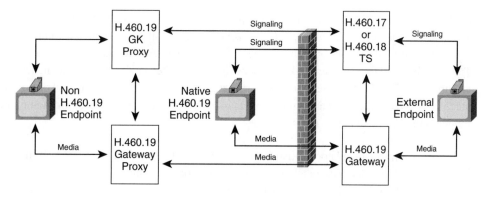

All media packets flow through the media relay in the DMZ, which must be accompanied by a DMZ GK that implements a NAT/FW traversal scheme for H.323 signaling, such as H.460.17 or H.460.18. The GK must also be able to control the operation of the media gateway. In addition:

- Internal client endpoints that do not support the H.460.19 protocol must use a gateway proxy endpoint inside the network.

- The administrator must configure the NAT/FW to allow bidirectional symmetric pinholes between internal endpoints and the media relay.

In normal H.323 signaling, endpoints signal the media channels to each other by exchanging H.245 packets containing the destination addresses/ports for the media. In H.460.19, the GK intercepts these packets and modifies the IP addresses/ports to ensure that media flows through the media gateway. When an external endpoint opens a channel to send media to an internal endpoint, the media first flows to the gateway, and then the gateway forwards the packet to the internal endpoint.

However, before the gateway can send media to the internal endpoint on a new RTP port, the internal endpoint must create a reverse pinhole for the media. The GK sends an H.245 message to the internal endpoint, instructing the endpoint to create this reverse pinhole by sending an empty RTP packet outbound to the gateway. The H.245 message contains the port on the gateway from which packets will originate. The endpoint responds by sending empty RTP packets to this port on the gateway, from a source port on the internal endpoint that will be the destination for inbound packets. After the gateway receives the empty RTP packet, it observes the public mapped address of the source and forwards inbound RTP packets to this public mapped address.

The internal endpoint must also use the same mechanisms to open pinholes and maintain bindings for the RTCP packets. The keepalive packet for RTCP is the Sender Report (SR) message.

H.460.19 has one additional feature that endpoints can use to reduce the number of open RTP media ports. This feature is called *media multiplexing*, and it allows a sender to multiplex data from different RTP sessions onto the same RTP port. This feature requires the sender to add a 4-byte multiplexID value after the UDP packet header and before the RTP packet header. The multiplexID identifies the stream. For each one-way media stream, the receiver chooses the mapping between sessionID and multiplexID, and the receiver transmits this information to the sender in the H.245 signaling messages.

H.460.19 specifies a mandatory antispamming feature that mitigates DoS attacks. To implement antispamming, a sender adds an additional authentication tag to the end of an RTP packet, which authenticates items in the RTP header. The receiver can quickly determine whether the RTP packet is valid by performing a quick authentication operation on these RTP header values. The intent of the antispamming feature is to allow receivers to quickly identify malicious RTP packets without doing extensive processing.

Endpoints may use H.460.19 with encrypted media, and the authentication tag added by antispamming provides DoS protection (in addition to any authentication tags added by the media encryption protocol).

H.460.18 and H.460.19 Issues

Video conferencing vendors are moving to adopt H.460.18 along with H.460.19. This protocol combination has the following attributes:

■   Administrators must configure the NAT/FW to allow any device inside the enterprise to send packets to the GK and media relay servers in the DMZ. In addition, the NAT/FW must open bidirectional symmetric pinholes in response to packets sent out the NAT/FW by internal endpoints. These requirements apply to all high-valued ports ranging from 1024 to 65,535.

■   The firewall may not implement any protocol-level ALG processing or fixups.

■   Different enterprises may implement peering, which is shown in Figure 8-19.

Figure 8-19   *H.460.18/19 Peering*

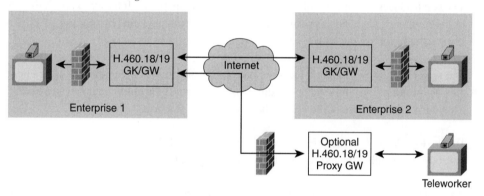

In the peering scenario, the administrators of the two enterprises cooperate and configure the DMZ GKs to work with each other. Without peering, an external H.323 endpoint must switch to a new GK when connecting to an endpoint in a different enterprise.

Figure 8-19 also shows a scenario with a teleworker at a remote location behind a NAT/FW. In this case, the enterprise TS also provides NAT traversal for the endpoint in the remote location. The remote endpoint must either be H.460.18/19 enabled, or it must use an H.460.18/19 proxy. Many teleworkers use PC-based desktop video conferencing endpoints, and the H.460.18/19 proxy can be in the form of a software client that runs on the desktop PC.

NAT/FW Traversal Using STUN/TURN/ICE

One means of NAT/FW traversal is to use a Session Border Controller (SBC) topology similar to the H.460 approach, with a server in the DMZ and a method of sending keepalives out through the NAT to maintain the address bindings.

However, an emerging standard for NAT/FW traversal is the method defined by Interactive Connectivity Establishment (ICE). This method is particularly suitable for SIP. ICE in turn uses other protocols, such as Simple Traversal Underneath NATs (STUN) and Traversal Using Relay NAT (TURN). The next sections discuss these protocols.

STUN

STUN is a client/server protocol that internal endpoints use to obtain their external public mapped address. STUN also provides a way for two endpoints to verify that they have connectivity through a NAT. The STUN protocol is still evolving as a standard in the IETF, but this section discusses the fundamental principles used by STUN that facilitate NAT traversal. These protocols are likely to appear in SIP endpoint products to enable enterprise-to-enterprise connections.

STUN introduces the concept of a server that exists on the public Internet to provides a service to endpoints that reside inside a private address space. The client begins by sending a STUN message to the default port on the STUN server.

The server replies by sending a message back to the apparent source address of the client. This message contains the public mapped address of the client. If the public mapped address is different from the private address of the client, the client knows that it is behind a NAT.

To avoid security vulnerabilities, a server that provides STUN functionality must allow the client to establish an authenticated session before exchanging messages.

If a client is behind a NAT that uses address-independent mapping and filtering, the client can use STUN to discover the public mapped address corresponding to one of its internal address/ports. It can then perform its own NAT fixup by using the public address/port combination inside protocol signaling messages. This endpoint-implemented fixup is possible because a NAT that provides address-independent mapping creates the same public mapped address for a single internal endpoint, and then uses that mapped address for all external destination endpoints. Therefore, an internal endpoint can use the public mapped address discovered via STUN as a return address when talking to other endpoints on the public Internet.

However, many NATs in large enterprises are symmetric NATs and create a new public mapped address/port for each external destination endpoint, even when an internal endpoint uses the same source address and port to talk to each of those external endpoints. Therefore, when an internal endpoint is behind a symmetric NAT, the endpoint cannot reuse a public mapped address discovered by STUN to connect with other external endpoints.

The ICE protocol, discussed later, allows endpoints to use a static public mapped address, discovered by STUN, if the client is behind a NAT that uses address-independent mapping and filtering. However, in the more likely case of a symmetric NAT, most clients must use a proxy gateway located in the public address space, discussed next.

TURN

TURN is a protocol under development in the IETF. The protocol is evolving, but this section discusses the fundamental principles of the TURN approach for NAT traversal. The TURN protocol defines a TURN server, which is a media relay located in the public address space that allocates static public addresses to clients behind a NAT. Clients can then perform their own NAT fixup by using this public address when connecting to other SIP endpoints through the TURN server. Figure 8-20 shows this NAT topology.

Figure 8-20   *TURN Server Topology*

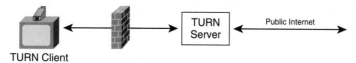

The client starts the sequence of events by sending an allocate message to the TURN server to allocate a static public IP address. The TURN server allocates the address in the public address space and then replies to the client with a message containing the allocated address. The TURN server observes the apparent source address of the client and associates this source address with the allocated public TURN address. The client can now forward packets to the TURN server, and the TURN server sends the packets out this allocated address. The TURN server also relays packets arriving at the allocated address back to the client. The originating endpoint can implement its own NAT fixup by creating protocol messages using the public address provided by the TURN server.

The client initially forwards packets through the TURN server by encapsulating the packet inside a TURN send message. When the TURN server receives a send message, it strips off the encapsulation and forwards the packet to the specified address. The TURN server sends the packet out the allocated address/port associated with the apparent source address of packets from the client.

There is another way to describe the functionality of the TURN server: It acts like an address-restricted NAT. After the client forwards data through the TURN server to a destination endpoint address/port, the TURN server allows packets from that external endpoint address, and any port, to flow back to the client encapsulated in TURN messages.

The client may also set one of the external address/port destinations to be the active destination. After the active destination has been set:

■   The TURN server forwards packets originating from the active address/port directly to the client, without TURN packet encapsulation.

■   When the TURN server receives nonencapsulated packets from the client, the TURN server forwards those messages to the active destination.

The downside of using TURN is that endpoints require modification to use the protocol. In addition, the client must send keepalive messages to maintain the NAT binding that connects the client and the TURN server. Clients can implement a keepalive by resending the TURN allocate request.

Like STUN, the TURN server operates only if the administrator configures the NAT/FW to allow bidirectional symmetric pinholes.

Like other NAT/FW traversal solutions that use an intermediate proxy or gateway, a TURN server imposes a delay in the signaling and media paths.

ICE

ICE is an evolving protocol in the IETF that allows two endpoints to exchange a set of candidate addresses for connectivity. Some of the addresses may be in the local private address space, and others may be in the public mapped address space. For the endpoints to discover the most optimal path, both endpoints must support ICE.

In the ICE protocol, each endpoint gathers a list of possible candidate public IP addresses that could allow an incoming packet to reach the endpoint. Endpoints gather these candidate addresses by locating STUN and TURN servers and then interrogating these servers for public mapped addresses. Endpoints may also use UPnP to obtain a public NAT address. In addition, the endpoint uses a local address as a candidate in case both endpoints are behind the same NAT. The endpoint prioritizes these addresses.

The SIP endpoint that initiates a SIP connection sends a SIP INVITE message containing a list of candidate IP addresses in prioritized order.

When the remote endpoint receives the list in the SIP INVITE, it replies with a list of addresses obtained in a similar manner. Each endpoint proceeds to attempt connectivity to the addresses provided by the other endpoint by sending STUN messages to each address. In this mode, the endpoints themselves must implement STUN server functionality and respond to STUN request messages from the other endpoint. When an endpoint receives a STUN return message, it knows that it has found an IP address that permits connectivity. Each endpoint chooses the highest-ranked address that offers connectivity to the other endpoint. Then the SIP endpoints exchange INVITE messages again, this time using the addresses obtained during the connectivity-testing phase.

The benefit of ICE is that if a public IP address exists, ICE will find it. In addition, if one of the endpoints is behind a NAT that uses endpoint-independent mapping and endpoint-independent filtering, ICE finds this low-latency direct route, instead of using a high-latency TURN relay. In addition, ICE allows endpoints to use local private addresses if each endpoint is behind the same NAT.

Similar to other NAT traversal approaches, the endpoints must issue periodic STUN keepalive messages to each other to preserve the NAT bindings.

ICE is beneficial even if one endpoint is behind a NAT and one endpoint is on the public Internet. If both endpoints implement ICE, the endpoints may find a direct connection through a NAT that has lower latency than a TURN server. Also, the endpoint behind the NAT can use the STUN keepalive messages to maintain the NAT bindings and reverse pinholes.

Encryption Basics

Before undertaking an analysis of encryption for video conferencing, it is necessary to have a fundamental understanding of cryptography.

Symmetric Encryption

Data encryption allows a sender and receiver to ensure the confidentiality of data. Video conferencing algorithms encrypt signaling or media using symmetric encryption schemes, which use a single fixed-length key to both encrypt and decrypt the data. Figure 8-21 shows the operation of symmetric encryption.

Figure 8-21 *Symmetric Encryption*

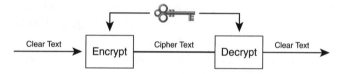

The original, unencrypted data is called the *cleartext*, and the encrypted data is called the *ciphertext*. The conferencing industry is moving to adopt the Advanced Encryption Standard (AES) for encryption. AES-128 is considered to be highly secure and uses a 128-bit key. Symmetric encryption algorithms such as AES-128 are generally fast enough for real-time media. To work effectively, the sending and receiving endpoints must use a method of secure key distribution. The most simple, but also most cumbersome, method of key distribution is to use a preshared key, distributed to the endpoints in an out-of-band, secure manner. A password is an example of a rudimentary preshared key. However, preshared key distribution usually does not scale well. A later section, "Media Encryption," describes other forms of key distribution.

Secure Hashes

Data integrity is the ability of a receiver to guarantee that an attacker has not tampered with data in transit on the network. Data integrity prevents MitM attacks on either signaling or media streams. A sender provides a mechanism for the receiver to verify data integrity by adding a secure hash to the end of the data packet.

A hash is a function that takes any number of bytes as an input and produces a small fixed-length output value. One of the widely adopted hash algorithms is SHA-1, which generates a 128-bit hash output value. Most important, hashes are one-way functions, meaning that it is computationally infeasible to perform the hash in reverse: Given a hash output value, attackers will not be able to assemble a string of input bytes that generate the output hash. Because the hash is a one-way function, it is like a checksum that cannot be spoofed. Another characteristic of a hash is that even the smallest change to the input string of bytes will result in a very different value for the output hash.

A secure hash adds a feature: In addition to an input stream of bytes, the secure hash incorporates a key value. Given the stream of bytes and the key value, the secure hash generates a unique output value, which changes if an attacker makes any change to either the string of bytes or the key. The universal standard method of using a key with any hash function is referred to as *hashed message authentication code* (HMAC), defined in RFC 2104. Any hash function may be converted into a secure hash using RFC 2104, and the name of the resulting secure hash is created by prepending HMAC to the hash name. The secure hash that uses SHA-1 is HMAC-SHA1.

Endpoints can authenticate a packet by calculating the HMAC value for the packet and then appending this value to the packet. In this case, the input to the HMAC algorithm is all bytes in the packet and a key. A receiver that has the key can recalculate the HMAC value and verify that it matches the HMAC value appended to the packet. If the values differ, an attacker has changed either a value in the packet or the HMAC value. An attacker cannot modify the packet and create a new valid HMAC without knowing the key.

However, when a sender and receiver use an HMAC tag for integrity protection, they must still solve the problem of key distribution, just like the case of symmetric encryption.

Video conference endpoints that send encrypted media generally provide both confidentiality and integrity: Encryption of the media provides confidentiality, and an HMAC tag provides integrity.

Asymmetric Encryption: Public Key Cryptography

Unlike symmetric encryption, where both sender and receiver use the same key, public key encryption uses two keys. In this approach, each endpoint creates a public key and a private key. Each endpoint keeps the private key secret but makes the public key widely available. Public key cryptography can perform two major functions: encryption and integrity protection.

Public Key Encryption

When used for encryption, public key cryptography relies on the fact that data encrypted with the public key can be decrypted only using the private key.

Figure 8-22 shows the process of encryption with public key cryptography.

Figure 8-22   *Public Key Encryption*

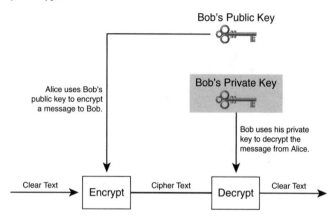

After an endpoint encrypts data with a public key, another endpoint can decrypt the data only with a private key. In this diagram, Bob has a public/private key pair and publishes his public key widely. Alice uses the public key from Bob to encrypt a message and then sends the encrypted message to Bob. Because only Bob possesses the private key, Alice can send the encrypted message to Bob in the clear, knowing that only Bob can decrypt it.

However, asymmetric encryption or decryption has a problem: It is highly CPU-intensive. For this reason, endpoints do not use asymmetric encryption to encrypt media streams directly. Instead, the endpoints typically use public key encryption to securely share symmetric keys. In this approach, each endpoint uses the public key from the other endpoint to exchange encrypted symmetric keys, and then the endpoints use the symmetric keys for symmetric encryption of the media or signaling streams.

Digital Signatures

Endpoints can achieve authentication or integrity by using public key cryptography to encrypt hash values, a process called *message signing*. Message signing relies on the fact that data decrypted by the public key could have only been encrypted with the private key.

Figure 8-23 shows the process of message signing, which is similar to creating an HMAC value.

Figure 8-23 *Creating a Digital Signature*

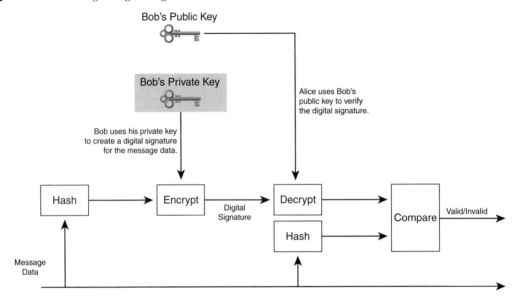

The sender calculates the hash of a message, using either MD5 or SHA-1 hashing, and then encrypts the hash using a private key. The resulting encrypted hash is called a *digital signature*. Any endpoint with the public key of the sender can decrypt the hash and then verify the hash against the contents of the message. Just as with encryption, endpoints must distribute their public key widely to allow other endpoints to perform the secure hash verification.

Certificates

X.509 certificates provide a method for endpoints to present their public keys to other endpoints in the network. The X.509 certificate defines a data structure, shown here:

Certificate

- Version

- Serial number

- Algorithm ID

- Issuer

- Validity

  — Not before

  — Not after

- Subject

- Subject public key info

  — Public key algorithm

  — Subject public key

- Issuer unique identifier (optional)

- Subject unique identifier (optional)

- Extensions (optional)

- Certificate signature algorithm

- Certificate signature

The certificate contains the public key of the endpoint and a list of permissions in the extensions item, which includes an indication of whether the certificate is authorized to use its private key to encrypt data or sign messages. The Subject field of the certificate contains subfields that include the identity of the certificate holder. Endpoints often use the distinguished name (DN) subfield to hold the identity.

When two endpoints want to communicate securely, they can exchange their certificates and then use the public keys in the certificates for the purposes of encryption, message authentication, and identity authentication.

However, for the endpoints to trust the identity (such as the Distinguished Name subfield) in the certificate presented to them, the endpoints use a Public Key Infrastructure (PKI). At the heart of a PKI is a device called a *certificate authority* (CA). The CA creates certificates and issues a certificate to each endpoint. The CA also has its own certificate, called a *CA certificate*. The CA validates each new certificate by signing the new certificate with the private key of the CA certificate, a process shown in Figure 8-24. To create the signature, the CA calculates the hash over the certificate, then encrypts the hash, and then inserts the result into the signature field of the certificate.

Figure 8-24 *Certificate Signature Creation*

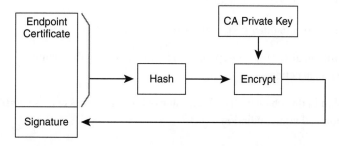

To complete the PKI, each endpoint must also have a copy of the CA certificate. An endpoint can validate the certificate from another endpoint by confirming the signature, using the public key in the CA certificate. Each certificate holds a pointer to the CA that provided the signature. Figure 8-25 shows the process.

Figure 8-25 *Certificate Signature Verification*

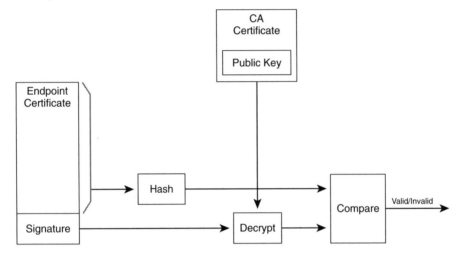

Web browsers use this method to validate certificates presented by websites. When a browser connects to a website, the website presents a certificate, and the certificate specifies which CA certificate provided the signature. The web browser must have a copy of the corresponding CA certificate. The browser uses this CA certificate to recalculate the signature of the certificate from the website. If the calculated signature matches the signature in the presented certificate, the certificate is valid.

When a CA issues a certificate, the CA sets attribute values in the certificate to specify how the certificate may be used. A CA may grant a certificate with one or more capabilities:

- The ability to provide security for encrypted TCP connections, such as Transport Layer Security (TLS)

- The ability to sign downloadable firmware

- The ability to sign other certificates (to operate as a CA)

- The ability to allow for nonrepudiation by guaranteeing the identity of endpoints that establish connections

A later section in this chapter, "H.323.2," shows how endpoints can use certificates to provide authentication and nonrepudiation.

Certificate Management

When a PKI infrastructure is in place, it provides an elegant way to exchange certificate-based credentials and key material among a large number of endpoints, because each endpoint only needs the CA certificate to validate certificates from other endpoints. However, a certificate-based PKI requires certificate management on both the CA and the endpoints. In addition, the administrator or the endpoint must perform certificate management both at the time of initial certificate distribution and in an ongoing manner.

CA Certificate Installation

When installing certificates on an endpoint, the first step is for the administrator to obtain the CA certificate and install it in the certificate store of the endpoint. The administrator can transfer this certificate in one of several ways:

- In the most low-tech method, the administrator can use sneakernet. The administrator logs on to the console of the CA, copies the CA certificate to a Universal Serial Bus (USB) drive, and then walks over to the endpoint and transfers the CA certificate to the endpoint.

- In the most common method for PC-based endpoints, the administrator can log on to the endpoint and then connect to the CA GUI using a web browser. The CA GUI can display the certificate on a web page, and the administrator can copy and paste the certificate into a file on the endpoint. The administrator then places the file into the certificate store on the endpoint. For this method to be secure, the administrator should follow several guidelines:

    — The GUI exposed by the CA should offer Secure Sockets Layer (SSL) connectivity, which allows the CA server to authenticate to the web browser user.

    — The CA should ask the administrator for a password preconfigured on the CA, which allows the administrator to authenticate to the CA server.

    — The administrator should verify the thumbprint of the endpoint certificate, which is a hash of the certificate contents.

- The endpoint can use a certificate management protocol to obtain the CA certificate from the CA server. Two such protocols are Simple Certificate Enrollment Protocol (SCEP) and Certificate Management Protocol (CMP). A CA can support one of these protocols to allow endpoints to automatically obtain certificate credentials. SCEP is a popular protocol because it is simple. SCEP allows endpoints to include a password (a preshared key) with the request.

When using the last two methods, the administrator should verify that attackers have not tampered with the CA certificate in transit. The administrator should perform this verification manually using a certificate thumbprint, which contains a hash of the certificate contents. The CA can provide the thumbprint out-of-band, either at the CA console or via e-mail. After the administrator copies over the certificate to the endpoint, the administrator calculates the thumbprint of the certificate using a simple thumbprint generator program and compares the two values.

Requesting an Endpoint Certificate

After installing the CA certificate on the endpoint, the next step is for the administrator to request the CA to issue a unique certificate to the endpoint by creating a certificate request. This process is called *enrollment*. However, the endpoint needs a public/private key pair before it can create the certificate request. There are several ways to create this key pair:

- The endpoint can generate the public/private key pair directly and keep the private key stored on the endpoint in a secure manner. Typically, the endpoint stores the private key in an encrypted file on disk, using a password. Applications that use the private key may prompt the user for the password to access the private key.

- Alternatively, the CA can generate the public/private key pair on behalf of the endpoint. After the CA generates the key pair, the administrator must encrypt the private key with a password, transfer the encrypted private key to the endpoint, and then inform the endpoint what the password is. This method of key generation is secure. However, if possible, it is more desirable for the endpoint to generate the private key directly and for the private key to never leave the endpoint.

- Another method of obtaining a key pair is to use a special hardware device called a *hardware security module* (HSM), which is usually in the form of a small USB device. The HSM module consists of a keystore, which is a special-purpose hardware device that contains the public and private key. It also has a processor that performs PKI functions using these keys. The keystore provides its public key, but the keystore is designed to never expose its private key.

After the administrator creates a public/private key pair, the next step is for the endpoint to create a certificate request. The certificate request contains the public key of the endpoint and other attributes for the certificate such as the name of the endpoint, the requested expiration time of the certificate, and the requested capabilities of the certificate, such as TLS encryption. Typically, the endpoint creates this certificate request, in which case the administrator must transfer this request to the CA. Alternatively, the CA can generate this request on behalf of the endpoint. The CA then processes this certificate request, creates a certificate, and signs the certificate using the private CA key. The administrator then transfers this certificate back to the endpoint and installs the certificate in the certificate store of the endpoint. The process of transferring the endpoint certificate from the CA to the endpoint is generally the same as the original process of transferring the CA certificate to the endpoint and uses one of three methods:

- Sneakernet

- The web-base GUI provided by a CA

- SCEP or CMP

> **NOTE**   The SCEP protocol can accept a password. However, when distributing initial certificate credentials, administrators should verify the certificate thumbprint.

The previous steps reveal a sticking point when deploying a PKI infrastructure: There are no well-developed methods of installing initial credentials on a large number of endpoints in a manner that scales well; all these methods require manual intervention.

Endpoint Authentication

After the endpoint has its own signed certificate and the CA certificate, the endpoint may securely connect to other endpoints using certificate-based credentials. In the simplest case, an endpoint can trust the certificate of a remote entity if the certificate of that remote entity is signed by a CA trusted by the endpoint. In addition, endpoints often implement an authorization scheme by accessing an identifier in the certificate. The usual identifier is the Distinguished Name subfield of the Subject field of the certificate. Enterprises typically create directories that list these identifiers, along with the permissions associated with each identifier. Most commonly, enterprises store these mappings in a directory based on the Lightweight Directory Access Protocol (LDAP). The endpoint can look up an identifier in a corporate LDAP directory to determine the list of permissions authorized for that identifier. Administrators can easily use such an LDAP directory to grant fine-grained permissions for each endpoint.

Certificate Revocation

However, before an entity can trust a certificate from a remote endpoint, the entity must check to see whether the administrator has revoked the certificate of the remote entity. The administrator may revoke a certificate if the private key of the certificate is exposed or if the machine on which the certificate resides is stolen. An endpoint checks the revocation status of a certificate by accessing a Certificate Revocation List (CRL). The CA generates the CRL and authenticates the CRL by signing it with the CA private key. The CA often transfers the CRL to a server that publishes the CRL. This publisher is called a *CRL Distribution Point* (CDP). Each certificate includes fields that list one or more CDPs that other endpoints may use to download the associated CRL. A CA may publish a CRL using an HTTP server or an LDAP directory.

The CRL has an expiration time, typically on the order of six months, and the CA must push a new CRL to the CDP before the current CRL expires. In addition, the CA may push a new CRL to the CDP at any time. Endpoints should download a CRL on a regular basis and *must* download a new

CRL before the current CRL expires. If the risk associated with using a revoked certificate is high, endpoints should download the CRL more often. The endpoints cache the CRL and may update it based on different policies:

■ For the lowest level of security, an endpoint may decide to cache the CRL and then download a new CRL shortly before the current CRL expires. If the endpoint cannot download a new CRL before the current CRL expires, the endpoint can choose to use the old (stale) CRL until a new CRL is available and continually attempt to download the fresh CRL on a best-effort basis. This level of security may suffice for closed environments in which it is unlikely for certificates or servers to be stolen or compromised.

■ The endpoint can add a level of security by refusing to trust any certificates if the endpoint does not have an unexpired CRL list in the cache. This case presents a potential problem because the CDP becomes a single point of failure. If endpoints cannot access a new CRL after the current one expires, all certificate-based secure communication comes to a screeching halt. To avoid this weakness, administrators must take several precautions:

— Administrators should install multiple CDPs for redundancy. For instance, each certificate may include links to an HTTP-based CDP and an LDAP-based CDP.

— Administrators should deploy HTTP-based CDPs that are highly available. This level of robustness is generally easy to achieve by using the same techniques used to deploy highly available web servers. CRL distribution using a web server does not need to provide Secure HTTP (HTTPS), because the CRL is already cryptographically signed by the CA, and no confidentiality is necessary when transferring the CRL to an endpoint. Configuring LDAP deployments for high availability is a more involved process.

■ For an additional level of security, the endpoint can periodically download a new CRL on a more frequent basis. Even though the current CRL cache might have an expiration date far into the future, an administrator may revoke a certificate at any time, which means the CA may add a certificate to the published CRL at any time. By checking the CRL more frequently, endpoints can recognize revoked certificates sooner.

■ For the highest level of security, the endpoint can download the CRL each time it attempts to validate a remote certificate. In this case, downloading an entire CRL may result in a large bandwidth transaction, in which case the endpoint can use the Online Certificate Status Protocol (OCSP). OCSP allows endpoints to query the status of individual certificates in a more efficient manner.

All certificates have expiration dates; if an attacker compromises the private key of a certificate, the attacker can only make use of the certificate until it expires. CAs grant certificates with lifetimes that typically vary from six months to two years. For certificates deployed in high-risk, public-facing networks, operators can configure shorter certificate lifetimes. In addition to verifying the validity of certificates from other endpoints, endpoints need to keep tabs on the expiration date of their own certificates. An endpoint must obtain a new certificate before the old certificate expires. The process of obtaining a new endpoint certificate is called *reenrollment*. The mechanism for reenrollment is the same as for enrollment, with one difference: The endpoint can use a certificate management protocol such as SCEP to connect over the network to a CA. SCEP allows existing endpoints to connect to a CA in a secure manner, using credentials from a current valid certificate, and obtain a new certificate without operator intervention. After the CA issues a new certificate, the CA usually revokes the old certificate to avoid having two different certificates active for the same endpoint at the same time.

Finally, like all certificates, CA certificates eventually expire. In the time period shortly before the CA certificate expires, the CA creates a new CA certificate, and endpoints must obtain this new CA certificate. Endpoints obtain the new CA certificate using the same mechanisms used to obtain the original CA certificate. When a new CA certificate is active, endpoints must get their own certificates re-signed by this new CA certificate by issuing certificate requests to the CA.

Nonrepudiation

Nonrepudiation provides a means to establish the identity of an endpoint that places a call, usually for billing purposes. If the endpoint establishes identity in a secure way, the endpoint cannot repudiate the act of placing the call.

Video conferencing infrastructure can implement nonrepudiation by requiring endpoints to use certificates for authentication and requiring those certificates to have attributes that allow the certificate to assert identity for nonrepudiation. When obtaining certificates, endpoints must specifically ask the CA to grant nonrepudiation capability for those certificates.

Key Distribution

For two endpoints to use symmetric encryption for media or signaling, the endpoints must agree to use a common key for both encryption and decryption, a process called *key distribution* or *key agreement*. As mentioned previously, one method of performing key distribution is to distribute preshared keys out-of-band in a secure manner. However, this method of key distribution does not scale well. Two other methods of key distribution include certificate-based distribution and Diffie-Hellman key exchange, as described in the next sections.

Certificates

An endpoint may send a symmetric key to a remote endpoint in a secure manner by encrypting the key with the public key listed in the certificate of the remote endpoint. This method assumes that endpoints in an enterprise participate in a PKI to obtain certificates from a CA.

Diffie-Hellman

Diffie-Hellman key exchange is a method by which two endpoints can agree on a common shared secret. Both endpoints then use the shared secret directly as a symmetric key, or they can use the shared secret to encrypt symmetric keys. Figure 8-26 shows the Diffie-Hellman mechanism.

Figure 8-26 *Diffie-Hellman Key Exchange*

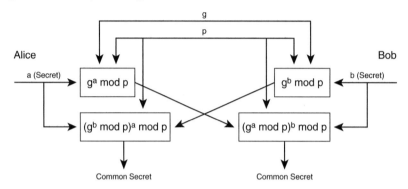

The Diffie-Hellman key exchange has public values and private values. The endpoints first agree on the values of p and g, which are public. Each endpoint then creates a secret private value: Alice creates the secret value a, and Bob creates the secret value b. Each endpoint performs calculations using its private value and the public p and g values to create intermediate values. Then the endpoints exchange these intermediate values. Based on the exchanged values, each endpoint calculates the same common shared secret value. Third-party attackers who snoop the Diffie-Hellman exchange cannot compute the secret value, because only someone with one of the private Diffie-Hellman values a or b can compute the secret value.

The problem with Diffie-Hellman key exchange is that it is susceptible to a MitM attack. In this attack scenario, the MitM performs the Diffie-Hellman key exchange with each endpoint, creating two different Diffie-Hellman secrets. After encrypted data starts to flow in each direction, the MitM can decrypt and then re-encrypt the data, acting as a router between the two endpoints. To use Diffie-Hellman key exchange without the threat of a MitM, endpoints must also use some additional means to authenticate each other. A common way of performing this type of authentication is to use the identity established by certificates.

IPsec and TLS for Secure Signaling

Two common methods to provide security for endpoint signaling are IPsec and TLS.

IPsec

IPsec operates by applying encryption at the IP layer, below the TCP and UDP stack. Because IPsec applies to the lowest layers of the IP stack, endpoints typically implement it as part of the operating system kernel, independently of the upper-layer application. Therefore, the applications are unaware of the underlying security, but the IPsec tunnel protects the UDP and TCP packets. However, administrators and users must manually configure IPsec on the originating and terminating endpoints and distribute IPsec credentials to these endpoints.

These constraints make IPsec ideal for teleworkers with a PC-based video conferencing endpoint at home. By establishing an IPsec VPN connection from a remote site to the enterprise, the teleworker can establish a direct secure connection. At the remote site, the user can use either a software-based VPN on the PC or a hardware-based VPN on the router. The enterprise hosts a VPN concentrator to allow the teleworker to connect.

However, IPsec is impractical for endpoints other than those used by teleworkers to dial into an enterprise remotely. IPsec is generally not practical for endpoint-to-endpoint connections within an enterprise, or between an endpoint in the enterprise and a nonteleworker in the public Internet, because administrators need to manually configure the VPN credentials and IP addresses of both endpoints. In addition, only some NATs offer a pass-through or tunnel mode that allows IPsec to traverse the NAT using the NAT-T standard.

TLS

TLS is an application layer protocol, because it requires applications on the two endpoints to establish the TLS connection. Unlike IPsec, which is usually hidden in the kernel of the operating system, the endpoint application must generally support TLS to use it. One exception is *Stunnel*, an application that provides a TLS wrapper that transparently protects network connections created by non-TLS-aware applications.

Endpoints most often use TLS in a client/server paradigm, where the server presents a certificate to the client to establish server-side authentication. However, TLS also provides a mechanism for mutual authentication, in which both sides of the conversation exchange certificates. TLS imposes one additional restriction: It requires a TCP connection, which means that UDP-based messages, such as RAS messages, cannot make use of TLS. The IETF is working to develop secure solutions for UDP, and one of those efforts is DTLS (TLS over UDP).

H.323 endpoints can tunnel H.225 and H.245 TCP connections over TLS, but there is no widely adopted method for endpoints to negotiate TLS protection.

On the other hand, SIP provides a way of supporting TLS. Normally, SIP addresses consist of a URL that begins with the characters sip:. One example of such an address is sip:bernie523@cisco.com. The SIP specification defines a sips: URL format for the destination address of TLS-protected connections. An example of a SIP address used to invoke TSL-protected SIP is sips:bernie523@cisco.com.

Media Encryption

Video endpoints encrypt RTP media in one of two ways:

- **Secure RTP (SRTP)**—SIP endpoints and SCCP endpoints use SRTP exclusively for media encryption. H.323 endpoints may also use SRTP, but H.323 does not provide a well-defined way of establishing SRTP, and the procedures are generally not interoperable between different vendors.

- **H.235.6**—H.235.6 is an encryption standard for H.323 endpoints, as discussed in the section "H.235.6."

In both cases, two endpoints must exchange a symmetric key and then use that key to encrypt and decrypt the data. For both SRTP and H.235.6, only the media portion of the RTP packet gets encrypted; the RTP header remains unencrypted.

In addition to encrypting the RTP media, SRTP also adds a 4-byte value to the end of the RTP packet to provide an HMAC authentication code. This HMAC code authenticates the RTP header and the RTP payload.

In practice, the complication of encrypting media is not the actual encryption process itself, but rather the mechanism of key exchange. H.235.6 specifies a built-in mechanism for key exchange. For SRTP, endpoints may use several mechanisms to perform key exchange; two examples are security-descriptions and Multimedia Internet Keying (MIKEY).

security-descriptions

SIP endpoints negotiate capabilities, media formats, and network ports by using the Session Description Protocol (SDP), defined in RFC 4566. SDP specifies the syntax for a text-based description of a session, and SIP messages include this SDP information. The SDP security descriptions specification RFC 4568 extends the SDP protocol by specifying how endpoints can include key material inside the SDP section of a SIP message. The SDP security descriptions specification is commonly referred to as *security-descriptions* or *s-descriptions*. The endpoint does not encrypt the key information or the SDP section of the message, which means that the endpoints must use encryption to secure the SIP messages. For this purpose, endpoints generally use secure SIP with TLS. By relying on encryption to protect SIP messages, s-descriptions provide a simple method of key exchange.

MIKEY

Another key exchange method is Multimedia Internet Keying (MIKEY). The base MIKEY specification is defined in RFC 3830, and the method that describes using it with SDP information is RFC 4567. Like s-descriptions, MIKEY inserts the key material as a parameter entry inside the SDP section of the SIP message. However, unlike s-descriptions, MIKEY encrypts this SDP entry. One of the benefits of MIKEY is that the SDP information, and therefore the SIP messaging, can transit in the clear, without an encrypted tunnel, while keeping the key material confidential. The downside of MIKEY is that it specifies a rather complex procedure for protecting the key material. MIKEY has four modes of operation:

- **Preshared key**—In this mode, both endpoints use preshared keys to protect the key material. However, preshared key distribution does not scale well.

- **Signed public key using certificates**—Each endpoint must obtain the certificate from the other endpoint before initiating the call. However, if both endpoints have certificates, a more straightforward approach is to use mutually authenticated TLS, which protects the entire SIP message.

- **Signed Diffie-Hellman**—Endpoints exchange Diffie-Hellman parameters to derive a common secret, which the endpoints use to derive the final key material. However, this mode also requires a certificate-based mechanism to authenticate the Diffie-Hellman parameters and prevent a MitM attack.

- **Null**—Endpoints send keys in the clear. Endpoints can use this mode if the SIP messages are encrypted.

H.323 Encryption: H.235

H.235 is part of H.323v4 and is the emerging standard for authenticating signaling and encrypting media for H.323 endpoints. H.235 messages expand upon H.323 signaling by defining crypto-tokens, which are data structures containing cryptographic information. H.323 signaling messages may contain one or more cryptotokens. H.235 was originally a single specification that featured three significant annexes:

- **Annex D**—Baseline security profile. It provides authentication for signaling, and encryption for media, based on preshared keys.

- **Annex E**—Signature security profile. It provides authentication for signaling based on certificates.

- **Annex F**—Hybrid security profile. A combination of annex D and E. Certificates establish initial authentication/identity, and then Diffie-Hellman-derived keys provide symmetric encryption.

In later versions of H.235, the standards committee broke the annexes into separate standards. Commercially available video endpoints use the following H.235 standards:

- **H.235.1**—Baseline security profile (previously part of annex D).

- **H.235.2**—Signature security profile (previously annex E).

- **H.235.3**—Hybrid security profile (previously annex F).

- **H.235.6**—Media encryption (previously part of annex D).

H.235 provides several cryptographic security features:

- Confidentiality

- Authentication

- Integrity

- Nonrepudiation

In addition, H.235 has modes of operation that can work with NATs that rewrite IP addresses in signaling messages.

H.235.1

H.235.1 is the baseline security profile for H.323. It uses preshared keys to provide integrity protection and authentication for H.323 signaling, using the HMAC-SHA1-96 secure hash, which is a 96-bit HMAC algorithm. In addition, H.235.1 allows endpoints to exchange Diffie-Hellman parameters in the H.225 setup and connect messages. The endpoints use the resulting Diffie-Hellman secret for media encryption, described in H.235.6. However, H.235.1 does not provide any type of confidentiality or encryption for H.323 signaling.

In practice, endpoints may use passwords for preshared secrets. In this case, endpoints add a level of security by performing a simple hash on the password; this hash becomes the preshared secret.

H.235.1 requires the use of GKRCS and provides protection for RAS messages, H.225 messages, and H.245 messages tunneled over H.225. H.235.1 does not provide protection for directly routed H.245 messages. Endpoints generally use the same preshared key for protecting RAS and H.225 messages.

H.235.1 makes use of the H.323 cryptotoken data structure to facilitate authentication and integrity protection. The cryptotoken has the following fields:

- SenderID, which is the identifier of the sender

- ReceiverID, which is the identifier of the receiver

- A time stamp and a random value, both of which prevent replay attacks

- An HMAC, which is generated with the preshared key

H.235.1 does not provide a means of end-to-end authentication: The authentication is strictly hop by hop. At each hop, a device verifies the authentication and then re-creates authentication tags for the next hop. In this hop-by-hop scenario, all devices in the end-to-end path must trust each other. For each hop-to-hop link, H.235.1 may apply protection in both directions or just one direction. When endpoints authenticate signaling in one direction, this scenario is called *single-sided authentication*. Signaling authenticated in both directions is referred to as *mutually authenticated*.

H.235.1 avoids replay attacks by including a time stamp in the message. In case the value of the time stamp is the same for two sequential messages, the H.235.1 message also includes a random value, which differs for each message. The secure hash always includes the time stamp and the random value.

In addition to providing authentication and identity, H.235.1 allows endpoints to transmit Diffie-Hellman parameters within H.225 setup and connect messages. The two endpoints use the Diffie-Hellman values to derive a common secret for use in media encryption, defined in H.235.6. Because the endpoints send the Diffie-Hellman parameters end to end, each hop in the end-to-end path must leave the Diffie-Hellman values untouched.

H.235.1 defines two procedures, each of which uses different structures in the cryptotokens:

- **Procedure I: authentication and integrity**—In this mode, the sender applies the HMAC hash to the entire signaling message, including any IP addresses included in the message. As a result, the hash becomes invalid if the message passes through an ALG NAT that rewrites addresses in the signaling protocol.

- **Procedure IA: authentication only**—In this mode, the hash protects a small subset of elements in the protocol message, including the following:

  — The endpoint identifiers

  — The time stamp and random number

  — The Diffie-Hellman values

  However, the hash does not protect the IP address in the message. Using this mode, the hash remains valid even if a NAT ALG rewrites the addresses in the signaling protocol. However, the message elements not protected by the hash will have no integrity protection.

For both procedures, a firewall cannot inspect the signaling and open pinholes for media ports.

With H.235.1, each pair of communicating devices must have a preshared key, which means that a central administrator must issue keys to each endpoint. To allow H.235.1 protection for calls placed between enterprises, the administrators of different enterprises must collaborate to distribute keys to all the gatekeepers so that two gatekeepers in different administrative domains have preshared keys. Because of this requirement, H.235.1 does not scale well.

H.235.1 protects against the following security threats:

- **DoS**—H.323 entities can use H.235.1 to authenticate signaling messages and thus avoid servicing bogus H.323 connection requests, which would deplete resources.

- **MitM attacks**—Assuming that all hops in the end-to-end signaling path are trusted, a potential MitM may take the form of a compromised router. Because H.235.1 signaling has no confidentiality protection, a MitM can read the packet contents. However, integrity protection (Procedure I) prevents a MitM from modifying protocol message data. In addition, authentication (Procedure I or IA) prevents a MitM from spoofing the identity of a sender.

- **Replay attacks**—The time stamp and random value prevent replay attacks.

- **Spoofing**—Authentication prevents identity spoofing.

- **Connection hijacking**—Authentication prevents connection hijacking.

H.235.2

H.235.2 is a protocol that uses certificates to provide authentication and integrity for H.323 signaling. In addition, H.235.2 can provide nonrepudiation.

When used within a single administrative domain, a certificate-based PKI provides a much more scalable way of distributing credentials than using preshared keys. H.235.2 does not specify how certificates should be distributed or how endpoints should validate certificates.

H.235.2 allows endpoints to create a digital signature for a packet by performing a hash on the data and then encrypting the data with the private key of the certificate. The endpoint may use either MD5 or SHA-1 hashing.

Each certificate contains a field that has an identifier that names the endpoint. This name can take the form of either an H.323 alias or a username. A gatekeeper can use the gatekeeper ID. Devices should not use an IP address as an identifier because a NAT may rewrite an IP address in the signaling header, causing a mismatch between the apparent source of the packets and the identifier.

Like H.235.1, H.235.2 has several attributes:

■   H.235.2 requires the use of GKRCS and provides protection for RAS messages, H.225 messages, and H.245 messages tunneled over H.225. H.235.2 does not provide protection for directly routed H.245 messages.

■   Endpoints can use single-sided authentication or mutual authentication.

■   H.235.2 allows endpoints to exchange Diffie-Hellman parameters in the H.225 setup and connect messages for use with media encryption, described in H.235.6. The authentication mechanism of H.235.2 prevents a MitM attack on the Diffie-Hellman exchange. However, H.235.2 does not provide any type of confidentiality for the signaling.

■   H.235.2 avoids replay attacks by including a time stamp in the message; the digital signature covers this time stamp. In case the value of the time stamp is the same for two sequential messages, the H.235.2 message also includes a random value, which differs for each message.

■   Because the signaling is not encrypted, a firewall cannot inspect the signaling and open pinholes for media ports.

H.235.2-enabled endpoints use their certificates to sign all or part of H.323 signaling messages. Each endpoint must transmit its certificate in the first message that makes use of H.235.2, but there is no need to send the certificate in subsequent messages.

The cryptotoken has the following fields:

■   SenderID, which is the identifier of the sender

■   ReceiverID, which is the identifier of the receiver

■   A time stamp and a random value, both of which prevent replay attacks

■   A digital signature

■   A certificate

An endpoint creates the digital signature by using the private key associated with a certificate to encrypt the hash. The remote endpoint verifies the signature by using the public key in the certificate to decrypt the hash.

H.235.2 defines two procedures to create cryptotokens:

- **Procedure II: authentication + integrity, hop by hop**—In this mode, each hop in the network removes the cryptotoken and creates a new cryptotoken, containing a new certificate-based digital signature. This mode has two submodes:

  — Mode A: The endpoint uses the certificate to create a signature that covers the entire signaling protocol message.

  — Mode B: The endpoint uses the certificate to create a signature that covers a subset of the signaling protocol message. This subset includes the time stamp, random value, senderID, receiverID, Diffie-Hellman parameters, and the certificate itself. Messages using this mode of authentication can pass through a NAT that rewrites IP addresses in signaling messages.

- **Procedure III: end-to-end authentication**—In this case, the cryptotoken travels end to end, and intermediate hops do not modify or remove the token. It also has two modes of operation:

  — Mode A: The endpoint uses the certificate to create a signature that covers the entire signaling protocol message. This mode provides authentication and integrity only if intervening hops do not change any part of the signaling message.

  — Mode B: Authentication covers only a subset of the message. The endpoint uses the certificate to create a signature that covers a subset of the signaling protocol message. The subset includes the time stamp, random value, senderID, receiverID, Diffie-Hellman parameters, and the certificate itself. This mode of authentication can pass through a NAT that rewrites IP addresses in signaling messages.

An endpoint may include multiple cryptotokens in the H.323 signaling message, and the message may contain both hop-by-hop tokens and end-to-end tokens. Each hop must replace the hop-by-hop tokens with newly generated tokens but leave the end-to-end tokens untouched.

H.235.2 provides protection against the same threats listed for H.235.1 (DoS, MitM attacks, replay attacks, spoofing, and connection hijacking). In addition, endpoints can use H.235.2 to provide nonrepudiation as long as two conditions are met:

- The original message must use Procedure III and include a cryptotoken that allows end-to-end authentication.

- The endpoint must possess a certificate with authority to assert nonrepudiation. The CA that issues the certificate must grant this authority by setting the appropriate attributes in the certificate.

H.235.2 also provides a means for participants in a multiparty video conference to obtain the certificates of other endpoints in the conference. Typically, multiparty conferences are hosted on a multipoint control unit (MCU). In an MCU-hosted video conference, the endpoints can use H.235.2 to request the certificates of other endpoints from the MCU to create an authenticated list of participants.

H.235.3

H.235.3 is a hybrid security profile that combines the certificate method of H.235.2 with symmetric keys of H.235.1. This profile uses certificates to establish authentication for the initial connection, as defined in H.235.2. Endpoints then exchange Diffie-Hellman info and use the Diffie-Hellman secret as the key for generating HMAC authentication tags in subsequent messages, as defined in H.235.1. This scheme benefits from the scalability of certificate-based PKI to establish identity and authenticated Diffie-Hellman parameters, which avoids the need for preshared keys.

H.235.3 deviates in one aspect from H.235.2: H.235.3 specifically disallows MD5 hashing, which reflects the fact that MD5 is considered a weaker algorithm than SHA-1.

H.235.3 defines one procedure:

- **Procedure IV**—Endpoints use Procedure II of H.235.2 to exchange certificates for the first message. This message includes Diffie-Hellman parameters that each side must use to derive a secret link key. Subsequent messages use the link key with Procedure I of H.235.1. Endpoints may also exchange additional Diffie-Hellman parameter sets in the setup and connect messages to establish keys for media encryption, as described in H.235.6.

Either endpoint may update the link key by sending new Diffie-Hellman parameters. H.235.3 dictates that endpoints must authenticate messages with new Diffie-Hellman parameters using certificates, as defined in Procedure II, instead of using the current link key.

H.235.6

Whereas most SIP endpoints use SRTP to encrypt media, most interoperable H.323 implementations use H.235.6 for media encryption. Like SRTP, H.235.6 uses a session key to encrypt the payload section of an RTP packet. However, unlike SRTP, H.235.6 does not authenticate the entire RTP packet.

H.235.6 defines the voice encryption profile for H.235 to encrypt voice or video media. H.235.6 allows several encryption algorithms: AES, RC2, DES, and Triple DES. However, the most secure of these is AES-128, the only recommended algorithm. To support H.235.6, endpoints exchange Diffie-Hellman parameters during the setup and connect messages as part of H.235.1, H.235.2, or

H.235.3. The endpoints derive a Diffie-Hellman shared secret from these parameters, which the endpoints use as a master key. Endpoints typically do not use this master key directly to encrypt media. Instead, endpoints use the master key to encrypt and exchange a session key and then use this session key to encrypt media. Endpoints should exchange a new encrypted session key periodically to reduce the possibility that an attacker can use a brute-force method to discover the session key.

NOTE H.235.6 endpoints encrypt the RTP payload data only. Endpoints do not encrypt the RTP headers.

When two endpoints connect, the H.323 protocol specifies that one of the endpoints will become the master. When an endpoint connects to an MCU, the MCU is always the master. H.235.6 specifies that after connection, the master endpoint creates a session key and encrypts it with the Diffie-Hellman master key. The endpoint then sends the encrypted session key to the other endpoint inside an H.245 OpenLogicalChannel message. The master endpoint may reissue a new session key at any time, and the slave may request a new session key from the master at any time.

When an endpoint disconnects from an MCU conference, the MCU should issue new session keys to the remaining endpoints to prevent the disconnected endpoint from listening in on the remainder of the conversation.

H.235.6 has gone through several version iterations. Starting with Version 3 of H.235.6, the specification now permits the use of a salt value for the encryption algorithm. A *salt value* provides both sides with an initial starting point for the encryption procedure, which prevents precomputation attacks on the media. As a result, H.235.6v3 is considered more secure than earlier versions of H.235.6.

Much like H.460.19, H.235.6 adds a mandatory antispamming authentication tag to the media packets, which mitigates DoS attacks. To implement antispamming, the sender adds an additional authentication tag to the end of an RTP packet, which authenticates items in the RTP header. The intent of the antispamming feature is to allow receivers to quickly identify malicious RTP packets without doing extensive processing. H.235.6 antispamming specifies an HMAC-SHA1 hash, which covers the RTP time stamp and RTP sequence number in the RTP packet header. Endpoints use the current RTP session key to generate and verify the HMAC.

H.235.6 provides protection against several media-related threats:

■   Antispamming prevents DoS and replay attacks.

■   Encryption prevents MitM attacks.

■   Encryption prevents confidentiality attacks.

SIP Encryption

The SIP standard defines a method of establishing a secure SIP signaling connection by using TLS on port 5061. In this case, endpoints use a sips: URL rather than the usual sip: URL. TLS offers either single-sided authentication or mutual authentication, and it provides encryption and integrity for data flow in both directions. The downside of TLS is that it is hop by hop: For the end-to-end connection to be secure, devices at all hops in the end-to-end path must trust each other. An example of a hop is a connection between an endpoint and a transcoder.

SIP may also make use of an end-to-end encryption scheme called *Secure/Multipurpose Internet Mail Extensions* (S/MIME). S/MIME encrypts SIP signaling end to end using a PKI and requires both sides in the conversation to use certificate-based encryption.

SIP signaling messages may specify Secure RTP (SRTP) for media encryption.

SIP-Digest

SIP-Digest is a password-based mechanism that allows SIP endpoints to authenticate to SIP proxies or SIP servers. In a SIP-Digest exchange, the endpoint always authenticates to the server. Optionally, the server may authenticate to the client. SIP-Digest also supports optional integrity protection, but few endpoints use this capability. SIP-Digest does not provide any sort of confidentiality protection via encryption.

SIP-Digest is almost identical to HTTP-Digest, which is a password-based protocol used to grant users access to websites. When a user accesses a password-protected directory on a web server that is protected with HTTP-Digest, the web server challenges the web browser, and in turn, the web browser pops up a small window that asks the user for credentials. The window displays a text string showing the name of the protected resource. This name is called the *realm*. The window typically has entry boxes for a username and password that the user must enter to gain access to resources associated with that realm. When the user enters the correct username and password, the browser automatically supplies the same username and password for all further HTTP messages that request access to directories under the same realm.

The operation of SIP-Digest is basically the same: When a SIP endpoint attempts to connect to a SIP server protected by a realm, the SIP server challenges the endpoint for a username and password associated with that realm, and the end user supplies these credentials. The username and password comprise a preshared secret known to both the client and the server.

Figure 8-27 shows the challenge-response call flow of SIP-Digest.

Figure 8-27 *SIP-Digest*

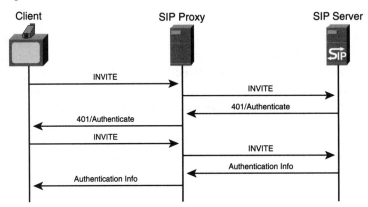

The SIP client issues an INVITE to the server, attempting to connect to a protected resource. The server rejects this initial request and issues a challenge to the client. In the case of a SIP server, this message is an HTTP WWW-Authenticate message, along with an HTTP 401 error message. The following shows some of the information contained in the challenge message:

```
realm="bigdatabase.com",
nonce="9dfe919a99345037d9f9b8c999263d9ef9"
...
```

The message contains several parameters, and included in this parameter list are the name of the realm and a nonce value. The nonce is a randomly generated value that the client includes in a secure hash calculation.

The client responds by resending the SIP invite message, this time inside an HTTP Authorization message, containing the client credentials. The following shows an example of part of the response message:

```
username="bob",
realm="bigdatabase.com",
nonce-count="00000001"
response="6629fae49393a05397450978507c4ef1",
...
```

In addition to the username and the realm, the message includes a response value and a nonce count. The client creates the response value by applying a hash to a series of values. Included with these values are the shared password, the nonce from the server, and other values from the SIP-Digest protocol. A nonce count is a value that counts how many times the client has used the currently active nonce.

When the server receives this response, it recalculates the secure hash using the preshared password, the nonce, and other values. If the calculated value matches the response entry, the server has authenticated the client.

The server nonce value is required to prevent precomputation dictionary attacks. Without the nonce value, an attacker can prepare for an attack by sequencing through a dictionary of likely passwords and calculating the hash value corresponding to each password. Over time, the attacker can create a large table of hash/password pairs. Armed with this table, the attacker can then snoop the signaling, extract the hash, and attempt to look up this hash value in the table, revealing the password. Because the server randomly selects the nonce at the time of the connection, however, the attacker cannot know this value in advance and has no time to precompute the table. To provide a greater level of security, the server may use the same nonce for several transactions and then change the nonce to minimize the time that any one nonce is in effect. The server also uses the nonce count as a sequence number to prevent replay attacks.

> **NOTE**   The server sends the nonce to the client in the clear. The nonce does not have to be secret; it only has to be unknown beforehand.

Even though an attacker cannot make use of a precomputed dictionary, the attacker can still snoop the signaling and then attempt to derive the password using an offline dictionary attack that incorporates the observed nonce. If the attacker can derive the password in this manner before the client and server change the password, the attacker can access all resources protected by the realm. This weakness is one of the downsides of SIP-Digest. A way to thwart this attack is to enforce strong passwords that are unlikely to be found in password dictionaries.

One scenario in which the server nonce fails to prevent a precomputation attack arises if an attacker can operate as a MitM by spoofing the server to the client. In this case, the client unwittingly performs a SIP-Digest exchange with the MitM, and the MitM returns a bogus challenge that contains a nonce previously used to create a precomputed table of password/hash values. When the MitM receives the response from the client, the MitM can then make use of the precomputation attack.

To thwart this attack, an optional mode of SIP-Digest allows the client to send a response that includes yet another nonce, called the *client nonce* or *cnonce*. The client calculates the hash as before but also includes the cnonce as one of the inputs to the hash. In addition, the client adds the cnonce as one of the parameters included in the message. The MitM cannot know the value of the cnonce in advance and has no time to precompute a password/hash table. Of course, the attacker can still use an offline dictionary attack after the exchange.

After the challenge/response, SIP-Digest allows for a third exchange, consisting of an HTTP AuthenticationInfo message from the server to the client, to allow the server to acknowledge the receipt of the client response. Similar to the response from the client, this message contains a hash that includes a series of values, among them the password, the nonce, and the cnonce. By including the password in the hash, the server proves that it knows the password and therefore authenticates to the client. In addition, the server can include a new nonce value that will be active for future handshakes; this value is referred to as the *nextnonce*. The following shows some of the values in this message:

```
nextnonce="49d28ef84022ab38153859d28ef8402102",
response-auth="6629fae49393a05397450978507c4ef1",
cnonce="0a4f113b"
...
```

The response-auth entry is the hash from the server. The server also includes the value of the cnonce.

SIP-Digest optionally provides integrity protection of SIP messages. In this mode, the input to the hash function includes the contents of the HTTP entity-body, which is the actual payload that includes the SIP message. This integrity protection is available for both the Authentication message response from the client and the AuthenticationInfo message from the server.

However, system administrators who use SIP-Digest must enforce strong passwords to thwart offline dictionary attacks.

One benefit of SIP-Digest is that the server and client need not store the password in the clear. Instead, both sides can store a hash of the username, realm, and password and then use this hashed value along with any values for the nonce and cnonce.

SCCP Encryption

The Cisco SCCP VoIP scheme is similar to SIP in its use of secure protocols. SCCP specifies the use of TLS for signaling encryption over port 2443. This use of TLS is similar to the secure SIP protocol. The CallManager distributes key material over this encrypted link, similar to the SIP methodology of using s-descriptions to send keying material in an SDP message. SCCP uses SRTP for media encryption in a way that is identical to secure SIP endpoints.

Summary

This chapter shows that security is a complex topic and that it requires protection at several layers of the network: Layer 2, Layer 3, and the stateful session layer. In addition, the security methods vary depending on the protocol: SIP, H.323, or SCCP. The challenge is to deploy secure protection of voice and video, while at the same time using techniques that allow the voice and video protocols to work in the presence of NATs and firewalls. One area where video conferencing will see significant progress is interoperability. As SIP endpoints adopt STUN/TURN/ICE, and as H.323 endpoints adopt H.460, connections between endpoints in the enterprise and endpoints in the public Internet will get easier. As SIP endpoints adopt TLS and SRTP, and as H.323 endpoints adopt H.235, more video calls will be encrypted. With this additional level of interoperability, video conferencing has the potential for accelerated future growth.

References

H.235.1: H.323 security: Baseline security profile. ITU-T Recommendation H.235.1. September 2005.

H.235.2: H.323 security: Signature security profile. ITU-T Recommendation H.235.2. September 2005.

H.235.3: H.323 security: Hybrid security profile. ITU-T Recommendation H.235.3. September 2005.

H.235.6: H.323 security: Voice encryption profile with native H.235/H.245 key management. ITU-T Recommendation H.235.6. September 2005.

H.323v5: Packet-based multimedia communications systems. ITU-T Recommendation H.323. July 2003.

H.460.17: Using H.225.0 call signaling connection as transport for H.323 RAS messages. ITU-T Recommendation H.460.17. September 2005.

H.460.18: Traversal of H.323 signaling across network address translators and firewalls. ITU-T Recommendation H.460.18. September 2005.

H.460.19: Traversal of H.323 media across network address translators and firewalls. ITU-T Recommendation H.460.19. September 2005.

UPnP Forum: http://www.upnp.org/

Dierks, T., and C. Allen. *The TLS Protocol Version 1.0*. IETF RFC 2246. 1999.

Franks, J., P. Hallam-Baker, J. Hostetler, S. Lawrence, P. Leach, A. Luotonen, and L. Stewart. *HTTP Authentication: Basic and Digest Access Authentication*. RFC 2617. 1999.

Krawczyk, H., M. Bellare, and R. Canetti. *HMAC: Keyed-Hashing for Message Authentication*. IETF RFC 2104. 1997.

Postel, Jon, ed. *Transmission Control Protocol*. IETF RFC 793. 1981.

Rescorla, E. *Diffie-Hellman Key Agreement Method*. IETF RFC 2631. 1999.

Rosenberg, J., H. Schulzrinne, G. Camarillo, A. Johnston, J. Peterson, R. Sparks, M. Handley, and E. Schooler. *SIP: Session Initiation Protocol*. IETF RFC 3261. 2002.

Santesson, S., and R. Housley. *Internet X.509 Public Key Infrastructure Authority Information Access Certificate Revocation List (CRL) Extension*. IETF RFC 4325. 2005.

Video Codec Standards

Chapter 3, "Fundamentals of Video Compression," covered the basic principles of video coding algorithms. This appendix describes the details of four standard codecs: H.261, H.263, H.264, and MPEG-4, Part 2.

H.261 Compression Standard

The H.261 codec was developed by the ITU (International Telecommunications Union). H.261 is a legacy codec used for only two purposes:

- H.323 requires that video endpoints support the H.261 format.

- H.261 provides interoperability with legacy endpoints.

Table A-1 shows the video frame parameters for H.261.

Table A-1 *Video Format for H.261*

Video Parameter	Parameter Options
Interlace-specific coding	No
Color format	YCbCr, 4:2:0 interstitial
Frame sizes	QCIF (mandatory) and CIF (optional)
Frame rate	Supports frame positions at intervals corresponding to 29.97 Hz
Aspect ratio	4:3

Technically, H.261 defines frames that may occur only at intervals corresponding to 29.97 Hz. However, it allows the encoder to send a lower frame rate, achieved by "dropping" a pre-fixed number of consecutive frames between each sent frame. If the encoder plans to send video at a fixed lower frame rate, that lower frame rate is not signaled in the bitstream, but it can be transmitted out of band.

Table A-2 shows the characteristics of motion vectors (MV) for H.261 coding. The allowable options are the simplest for any of the standard codecs and allow a single MV per macroblock (MB).

Table A-2   *Motion Vector Attributes for H.261*

Motion Vector Attribute	Attribute Options
MV per MB	1.
MV H / V range	[−15, +16].
MV resolution	Single pel for luma and chroma.
Chroma MV calculation	Divide the luma MV by 2, and then truncate to single pel accuracy.
MV inter groups of blocks (GOB) restrictions	Not restricted to the same GOB.
MV frame restrictions	MVs are restricted to within frame boundaries.
MV prediction	H.261 codes the MV difference from an inter MB to the left.
Overlapped block motion compensation (OBMC)	None.

H.261 does not perform prediction of pixel values in the spatial domain; the algorithm applies a discrete cosine transform (DCT) directly to either original pixel values or residual pixel values. Table A-3 shows the characteristics of DCT coding for H.261.

Table A-3   *DCT Attributes for H.261*

DCT Attribute	Attribute Options
Transform	8×8 DCT
Prediction of DCT coefficients	No

Table A-4 shows the characteristics of the quantization process used in the H.261 standard, after the DCT.

Table A-4   *Quantization Attributes for H.261*

Quantization Attribute	Attribute Options
Step size changes	The step size can change by any amount from MB to MB.
Intra DC coefficient	This value is quantized without a dead zone, with a step size of 8, represented in 8 bits.

Table A-4 *Quantization Attributes for H.261 (Continued)*

Quantization Attribute	Attribute Options
Intra AC coefficient and all inter coefficients	Matrix quantization: No
	Quantizer step size range: 31
	Values: [2, 4, 6, ... 60, 62], with a dead zone
	Quantizer clipping: [−127, +127]

Table A-5 shows the methods by which the H.261 codec applies entropy coding to each bitstream element. H.261 uses a fixed-length code for the intra DC coefficients and variable-length coding (VLC) for other elements of the bitstream. H.261 does not use an arithmetic coder.

Table A-5 *Entropy Coding for H.261*

Attribute	Characteristics
Intra DC coefficient	Fixed-length 8 bits.
Other coefficients	The run and length are coded jointly. For the inter DC coefficient, H.261 uses a slightly modified VLC table.
MV	VLC.
Scanning options	One fixed zigzag scan.

Table A-6 shows that two of the more significant advanced features commonly available in other codecs are not options for H.261.

Table A-6 *Special Features for H.261*

Advanced Feature	Present in Codec?
Deblocking filter	No
Temporal, signal-to-noise ratio (SNR), and spatial scalability	No

Table A-7 shows that H.261 offers forward error correction as the only kind of built-in data resiliency.

Table A-7 *Data Resiliency for H.261*

Resiliency Attribute	Available in H.261?
Forward error correction (FEC)	Yes
Slices	No
Data independence	No
Data partitioning	No
Redundant slices	No

The H.261 codec is the only codec in this appendix that applies a loop filter to the predicted frame. This loop filter simply blurs the reconstructed frame before the frame is used as a predicted frame. The loop filter might be necessary when the video sequence has objects with sharp edges. Because H.261 is limited to MVs with single-pel accuracy, sharp edges in the original frame and predicted frame might not line up. The result is a residual image containing high-frequency edge-difference information. These high frequency-edges result in larger values for AC DCT coefficients and in turn increase the bit rate of the output stream. The goal of the loop filter is to blur the predicted frame slightly, to soften the sharp edges of the residual image. Other codecs use MVs with subpixel accuracy and do not have this alignment problem.

H.263 Compression Standard

The H.263 codec was developed by the ITU. H.263 and went through three iterations. The first version of the standard was finalized in 1995 and added many enhancements relative to H.261. In the following tables, this version is referred to as *Base H.263*. The next two iterations of H.263 were issued in 1998 and 2000, with the following further enhancements:

- **H.263v2 (aka, H.263+ or H.263 1998)**—Sixteen annexes were added, up to annex T. In addition, the specification added supplemental enhancement info.

- **H.263v3 (aka H.263++ or H.263 2000)**—This version added annexes U, V, W, and X.

H.263v3 encompasses Base H.263 and H.263v2. This discussion covers H.263v3 and includes the common annexes supported by many codecs. The next section, "Additional H.263 Annexes," covers the remaining annexes.

The H.263 codec defines nine profiles and multiple levels in annex X. The profiles define the allowed features, such as the use of B-frames. Levels define allowable frame sizes, bit rates, and frame rates.

Table A-8 shows the source video formats possible with H.263.

Table A-8   *Video Formats for H.263*

Video Parameter	Parameter Options
Interlace-specific coding	No. However, encoders can flag an image as being from either the top field or bottom field.
Color format	YCbCr, 4:2:0 interstitial.
Frame sizes	Five standard sizes: sub-QCIF, QCIF, CIF, 4CIF, 16CIF, plus a custom size.
Aspect ratios	Standard aspect ratios and custom aspect ratios.
Frame rate	Standard 29.97 or a custom frequency. The encoder can also skip frames to lower the final frame rate.

The segmentation of each frame into GOBs and MBs is similar to H.261: Each frame is segmented into GOBs or slices. GOBs span the entire width of an image and consist of rows of MBs.

Table A-9 shows the features and limitations of MVs in H.263.

Table A-9   *Motion Vector Attributes for H.263*

Motion Vector Attribute	Attribute Options
MV per MB	Base H.263: 1.
	Annex F: 4 MV per MB (cannot be used with B pictures from annex O).
MV H / V range	Base H.263: [−16, 15.5] (also applies to B pictures).
	Annex D: The maximum possible range is [−31.5, 31.5], but complex rules restrict the final range.
MV resolution	1/2 pel for luma and chroma.
Chroma MV calculation	Average of all MV in the MB, rounded to the nearest 1/2 pel.
MV inter GOB or slice restrictions	Base H.263: not restricted to the same GOB.
	Annex K: slice mode: no interslice dependencies allowed.
	Annex R: independent segment decoding mode: no inter GOB dependencies allowed.
MV frame restrictions	Base H.263: MV restricted to within frame boundaries.
	Annex D, F, J, or the B and EP pictures of annex O: MV can refer to pixels outside the frame.

continues

Table A-9   *Motion Vector Attributes for H.263 (Continued)*

Motion Vector Attribute	Attribute Options
MV prediction	Base H.263: (1 MV per MB): The MV prediction is obtained by applying a median filter to the MVs from three surrounding MBs.
	Annex F, four MVs per MB (1 MV per 8×8 block): The MV prediction is obtained by applying a median filter to the MVs from three surrounding 8×8 blocks.
OBMC	Base H.263: No.
	Annex F, for P pictures only, not B pictures.

Table A-10 shows the attributes and characteristics of the H.263 DCT.

Table A-10   *Prediction of DCT Coefficients for H.263*

DCT Attribute	Attribute Options
Transform	8×8 DCT
Prediction of DCT coefficients	Base H.263: No
	Annex: Yes, for intra coefficients only

For intrablocks in either intra- or interframes, annex I allows three possible modes for intra coefficient prediction, signaled explicitly. This prediction uses information from the block to the left and the block above the current block. Figure A-1 shows the blocks used in the calculations.

Figure A-1   *Coefficient Prediction in H.263*

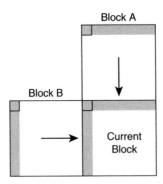

Using these surrounding blocks, the calculations for the three modes are as follows:

■   DC mode, which involves the prediction of only the DC coefficient by taking the average of the DC coefficients from blocks A and B. The resulting MB uses the normal zigzag scan.

- Vertical+DC mode, which predicts the DC coefficient plus the first row of AC coefficients. The prediction comes from the corresponding row of coefficients in the adjacent block above the current block. This mode uses an alternate-horizontal scanning pattern.

- Horizontal+DC mode, which predicts the DC coefficient plus the first column of AC coefficients. The prediction comes from the corresponding column of coefficients in the adjacent block to the left of the current block. This mode uses an alternate-vertical scanning pattern.

Table A-11 shows the basic attributes and characteristics of the quantization process in H.263.

Table A-11 *Quantization for H.263*

Quantization Attribute	Attribute Options
Matrix quantization	No.
Step size change	Base H.263: The quantization step size can change by a small amount from MB to MB; the change is restricted to –2, –1, 0, 1, 2.
	Annex T: The quantization value can change by a large amount.
Intra DC coefficient	Base H.263: exactly the same as H.261; no dead zone, step size = 8.
	Annex I: The intra DC coefficient uses the same quantization value as the intra AC coefficients.

Table A-12 shows the variations in quantizer capabilities for intra AC coefficients and inter AC + inter DC coefficients for H.263.

Table A-12 *Quantization for Intra AC and Inter AC + DC Coefficients for H.263*

Quantizer Attribute	Attribute Options
Quantizer step size range	31 values: [2, 4, 6, ... 60, 62], with a dead zone.
Quantizer clipping	For DC and AC: [–127, +127].
Quantizer variations	Annex T: Step sizes for chroma are lower than for luma, and clipping values are higher, to accommodate lower values of the quantizer.

In H.263 annex I (advanced intra coding mode), all modes use a special VLC table for both DC and AC coefficients. In addition, the DC coefficient is handled the same as the AC coefficients.

Table A-13 shows the attributes and characteristics of entropy coding in H.263.

Table A-13   *Entropy Coding for H.263*

Attribute	Characteristics
Intra DC coefficients	Base H.263: 8 bits, fixed length
	Annex I: same as the AC coefficients
Other coefficients	Nonreversible VLC; run and length coded jointly
	Annex S: use intra VLC for all inter coefficients
	Annex T: extended nonreversible VLC table
MV	Nonreversible VLC
	Annex D: special VLC table, reversible VLC
Arithmetic coder options	Base H.263: no
	Annex E: N-array arithmetic coder, which applies to all elements in the bitstream
Zigzag scanning options	Base H.263: normal zigzag
	Annex I: one of three selections for advanced intra prediction

Base H.263 does not support B-frames; however, B-frames are supported in annex O. B-frames in direct mode do not include a delta MV to compensate for a deviation from linear prediction. The possible prediction modes for B-frames include the following:

- Direct mode, with no delta vector

- Bidirectional prediction, using two MVs

- Forward prediction only, using one MV

- Backward prediction only, using one MV

In addition to B-frames in annex O, H.263 offers PB-frames, defined in annexes G and M. A single PB-frame consolidates two consecutive frames: a frame represented by the B-part of a PB-frame, followed by a frame represented by the P-part of a PB-frame. To prevent confusion, use the term *B-frame* to refer to only the standalone B-frames of annex O, and use the terms *B-part* and *P-part* to refer to the respective parts of a PB-frame, defined in annexes G and M. For PB-frames, H.263 consolidates the B-part and the P-part for several reasons:

- To process the B-part, both the encoder and decoder must first process the following P-part. Therefore, because the B-part must be delayed by a frame time, no latency hit occurs by packaging the B- and P-parts together in one unit.

- By using PB-frames, the encoder avoids reordering frames in the IPB sequence.

- PB-frames are intended to be used in IPB frame sequences where B-type frames occur only once in a row. Therefore, it is allowable to include the next P-frame along with the current B-frame.

For the definition of PB-frames, annex M supersedes annex G: Use Annex G only if you need to interoperate with legacy equipment that is limited to annex G.

Table A-14 shows the PB-frame capabilities of the Base H.263 codec and the enhanced capabilities of annexes G and M.

Table A-14 *PB-Frames for H.263*

Codec Implementation	PB-Frame Capabilities
Base H.263	No PB-frames.
Annex G	PB-frames consist of a B-part and a P-part.
	The B-part uses the direct mode only: It uses the P MV plus a delta vector.
	Intrablocks in the P-frame must still have MVs to provide an MV for the direct mode of the B-part.
	All blocks in the B-part of a PB-frame are intercoded.
Annex M	All features of annex G.
	Bidirectional mode: It is actually a direct mode, but with no delta vector.
	Forward prediction, using 1 MV (predicted from the block to the left).
	Backward prediction only mode: No MV is used for this mode; instead, the corresponding block in the next frame is used.

The forward prediction mode of annex M applies only a single forward MV to the B-part of the MB. This mode is useful if there is a scene cut immediately after the B-part and before the next P-part.

The backward prediction mode of annex M is used if the B-part of the PB-frame immediately follows a scene cut. In this case, the prediction just uses the corresponding block in the following P-part, without using MVs.

The Base H.263 codec cannot implement scalability. However, annex O supports three scalability options:

- **Temporal scalability**—B-frames allow either the encoder or decoder to discard frames.

- **SNR scalability**—The encoder provides an enhancement layer with the same image dimensions as the base layer.

- **Spatial scalability**—Base layer pictures can be scaled up by a factor of 2 in the horizontal direction, the vertical direction, or both directions, before the addition of an enhancement layer.

In H.263, spatial and SNR scalability is achieved with layers of enhancement. Each layer of enhancement provides a residual layer, which is added to the underlying reconstructed layer to produce a new reconstructed layer. Each residual layer is created by taking the difference between the original image sequence and the underlying reconstructed layer. This process is essentially a prediction loop, which uses the underlying reconstructed layer as the prediction. The prediction loop then codes the residual difference between the prediction layer and the original layer. However, in this case, no MVs are used to create the prediction.

The residual layer can be coded using EI pictures and EP pictures:

- An EI picture is an intraframe because it does not depend on other frames in the same enhancement layer. An EI picture codes the residual enhancement layer. EI pictures of annex O cannot be used with annexes D, E, F, P, Q, or S.

- An EP picture is an interframe because it may apply motion-compensated prediction to previous frames in the same enhancement layer. An EP picture codes the residual enhancement layer. To create a residual layer picture, the EP picture codes the residual created by subtracting the residual layer picture from the previous motion-compensated frame in the same layer. EP pictures of annex O cannot be used with annex E or F.

The Base H.263 codec supports GOBs, but not slices. Annex K supports slices and provides two features related to slices:

- **Arbitrary-shaped slices**—Slices can either have a collection of MBs or be defined as a rectangular selection of MBs.

- **Arbitrary slice ordering**—Slices may appear in the bitstream in any order.

Annex K imposes several restrictions on slices:

- Prediction is restricted to the slice, which means that MVs or intra coefficients from outside the slice cannot be used as part of a prediction loop.

- Independent segment decoding (annex R) may impose more restrictions on usage of slices.

Data independence is supported in annex R, which ensures that no slices have dependencies with each other. When the bitstream uses GOBs rather than slices, a GOB may omit the GOB header, which indicates that the GOB uses the same state information from the previous GOB. However, when a GOB header is present, it means that the GOB changes the state information. Annex R prevents inter GOB dependency if a GOB header is present. Annex R ensures data independence for the following:

- MVs

- Deblocking filters

- Bilinear prediction used for spatial scalability

Annex R imposes several restrictions:

- When used with slices, the bitstream must use the rectangular slice submode.

- Boundary extrapolation must be used when referring to regions outside the current segment.

- In OBMC mode, MVs from other segments are not used; instead, the MV of the current block is used.

- Annex R cannot be used with annex P (reference picture resampling mode).

Annex V provides data partitioning. It reorganizes the bitstream as follows:

- All the MB headers are sent together, using a reversible VLC.

- All the coded MVs in the slice are sent together.

- All the coded DCT coefficients in the slice are sent together.

Markers separate each of the sections. Annex V also specifies the use of a reversible VLC table for the MVs. In addition, annex V must be used with annex K. Annex V can be used with annex O, cannot use annex E (arithmetic coding) or U, and should not be used with annex H.

Finally, H.263 allows the use of FEC, detailed in annex H.

Additional H.263 Annexes

This section delves into less frequently used annexes. These annexes might be used in video conferencing endpoints in the future to implement specialized functionality.

Annex C

Annex C provides facilities to support switched multipoint operation. The following facilities are defined:

- Freeze picture request causes the decoder to freeze the displayed picture until a freeze picture release signal is received or a timeout period of at least 6 seconds has expired. This signal is transmitted either by external means such as H.245 or by using supplemental services (annex L).

- Fast update request causes the encoder to encode its next picture in intra mode. This signal is transmitted using external signaling.

- Freeze picture release is a signal from an encoder that has responded to a fast update request. It allows the decoder to exit its freeze picture mode and display the picture. This signal is transmitted in the PTYPE field of the H.263 bitstream in the first picture header coded in response to a fast update.

- Continuous Presence and Video Multiplexing (CPM) is a feature that can be negotiated via external means such as H.245. It allows up to four H.263 bitstreams to be multiplexed as independent "subbitstreams" in one video bitstream. Encoders may signal this mode using the CPM field in the picture header in the H.263 bitstream. This mode is intended for circuit-switched networks such as ISDN, which have no support for bitstream multiplexing.

Annex L

This annex provides an opportunity for an encoder to send commands to the decoder. These command requests include the following:

- Full picture freeze request.

- Partial picture freeze request.

- Resizing partial picture freeze request.

- Partial picture freeze release.

- Full picture snapshot tag. This indicates that the current picture is labeled for external use as a still image snapshot of the video content. This option is useful for conference recording.

- Partial picture snapshot tag. The same as the preceding except that it indicates a partial rectangle within a picture.

- Video time segment start tag. It indicates the start of a video sequence label for external use.

- Video time segment end tag. It indicates the end of the labeling of a video sequence for external use.

- Progressive refinement segment start tag.

- Progressive refinement segment end tag.

- Chroma keying information. This indicates that the "chroma keying" technique is used to represent transparent and semitransparent pixels in the decoded video picture. This mode might be interesting in the case of text overlay.

The use of this annex is signaled in the picture header of the H.263 bitstream using the PEI/PSUPP fields. Decoders not implementing annex L can discard the supplementary information.

Annex N

This annex provides a reference picture selection mode. This mode provides two features:

- The encoder can use a number of picture memories and select one of them as the reference picture in the encoding of the current frame. The amount of picture memory available at the decoder might be signaled via external means to help the memory management in the encoder.

- The decoder may use a back channel to send the encoder information on which parts of which pictures have been correctly decoded at the decoder. This mode can help the encoder choose a reference picture from its picture memories that suppresses the temporal error propagation because of interframe coding.

This mode has low computational complexity but high memory requirements on both the encoder and the decoder. The use of this annex is indicated in the picture header of the bitstream using bit 11 of the OPPTYPE subfield in the PLUSPTYPE field.

Annex P

This annex provides a reference picture resampling mode. This feature is a resampling process that can be applied to the previous decoded picture to generate a warped picture for use in predicting the current picture. This mode is used in specifying the relationship between the current picture and its reference if the source format differs. This mode may be used in restricted scenarios defined during capability negotiations. For example, encoders/decoders might support only factor of 4 picture resizing. This mode gives the encoder the capability to make trade-offs between spatial and temporal resolutions. The factor of 4 upsampling/downsampling does not add much computational complexity on the encoder or the decoder, because it requires a simple fixed filter.

The use of this annex is indicated in the picture header of the bitstream using bit 4 of the mandatory MPPTYPE subfield in the PLUSPTYPE field.

Annex Q

This annex provides a reduced resolution update mode. This mode is used for fast-moving video sequences. The encoder is allowed to send update information for a picture that is encoded at a reduced resolution while preserving the detail in a higher-resolution reference image. This creates a final image at the higher resolution. This capability allows the coder to increase the picture update rate while maintaining its subjective quality.

The syntax of the bitstream when using this mode is identical to the syntax when the mode is not used; however, the semantics differ. In this mode, the portion of the picture covered by an MB is twice as wide and twice as high as normal. Hence, approximately a quarter of the number of MBs are available in the normal picture. MVs are calculated for blocks twice the size (32×32 and 16×16). However, the DCT is describing an 8×8 block on a reduced-resolution version of the picture.

The use of this annex is indicated in the picture header using bit 5 of the mandatory MPPTYPE subfield in the PLUSPTYPE field.

Annex U

This annex provides an enhanced reference picture selection mode. Annex U provides benefits for both error resilience and coding efficiency by using a memory buffer of reference pictures. It allows the following:

- Pictures to be predicted from multiple reference pictures at the MB level. This mode enhances the coding efficiency.

- Motion compensation to be extended to prediction from multiple pictures. Each MV is extended by a picture reference number that may index any of the multiple reference pictures. This added flexibility enhances the coding efficiency.

- A multibuffer control mechanism is used. The mechanism is either a sliding window mechanism or an "Adaptive Memory Control" that provides more flexibility.

- A submode can be used for subpicture removal. This feature reduces the amount of memory needed to store the reference pictures. The support of this submode and the allowed fragmentation of the pictures into subpictures are negotiated via external means such as H.245.

- A submode can be used for enabling two-picture backward prediction in B pictures. The support of this submode is negotiated via external means.

- For error resilience, a backward channel message can be used to allow the decoder to inform the encoder which pictures or parts of pictures have been correctly decoded. The signaling of this channel is outside the scope of this annex.

The use of this annex is indicated in the picture header of the bitstream using bit 16 of the OPPTYPE subfield of the PLUSPTYPE field.

Annex W

This annex provides additional supplemental enhancement information. Annex W defines two values that were reserved in annex L:

■   Fixed-point inverse DCT (IDCT) indicates that a particular IDCT approximation is used to construct the bitstream. The annex specifies a particular reference IDCT implementation.

■   Picture message indicates one or more octets representing message data. The annex specifies several message types:

— Arbitrary binary data.

— Arbitrary text.

— Copyright text.

— Caption text. Note that this recommendation puts no restriction on how caption text is actually displayed and stored at the decoder.

— Video description text. Again, this recommendation puts no restriction on how this text is actually displayed and stored at the decoder.

— Uniform resource identifier. This recommendation does not specify how the decoder might use this identifier.

— Current picture header repetition.

— Previous picture header repetition.

— Next picture header repetition, reliable temporal reference (TR).

— Next picture header repetition, unreliable TR.

— Interlaced field indication. This message indicates that the current picture was not actually scanned as a progressive-scan picture; that is, it contains only half of the lines of the full-resolution source picture. This message will not be used except if the decoder signals its capability using external means such as H.245.

— Picture number.

The use of this annex is signaled in the picture header of the H.263 bitstream using the PEI/PSUPP fields, similar to annex L.

Annex X

Annex X defines profiles and levels for H.263. Of particular interest for video conferencing is section 2.6, which defines profile 5, also known as the *Conversational High Compression* (CHC) profile. This profile allows low-latency, real-time video encoding for video conferencing endpoints. This profile defines several features and limitations:

- All the attributes of the H.263 Baseline profile, in addition to the following.

- Annex F, advanced prediction mode, which allows four MVs per MB, and the use of OBMC.

- Annex D, unrestricted motion Vector Mode. MVs can refer to areas outside the frame. In addition, this mode allows for larger MV ranges.

- Annex U, enhanced reference picture selection mode, which allows the bitstream to refer to multiple previous reference frames for motion compensation.

H.264 Compression Standard

The H.264 codec was jointly developed by two standards bodies: the ITU and the ISO/IEC (International Organization for Standardization / International Electrotechnical Commission). As a result, H.264 can be found in two different documents: the ITU document H.264, and the ISO document MPEG-4, Part 10. H.264 is also known by its more generic name AVC, for *Advanced Video Codec*.

H.264 has superior performance compared to previous standards such as H.263 or MPEG-4, Part 2. For the same perceptual quality or peak signal-to-noise ratio (PSNR), H.264 generates bit rates that are 30 percent to 50 percent less than H.263 or a MPEG-4 simple profile. However, this improvement in performance comes at a cost of CPU cycles. H.264 encoders may have a CPU load that is about four times that of other codecs, and H.264 decoders may consume up to three times the CPU load of other decoders.

All profiles of H.264 have several distinguishing features:

- Deblocking filter.

- MVs may apply to blocks as small as 4×4 pixels.

- Each MV may specify a different reference image.

- 1/4 pel MVs for luma.

- 1/8 pel MVs for chroma.

- Content-adaptive VLC-based entropy coding (CAVLC).

Each profile also defines a set of features optimized for a particular application. The H.264 Baseline profile is intended for video conferencing and wireless, with the following attributes:

- I and P picture types only

- No interlace: no field coding or MB switching between field and frame

- No support for switching P- frames or switching I-frames

- No arithmetic coder

- Supports flexible MB ordering (FMO), arbitrary slice ordering (ASO), and redundant slices (RS)

H.264 Extended profile is designed for streaming over the Internet and contains all baseline features in addition to these attributes:

- No arithmetic coder

- Support for I-, P-, and B-frames

- Interlace support: picture and MB-level frame/field switching

- Support for switching P- frame and switching I-frames

- Data partitioning

- Supports FMO, ASO, and RS

H.264 Main profile is intended for broadcast and entertainment, with these characteristics:

- All baseline features except enhanced error resilience features (FMO, ASO, RS)

- Support for I-, P-, and B-frames

- Interlace support: picture and MB-level frame/field switching

- Content-adaptive binary arithmetic coder (CABAC)

A later addition to H.264 included the Fidelity Range Extensions (FRExt), which added the following capabilities:

- 8×8 integer transform

- Custom quantization matrices

- Lossless encoding

- Support for color spaces

- Support for arbitrary colorspace transformation matrices

Profiles added by FRExt include the following:

- H.264 High profile (HP), which includes support for the Main profile, in addition to the following:

  — 8×8 transform mode

  — Custom quantization scaling matrices

  — Separate Cb and Cr quantization control

  — Monochrome format

  — H.264 High 10 profile (Hi10P), which includes support for the High profile, plus 9 and 10 bits per sample

- H.264 High 4:2:2 profile (H422P), which includes support for the High 10 profile, plus 4:2:2 support

- H.264 High 4:4:4 profile (H444P), which includes support for the High 4:2:2 profile, plus 4:4:4 support

H.264 also defines multiple levels that place upper limits on the bit rate, frame size, total buffer size, and so on.

Video Formats

Table A-15 shows the source video formats possible with H.264.

Table A-15   *Video Formats for H.264*

Video Parameter	Parameter Options
Interlace-specific coding	Yes, on a per-MB basis
Types of interlace coding	Merged, or field/frame coding per MB pair (each MB representing a different field)
Color format	Base: YCbCr, 4:2:0 co-sited/interstitial
	FRExt: also 4:2:2 and 4:4:4
Frame sizes	Limited by the level definitions
Aspect ratios	Many preset aspect ratios, plus a custom aspect ratio
Frame rate	No settings or limits

Motion Vectors

For the purpose of assigning MVs, each 16×16 MB may be segmented in several ways: as a 16×16 block, as two 8×16 blocks, as two 16×8 blocks, or as four 8×8 blocks. The four 8×8 segmentation mode allows any of the 8×8 blocks to be further subdivided as two 4×8 blocks, two 8×4 blocks, or four 4×4 blocks, as shown in Figure A-2.

Figure A-2 *Segmentation of a Macroblock in H.264*

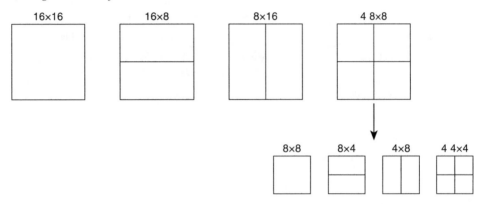

As a result, an H.264 MB may contain 16 4×4 blocks, and in a B-frame, each block may have up to two MVs, for a total of 32 possible MVs per MB. Further, each MV may refer to a different reference frame. Each MV may also have an associated weighting, w, and offset, o, and these parameters are applied to the predicted pixels referenced by the MV. The weighting and offset are useful to generate predictions for scene cuts and cross-fades.

Luma MVs with an accuracy of 1/4 pel may be specified. Given a 1/4 pel accurate MV, the predicted pixels are interpolated in a two-step process:

1. MVs at 1/2 pel locations are calculated with high precision using a six-tap one-dimensional filter.

2. If necessary, 1/4 pel MVs are interpolated using bilinear interpolation on the 1/2 pel accurate values.

The codec achieves 1/8 pel resolution for chroma predicted blocks by using linear interpolation.

Table A-16 shows the features and limitations of MVs in H.264.

Table A-16 *Motion Vectors for H.264*

Motion Vector Attribute	Attribute Options
MV block sizes	Motion vectors can apply to block sizes of 16×16, 16×8, 8×16, 8×8, 8×4, 4×8, or 4×4
MVs per MB	Up to 32
MV prediction	Uses a median filter, applied to the MV of three nearby blocks
MV resolution	1/4 pel for luma, 1/8 pel for chroma
Luma 1/2 pel	Attained with a one-dimensional six-tap filter
Luma 1/4 pel	Attained with a bilinear filter applied to the two nearest 1/2 pel interpolated values
Chroma 1/8 pel interpolation	Linear interpolation
MV H / V range	Set by the level
Unrestricted MVs	Yes
MV restricted to the same slice	Yes

B-Frames

H.264 supports B-frames, with four different modes:

- Forward only (1 MV)

- Backward only (1 MV)

- Bidirectional (2 MV)

- Direct mode, with no delta vector

Intra Prediction

H.264 has an intra prediction mode that predicts pixels in the spatial domain before the intra transform process. For luminance, the encoder can use two different modes: a 16×16 prediction mode or a 4×4 prediction mode. For chrominance, the encoder can use an 8×8 prediction mode. In both cases, the pixels inside the block are predicted from previously decoded pixels adjacent to the block.

The 16×16 prediction mode has four methods of prediction. Figure A-3 shows two modes.

Figure A-3 *Two of the Four Modes for 16×16 Intra Prediction in H.264, Showing Vertical Prediction and Horizontal Prediction*

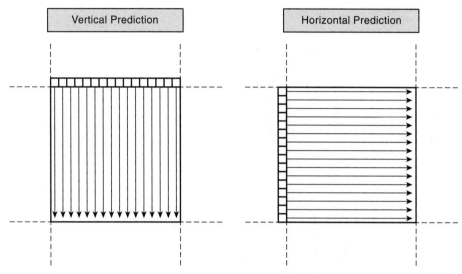

In the vertical prediction mode, the horizontal sequence of pixels just above the current block is used to predict the pixels inside the block by sweeping these pixels downward. The horizontal prediction mode uses the vertical line of pixels to the left and sweeps them horizontally. The 16×16 prediction mode also has two other variations:

■ A DC prediction mode, where all interior pixels are estimated with a single value by using the average value of surrounding edge pixels.

■ A planar prediction mode, which uses surrounding pixels at the top and left of the block to interpolate each pixel in the interior of the 16×16 block. The interpolation process operates by modeling the interior pixels as a plane in three dimensions, with the pixel values defining the height of the plane above the 16×16 grid.

Figure A-4 shows the edge pixels used for the 4×4 intra prediction modes.

Figure A-4 *Intra Prediction for 4×4 Blocks for H.264*

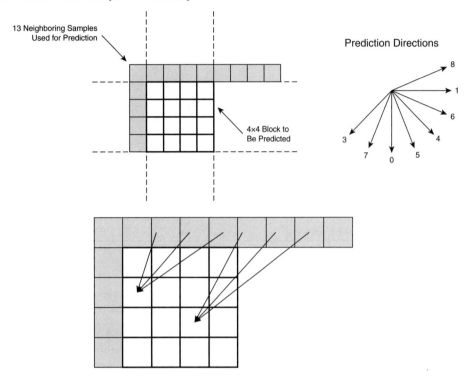

In addition to the nine neighboring pixels to the left and above the 4×4 block, this prediction mode uses four previously decoded pixels to the right. Eight of the nine variations of the 4×4 intra prediction mode use simulated motion to interpolate the interior pixels. Each of these modes corresponds to a direction, shown by the eight direction arrows. The edge pixels are "swept" over the 4×4 pixel block to interpolate the interior pixels. The bottom diagram in Figure A-4 shows the interpolation dependencies of two interior pixels for mode 3 as a function of edge pixels. In addition to the eight simulated motion directions, the 4×4 intra prediction mode has a DC prediction, where all interior pixels are estimated with a single value by using the average value of surrounding edge pixels.

Figure A-5 shows two of the four prediction modes for 8×8 chrominance blocks.

Figure A-5 *Two of the Four Modes for 8×8 Intra Prediction in H.264 for Chrominance Blocks, Showing Vertical Prediction and Horizontal Prediction*

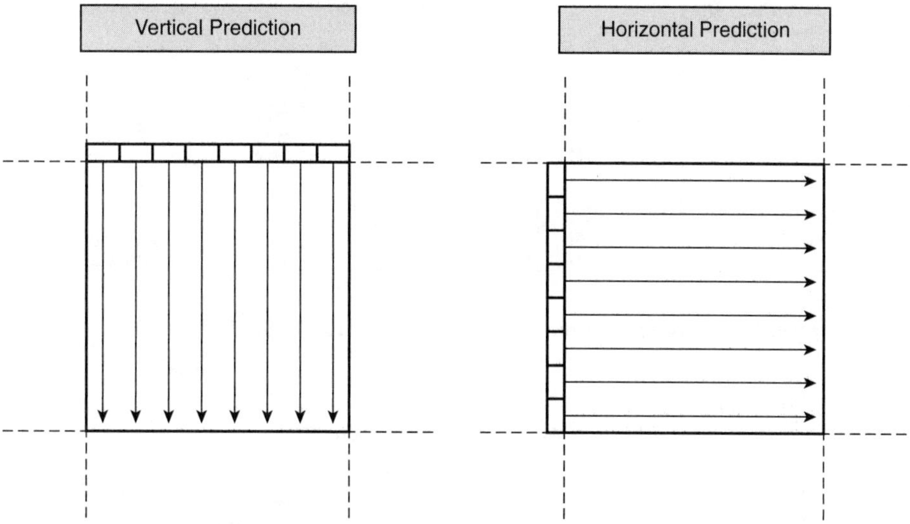

Like the 16×16 prediction mode, the other two modes for chrominance consist of a DC prediction mode and a planar prediction mode.

Integer Transform

Unlike the 8×8 transform of most other codecs, H.264 initially defined a 4×4 integer-based transform. The transform provides almost as much frequency separation as the 8×8 DCT but has a simpler integer implementation. The FRExt subsequently added the option of an 8×8 integer-based transform.

H.264 takes a two-stage approach when applying the 4×4 transform:

■ As shown in Figure A-6, when the MB is segmented into 16 4×4 blocks, *and* when the MB is entirely intracoded, the DC coefficients from each 4×4 block are arranged in a new 4×4 block and then are transformed using a simplified 4×4 transform.

■ As shown in Figure A-7, for all modes (intra and inter), a similar process is applied to the DC coefficients of the chroma blocks: The DC values are arranged into a 2×2 array and then are processed with a 2×2 transform.

Figure A-6   *H.264 Transform Processing for Luminance (Intra Mode Only)*

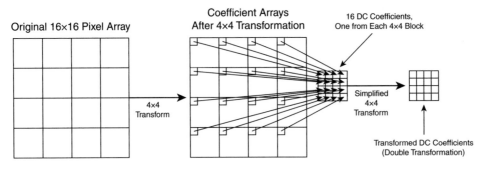

Figure A-7   *Transform Processing for Chrominance (Intra or Inter Modes)*

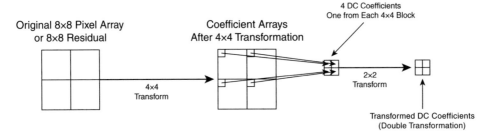

Quantization

Table A-17 shows the characteristics of the quantizer for H.264.

Table A-17   *Quantization for H.264*

Quantization Attribute	Attribute Options
Quantizer dead zone	No.
Quantizer clipping	No upper limit on the input quantizer value.
Matrix quantization	Except for secondary DC 4×4 luma and DC 2×2 chroma mode, H.264 always uses matrix quantization, based on fixed quantization tables.
Step size	Q has a range of [0, 51] and is used to generate the matrix of quantization values.
	Q can change by a large amount per MB [−26, +25].
Intra DC coefficient	The quantizer is less coarse than for other coefficients.
Chroma Q values	For higher Q values, step sizes for chroma are lower.

An innovation in the H.264 codec is backward zigzag scanning in the entropy coder. Instead of scanning from large-coefficient values (upper left of the transform) to small-coefficient values (lower right of the transform), the entropy coder scans in the reverse direction. This approach allows the adaptive VLC process to better predict future coefficient values.

In addition, the codec takes advantage of a characteristic of most transform coefficients: Nonzero coefficients near the lower-right corner of the transform often have a value of either +1 or –1. The entropy coder has a "trailing 1s" special case to efficiently code these values.

The only variation on the zigzag scan is used for field coding, as shown in Figure A-8.

Figure A-8 *Two Zigzag Scanning Patterns of H.264*

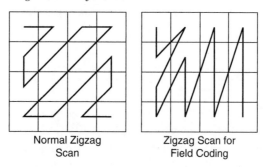

Normal Zigzag
Scan

Zigzag Scan for
Field Coding

When field coding, each MB contains data from only a single field. As a result, the content in a field-coded MB contains every other line of video from the frame, which means there is less vertical pixel-to-pixel correlation. As a result, the MBs tend to have high vertical frequencies, corresponding to larger coefficients on the left half of the 4×4 block. As a result, the zigzag pattern for field coding scans the block from left to right.

Entropy Coding

Table A-18 shows the attributes of entropy coding in H.264.

Table A-18 *Entropy Coding for H.264*

Attribute	Characteristics
Reversible VLC tables	No.
Regular syntax	Exp-Golomb table.

continues

Table A-18 *Entropy Coding for H.264 (Continued)*

Attribute	Characteristics
Coefficients	Backward zigzag scanning.
	The run and level are not coded jointly.
	H.264 codes the number of coefficients using a context-adaptive VLC table.
	H.264 codes the zero-run length sequence using a context-adaptive VLC.
	H.264 codes the coefficient levels using a fixed VLC table.
	H.264 codes trailing ones (+1 or –1) as a special case.
MV	Motion vectors are coded using a modified Exp-Golomb, nonadaptive VLC.
Arithmetic coder	CABAC.
Zigzag DCT scanning options	Two zigzag patterns: one for frame coding and one for field coding.

Deblocking Filter

H.264 has a deblocking filter that may be applied to the 16×16 MB boundary, or optionally to 4×4 block boundaries. The deblocking filter is an adaptive one-dimensional filter applied to vertical edges and then to horizontal edges. The filter is highly adaptive and modifies two edge pixels on each side of the block boundary. For chrominance pixels, the deblocking filter is applied to the 8×8 block boundary only.

H.264 Error Resilience

Table A-19 shows that H.264 offers many types of data resiliency.

Table A-19 *Data Resiliency for H.264*

Resiliency Attribute	Available in H.264?
Slice structured coding	Yes
Flexible MB ordering	Yes
Arbitrary slice ordering	Yes
Redundant slices	Yes
Data partitioning	Yes

The higher complexity and flexibility of the H.264 codec allows it to deliver superior performance relative to the other codecs. An article published by the IEEE in 2003, "Rate-Constrained Coder Control and Comparison of Video Coding Standards," provides PSNR/bit rate graphs for several test sequences using real-time encoding. The results show H.264, Baseline profile, as the clear leader:

- The H.264 Baseline profile had a 28 percent bit rate reduction compared to the H.263 Conversational High Compression profile.

- The H.264 Baseline profile had a 30 percent bit rate reduction compared to MPEG-4, Part 2 (Simple profile).

- The H.264 Baseline profile had a 41 percent bit rate reduction compared to the H.263 Baseline profile.

H.264-SVC

H.264-SVC is a scalable extension to H.264. It allows scalability in the spatial domain and the temporal domain. The essential innovation of H.264-SVC is the ability to incorporate motion-compensated temporal filtering (MCTF). This scheme separates the video sequence into temporal sub-bands and also minimizes the bit rate of the coded sub-bands by motion-compensating them.

MPEG-4, Part 2

The MPEG-4, Part 2 codec was developed by the ISO/IEC. The formal codec designation is ISO/IEC 14496-2. It is used mostly in 3G mobile phones, still cameras, and IP video cameras.

MPEG-4, Part 2 defines several profiles. One of the profiles is called the *Short Header profile*, which is simply the H.263 video stream encapsulated with MPEG-4 video stream headers.

For video conferencing, the common profiles for MPEG-4, Part 2 consist of the Simple profile and the Advanced Simple profile (ASP).

The following list describes the Simple profile:

- Used primarily in cell phones

- Uses the short header option, which is identical to H.263

- I- and P-frames only (no B-frames)

- Uses a simpler quantization algorithm called *Method 2*

- Motion estimation limited to 1/2 pel accuracy

- Goes up to CIF resolution and 384 kbps (at the L3 level)

ASP includes all features in the Simple profile, plus the following:

- Interlacing

- B-frames

- An alternative quantization method called *Method 1*

- 1/4 pel accurate MVs

- Global motion compensation, in which four MVs are applied to edges of the picture

Video Formats

Table A-20 shows the source video formats and options possible with MPEG-4, Part 2.

Table A-20 *Video Formats for MPEG-4, Part 2*

Video Parameter	Parameter Options
Interlace support	Field/frame coding per MB: The top half of the MB is one field, and the bottom half is the other field.
Color format	YCbCr, 4:2:0 interstitial/co-sited.
Frame sizes	There are no standard sizes: All sizes are custom.
Aspect ratios	Five standard aspect ratios, and custom aspect ratios.
Frame rate	There are no standard frame rates: All frame rates are custom.

Motion Vectors

Table A-21 shows the features and limitations of MVs in H.264.

Table A-21 *Motion Vectors for MPEG-4, Part 2*

Motion Vector Attribute	Attribute Options
MV block sizes	Progressive: 16×16 or 8×8 frame blocks.
	Interlaced: 16×8 field blocks.
MV resolution	1/4 pel for luma, 1/2 pel for chroma.
Luma 1/2 pel interpolation	Attained with a two-dimensional linear filter.
Chroma 1/2 pel interpolation	Attained with a two-dimensional linear filter.
Luma 1/4 pel interpolation	1/4 pel accuracy for luma is a two-stage process: First, a one-dimensional eight-tap filter is used to get 1/2 pel sample values. Then 1/4 pel sample values are calculated using a linear interpolation on the 1/2 pel values.
MV per MB	Up to four.

Table A-21 *Motion Vectors for MPEG-4, Part 2 (Continued)*

Motion Vector Attribute	Attribute Options
OBMC	Yes.
Unrestricted MVs	Yes.
MV prediction	Uses a median filter, applied to the MV of three nearby blocks.
Impact on field coding	A field-predicted MV has only two MVs: one for the top field, and one for the bottom field.

The transform used for MPEG-4, Part 2 is an 8×8 DCT.

Prediction of DCT Coefficients

MPEG-4, Part 2 has a method of predicting intrablock coefficients for 8×8 blocks that is similar to H.263 annex I. The method of prediction is implicitly specified using two gradients calculated from surrounding blocks:

- The horizontal gradient, between the 8×8 block above and to the left of the current block and the 8×8 block above the current block. This gradient is calculated using the inverse quantized DC values of those blocks.

- The vertical gradient, between the 8×8 block above and to the left of the current block and the 8×8 block to the left of the current block. This gradient is calculated using the inverse quantized DC values of those blocks.

If the horizontal gradient is larger, the encoder uses the block above the current block to predict values in the current block:

- For the DC coefficient: Use the decoded DC value from the block above.

- For the AC coefficients: Predict the top row of AC coefficients using the top row from the block above.

- This mode uses an alternate-horizontal zigzag scan.

If the vertical gradient is larger, the encoder uses the block to the left to predict values in the current block:

- For the DC coefficient: Use the decoded DC value from the block to the left.

- For the AC coefficients: Predict the left column of AC coefficients using the left column from the block to the left.

- This mode uses the alternate-vertical zigzag scan.

Quantization

MPEG-4, Part 2 has two quantization methods, referred to as the *first* and *second quantization methods*.

The first quantization method includes the following characteristics:

■ The intra DC coefficient is quantized using a quantizer that is a function of the overall quantization parameter.

■ Other coefficients are quantized using matrix quantization. The algorithm uses one matrix for the intra coefficients and one for inter coefficients.

■ The bitstream can specify a custom quantization matrix.

The second quantization method includes the following characteristics:

■ The intra DC coefficient is quantized using a quantizer that is a function of the overall quantization parameter.

■ Other coefficients are quantized using a simple static quantizer value (no matrix).

Entropy Coding

Table A-22 shows the attributes of entropy coding in MPEG-4, Part 2.

Table A-22   *Entropy Coding for MPEG-4, Part 2*

Attribute	Characteristics
Coefficients	Run and level coded jointly
MV	Nonreversible VLC
Arithmetic coder	Yes
Allowable DCT scanning patterns	Normal zigzag scanning
	Alternate-horizontal scanning
	Alternate-vertical scanning

B-Frames

MPEG-4, Part 2 supports B-frames, with four different modes:

■ Backward only

■ Forward only

- Bidirectional

- Direct mode, which also includes a delta vector

Scalability

Scalability in MPEG-4 is not defined in the Part 2 specification for video coding. Instead, scalability is defined in Part 1 of the specification, and it is defined in a generic way to apply to any video codec. MPEG-4 supports temporal and spatial scalability.

Codecs, Bit Rates, and Annexes Supported by Endpoints

Table A-23 identifies the annexes and codecs supported by different enterprise endpoints.

Table A-23   *Endpoint Codec Support*

Endpoint	Bit Rate	Codecs	H.263 Annexes Supported	Comments
Polycom View Station	64 kbps or 128 kbps	G.728, H.263	F, I, T	Polycom View Station shows that it supports annexes F, I, and T at 64K and 128K bit rates.
Polycom VSX 3000/ 7000	128 kbps to 2 Mbps	PCMU, PCMA, G.722, G.722.1, G.728, G.729, H.261, H.263, H.263-1998, H.264	—	VSX 3000 and VSX 7000 also support SIP signaling.
Cisco soft clients: Cisco Unified Personal Communicator (CUPC), Cisco Unified Video Advantage (CUVA)	64 kbps to 1.5 Mbps	H.263, H.263-1998, H.264, G.711	—	—
Tandberg 7980 IP phones	128 kbps to 1.5 Mbps	G.711, H.263	None	—
E-Conf	128 kbps to 768 kbps	PCMA, PCMU, G.722, G.723, H.261, H.263, and H.263-1998	I, J, K, T	E-Conf Version 4 supports H.264 baseline profile.
Windows Messenger	128 kbps	PCMU, H.261, and H.263	None	—

Summary

Table A-24 summarizes the major features of each codec. This table reflects the capabilities of all optional annexes of each codec.

Table A-24   *Codec Feature Comparison*

	H.261	H.263	MPEG-4, Part 2	H.264
Maximum MVs per MB	1	4	4	32
Interlace support	No	No	Yes	Yes
Luma MV accuracy	1	1/2	1/4	1/4
Smallest luma block sizes for MV	16×16	8×8	8×8	4×4
OBMC	No	Yes	Yes	No
Transform	8×8 DCT	8×8 DCT	8×8 DCT	4×4 integer, 8×8 integer
Prediction of DCT coefficients	No	Yes	Yes	No
Prediction of spatial values	No	No	No	Yes
Arithmetic coder	No	Yes	Yes	Yes
Reversible VLC	No	Yes	Yes	No
B-frames	No	Yes	Yes	Yes
Deblocking filter	No	Yes	Yes	Yes
Scalability mode	No	Yes	Yes	Yes

In general, the codec descriptions reveal that advanced codecs offer more flexibility for the encoder at each stage of the pipeline. The H.264 codec can assign up to 32 MVs per MB, with each MV pointing to a different reference image and carrying a different weighting value. In contrast, the simpler H.261 codec applies a single MV to an MB. However, to take full advantage of this flexibility, the H.264 encoder requires significantly more CPU power.

References

ITU-T Recommendation H.264 / ISO/IEC 14496-10, March 2005. Advanced video coding for generic audiovisual services.

ITU-T Recommendation H.261, March 1993. Video Codec for Audiovisual Services at p x 64 kbits.

ITU-T Recommendation H.263, January 2005. Video coding for low bit rate communications.

MPEG-4, Part 2: ISO/IEC 14496-2: Coding of audio-visual objects—Part 2, Visual, Third Edition. May 2004.

Wiegand, T., H. Schwarz, A. Joch, F. Kossentini, and G. J. Sullivan. Rate-Constrained Coder Control and Comparison of Video Coding Standards. *IEEE Transactions on Circuits and Systems for Video Technology*, Vol. 13, Issue 7. July 2003.

Index

Numerics

A

H

W-X-Y-Z

CISCO SYSTEMS

Cisco Press

3 STEPS TO LEARNING

STEP 1

First-Step

STEP 2

Fundamentals

STEP 3

Networking
Technology Guides

STEP 1 **First-Step**—Benefit from easy-to-grasp explanations.
No experience required!

STEP 2 **Fundamentals**—Understand the purpose, application,
and management of technology.

STEP 3 **Networking Technology Guides**—Gain the knowledge
to master the challenge of the network.

NETWORK BUSINESS SERIES

The Network Business series helps professionals tackle the
business issues surrounding the network. Whether you are a
seasoned IT professional or a business manager with minimal
technical expertise, this series will help you understand the
business case for technologies.

Justify Your Network Investment.

Look for Cisco Press titles at your favorite bookseller today.

Visit **www.ciscopress.com/series** for details on each of these book series.

CISCO SYSTEMS

Cisco Press

CISCO CERTIFICATION SELF-STUDY
#1 BEST-SELLING TITLES FROM CCNA® TO CCIE®

Look for Cisco Press Certification Self-Study resources at your favorite bookseller

Learn the test topics with **Self-Study Guides**

1-58705-142-7

Gain hands-on experience with **Practical Studies** books

1-58720-046-5

Prepare for the exam with **Exam Certification Guides**

1-58720-083-X

Practice testing skills and build confidence with **Flash Cards and Exam Practice Packs**

1-58720-079-1

SAVE UP TO 30%

Become a member and save at **ciscopress.com**!

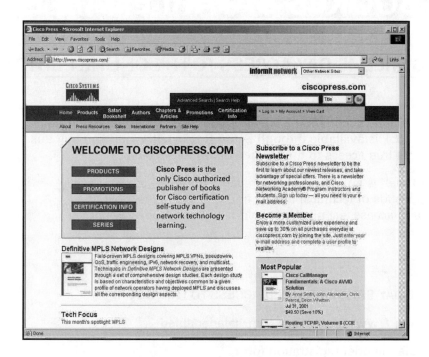

Complete a **user profile** at ciscopress.com today to become a member and benefit from **discounts up to 30% on every purchase** at ciscopress.com, as well as a more customized user experience. Your membership will also allow you access to the entire Informit network of sites.

Don't forget to subscribe to the monthly Cisco Press newsletter to be the first to learn about new releases and special promotions. You can also sign up to get your first **30 days FREE on Safari Bookshelf** and preview Cisco Press content. Safari Bookshelf lets you access Cisco Press books online and build your own customized, searchable electronic reference library.

Visit **www.ciscopress.com/register** to sign up and start saving today!

The profile information we collect is used in aggregate to provide us with better insight into your technology interests and to create a better user experience for you. You must be logged into ciscopress.com to receive your discount. Discount is on Cisco Press products only; shipping and handling are not included.

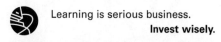

Learning is serious business.
Invest wisely.

THIS BOOK IS SAFARI ENABLED

INCLUDES FREE 45-DAY ACCESS TO THE ONLINE EDITION

The Safari® Enabled icon on the cover of your favorite technology book means the book is available through Safari Bookshelf. When you buy this book, you get free access to the online edition for 45 days.

Safari Bookshelf is an electronic reference library that lets you easily search thousands of technical books, find code samples, download chapters, and access technical information whenever and wherever you need it.

TO GAIN 45-DAY SAFARI ENABLED ACCESS TO THIS BOOK:

- Go to **http://www.ciscopress.com/safarienabled**

- Complete the brief registration form

- Enter the coupon code found in the front of this book before the "Contents at a Glance" page

If you have difficulty registering on Safari Bookshelf or accessing the online edition, please e-mail customer-service@safaribooksonline.com.